Every Decker book is accompanied by a CD-ROM.

The disc appears in the front of each copy, in its own sealed jacket.

The disc contains the complete text and illustrations of the book, in fully searchable PDF files. The book and disc are sold *only* as a package; neither is available independently, and no prices are available for the items individually.

BC Decker Inc is committed to providing high-quality electronic publications that complement traditional information and learning methods.

We trust you will find the book/CD package invaluable and invite your comments and suggestions.

Brian C. Decker
CEO and Publisher

Ballenger's

Manual of Otorhinolaryngology Head and Neck Surgery

James B. Snow Jr, MD
Professor Emeritus,
University of Pennsylvania School of Medicine
Philadelphia, Pennsylvania

Former Director,
National Institute of Deafness and
other Communicative Disorders,
National Institutes of Health
Bethesda, Maryland

2003
BC Decker
Hamilton • London

BC Decker Inc
P.O. Box 620, L.C.D. 1
Hamilton, Ontario L8N 3K7
Tel: 905-522-7017; 800-568-7281
Fax: 905-522-7839; 888-311-4987
E-mail: info@bcdecker.com
www.bcdecker.com

02 03 04 05/GSA/9 8 7 6 5 4 3 2 1

ISBN 1-55009-199-9
Printed in Spain

Sales and Distribution

United States
BC Decker Inc
P.O. Box 785
Lewiston, NY 14092-0785
Tel: 905-522-7017;
    800-568-7281
Fax: 905-522-7839;
    888-311-4987
E-mail: info@bcdecker.com
www.bcdecker.com

Canada
BC Decker Inc
20 Hughson Street South
P.O. Box 620, LCD 1
Hamilton, Ontario L8N 3K7
Tel: 905-522-7017;
    800-568-7281
Fax: 905-522-7839;
    888-311-4987
E-mail: info@bcdecker.com
www.bcdecker.com

Japan
Igaku-Shoin Ltd.
Foreign Publications Department
3-24-17 Hongo
Bunkyo-ku, Tokyo, Japan
113-8719
Tel: 3 3817 5680
Fax: 3 3815 6776
E-mail: fd@igaku-shoin.co.jp

*U.K., Europe, Scandinavia,
Middle East*
Elsevier Science
Customer Service Department
Foots Cray High Street
Sidcup, Kent
DA14 5HP, UK
Tel: 44 (0) 208 308 5760
Fax: 44 (0) 181 308 5702
E-mail: cservice@harcourt.com

*Singapore, Malaysia, Thailand,
Philippines, Indonesia, Vietnam,
Pacific Rim, Korea*
Elsevier Science Asia
583 Orchard Road
#09/01, Forum
Singapore 238884
Tel: 65-737-3593
Fax: 65-753-2145

Australia, New Zealand
Elsevier Science Australia
Customer Service Department
STM Division
Locked Bag 16
St. Peters, New South Wales, 2044
Australia
Tel: 61 02 9517-8999
Fax: 61 02 9517-2249
E-mail: stmp@harcourt.com.au
www.harcourt.com.au

Mexico and Central America
ETM SA de CV
Calle de Tula 59
Colonia Condesa
06140 Mexico DF, Mexico
Tel: 52-5-5553-6657
Fax: 52-5-5211-8468
E-mail: editoresdetextosmex@
prodigy.net.mx

Argentina
CLM (Cuspide Libros Medicos)
Av. Córdoba 2067 - (1120)
Buenos Aires, Argentina
Tel: (5411) 4961-0042/(5411)
    4964-0848
Fax: (5411) 4963-7988
E-mail: clm@cuspide.com

Brazil
Tecmedd
Av. Maurílio Biagi, 2850
City Ribeirão Preto – SP – CEP:
14021-000
Tel: 0800 992236
Fax: (16) 3993-9000
E-mail: tecmedd@tecmedd.com.br

Foreign Rights
John Scott & Company
International Publishers' Agency
P.O. Box 878
Kimberton, PA 19442
Tel: 610-827-1640
Fax: 610-827-1671
E-mail: jsco@voicenet.com

CONTENTS

PREFACE

The *Manual* of the Sixteenth Edition of *Ballenger's Otorhinolaryngology Head and Neck Surgery* provides a new approach to the development and maintenance of competency in the field. It presents synopses of 46 of the chapters in the main book that address clinical problems, and provides a handy, easily portable source of clinical knowledge emphasizing diagnosis and therapeutic management. Each synopsis is accompanied in the CD-ROM version by a group of multiple-choice examination items to allow the reader to assess his or her comprehension of the subject matter. Each examination item has a teaching commentary that indicates why the best response is favored and includes teaching points relevant to the subject matter of the examination item. The format is based on the educational concepts of immediate review and analysis of comprehension. The process has the important added benefit of giving the participant a prompt reinforcement of what the author(s) consider important. It gives the participant an opportunity to review the contents with a new perspective of the author's orientation and emphasis.

The informational content of the *Manual* is presented in clinically oriented synopses of commonly encountered problems in otology/neurotology, rhinology, facial plastic and reconstructive surgery, pediatric otorhinolaryngology, laryngology, head and neck surgery, and bronchoesophagology. For each topic, the reader is referred to the main book for a more comprehensive source of information. The content reflects the central responsibility of the otorhinolaryngologist in treating patients with diseases affecting the senses of smell, taste, and balance, and with disorders of human communication affecting hearing, voice, speech, and language.

The senior authors have been chosen not only for their contribution of new knowledge to their topics through highly regarded research, but also for their intellectual leadership in the specialty, and, thereby, are truly authoritative in the subject matter of their chapters and synopses.

The synopses stress the important role of molecular biology in understanding the pathogenesis of disease. Throughout the *Manual*, the genetic basis of disease is emphasized. This book provides students, residents, fellows, and practitioners with a ready reference to the current understanding necessary for the diagnosis and management of common problems in otorhinolaryngology head and neck surgery. The sum of these synopses will provide developing specialists and specialists wanting to maintain their competence with an efficient and compelling source of contemporary knowledge.

James B. Snow Jr, MD

CONTRIBUTORS

Omid Abbassi, MD, PhD
Department of
  Otorhinolaryngology and
  Communicative Sciences
Baylor College of Medicine
Houston, Texas

Peter W. Alberti, MB, PhD
Department of Otolaryngology
University of Toronto
Toronto, Ontario

Daniel G. Becker, MD
Department of
  Otorhinolaryngology–
  Head and Neck Surgery
University of Pennsylvania
Philadelphia, Pennsylvania

Peter C. Belafsky, MD, PhD
Department of Otolaryngology
Bowman Gray School of
  Medicine
Winston-Salem, North Carolina

John L. Boone, MD
Department of Otolaryngology
Camp Pendleton Naval Hospital
Camp Pendleton, California

Steven M. Bromley, MD
Department of Neurology
University of Pennsylvania
Philadelphia, Pennsylvania

Brian B. Burkey, MD
Department of Otolaryngology
Vanderbilt University
Nashville, Tennessee

William R. Carroll, MD
Department of
  Otorhinolaryngology–
  Head and Neck Surgery
University of Alabama
Birmingham, Alabama

Ara A. Chalian, MD
Department of
  Otorhinolaryngology–
  Head and Neck Surgery
University of Pennsylvania
Philadelphia, Pennsylvania

Richard A. Chole, MD, PhD
Department of Otolaryngology
Washington University
St. Louis, Missouri

Ellen S. Deutsch, MD
Department of Otolaryngology
Thomas Jefferson University
Philadelphia, Pennsylvania

Robert A. Dobie, MD
Division of Extramural Research
  National Institute on
  Deafness and Other
  Communication Disorders
Bethesda, Maryland

Paul J. Donald, MD
Department of Otolaryngology
University of California
Sacramento, California

Richard L. Doty, PhD
Department of
 Otorhinolaryngology–
 Head and Neck Surgery
University of Pennsylvania
Philadelphia, Pennsylvania

Jose N. Fayad, MD
Department of Otolaryngology
Columbia University
New York, New York

James W. Hall III, PhD
Department of Communicative
 Sciences and Disorders
University of Florida
Gainesville, Florida

Lee A. Harker, MD
Department of Surgery
Creighton University
Omaha, Nebraska

Jeffrey P. Harris, MD, PhD
Department of
 Otorhinolaryngology–
 Head and Neck Surgery
University of California
San Diego, California

James M. Hartman, MD
Department of Otolaryngology
Washington University
St. Louis, Missouri

Gerald B. Healy, MD
Department of Otology
 and Laryngology
Harvard Medical School
Boston, Massachusetts

Robert A. Hendrix, MD
Department of Surgery
Nash General Hospital
Rocky Mount, California

Stephen W. Hone, MD
Department of Otolaryngology
University of Iowa
Iowa City, Iowa

Ian N. Jacobs, MD
Department of
 Otorhinolaryngology–
 Head and Neck Surgery
University of Pennsylvania
Philadelphia, Pennsylvania

Margaret M. Jastreboff, PhD
Department of Otolaryngology
Emory University
Atlanta, Georgia

Pawel J. Jastreboff, PhD, ScD
Department of Otolaryngology
Emory University
Atlanta, Georgia

Herman A. Jenkins, MD
Department of Otolaryngology
University of Colorado
Denver, Colorado

Tae Hoon Jinn, MD
Division of
  Otorhinolaryngology–
  Head and Neck Surgery
Loma Linda University
Loma Linda, California

John K. Joe, MD
Department of Surgery
Memorial Sloan-Kettering
  Cancer Center
New York, New York

Jacob Johnson, MD
Department of
  Otorhinolaryngology–
  Head and Neck Surgery
University of California
San Francisco, California

Timothy T.K. Jung, MD, PhD
Division of
  Otorhinolaryngology–
  Head and Neck Surgery
Loma Linda University
Loma Linda, California

Elizabeth M. Keithley, PhD
Division of
  Otorhinolaryngology–
  Head and Neck Surgery
University of California
San Diego, California

David W. Kennedy, MD
Department of
  Otorhinolaryngology–
  Head and Neck Surgery
University of Pennsylvania
Philadelphia, Pennsylvania

Charles P. Kimmelman, MD
Department of Otolaryngology
Cornell University
New York, New York

Karen Iler Kirk, PhD
Department of Otolaryngology
University of Indiana
Indianapolis, Indiana

Robert I. Kohut, MD
Department of Otolaryngology
Bowman Gray School of
  Medicine
Winston-Salem, North Carolina

James A. Koufman, MD
Department of Otolaryngology
Bowman Gray School of
  Medicine
Winston-Salem, North Carolina

Dennis H. Kraus, MD
Department of Otolaryngology
Cornell University
New York, New York

Stephen Y. Lai, MD, PhD
Department of
  Otorhinolaryngology–
  Head and Neck Surgery
University of Pennsylvania
Philadelphia, Pennsylvania

Anil K. Lalwani, MD
Department of
  Otorhinolaryngology–
  Head and Neck Surgery
University of California
San Francisco, California

Paul R. Lambert, MD
Department of Otolaryngology
University of South Carolina
Charleston, South Carolina

Andrew P. Lane, MD
Department of
  Otorhinolaryngology–
  Head and Neck Surgery
Johns Hopkins University
Baltimore, Maryland

M. Samantha Lewis, MA
Department of Communicative
  Sciences and Disorders
University of Florida
Gainesville, Florida

David Litman, MD
Department of
  Otorhinolaryngology–
  Head and Neck Surgery
University of Pennsylvania
Philadelphia, Pennsylvania

Frank E. Lucente, MD
Department of Otolaryngology
State University of New York
Brooklyn, New York

Christy L. Ludlow, PhD
Laryngeal and Speech Section
National Institute of
  Neurological Disorders
  and Stroke
Bethesda, Maryland

**Valerie J. Lund, MS, FRCS,
  FRCS(Ed)**
Department of Otolaryngology
University College of London
London, England

Rodney P. Lusk, MD
Department of Otolaryngology
Washington University
St. Louis, Missouri

Eric A. Mann, MD, PhD
Laryngeal and Speech Section
National Institute of
  Neurological Disorders
  and Stroke
National Institutes of Health
Bethesda, Maryland

John H. Mills, PhD
Department of Otolaryngology
University of South Carolina
Charleston, South Carolina

Fred D. Minifie, PhD
Department of Speech and
  Hearing Sciences
University of Washington
Seattle, Washington

Richard T. Miyamoto, MD
Department of Otolaryngology
University of Indiana
Indianapolis, Indiana

Kris S. Moe, MD
Department of Surgery
University of California
San Diego, California

C. Elliott Morgan, DMD, MD
Department of
  Otorhinolaryngology–
  Head and Neck Surgery
University of Alabama
Birmingham, Alabama

Robert M. Naclerio, MD
Department of Otolaryngology
University of Chicago
Chicago, Illinois

Frank G. Ondrey, MD, PhD
Department of Otolaryngology
University of Minnesota
Minneapolis, Minnesota

Lisa A. Orloff, MD
Department of Surgery
University of California
San Diego, California

Simon C. Parisier, MD
Department of Otolaryngology
Mount Sinai School of Medicine
New York, New York

Philip Passalaqua, MD
Department of Otolaryngology
Mount Sinai School of Medicine
New York, New York

Jayant M. Pinto, MD
Department of Otolaryngology
University of Chicago
Chicago, Illinois

James S. Reilly, MD
Department of Otolaryngology
Thomas Jefferson University
Philadelphia, Pennsylvania

John S. Rhee, MD
Department of Otolaryngology
Medical College of Wisconsin
Milwaukee, Wisconsin

Kristina W. Rosbe, MD
Department of
  Otorhinolaryngology–
  Head and Neck Surgery
University of California
San Francisco, California

Lee D. Rowe, MD
Department of Otolaryngology
Thomas Jefferson University
Philadelphia, Pennsylvania

Michael Ruckenstein, MD
Department of
  Otorhinolaryngology–
  Head and Neck Surgery
University of Pennsylvania
Philadelphia, Pennsylvania

Leonard P. Rybak, MD, PhD
Department of Otolaryngology
University of Southern Illinois
Springfield, Illinois

Cecelia E. Schmalbach, MD
Department of
  Otorhinolaryngology
University of Michigan
Ann Arbor, Michigan

Mitchell K. Schwaber, MD
St. Thomas Neuroscience
  Institute
Nashville Hearing and
  Balance Center
Nashville, Tennessee

Samir Shah, MD
Department of Otolaryngology
Thomas Jefferson University
Philadelphia, Pennsylvania

Neil T. Shepard, PhD
Department of
  Otorhinolaryngology
University of Pennsylvania
Philadelphia, Pennsylvania

Richard J.H. Smith, MD
Department of
  Otorhinolaryngology–
  Head and Neck Surgery
University of Iowa
Iowa City, Iowa

Joseph C. Sniezek, MD
Department of Otolaryngology
Tripler Army Medical Center
Honolulu, Hawaii

David Solomon, MD, PhD
Department of Neurology
University of Pennsylvania
Philadelphia, Pennsylvania

Jeffery Staab, MD
Department of Psychiatry
University of Pennsylvania
Philadelphia, Pennsylvania

Jonathan M. Sykes, MD
Department of
  Otorhinolaryngology
University of California
Sacramento, California

M. Eugene Tardy Jr, MD
Department of
  Otorhinolaryngology–
  Head and Neck Surgery
University of Illinois
Chicago, Illinois

Steven A. Telian, MD
Department of
  Otorhinolaryngology
University of Michigan
Ann Arbor, Michigan

Lawrence W.C. Tom, MD
Department of
  Otorhinolaryngology–
  Head and Neck Surgery
University of Pennsylvania
Philadelphia, Pennsylvania

John Touliatos, MD
Department of Otolaryngology
University of Southern Illinois
Springfield, Illinois

Jeffrey Vierra, MD
Department of Medicine
State University of New York
Brooklyn, New York

Phillip A. Wackym, MD
Department of Otolaryngology
Medical College of Wisconsin
Milwaukee, Wisconsin

Robert A. Weisman, MD
Department of Surgery
University of California
San Diego, California

Peak Woo, MD
Department of Otolaryngology
Mount Sinai School of
  Medicine
New York, New York

Simon K. Wright, MD
Department of Otolaryngology
University of Minnesota
Minneapolis, Minnesota

Jane Y. Yang, MD
Department of Otolaryngology
Thomas Jefferson University
Philadelphia, Pennsylvania

DIAGNOSTIC AUDIOLOGY, HEARING AIDS, AND HABILITATION OPTIONS

James W. Hall III, PhD
M. Samantha Lewis, MA

This synopsis presents current techniques and strategies for hearing assessment, with an emphasis on the application of a test battery approach that maximizes diagnostic accuracy and efficiency while minimizing test time and costs. It also includes a review of current hearing aid technology for non-medical management of hearing impairment and a précis of pediatric habilitation approaches.

BASIC AUDIOLOGIC TEST BATTERY

Pure-Tone Audiometry

Pure-tone audiometry is a measure of hearing sensitivity using pure-tone signals at octave frequencies from 250 Hz up to 8,000 Hz. The unit of stimulus is the decibel (dB), a logarithmic unit of the ratio of a given sound pressure to a reference sound pressure. The reference sound pressure is the amount of pressure against the tympanic membrane just to be detected by a normal human ear as sound defined as 0 dB hearing level (HL). For other audiologic purposes, the sound pressure reference is 0.0002 dynes/cm^2, defined as 0 dB sound pressure level (SPL). The audiogram is a graph of hearing sensitivity in dB HL as a function of the above-mentioned frequencies and often 3,000 Hz. Hearing thresholds for air-conduction tonal or speech signals are measured separately for each ear with earphones. Pure-tone audiometry can also be performed with stimuli presented by a bone-conduction oscillator or vibrator placed on the mastoid bone.

The clinically normal region on the audiogram is from 0 to 20 dB HL for adults and 0 to 15 dB HL for children. Thresholds in the 20 to 40 dB HL region constitute a mild hearing loss, 40 to 60 dB HL thresholds define a moderate loss, and threshold levels greater than 60 dB HL are considered a severe hearing loss. The essential frequencies for understanding speech are in the 500 through 4,000 Hz region. Hearing sensitivity within the "speech frequency" region is traditionally summarized by calculating the pure-tone average or PTA (hearing thresholds for 500, 1,000, and 2,000 Hz divided by three and reported in dB).

Type of hearing loss can be described by comparison of the hearing thresholds for air- versus bone-conduction signals. The major types of hearing loss are conductive (normal bone conduction and a loss by air conduction), sensorineural (no air–bone gap), and mixed (combination of conductive and sensorineural). The configuration of a hearing loss refers to the shape of the hearing loss as a function of the test frequency. The most common configuration is a sloping high-frequency hearing loss that is sensorineural in type.

Masking is the audiometric technique used to eliminate participation of the nontest ear whenever air- and bone-conduction stimulation exceeds the level that might cross over to the nontest ear (interaural attenuation). A noise signal is presented to the nontest ear when the stimulus is presented to the test ear. With adequate masking, any signal crossing over to the nontest ear is masked by the noise.

A problem encountered in audiometric assessment of patients with a severe conductive hearing loss is the *masking dilemma*. The level of masking noise necessary to overcome the conductive component and adequately mask the nontest ear exceeds the interaural attenuation levels. The masking noise may then cross over to the test ear and mask the test signal. In the masking dilemma, enough masking is too much masking.

Speech Audiometry

Speech audiometry measures how well a person hears and understands speech signals. Even though it was introduced more than 50 years ago, the most common clinical approach for estimating a person's ability to hear and understand speech is still speech recognition for a list of 25 or 50 words in which specific speech sounds (phonemes) occur approximately as often as they would in everyday conversational English; hence they are phonetically balanced (PB) words. With adult patients, it is always preferable to use professionally produced (and commercially available) speech materials presented via compact disc player and an audiometer. Diagnostic speech audiometry using more sophisticated materials (eg, spectrally degraded or temporally distorted speech or speech-in-noise materials) is feasible for assessment of the function of the central auditory system.

Immittance Measurement

Immittance (*im*pedance and/or ad*mittance*) characteristics of the middle ear system can be inferred objectively with quick and noninvasive electrophysiologic techniques and then related to well-known patterns of findings for various types of middle ear lesions. Tympanometry is the continuous recording of middle ear impedance as air pressure in the ear canal is systematically increased or decreased. Initially in the testing, the volume of the ear canal is estimated. If it exceeds 2 cm^3, the possibility of a perforation of the tympanic membrane is to be considered. A middle ear system with low impedance (high admittance) more readily accepts acoustic energy, whereas a middle ear with high impedance (low admittance) tends to reject acoustic energy. In the tympanogram, static compliance (the reciprocol of stiffness) of the middle ear components is plotted as a function of the pressure in the ear canal. There are three general tympanogram types: A (normal with a peak between 0 and -100 mm H_2O), B (there is no peak but rather a flat pattern, most often associated with fluid in the middle ear), and C (with a peak within the negative pressure region beyond -150 mm H_2O indicative of poor middle ear ventilation owing to eustachian tube dysfunction). Tympanometric patterns, in combination with audiogram patterns, permit differentiation among and classification of middle ear disorders.

Measurement of contractions of the middle ear stapedial muscle to high sound intensity levels (usually 80 dB or greater) is the basis of the test for the acoustic reflex. Acoustic reflex measurement is clinically useful for estimating hearing sensitivity and for differentiating among sites of auditory disorders, including the middle ear, inner ear, eighth cranial nerve, and auditory brainstem. This objective measure can be accomplished quickly and is especially valuable in children and difficult-to-test patients.

AUDITORY EVOKED RESPONSES

Auditory Brainstem Response

Among the many auditory evoked responses, the auditory brainstem response or ABR (often referred to by neurologists as the brainstem auditory evoked response or BAER) and electrocochleography (ECochG) are applied most often clinically. The ABR is generated with transient acoustic stimuli (eg, clicks or tone bursts) and is detected with surface electrodes placed on the forehead and near the ears (earlobe or within the external ear canal). Using a computer-based device, thousands of sound stimuli are presented at rates of 20 to 30 per second, and reliable ABR waveforms can be averaged in a matter of minutes. ABR wave components I through V are generated mostly by axonal fiber tracts from the auditory (eighth cranial) nerve through the lateral lemniscus. Auditory brainstem response analysis consists of the calculation of latencies for each of the ABR waves under different stimulus conditions (right and left ear and varying intensity levels). With pediatric applications of the ABR, the main objective is to estimate hearing sensitivity with air-conducted (and sometimes bone-conducted) click and tone-burst signals when this cannot be reliably done with behavioral audiometry. A primary goal in any neurodiagnostic ABR is to record a clear and reliable wave I component. Wave I serves as the benchmark for peripheral auditory function. Subsequent interwave latencies offer indices of retrocochlear (eighth nerve and brainstem) function that are relatively unaffected by conductive or sensory hearing loss.

Electrocochleography

Electrocochleography is an electrophysiologic measure of cochlear auditory function. The three major components of the ECochG are the cochlear microphonic (CM), the summating potential (SP), and the action potential (AP). The CM and SP reflect cochlear bioelectric activity, whereas the AP is generated by synchronous firing of distal afferent eighth nerve fibers and is equivalent to ABR wave I. Currently, ECochG is performed most often for intraoperative monitoring of cochlear and eighth nerve status and in the diagnosis of Meniere's disease. Optimal ECochG waveforms are recorded when the electrode is placed close to the cochlea, for example, through the tympanic membrane onto the promontory, although tympanic membrane and, to a lesser extent, ear canal electrode locations are also clinically useful. The characteristic ECochG finding for patients with Meniere's disease is an abnormal increase in the SP amplitude relative to the AP amplitude.

OTOACOUSTIC EMISSIONS

Otoacoustic emissions (OAEs) are low-intensity sounds produced by the cochlea. A moderate-intensity click, or an appropriate combination of two tones, activates outer hair cell movement or motility. Outer hair cell motility generates mechanical energy within the cochlea that is propagated outward via the middle ear system and the tympanic membrane to the ear canal. Vibration of the tympanic membrane then produces an acoustic signal that can be detected with a sensitive microphone. There are two broad classes of OAEs: spontaneous and evoked. Evoked OAEs, most useful clinically, are elicited by moderate levels of acoustic stimulation at 50 to 80 dB SPL in the external ear canal.

When outer hair cells are structurally damaged or at least nonfunctional, OAEs cannot be evoked by acoustic stimuli. Among patients with mild cochlear dysfunction, OAEs may be recorded, but amplitudes are below normal limits for some or all stimulus frequencies. Importantly, some patients with abnormal OAE, consistent with cochlear dysfunction, will have normal pure-tone audiograms. The noninvasive nature of OAE recording, coupled with their accuracy and objectivity in assessing cochlear, in particular outer hair cell, function, has led to diverse clinical applications, ranging from neonatal auditory screening, to monitoring for ototoxicity, to differential diagnosis of sensorineural auditory dysfunction.

INDICATIONS FOR DIAGNOSTIC AUDIOLOGIC ASSESSMENT

Children

Hearing loss influences speech and language development of infants and young children, and these effects begin within the first 6 months of life. Therefore, early identification of hearing loss, coupled with timely and appropriate intervention and management, is necessary for a child to reach his or her full communicative and educational potential. Over 10 specific factors put children at risk for hearing impairment, for example, perinatal infection, congenital anomalies of the ear, and ototoxicity, as identified by the 2000 Joint Committee on Infant Hearing. Recognition that only about 50% of pediatric hearing loss, however, is associated with these risk factors has led to widespread professional and legislative support for universal newborn hearing screening, that is, hearing screening of all infants at or soon after birth. In addition to peripheral hearing impairment secondary to common causes, such as conductive hearing loss with otitis media or sensorineural hearing loss in ototoxicity, it is also important to consider the possibility of auditory processing disorders in children. Auditory processing disorders are defined as "deficits in the processing of information that is specific to the auditory modality."

Adults

In adults, hearing loss can be associated with multiple and diverse diseases. The initial step is thorough medical and audiologic assessment, as outlined above. However, for the majority of adult patients, hearing loss is secondary to either noise exposure and/or advancing age. Management for these persons typically involves attempts to improve communication and quality of life with nonmedical and nonsurgical treatment approaches, such as hearing aids.

HEARING AIDS

A hearing aid is a device that delivers an amplified acoustic signal to the ear. Hearing aids consist of three basic components: a microphone, an amplifier, and a receiver, which are housed in a plastic case designed to fit behind or in the ear. There are two main ways of classifying hearing aids. The first is by the style of the hearing aid, which usually refers to the size and placement of the aid. The second is by the technological features of the device.

The most commonly used hearing aid styles are the behind-the-ear (BTE), in-the-ear (ITE), in-the-canal (ITC), and completely-in-the-canal (CIC) hearing instruments. Although each style is associated with strengths and limitations, the clear trend in hearing aid design and popularity has been toward smaller hearing aids. Behind-the-ear hearing aids are the most widely used style for children. The BTE style allows an inexpensive means of accommodating growth of the auricle and ear canal, is more resistant to feedback, and is more readily retained on the ear.

Hearing Aid Technology

In the past few years, hearing aid technology has advanced rapidly. Disposable and instant fit hearing aids are the newest development to emerge on the hearing aid market. These devices are receiving increased attention because they can be fit immediately. The products are available in a wide range of sizes and technologies and in styles from BTE to CIC. An advantage of these devices is their significantly reduced price in comparison to custom-made products. Disposable hearing aids have an added benefit in that there is never a need to replace the battery since the entire hearing aid is replaced after a specific number of days (eg, 40). However, these devices are suitable only for milder degrees of hearing impairment. Another technological advance, the programmable hearing aid, provides increased flexibility and options for the wearer. Many of these devices offer multiple memories or programs, allowing the patient access to different settings that may be more appropriate for various listening environments. Digital hearing aids are the most popular new hearing aid technology available in today's market. A digital hearing aid processes the acoustic signal differently than an analog instrument. These devices offer a number of advantages, which include increased flexibility of shaping the frequency response of the instrument, feedback suppression capabilities, improved sound quality, decreased battery drain, and less internal circuit noise. These devices may also have multiple memories and be adjusted via a computer or hand-held programmer. The memories may be accessed via a remote control or a switch on the device. The major complaint of individuals with sensorineural hearing loss is the inability to hear in background noise. Directional microphones provide a person with a hearing impairment with the opportunity for understanding in noise.

Indications for and Benefits from Amplification

Hearing aids are indicated whenever it can be demonstrated that the patient's ability to communicate will be significantly improved through the use of amplification.

Amplification is an extremely effective means of improving the hearing of patients with conductive hearing loss. A hearing aid is clearly not an acceptable alternative to effective medical treatment of a pathologic condition, but it may be used after the course of treatment to offset residual peripheral hearing impairment. The use of amplification must be carefully evaluated in all cases of central impairment. However, there are alternatives for these patients. Perhaps the most common approach is the recommendation of an assistive listening device, like an FM system, for improvement of speech understanding by significantly enhancing the speech signal in relation to background noise.

There are a number of means to assess the efficacy of amplification, including electroacoustic analysis, functional gain measures, real-ear measures, and self-assessment inventories. An individual with hearing impairment requires a period of adjustment to become accustomed to wearing a hearing aid. According to federal law, a customer may return a hearing aid to the dispenser within 30 days for a refund.

Unfortunately, 30 days are often not sufficient time for complete accommodation and/or modification of the instrument.

It is readily apparent that the use of amplification significantly improves the communicative ability of an individual with hearing impairment. However, recent research has revealed additional benefits in psychosocial and functional health measures. These studies have shown that most individuals using amplification reported less depressive feelings, richer social relationships, and less anxiety and paranoia.

If the hearing loss is bilateral, binaural amplification has been documented to

- improve word identification, particularly in adverse listening conditions;
- improve localization of the sound source;
- provide a sense of "balanced hearing";
- require less gain;
- eliminate the head shadow effect; and
- increase perception of high-frequency consonants.

ADVISING THE PARENTS OF YOUNG CHILDREN WITH HEARING IMPAIRMENT

Although otolaryngologists are principally concerned with the medical or surgical management of aural disease and disorders, it is important that they have an understanding of and an appreciation for the various educational options and communication modalities available to the families of children with hearing impairments. There is no single communication modality that is right for every child. This decision must be made on an individual basis, and consideration should be given to issues such as the characteristics of the child (ie, age of diagnosis and accompanying learning disabilities), available community resources, and the commitment of the family to the child and the chosen communication modality. The various communication modes and educational strategies include oral approaches, manual approaches (eg, signing techniques), bilingual-bicultural approaches, and combination approaches (the most popular of which is total communication).

Thus, a variety of educational methods are available to the individual with hearing impairment. For the vast majority of families, this important educational decision is often made during a period of emotional turmoil. These parents view the identification of a hearing loss as a loss of their dreams of a normal child and may grieve accordingly. Unfortunately, a lack of understanding of the hearing loss, its implications, and remedial interventions can only exacerbate this emotional reaction.

The concept of a critical period of development during which the central nervous system exhibits maximal plasticity is central to any discussion about the education of the individual with hearing impairment.

In summary, each of the currently available educational methods has its proponents and opponents. Whenever appropriate, and with the support of the parents and other caregivers, otolaryngologists should encourage and facilitate maximal use of residual hearing and language development in an attempt to help these children reach their full communicative potential. It is essential that the otolaryngologist provide the parent with supportive, unbiased information regarding the benefits and limitations of the aforementioned modalities. No matter what the family's educational decision, early intervention services should be highly encouraged.

2

EVALUATION OF THE VESTIBULAR (BALANCE) SYSTEM

Neil T. Shepard, PhD
David Solomon, MD, PhD
Michael Ruckenstein, MD
Jeffery Staab, MD

In considering the evaluation of the patient with complaints of vertigo, light-headedness, imbalance, or combinations of these descriptors, one must look beyond just the peripheral and central parts of the vestibular system with its oculomotor connections. The various pathways involved in postural control, only part of which have direct or indirect vestibular input, should be kept in mind during an evaluation. Additionally, significant variations in symptoms and test findings can be generated by migraine and/or anxiety disorders, yet these are diagnosed primarily by history, requiring a specific line of questioning. Additionally, the principles and techniques behind the laboratory investigations can be applied in detailed direct office examinations of these patients.

The evaluation of the dizzy patient should be guided by what information is needed to make initial and subsequent management decisions. The following are considered required elements to management decisions for the chronic dizzy patient: detailed neurotologic history, office vestibular and physical examination, and formal audiometric testing given the inescapable anatomic relationship between the peripheral parts of the auditory and vestibular systems. The following are considered important but less likely to drive directly the management in the typical case: laboratory vestibular and balance function studies, neuroradiographic evaluations, and serologic tests. It is important to realize that there will be patients for whom unexpected findings on any one of these latter studies will either alter the complete course of the management or add dimensions to the management not originally considered. But for the majority of patients, the vestibular and balance tests will be confirmatory in nature.

Given the various tools for assessment, the history is the single most important factor in determining the course of management and therefore requires discussion. The differentiation among the various peripheral vestibular disorders is particularly dependent on historical information and the conclusions that the physician draws from the interview. Most vestibular disorders cannot be distinguished from one another simply by vestibular testing or other diagnostic interventions. Failure to discriminate properly these disorders on historical grounds may be the source of considerable ongoing distress for the patient and may lead to improper management by the physician. Since subsequent treatment decisions will be based on the clinical diagnosis, it is particularly appropriate to spend additional time during the history to clarify important features. Two of the critical elements in developing a differential diagnosis involve the determination of spontaneity versus visual or head movement provocation together with the temporal characteristics of the symptoms. These two features play a major role in the development of the working diagnosis.

Specifically, one wishes to know if the spells are continuous or occur in discrete episodes. If the symptoms are episodic, it is extremely important to distinguish whether they are spontaneous or motion provoked. If the symptoms are brief and predictably produced by head movements or body position changes, the patient most likely has a stable lesion but has not completed central nervous system compensation. Those who describe these symptoms also note a chronic underlying sense of dysequilibrium or light-headedness. The chronic symptoms may be quite troublesome, but any intense vertigo should be primarily motion provoked. These patients are suitable candidates for vestibular rehabilitation therapy. If the episodes last longer with intense vertigo and occur spontaneously, they probably represent progressive or unstable peripheral dysfunction. One must suspect a progressive lesion if the vertigo is accompanied by fluctuating or progressive sensorineural hearing loss. Patients with progressive lesions are not suitable candidates for vestibular rehabilitation therapy.

Other psychosocial aspects can be important in understanding the patient's situation. Complicating features of anxiety, depression, or excessive dependence on psychotropic medications should be identified.

The principal tests that are found in most dedicated balance centers are electronystagmography (ENG), rotational chair, and computerized dynamic posturography (CDP). Other evaluation tools are available for specific tasks. These include head on body studies (autorotation tests), special protocols that use eye movement recordings that can quantify linear horizontal and vertical as well as torsional activity, dynamic visual acuity, and protocols to assess the otolith organs specifically. Assuming that all of the studies are available, it is not necessary for each patient to have all aspects of the major evaluative tools as a selection of the tests may be adequate. One suggested strategy for determining which tests are needed is based on a core set of studies that would be appropriate for all patients, and the use of those studies together with the neurotologic history determine when the other tests are needed. A possible core would be the ENG with full oculomotor studies (by computerized system), full history, and screening evaluation of postural control. The basic site-of-lesion investigation and first approximation of the functional assessment of balance can be obtained in this manner.

Traditional ENG, using electro-oculography for eye movement recordings, is a process that estimates the position of the eye as a function of time indirectly. The estimates are reliable whether recorded with eyes open or closed and in a darkened or well-lit environment. Changes in eye position are indicated by the polarity of the corneal-retinal potential (dipole) relative to each electrode placed near the eyes. These electrodes are typically placed at each lateral canthus and above and below at least one eye with a common electrode on the forehead. Since the primary purpose of the vestibular apparatus is to control eye movements, the movements of the eyes may be used to examine the activity of the vestibular end-organs and their central vestibulo-ocular pathways. More recently, the technique of infrared video-oculography has begun to replace the standard electro-oculography. This technique has the advantages of direct estimate of the eye position as a function of time and reduction in electrical artifacts. It is important to understand that assessment of the peripheral part of the vestibular system with ENG is significantly limited, typically reflecting the function of the horizontal semicircular canal with restricted information from vertical canals and otolith organs. With the use of computerized ENG systems, which afford significant visual stimulus control and quantitative analysis, evaluation of the central vestibulo-ocular pathways can be quite thorough.

Spontaneous nystagmus of peripheral origin is usually suppressed with visual fixation. It frequently occurs after unilateral labyrinthine injury. Direction-changing nystagmus, vertical nystagmus, and nystagmus not suppressed by fixation suggest a lesion in the central nervous system.

The ENG consists of the following groups of subtests: oculomotor evaluation, typically with smooth pursuit tracking, saccade analysis, gaze fixation, and optokinetic stimulation; spontaneous nystagmus; rapid positioning (Dix-Hallpike maneuver); positional nystagmus; and caloric irrigations. The slow component eye velocity of the nystagmus is the measurement of interest as it reflects the portion of the nystagmus that is generated by the vestibulo-ocular reflex (with the fast component generated from the pons area of the brainstem in response to the position of the eye in the orbit). The responses to caloric stimulation are equivalent to the angular acceleration in the low-frequency range. Therefore, absence of caloric response to warm, cool, or ice water irrigations cannot be taken as an indication of complete lack of function. Although traditionally part of the ENG, the Dix-Hallpike maneuver should be analyzed by direct examination, not requiring quantification with recording, and should not be analyzed by the typical two-dimensional (horizontal and vertical) recorded eye movements from an ENG. The findings from the Dix-Hallpike maneuver should be interpreted with the knowledge of the patient's complaints. The oculomotor tests are quantified according to the eye movements generated during the task and analyzed by comparison to normative data when a computerized system is used.

Rotary chair testing has been used to expand the evaluation of the peripheral part of the vestibular system. As with the ENG findings, the rotational chair evaluation can assist in site-of-lesion determination, counseling the patient, and confirmation of clinical suspicion of diagnosis and lesion site but is not likely to alter or impact significantly the course of patient management, excepting the patient with bilateral peripheral weakness. The rotational chair is the only tool currently available for defining the extent of suspected bilateral peripheral lesions. When considering the use of the chair protocols, it is important to remember that the sides of the peripheral parts of the vestibular system have a "push-pull" arrangement, such that if one side is stimulated with angular acceleration, the opposite side is inhibited in its neural activity. Therefore, the chair is not a tool that can be easily used to isolate one side of the peripheral part of the system from the other for evaluation as each stimulus affects both sides simultaneously.

As with the ENG, electro-oculography or video-oculography can be used to monitor and record the outcome measure of interest, jerk nystagmus, which is generated in response to the angular acceleration stimulus. The vestibulo-ocular reflex is the slow component of the jerk nystagmus and, as with ENG, is the portion of the eye movement for which velocity is calculated for analysis.

Just as all patients who are being evaluated in the laboratory need tests for peripheral and central vestibulo-ocular pathway involvement, they also require some assessment of postural control ability. However, just as in the use of ENG and rotational chair testing, not all patients would need high-technology, formal postural control assessment. There are several different general approaches to formal postural control testing, each with specific technical equipment requirements and goals for the testing. To reduce the scope of this discussion, comments will be restricted to the most common formal assessment tool used in the United States, CDP, as formulated in the EquiTest® (Clackamas, OR) equipment.

The most important aspect of interpretation for the sensory organization test (SOT) is that it provides information as to which input system cues the patient is unable to use for performing the task of maintaining postural control. In other words, it provides a relative measure of the patient's ability to use the sensory input cues, visual, vestibular, and proprioceptive/somatosensory, to maintain quiet upright stance. The test does *not* provide relative information as to which of the sensory systems has lesions, causing postural control abnormalities. Therefore, the SOT of CDP provides no site-of-lesion information; it is strictly a test of functional ability.

The motor control test (MCT) is used less as a functional evaluation than the SOT and more to evaluate the long-loop neural pathway. This pathway begins with inputs from the ankle, knee, and hip regions (tendon and muscle stretch receptors) and projects to the motor cortex and back to the various muscles of postural control, including upper and lower body. When an abnormal latency to onset of active recovery from induced sway is noted, then problems in the long-loop pathway should be considered. The explanation may be as simple as ongoing joint or back pain, a congenital condition of the back or lower limbs, or an acquired lesion involving the neural pathways of the afferent or efferent tracts.

Postural evoked responses are used to define patterns of muscle response that have been associated with specific lesion sites and diseases. Normative results for the paradigm have been developed across age and have been shown to have sensitivity for identifying the site-of-lesion and/or specific disease entities reflected by the defined patterns of abnormal responses. As with the MCT, the electromyographic evaluation does not distinguish afferent from efferent disruptions that may underlie the abnormal muscle responses. With additional clinical investigations of sensitivity in the lower limbs and/or the use of lower limb somatosensory evoked responses, pathology affecting sensory input may be distinguished from motor output abnormalities.

The CDP tests provide data ranging from purely functional information to that of specific site-of-lesion, postural control pathways by changing the protocol and the output parameters. Lastly, CDP is useful for identification of patients who may be, for whatever reason, exaggerating their condition.

A discussion of the investigation of patients with dizziness and balance disorders would not be complete without a brief description of the use of neuroradiographic techniques, serologic studies, and when the pursuit of psychological issues may be useful.

Patients with dizziness often have psychological symptoms such as anxiety or depression. From a diagnostic standpoint, psychiatric disorders may be the sole cause of dizziness, but, just as often, they co-occur with neurotologic illnesses. The use of magnetic resonance imaging (MRI), magnetic resonance angiography (MRA), and computed tomography (CT) scans is widespread. There are bedside (office examination) signs that would warrant a referral for MRI as each of these is an indicator of possible central nervous system involvement. Some of these same findings are also appreciated on an ENG study. The most prominent central indicator is that of pure vertical nystagmus (especially when noted with fixation present) or a pure torsional nystagmus with fixation removed. There are signs that, when seen with acute-onset vertigo, should trigger an emergent imaging study. A diffusion-weighted MRI is the preferred technique over CT if it can be obtained within hours of the onset of symptoms. Cerebellar infarcts may mimic peripheral vestibular paresis. These may become hemorrhagic, and swelling during the first few days after the stroke can cause brainstem herniation and death. Patients with a history of brainstem or cerebellar symptoms typically lasting from 5 to 60 minutes may be having posterior circulation (vertebrobasilar) transient ischemic attacks. This is an indication for the use of MRA to rule out stenosis of the vertebral or basilar arteries.

Vestibular and balance rehabilitation therapy (VBRT) is a symptom-driven program for determination of who is an appropriate candidate. Therefore, it is during the history that the first possible indications for the use of this management technique would be developed. For the most part, other than the SOT of posturography, the laboratory tests described above do not provide indications for the use of this treatment option. There are situations when the symptom complaints are questionable for use of the program, yet findings on postural control studies suggest functional deficits that can be addressed with the VBRT techniques, and its use would be appropriate. In the case of bilateral vestibular paresis, the rotary chair is the only test that can provide information about the extent of bilateral weakness. With those chair results, VBRT programs can be altered for more realistic goals. Lastly, indications from ENG or rotary chair of a unilateral reduced vestibular response to caloric irrigation or abnormal timing relationship between eye and head movement from the rotary chair support the use of adaptation exercises to improve vestibulo-ocular reflex gain. It is unlikely that repeat use of ENG or the rotary chair following use of VBRT would be called for since the utility of these tools in determining compensation status is very limited, and the primary focus in a VBRT program is to enhance the compensation process in many dimensions. However, repeated use of various postural control and dynamic visual acuity assessments would be useful as a monitor and/or final outcome measure of the effectiveness of a VBRT program since these studies are primarily functional in nature.

3

DISEASES OF THE EXTERNAL EAR

Timothy T. K. Jung, MD, PhD
Tae Hoon Jinn, MD

TRAUMA TO THE EXTERNAL EAR

Auricular Hematoma

Hematoma of the auricle usually develops after blunt trauma and is common among wrestlers and boxers. The mechanism usually involves traumatic disruption of a perichondrial blood vessel. Blood accumulation in the subperichondrial space results in separation of perichondrium from the cartilage. The most effective treatment for auricular hematoma is adequate incision and drainage with through-and-through suture-secured bolsters such as dental rolls.

Frostbite

The auricle is particularly susceptible to frostbite because of its exposed location and lack of subcutaneous or adipose tissue to insulate the blood vessels. The frostbitten ear should be rapidly warmed. Wet sterile cotton pledgets at 38 to 42°C are applied until the ear is thawed. The ear should be treated gently owing to the risk of further damage to the already traumatized tissue. Necrotic tissue is débrided, the topical thromboxane inhibitor aloe vera is applied, and antiprostaglandin drugs such as ibuprofen may be beneficial.

Burns

Burns caused by scalding liquids or fire are often full thickness. Untreated, they may lead to perichondritis. It is important to avoid pressure on the ear, and gentle cleansing and topical antibiotic applications are advocated. Prophylactic use of antipseudomonal antibiotics is recommended. The antibiotics may be injected subperichondrially at several different injection sites over the anterior and posterior surfaces of the auricle.

Cerumen

Cerumen is a combination of the secretions produced by sebaceous (lipid producing) and apocrine (ceruminous) glands admixed with desquamated epithelial debris. This combination forms an acidic coat that aids in the prevention of external auditory canal (EAC) infection. The pH of the cerumen is high in diabetic patients compared with 6.5 to 6.8 in the normal EAC.

Several techniques are available for the removal of cerumen and may be used in a variety of ways such as mechanical removal with ring curet and alligator forceps, irrigation, and suction. Before starting to remove cerumen, one should make sure that the patient does not have a history of tympanic membrane perforation. If perforation is suspected, the irrigation method should not be used. If impaction of hard cerumen persists or is too painful to remove, the patient may be sent home with instructions for using an agent to soften the cerumen. Following its use for a few days, the cerumen can be removed with irrigation or suction.

Foreign Bodies

Foreign bodies in the EAC are found most frequently in the pediatric age group or in mentally retarded institutionalized patients. The removal of a foreign body can be safely done under direct visualization, preferably under an operating microscope with the patient in a supine position. A live insect in the EAC should be immobilized before removal by instilling mineral oil or alcohol into the canal. The best chance for removal of a foreign body in the EAC is the first attempt. When it fails, the ear may become extremely painful, and proper anesthesia may be necessary. Four-quadrant canal skin injection with a local anesthetic agent is sufficient in adults. In young children, it is best to use general anesthesia.

Fractures of the External Auditory Canal

A strong blow to the mandible can drive the mandibular condyle into the ear canal, resulting in fracture of the anterior canal wall. Fractures of the canal can be a part of temporal bone fractures. Longitudinal temporal bone fractures may extend into the bony ear canal, usually passing through the bony tympanic ring at the junction of the scutum and the tympanomastoid suture. Fracture of the anterior wall can be treated with closed reduction with packing in the canal. Tympanoplasty may be needed to restore hearing in fractures of the EAC with ossicular disruption.

INFECTION AND INFLAMMATION OF THE EXTERNAL EAR

Auricle

Cellulitis of the Auricle

Cellulitis is a bacterial infection usually following abrasion, laceration, or ear piercing. It is usually caused by gram-positive cocci such as *Staphylococcus* or *Streptococcus* and rarely other microorganisms such as *Pseudomonas*. Treatment includes oral or intravenous antibiotic and wound care.

Allergic Dermatitis of the Auricle

Allergic dermatitis of the auricle is characterized by localized erythema, swelling, and itching in the area of allergen exposure. A patient with neomycin allergy who has been using eardrops containing neomycin will present with swelling and redness in the area exposed to the drops such as the meatus, EAC, and inferior part of the auricle. A patient with metal allergy will present with a red swollen ear lobule owing to contact with the earring. Treatment includes removing the allergen, topical corticosteroid cream, and oral antihistamines.

Perichondritis and Chondritis

Perichondritis or chondritis is a bacterial infection of the perichondrium or cartilage of the auricle. This condition may follow inadequately treated auricular cellulitis, acute otitis externa, accidental or surgical trauma, or multiple ear piercing in the scapha. The affected ear is painful, red, and swollen and drains serous or purulent exudates. The surrounding soft tissues of the face and neck may be affected. The most common pathogen is *Pseudomonas*.

For treatment in the early stage of perichondritis or chondritis, oral fluoroquinolone antibiotics are sufficient. In the advanced stage with surrounding soft tissue involvement and lymphadenopathy, intravenous ceftazidime or a fluoroquinolone is needed.

Relapsing Polychondritis

Relapsing polychondritis is an autoimmune disease manifested by intermittent episodes of inflammation of cartilage throughout the body. Auricular cartilage is most commonly involved, whereas nasal and laryngeal cartilages are less frequently involved. The typical patient presents with a red, swollen tender auricle. Recurrent episodes may result in a floppy and distorted auricle. Treatment includes corticosteroids, antiprostaglandin drugs, or dapsone for chronic disease.

External Auditory Canal

Acute Localized Otitis Externa (Furuncle)

Acute localized otitis externa is an infection of a hair follicle, beginning as a folliculitis but usually extending to form
a small abscess, a furuncle. The infecting microorganism is
usually *Staphylococcus aureus*. Resolution may occur with
topical or systemic antibiotics. A localized abscess should be
drained.

Acute Diffuse Otitis Externa (Swimmer's Ear)

Acute diffuse otitis externa is a bacterial infection of the EAC
and the most common form of otitis externa. Predisposing
factors include frequent swimming, a warm and humid cli-
mate, a narrow and hairy ear canal, presence of exostosis in
the canal, trauma or foreign body in the canal, impacted or
absent cerumen, use of hearing aids or earplugs, diabetes or
immunocompromised state, skin conditions such as eczema,
seborrhea, and psoriasis, and excessive sweating. The usual
pathogens in acute diffuse otitis externa are *Pseudomonas
aeruginosa, Proteus mirabilis,* and *Staphylococcus aureus*.

Certain principles of management must be observed in
every case of otitis externa. These are frequent inspection
and cleansing of the canal, control of pain, use of specific
medication appropriate to the type and severity of disease,
acidification of the canal, and control of predisposing
causes. Frequent inspection, with cleaning using microscopic suction-débridement and drying of the ear canal, is
the single most important step in obtaining resolution of all
forms of otitis externa.

In the moderate stage of inflammation, treatment may
include gentle cleaning-débridement of the canal and application of acidifying/antiseptic/antibiotic agents. If the canal
is edematous and swollen, a cotton or Pope wick may be
inserted and otic drops instilled on it. A variety of eardrops

are available for treatment. Most of the eardrops contain a combination of antipseudomonal antibiotics with or without corticosteroids such as neomycin, colistin, and hydrocortisone (Cortisporin); ofloxacin (Floxin); and ciprofloxacin hydrochloride (Cipro HC). Most of these agents are acidic to inhibit the proliferation of bacteria and fungi. The major adverse reaction to the use of an acidic agent is burning on application. Ophthalmic preparations (gentamicin, tobramycin with dexamethasone [Tobradex], ciprofloxacin hydro chloride [Ciloxan]) are pH neutral and may be tolerated better than otic drops. An additional advantage of ophthalmic drops is a low viscosity, allowing improved penetration.

Chronic Otitis Externa

Chronic otitis externa is a low-grade, diffuse infection and inflammation of the EAC that persist for months or years. It is characterized by pruritus and dry hypertrophic skin of the EAC. The goal of treatment is to prevent stenosis and restore the EAC skin to its normal healthy state. Antibiotics and corticosteroid otic drops can decrease the inflammation and edema of the EAC. Patients are instructed not to touch the EAC or use cotton swabs. In case of medical treatment failure, especially with a stenotic canal, surgical procedures are indicated to restore canal patency and hearing.

NECROTIZING (MALIGNANT) EXTERNAL OTITIS

Malignant external otitis is a progressive, potentially lethal infection of the EAC, surrounding tissue, and skull base (osteomyelitis) typically seen in elderly diabetic or other immunocompromised patients. *Pseudomonas aeruginosa* is the most common pathogen.

The typical otoscopic finding is granulation tissue in the floor of the EAC near the bony-cartilaginous junction. Patients usually complain of severe otalgia. The erythrocyte sedimentation rate is a nonspecific test but is useful in following the response to antibiotics.

Radiologic tests are required to determine the extent of disease. High-resolution computed tomography (CT) is recommended to assess the extent of disease at initial evaluation. Magnetic resonance imaging (MRI) is of no use in detecting bony changes. Bony involvement in patients with early malignant external otitis can be detected with a technetium scan (bone scan). A gallium scan is a sensitive indicator of infection; therefore, it is best for monitoring resolution of infection and is useful in determining the duration of antimicrobial therapy.

The standard treatment is hospitalization of the patient and treatment of diabetes, if present, together with the use of high doses of antibiotics specific for *Pseudomonas* for an extended period of time. Daily débridement of the EAC is performed, and culture of débrided material and sensitivity testing should be repeated during the initial phase of management. Standard antibiotic therapy has been aminoglycosides combined with either an antipseudomonal penicillin or cephalosporin for dual drug therapy as primary intervention. Because of potential nephro-ototoxicity of aminoglycosides, oral quinolones (ciprofloxacin) have been used successfully as an alternative to treat for malignant external otitis. The duration of antimicrobial therapy depends on serial gallium scans performed at 4-week intervals. A strict control of diabetes is essential for the treatment of malignant external otitis. Lessening of pain is the first indication of a favorable therapeutic response.

Fungal Otitis Externa (Otomycosis)

Fungal infection of the EAC is usually caused by *Aspergillus* and/or *Candida*. The most common presenting symptom is pruritus. Treatment consists of frequent and meticulous cleansing and topical medication. Topical antifungal agents may be effective in powder form and/or in a cream such as nystatin and triamcinolone (Mycolog).

Herpes Zoster

Herpes zoster is the most frequent virus to affect the external ear. The virus causes blisters on the auricle, the EAC, and even on the lateral surface of the tympanic membrane. This clinical syndrome with facial palsy, with or without hearing loss and dizziness, caused by herpes zoster is called *herpes zoster oticus* or *Ramsay Hunt syndrome*. Patients with full-blown herpes zoster oticus may be treated with acyclovir (Zovirax) and corticosteroid.

Tympanic Membrane

Bullous Myringitis

Bullous myringitis is an infection of the tympanic membrane characterized by rapid onset, severe pain, and varying sizes of blister formation on the tympanic membrane and adjacent bony ear canal. Treatment includes analgesia, topical antibiotics, and corticosteroid drops. Rupturing the blisters and packing or irrigation of the canal should be avoided.

Granular Myringitis

Granular myringitis is an inflammation of the tympanic membrane characterized by persistent granulation tissue on the lateral surface of the pars tensa with an intact tympanic membrane. The etiology is not clear, but granular myringitis is believed to be caused by local trauma or infection that denudes the epithelial layer of the tympanic membrane. Treatment includes cauterization with silver nitrate sticks and topical antibiotic and corticosteroid drops.

BENIGN TUMORS OF THE EXTERNAL EAR

Vascular Tumors

A *capillary hemangioma* consists of masses of capillary-sized vessels and may form a large flat mass. *Cavernous hemangioma* is the most alarming of these lesions, consisting of raised masses of blood-filled endothelial space. Often termed a "strawberry tumor," it increases rapidly in size during the first year of life but usually regresses thereafter. Much less common is the *lymphangioma*. It has the appearance of multiple pale circumscribed lesions, like a cluster of fish or frog roe.

Cysts

Sebaceous cysts are common around the ear. They usually occur on the posterior surface of the lobule and in the skin over the mastoid process. The treatment for sebaceous cysts is excision.

Preauricular Pits and Sinuses

Preauricular pits and sinuses are of congenital origin, arising from faulty developmental closure of the hillocks of first and second branchial arches that form the auricle. They present as a small opening in the skin just anterior to the crus of the helix. Treatment includes complete removal of the cyst along with the fistula tract.

Keloids

Keloids represent an unchecked healing response in individuals with a genetic predisposition to their development. Keloid formation is seen most frequently in the dark-skinned races, particularly in blacks. Keloids around the ear are most frequently pedunculated tumors on the lobule following ear piercing. Treatment is excision followed by periodic injection of a small amount of corticosteroids, such as triamcinolone (Kenalog), into the surgical site to prevent keloid reformation.

Winkler's Nodule (Chondrodermatitis Nodularis Chronica Helicis)

Chondrodermatitis nodularis chronica helicis is a benign nodular growth usually occurring on the rim of the helix in older men. It appears as a firm elevated nodular lesion with a grayish crust on the surface. Definitive treatment requires full-thickness excision, including a wedge of cartilage.

Keratoacanthoma

Keratoacanthoma is a benign tumor resembling carcinoma and is believed to be related to actinic exposure. The common location of the tumor is anterior to the tragus. Although the disease is self-limiting, excisional biopsy is required to rule out a malignant tumor.

Keratosis Obturans

Keratosis obturans is characterized by the accumulation of large plugs of desquamated keratin in the bony portion of the EAC. There is marked inflammation in the subepithelial tissue but no bone erosion. It has been associated with chronic pulmonary disease and sinusitis. The disease may be controlled in most cases by regular cleaning. *Cholesteatoma of the EAC* consists of a localized erosion of the bone by squamous cell tissue. It is usually unilateral and not associated with systemic disease. Treatment consists of periodic cleaning and surgery.

Exostoses and Osteomas

Exostoses are not traditionally considered neoplastic. Exostoses are common in patients who have histories of swimming in cold water. They are usually bilateral and appear as two or three smooth sessile protrusions on opposing surfaces of the bony canal medial to the isthmus. An osteoma occurs as a single unilateral pedunculated cancellous (trabecular) bone formation near the lateral end of the bony canal resembling a foreign body or cysts.

Fibrous Dysplasia

The temporal bone may be the site of monostotic or, less commonly, polyostotic fibrous dysplasia. The most common presentation of temporal bone fibrous dysplasia is progressive conductive hearing loss secondary to occlusion of the EAC or impingement on the ossicular chain. Progressive narrowing of the ear canal may lead to the development of a cholesteatoma. Diagnosis of fibrous dysplasia is based on radiographic and histologic findings. On plain radiographs, a fibrous dysplastic lesion consists of varying degrees of radiolucency and sclerosis, giving a "ground-glass" appearance. Surgery is indicated for diagnostic biopsy, presence of cholesteatoma, hearing loss, and correction of significant cosmetic deformity.

Adenomas

Adenomas of various sorts occur in the EAC. These are derived from sweat glands, sebaceous glands, or aberrant salivary gland tissue. Symptoms are minimal unless the growth completely occludes the canal. The treatment is surgical excision. Some of these lesions occasionally become malignant, and pathologic examination is required in each case.

MALIGNANT TUMORS OF THE EXTERNAL EAR

Squamous Cell Carcinoma of the Auricle

Prolonged exposure to the sun is a risk factor for the development of skin malignancy. Malignancy of the auricle is common in fair-skinned Whites and rare in Blacks. Squamous cell carcinomas present as ulcerated lesions with an area of surrounding erythema and induration. They occur more often on the helix. The treatment of choice for squamous cell carcinoma of the auricle is wide excision and reconstruction.

Basal Cell Carcinoma of the Auricle

Basal cell carcinomas present as painless, well-circumscribed ulcers with raised margins. The tumors are often found in the preauricular or postauricular areas, and more often in the helix and anterior surface of the pinna. Treatment is wide excision with full-thickness skin graft as needed. The surgical margin need not be as large as that for squamous cell carcinoma.

Squamous Cell Carcinoma of the External Auditory Canal

Malignant tumors can arise from the EAC, middle ear, and temporal bone. The tumor type, clinical presentation, prognosis, and treatment are determined by the anatomic location of the tumor. When patients present with advanced neoplasms, it may not be possible to define the sites of origin. The majority of cancers of the middle ear and mastoid originate in the EAC. Squamous cell carcinoma is the most common malignant tumor arising from the EAC and middle ear space.

The most common finding is a growth in the EAC, which is clinically difficult to differentiate from an aural polyp, granulation tissue, and otitis externa. When a tumor is found in the canal, the location, size, and extent of the tumor should be thoroughly evaluated under an operating microscope. Both CT and MRI are helpful in defining the extent of a carcinoma. Computed tomography is unsurpassed for assessing the integrity of osseous structures of the temporal bone and middle ear. Magnetic resonance imaging is superior to CT in the evaluation of soft tissues and may be used to assess dural, intracranial, and extracranial soft tissue involvement.

Treatment consists of wide surgical excision and postoperative radiation therapy. When a malignant tumor is small, involving the posterior part of the EAC, and has not extended to the drumhead, a complete modified radical mastoidectomy is done. If the tumor is close to the drumhead, a radical mastoidectomy is performed. If the tumor is located in the anterior wall of the EAC, excision may include the anterior canal wall, parotid gland, and condyle of the mandible. If a malignant tumor is extensive and involves the middle ear and mastoid, subtotal or total temporal bone resection may be needed.

Malignant Melanoma

Melanoma may occur either on the auricle or in the EAC, more commonly in the former location. Diagnosis should be suspected when a pigmented lesion begins to increase in size or change in color. Lymphatic spread, treatment, and prognosis are greatly influenced by location. Treatment is wide excision.

4

OTITIS MEDIA AND MIDDLE EAR EFFUSIONS

Gerald B. Healy, MD
Kristina W. Rosbe, MD

It is estimated that 70% of children will have had one or more episodes of otitis media (OM) by their third birthday. This disease process knows no age boundaries but occurs mainly in children from the newborn period through approximately age 7 years, when the incidence begins to decrease. It occurs equally in males and females. A racial prevalence exists, with a higher incidence occurring in specific groups such as Native Americans, Alaskan and Canadian Natives, and Australian aboriginal children. African American children appear to have less disease than do American White children.

Important epidemiologic factors include a higher incidence of OM in children attending daycare centers, a seasonal variation with more disease being present in the fall and winter versus the spring and summer, and a genetic predisposition to middle ear infection. Other epidemiologic factors include a lower incidence and duration of OM in breast-fed children and a higher incidence in children with altered host defenses. Anatomic changes such as cleft palate and other craniofacial anomalies as well as congenital and acquired immune deficiencies are also important factors. One of the earliest signs of acquired immune deficiency syndrome (AIDS) in infants is recurring episodes of OM. This observation has been seen in more than 50% of neonates with AIDS.

DEFINITIONS

Otitis media represents an inflammatory condition of the middle ear space, without reference to cause or pathogenesis.

Middle ear effusion is the liquid resulting from OM. An effusion may be either serous (thin, watery), mucoid (viscid, thick), or purulent (pus). The process may be acute (0 to 3 weeks in duration), subacute (3 to 12 weeks in duration), or chronic (greater than 12 weeks in duration).

Otitis media may occur with or without effusion. In those cases without effusion, inflammation of the middle ear mucous membrane and tympanic membrane may be the only physical finding. Occasionally, infection may involve only the tympanic membrane (myringitis), without involving the mucosa of the middle ear space.

Acute otitis media (AOM) represents the rapid onset of an inflammatory process of the middle ear space associated with one or more symptoms or local or systemic signs. These usually include otalgia, fever, irritability, anorexia, vomiting, diarrhea, or otorrhea. Physical examination usually reveals a thickened, erythematous, or bulging tympanic membrane with limited or no mobility to pneumatic otoscopy. Erythema of the tympanic membrane may be an inconsistent finding and may be absent in certain systemic illnesses such as immune deficiency, when the patient cannot mount a sufficient inflammatory response to present this more classic finding. The acute onset of fever, otalgia, and, on occasion, a purulent discharge is usually evidence of AOM. Following such an episode, the patient may move into a subacute or even chronic phase during which fluid is present in the middle ear space, although active infection may be absent.

Chronic otitis media with effusion (COME) indicates the presence of asymptomatic middle ear fluid, usually resulting in conductive hearing loss. The tympanic membrane may present numerous physical findings including thickening, opacification, and impaired mobility. An air-fluid level and/or bubbles may be observed through a translucent tympanic membrane. This entity is distinguished from AOM in that the signs and symptoms of acute infection are lacking (eg, otalgia, fever, otorrhea).

ETIOLOGY

Eustachian tube (ET) dysfunction is considered the major etiologic factor in the development of middle ear disease. There are essentially two types of ET obstruction resulting in middle ear effusion: mechanical and functional. Mechanical obstruction may be either intrinsic or extrinsic. Intrinsic mechanical obstruction is usually caused by inflammation of the mucous membrane of the ET or an allergic diathesis causing edema of the tubal mucosa. Extrinsic mechanical obstruction is caused by obstructing masses such as adenoid tissue or nasopharyngeal neoplasms.

Some observers believe that infants and younger children may suffer from *functional ET obstruction* as a result of either decreased tubal stiffness or an inefficient active opening mechanism. Proponents of this theory believe that either form of obstruction results in inadequate ventilation of the middle ear with resulting negative middle ear pressure.

The ET has three functions:

1. Ventilation of the middle ear associated with equalization of air pressure in the middle ear with atmospheric pressure
2. Protection of the middle ear from sound and secretions
3. Drainage of middle ear secretions into the nasopharynx with the assistance of the mucociliary system of the ET and middle ear mucous membrane

The role of allergy in otitis media with effusion (OME) has been extensively investigated. Inhalant allergies are felt to play a greater role than food allergies. Most studies, however, have been unable to demonstrate an increase in serum immunoglobulin E (IgE) in children with OME. Allergy is felt to affect ET function in several ways. Nasal obstruction can occur secondary to mast cell degranulation with increased vascular permeability, increased mucosal blood flow, and increased mucus production. Retrograde extension of inflammatory mediators from the anterior nose to the nasopharynx as well as allergen contact with the nasopharynx can cause ET edema and obstruction with a secondary increase in the pressure gradient through nitrogen gas exchange and subsequent transudation of fluid.

Otitis media–prone children have been shown to have higher levels of IgG antibody and IgG-antigen immune complexes in their serum and middle ears versus a non-OM-prone cohort. Immunoglobulin G may be the predominant immune mechanism in the middle ear. It is felt that bacteria may actually cause immunosuppression of cell-mediated immunity. Immunoglobulin A is thought to be a late defense mechanism and may actually prevent bacteriolysis by IgG and its complement, acting as a blocking antibody. Others have proposed an IgE-mediated hypersensitivity reaction to viral antigens.

MICROBIOLOGY

The most common bacterial pathogens responsible for acute infection include *Streptococcus pneumoniae* and nontypable *Haemophilis influenzae*. These two microorganisms account for approximately 60% of the cases associated with bacterial infection. Group A *Streptococcus, Branhamella catarrhalis, Staphylococcus aureus*, and gram-negative enteric bacteria are less frequent causes of OM.

Because of the difficulty in obtaining viral cultures, less specific data are available regarding their occurrence in patients with OM. However, *respiratory syncytial virus* accounts for a majority of the viral infections of the middle ear space. Otitis media may accompany exanthematous viral infections such as infectious mononucleosis and measles.

Over the years, chronic effusions have been thought to be sterile. However, more recent studies have confirmed the presence of bacteria in middle ear fluid, and studies show that the bacterial spectrum closely resembles that found in AOM.

DIAGNOSIS

In most cases, a careful history and physical examination will lead to the accurate diagnosis of OM. A careful history should elicit classic symptoms of OM. In the patient with the acute form of the disease, otalgia, fever, irritability, vomiting, and diarrhea may be present. Less frequently, otorrhea, vertigo, and facial paralysis may be associated with an acute infection of the middle ear space. In those patients in whom infection has spread into the mastoid air cell system and beyond, swelling of the postauricular area may be present.

In COME, hearing loss may be the only symptom. The most definitive part of the diagnosis is an appropriate physical examination to confirm the presence or absence of middle ear pathology. A complete examination of the head and neck should be undertaken first to identify the possibility of any predisposing condition such as craniofacial anomaly, nasal obstruction, palatal defect, or adenoid hypertrophy. In patients with unilateral OM, the nasopharynx should be visualized to rule out the possibility of neoplasm.

Otoscopy represents the most critical part of the examination to establish the diagnosis of OM. Use of the pneumatic otoscope is essential. The existence of chronic middle ear effusion is most easily confirmed when there is a definite air-fluid level or when bubbles are clearly visible within the middle ear space. However, findings commonly associated with OME include a severely retracted tympanic membrane with apparent foreshortening of the handle of the malleus and a reduction in tympanic membrane mobility. Occasionally, the tympanic membrane may be dull or thickened and have an amber hue.

In severe cases, middle ear fluid may become purplish or blue, indicating hemorrhage within the tympanic cavity.

The color of the tympanic membrane is important but is not conclusive in making a diagnosis. An erythematous tympanic membrane alone may not be indicative of a pathologic condition because the vasculature of the tympanic membrane may be engorged as a result of the patient's crying or the presence of fever.

Acute otitis media usually presents with a hyperemic tympanic membrane that is frequently bulging and has poor mobility. Occasionally, perforation may be present, and purulent otorrhea is visible.

The use of tympanometry confirms the findings of pneumatic otoscopy. This modality provides an objective assessment of the mobility of the tympanic membrane as well as the ossicular chain. By measuring tympanic membrane impedance, one can accurately predict conditions of the middle ear space (see Chapter 1).

The ultimate diagnostic test to confirm the presence of OM involves aspiration of middle ear contents. In acute situations, myringotomy or tympanocentesis may be undertaken to confirm the diagnosis, obtain material for culture, and relieve pus under pressure in an effort to avoid further complications. This may be necessary in patients who are unusually ill or toxic secondary to OM or in patients with severe suppurative complications. It may also be necessary in those patients who are having an unsatisfactory response to antibiotic therapy, in toxic newborns, or in patients who are significantly immune deficient.

With the rise in bacteria resistant to initial antibiotic therapy, tympanocentesis has been examined for its role in more specific antibiotic therapy. Tympanocentesis has several indications: (1) OM in patients with severe otalgia or toxic patients; (2) unsatisfactory response to antimicrobial therapy; (3) onset of OM in a patient already receiving antibiotics; (4)

OM associated with a confirmed or potential suppurative complication; and (5) OM in a newborn, sick neonate, or immunosuppressed patient. This procedure does have significant risks, including conductive and sensorineural hearing losses if not done properly. Otolaryngologists and pediatricians must be well trained in the technique to prevent these serious complications.

The hearing loss associated with OM should be documented whenever possible, especially in patients in whom chronic effusion is present. Although the presence of a conductive hearing loss does not confirm the diagnosis of COME, its presence does contribute to the confirmation of middle ear fluid. It is also important in documenting response to therapy.

MANAGEMENT

Acute Otitis Media

Acute otitis media represents one point in a continuum of the disease process known as "otitis media." The current standard of care strongly indicates that patients diagnosed as having an acute middle ear process should receive antimicrobial therapy for at least 10 to 14 days. In light of the fact that culture material is usually not readily available, therapy is begun on an empiric basis, with treatment being aimed at the more common microorganisms found in the acute process. Some have recommended withholding antimicrobial agents in certain cases. However, in light of the fact that suppurative complications have markedly declined during the antibiotic era, antibiotic therapy is still strongly recommended in the acute process.

The standard initial treatment for AOM is amoxicillin, 40 mg/kg/24 h in three divided doses, or ampicillin, 50 to 100 mg/kg/24 h in four divided doses, for 10 days. In children allergic to penicillin, a combination of erythromycin, 40 mg/kg/24 h, and sulfisoxazole, 120 mg/kg/24 h, in four divided doses may be substituted. If β-lactamase-producing

H. influenzae or *B. catarrhalis* is suspected, either amoxicillin-clavulanate 40 mg/kg/24 h in three divided doses or trimethoprim-sulfamethoxazole, 8 mg of trimethoprim and 40 mg of sulfamethoxazole/kg/24 h, may be used in two divided doses. Cefixime (Suprax, Lederle Laboratories, Wayne, NJ), 8 mg/kg in one dose, or cefprozil (Cefzil, Bristol-Myer-Squibb, Princeton, NJ), 15 mg/kg/24 h in two divided doses, may also be used effectively. A single intramuscular injection of ceftriaxone (Rocephin, Hoffman-Roche, Nutley, NJ), 50 to 100 mg/kg mixed with 1% lidocaine, not to exceed 1.5 mL, may be used in patients with vomiting. Newer treatment for β-lactamase-producing microorganisms include high-dose amoxicillin at 80 mg/kg/24 h.

Most patients who are receiving antibiotic therapy for AOM have significant improvement within 48 hours. If the child has not improved or the condition has worsened, tympanocentesis for culture and possibly myringotomy for drainage may be indicated. The patient may be re-examined some time during the course of therapy to ensure that the treatment has been effective.

Most children will have an effusion present at the completion of a 10- to 14-day course of antibiotic therapy. Such effusions may last up to 12 weeks before spontaneous clearance can be expected.

Additional therapy such as analgesics, antipyretics, and oral decongestants (antihistamines and sympathomimetic amines) may be useful. Oral decongestants may relieve nasal congestion, providing some aeration of the ET. Their efficacy has not been proven, however.

Repeated episodes of AOM plague many children, especially during the first 3 to 4 years of life. Several issues should be considered and evaluated in the management of such patients. A search should be made for a concomitant source of infection in the upper respiratory tract such as chronic adenoiditis or chronic sinusitis. Mild immune immaturity, especially in the IgG subclass group, may be responsible for this relentless process. Testing of immuno-globulins should be considered in relentless cases.

Prevention

A heptavalent pneumococcal conjugate vaccine, PCV7 (Prevanar, Wyeth-Lederle Vaccines), has become available. PCV7 and other pneumococcal vaccines may prove to be an important step in the prevention of AOM. This vaccine is recommended for universal use in children 23 months and younger. The American Academy of Pediatrics recommends that if immunization is initiated in infants younger than 7 months, four doses of PCV7 should be given concurrently with other recommended childhood immunizations at 2, 4, 7, and 12 to 15 months. If immunization is initiated in infants who are between 7 and 23 months of age, who have not received their prior doses of PCV7, fewer doses are recom-mended. Children with congenital immune deficiency, chronic cardiac disease, infection with human immunodeficiency virus, chronic pulmonary disease, and other serious chronic condi-tions are especially vulnerable to pneumoccocal infection.

Chronic Otitis Media with Effusion

Medical Therapy

Chronic otitis media with effusion may occur as a sequela to AOM or in patients who have had no documented recent episodes of acute suppurative disease. Numerous associated factors must be considered; thus, a careful history should be taken for the possibility of underlying allergy, sinus disease, or nasopharyngeal obstruction, which may be secondary to hypertrophic adenoids or even neoplasm.

Numerous methods of management have been advocated over the years for the persistent form of the disease. Antihistamine-sympathomimetic amine preparations were used frequently to clear the effusion. However, controlled clinical trials have demonstrated a lack of efficacy. The use of corticosteroids, either applied topically in the nose or given systemically, has been reported to be advantageous in clearing middle ear fluid. The proposed therapeutic mechanisms of corticosteroids include stabilization of phospholipids to prevent arachidonic acid formation and subsequent inflammatory mediator formation, possible decrease in peritubal lymphoid tissue size, enhanced secretion of ET surfactant, and reduced middle ear fluid viscosity by action on mucoproteins. Unfortunately, there is a paucity of data to demonstrate efficacy; therefore, their use cannot be strongly recommended at this time.

The most effective medical therapy used to this point has been antibiotic administration. Numerous trials have concluded that some patients may respond to a 21- to 30-day course of full-dose antibiotic therapy. The demonstration of viable bacteria in the middle ear effusions of chronically diseased ears has led to this recommendation. In light of the similarity of the bacterial spectrum, the same antibiotics recommended for AOM may be used in this disease. This form of therapy is strongly recommended in any child who has not received antibiotic treatment before consideration is given to myringotomy and ventilation tube insertion and/or adenoidectomy.

In children with concomitant disease of the upper respiratory tract such as chronic sinusitis or adenoiditis, consideration must be given to the simultaneous control of these diseases. In addition, systemic problems such as allergy or immunodeficiency must also be addressed if long-term reversal of the middle ear abnormality is to be achieved.

Surgery

The use of ventilation tubes with or without adenoidectomy has become the ultimate treatment of COME. This surgical intervention immediately corrects the conductive hearing loss associated with the middle ear process and diminishes the patient's tendency toward recurrent infection. It should be strongly considered in the following situations:

1. Recurrent AOM
   a. Unresponsive to antibiotic therapy
   b. Significant antibiotic allergy or intolerance
2. Negative middle ear pressure with impending cholesteatoma
3. Chronic effusion of the middle ear space with a duration of greater than 3 months
   a. Conductive hearing loss of greater than 15 dB
   b. Nasopharyngeal neoplasm for which treatment such as radiation therapy may be necessary

Although some controversy exists over the use of ventilation tubes, they do provide a safe method for normalizing middle ear pressure and, in most cases, restoring hearing to normal. They are usually associated with minimal morbidity, although tympanosclerosis or persistent perforation may be seen in a few instances. In most circumstances, it is difficult to determine whether these findings are a result of the underlying middle ear pathology with middle ear atelectasis or secondary to the ventilation tube itself. Numerous types of tubes are available for ventilation of the middle ear space, but basically they are all designed to provide equalization of pressure across the tympanic membrane. Some designs favor intubation of greater duration but also carry a slight risk of an increased incidence of persistent perforation on extrusion.

Depending on the age of the patient, tube insertion may be carried out under local or general anesthesia.

It is usually advisable to allow spontaneous extrusion of the tubes to occur. Most tympanostomy tubes remain in the tympanic membrane for approximately 6 to 12 months, with some extruding earlier and some later.

Adenoidectomy may be useful as an adjunct to myringotomy in the treatment of middle ear effusion. Removal of adenoid tissue improves the ventilatory function of the ET, thus allowing for appropriate equalization of pressure. The adenoid has been felt to play a role in OM in two ways: when hypertrophic, by causing mechanical obstruction of the ET, and when small, as a bacterial reservoir. There is greater long-term efficacy in the treatment of OM in children 4 to 6 years of age when adenoidectomy was added to tympanostomy tube placement or myringotomies even if this was the first surgical intervention in a child. Some recommmend adenoidectomy only if a child fails initial tympanostomy tube placement. Studies have also shown that the recurrence rate of AOM may be reduced by adenoidectomy. In addition, other confounding factors may warrant adenoidectomy such as evidence of chronic adenoiditis, nasal obstruction, or recurrent or chronic sinusitis secondary to nasal obstruction.

5

CHRONIC OTITIS MEDIA

Steven A. Telian, MD
Cecelia E. Schmalbach, MD

CLASSIFICATION

A unifying definition of the term "chronic otitis media" is any structural change in the middle ear system associated with a permanent defect in the tympanic membrane (TM) for a period of greater than 3 months. Usually, there is associated inflammatory mucosal disease in the middle ear, which may also involve the mastoid cells.

Perforations of the TM are described according to their anatomic location. Central perforations involve the pars tensa and are circumferentially surrounded by residual TM. Marginal perforations involve loss of the posterior aspect of the TM. Unlike central perforations, marginal perforations are commonly associated with cholesteatomas that are pockets or cysts lined with squamous cell epithelium and filled with keratin debris occurring within the pneumatized spaces of the temporal bone. Cholesteatomas have a propensity for growth, bone destruction, and chronic infection. They are classified as congenital or acquired. Congenital cholesteatomas appear as white pearly masses deep to normal, intact TMs. Primary acquired cholesteatomas arise from retracted but intact drumheads, most often within an attic. Secondary acquired cholesteatomas result from ingrowth of squamous cell epithelium into the middle ear. Although not associated with an actual perforation of the TM, atelectatic and adhesive otitis media are also considered forms of chronic otitis media (COM). These conditions involve collapse and retraction of an atrophic TM into the middle ear cleft, causing obliteration of the middle ear space.

PATHOGENESIS

Chronic otitis media is an insidious process, and patients tend to present with long-standing disease. It has been suggested that all cases of otitis media represent different stages in a continuum of events that include infection, mucosal inflammation, granulation tissue formation, and fibrosis. Late changes include bone erosion, tympanosclerosis, and cholesterol granuloma. Both eustachian tube dysfunction and poor mastoid pneumatization play an important role in the development of COM.

Congenital cholesteatomas are thought to result from an error in embryogenesis that causes squamous epithelial cell arrest behind an intact TM. The pathogenesis of acquired cholesteatoma has been debated for well over a century. The most popular explanation for attic cholesteatomas is the invagination theory in which eustachian tube dysfunction leads to the development of a retraction pocket filled with desquamated keratin that cannot be cleared. It has also been theorized that cholesteatomas may develop as a result of the ingrowth of squamous cell epithelium from the lateral surface of the TM through a perforation. The implantation theory proposes that squamous cell epithelium is displaced into the middle ear from surgery, trauma, or a foreign body. The metaplasia theory involves the transformation of healthy cuboidal cells into squamous cell epithelium in the setting of chronic inflammation.

DIAGNOSIS

Approximately one-third of individuals with COM have their diagnosis made as an incidental finding during a routine physical examination. When symptomatic, the two hallmark presenting symptoms are otorrhea and mixed hearing loss. Pain is unusual and indicates either a reactive external otitis or the possibility of a developing intratemporal or intracranial complication. Profuse, intermittent, mucoid drainage is commonly noted in the setting of chronic suppurative otitis media without cholesteatoma. Conversely, patients with COM associated with cholesteatoma describe scant but persistent, purulent, and foul-smelling otorrhea. Blood-stained drainage is often noted in the setting of granulation tissue or polyps.

Every evaluation for COM should include binocular microscopic examination of the ear to assess the integrity of the TM as well as the presence of cholesteatoma, polyps, and granulation tissue. The examination should also include a fistula test if the patient reports vestibular symptoms, inspection of the nasopharynx including the eustachian tube orifices, and gross assessment of hearing with a 512 Hz tuning fork. Audiometric testing with air and bone pure-tone thresholds is also indicated. Computed tomography (CT) is warranted for revision cases in which previous anatomic modifications are unknown to the surgeon or when there is concern for recurrent cholesteatoma hidden from otoscopic view. Other indications for preoperative imaging include congenital ear malformation, vertigo, a positive fistula test, and facial nerve paralysis. Cholesteatoma does not enhance with intravenous contrast, which is not routinely administered unless there is a high suspicion for a vascular abnormality, tumor, or intracranial complication. Magnetic resonance imaging (MRI) with gadolinium enhancement is warranted in the setting of suspected central nervous system complications such as a brain abscess, cerebritis, or lateral sinus thrombosis when the diagnosis is uncertain after the CT scan.

BACTERIOLOGY

Staphylococcus aureus and *Pseudomonas aeruginosa* are common aerobic isolates in COM. The most common anaerobic microorganisms cultured include *Fusobacterium* spp, pigmented *Prevotella, Bacteroides fragilis*, and *Porphyromonas* (previously known as *B. acteroides melaninogenicus*). Overall, COM should be viewed as a polymicrobial disease since multiple isolates are usually recovered from a single culture. Nearly one half of all COM is caused by a combination of aerobic and anaerobic microorganisms.

MEDICAL MANAGEMENT

The treatment of COM generally begins with local care of the ear and outpatient medical management. For medical management to be successful, aural toilet is imperative. This intervention requires repeat microscopic examination of the ear and diligent suctioning. The main goal is to remove debris from the external auditory canal (EAC) overlying the TM and middle ear cleft so that topical antimicrobial agents can successfully penetrate to the middle ear mucosa.

Topical medications may include antibiotics, antifungals, antiseptics, and corticosteroid preparations alone or in combination with other medications. The use of neomycin in ototopical preparations continues to be extremely widespread owing to long-standing prescribing habits and low cost, despite the fact that almost no strains of *Pseudomonas* remain sensitive to this medication. In addition, there is a fairly high incidence of localized and diffuse allergic reactions to the topical use of neomycin. For these reasons, preparations containing neomycin should eventually fade from the ototopical armamentarium. More recently, fluoroquinolone antibiotic drops such as ciprofloxacin and ofloxacin have gained popularity because of their antipseudomonal properties, minimal bacterial resistance, and lack of ototoxicity. If otorrhea is profuse, it may be helpful to have the patient irrigate the ear daily with a body temperature half-strength solution of acetic acid (50% white vinegar diluted with warm water) prior to the application of otic drops.

The use of systemic antibiotics in COM is limited by several factors. Antibiotic penetration into the middle ear may be hampered by mucosal edema. Systemic aminoglycosides carry a risk of ototoxicity and require parenteral administration with monitoring of serum levels. Oral ciprofloxacin has proven to be a safe and effective treatment for adults with COM; however, safety in patients under 18 years of age has not been established.

For patients with otorrhea secondary to cholesteatoma, the hope is to minimize granulation tissue and perhaps achieve a dry ear prior to surgical intervention. Before addressing the granulation tissue with topical cautery, one must be reasonably convinced that the critical landmarks are properly identified and that there is no dural defect with an encephalocele present.

Medical management of COM may be difficult for both the patient and the physician. Multiple office visits are often required for adequate aural toilet. Patients are asked to comply with a regimen that may include not only daily irrigation but also multiple administrations of otic drops throughout the day. Medical treatment usually requires 14 to 21 days. Most often, it is appropriate to proceed to operation if the ear does not respond to microscopic débridement and ototopical management.

SURGICAL MANAGEMENT

The primary goal of surgery for COM is to eradicate disease and obtain a dry, safe ear. Restoration of hearing is by necessity a secondary consideration because any attempt at middle ear reconstruction will fail in the setting of persistent inflammation and otorrhea. Absolute indications for surgical intervention include impending or established intratemporal or intracranial complications. Various pathologic conditions within the middle ear, such as cholesteatoma and chronic fibrotic granulation tissue, are irreversible and require elective surgical attention. In addition, patients with otorrhea failing to respond to medical treatment are surgical candidates, as well as those who respond but are left with a correctable conductive hearing loss or a TM perforation.

Tympanoplasty

The goal of tympanoplasty is to repair the TM with a connective tissue graft in the hope that squamous cell epithelium will proliferate over the graft and seal the perforation. Various grafting materials are available. Autogenous temporalis fascia is used most often because it is readily available through a postauricular incision and is extremely effective. Other alternatives include tragal perichondrium, periosteum, and vein. Preserved homograft materials such as cadaveric TM, dura, and heart valve have limited application because of concern for disease transmission. The two most common approaches are the transcanal tympanomeatal flap and the postauricular approach with creation of a vascular strip. The two classic types of tympanoplasty are the lateral and the medial technique, which define the final relationship of the graft to the fibrous layer of the TM remnant and the anulus tympanicus. In both techniques, the graft is placed medial to the handle of the malleus. The lateral technique is more technically demanding but provides more reliable results when repairing large anterior or pantympanic perforations. It is useful when ear canal anatomy is unfavorable and extensive removal of bone from the anterior canal wall (canalplasty) is necessary. The canalplasty improves access to the anterior half of the TM. The lateral technique may be complicated by displacement of the graft laterally during healing and formation of cholesteatoma between the graft and the remnant of the TM. If, in the canalplasty, the soft tissue of the temporomandibular joint is violated, the posterior aspect of the joint can be eroded, allowing the condyle of the mandible to prolapse into the ear canal. This feared complication is difficult to correct and should be assiduously avoided. The medial technique is easier and less time consuming, and postoperative care is less compared with the lateral technique. Ultimately, the technique chosen will depend on the location of the perforation, the bony anatomy of the EAC, and the surgeon's experience.

Ossicular Chain Reconstruction

The numerous techniques and middle ear prostheses available to the otologic surgeon lend credence to the claim that ossicular chain reconstruction remains to be perfected. Reconstruction should achieve closure of the air–bone gap to within 20 dB in two-thirds of patients with an intact stapes arch and one half of patients missing the stapes superstructure. Autograft ossicles are removed from the patient and sculpted to serve as inter-position grafts. The incus is used most often. Immediate availability, obvious biocompatibility, and a low extrusion rate have made autograft ossiculoplasty very popular. However, extensive bone erosion caused by middle ear disease may limit availability. Homograft ossicles and en bloc tympanic membranes with attached ossicles can be harvested from human cadavers and are available, but the fear of potential disease transmission limits their use. More recently, biocompatible prostheses composed of Plastipore, Proplast, hydroxyapatite (HA), and HAPEX (HA and reinforced high-density polyethylene mixture) have been engineered. These allografts are expensive but offer the advantage of sterility, availability, and, in some cases, tissue bonding to the ossicular chain or TM. Success in the use of these prostheses is enhanced by good eustachian tube function and a healthy middle ear and mastoid.

The technique chosen for ossicular reconstruction will ultimately depend on the remaining ossicles, with the two most important structures being the stapes superstructure and the malleus handle. If only the tip of the long process of the incus is absent, ossicular continuity can be restored using bone cement or a biocompatible sleeve prosthesis that fits onto the remaining long process. If complete erosion of the long process is discovered, the incus body can be extracted, sculpted, and used as an autograft to bridge the gap between the malleus handle and the stapes capitulum. Biocompatible partial ossicular replacement prostheses are available to bridge the gap between the TM and stapes capitulum. In the absence of the stapes arch, a total ossicular replacement prosthesis is seated between the drumhead and footplate.

Cortical Mastoidectomy

Tympanoplasty failures occur in eustachian tube dysfunction and persistent inflammatory disease. For this reason, a cortical mastoidectomy is often recommended as an adjuvant to tympanoplasty. The goal is to eliminate all irreversible mucosal disease, improve mastoid ventilation, and increase the buffering action of the mastoid cavity by enlarging its volume.

Intact Canal Wall Tympanoplasty with Mastoidectomy

In an attempt to expose and eradicate middle ear disease better while preserving normal anatomic relationships for improved sound conduction, the posterior tympanotomy approach was introduced. This technique allows access from a cortical mastoidectomy defect into the posterior mesotympanum by removal of the bony wall bound by the fossa incudis, the second genu of the facial nerve, and the chorda tympani. Since the access point into the middle ear is the facial recess of the posterior part of the tympanum, this operation is often referred to as a "facial recess approach." The major advantage of the intact canal wall (ICW) tympanoplasty with mastoidectomy is the avoidance of a mastoid bowl that requires lifelong cleaning. However, this advantage comes with a higher risk of residual and recurrent disease because preservation of the posterior canal wall limits visualization and access to the middle ear. Because an ICW tympanoplasty with mastoidectomy does not address the problem of negative pressure within the middle ear, ideal candidates are individuals with large pneumatized mastoids and well-aerated middle ear clefts. As a result of the high rate of recidivism, most surgeons advocate a second-stage procedure when treating cholesteatoma in this manner.

Modified Radical Mastoidectomy

Today, the classic Bondy modified radical mastoidectomy is used infrequently since it only addresses the rare instance when one is treating isolated atticoantral cholesteatoma with disease lateral and posterior to the ossicles. Modifications have been made to the original approach to explore the middle ear and correct the conductive hearing loss that often results in the setting of cholesteatoma. This combination of the open mastoidectomy and tympanoplasty with or without ossicular chain reconstruction is what most surgeons mean today when they use the term "modified radical mastoidectomy." An alternate, less ambiguous term for this operation is "tympanoplasty with canal wall down (CWD) mastoidectomy." A small, sclerotic mastoid, a low-lying middle cranial fossa dura, and an anteriorly positioned sigmoid sinus will limit surgical exposure and often necessitate the removal of the canal wall. Other indications include operating on extensive cholesteatoma in the only hearing ear, presence of a large labyrinthine fistula, recurrent retraction cholesteatoma in the epitympanum, and significant destruction of the scutum or posterior canal wall. Patients who are unlikely to follow faithfully postoperative protocols, unwilling to undergo a second-stage procedure, or at high risk for general anesthesia will also benefit from a CWD mastoidectomy. Often the decision to remove the posterior canal wall is made intraoperatively.

The major advantage of a modified radical mastoidectomy is excellent exposure during dissection of cholesteatoma, which reduces the rate of residual or recurrent disease, usually precludes the need for a second-stage operation, and is therefore cost effective. Postoperative examination is ideal because only that disease hidden within the mesotympanum might go unnoticed. With removal of the canal wall, all other areas are exteriorized and can be inspected during follow-up. The major disadvantage of this approach is the need for periodic mastoid bowl cleaning. Success of a CWD mastoidectomy and long-term care of the mastoid cavity depend on key operative techniques, including opening air cells at the sinodural angle, along the tegmen and in the perilabyrinthine region; lowering the facial ridge to leave a thin layer of bone over the facial nerve; exenterating the mastoid tip cells and amputating the tip; saucerizing, by wide beveling, the cavity to form smooth walls; and creating a meatoplasty by resecting a crescent of conchal cartilage.

Open cavities take 6 to 10 weeks to heal. During this period, the patient is seen every 2 to 3 weeks for débridement of the cavity and management of granulation tissue. Early granulation tissue is suctioned away, and the base is cauterized. Early neomembrane formation is disrupted. Ototopical drops with an antibiotic and corticosteroid should be continued until there is no granulation tissue and the cavity is lined with skin.

Radical Mastoidectomy

Radical mastoidectomy entails exteriorization of the entire middle ear and mastoid by combining a CWD mastoidectomy with removal of the TM and the ossicles (with the exception of the stapes if present). In doing so, the mastoid, middle ear, and EAC become one common cavity. There is no attempt at middle ear reconstruction, and patients are left with a substantial conductive hearing loss. Given this significant functional deficit, radical mastoidectomy is considered a last resort, usually after previous surgical attempts have failed or when it is not possible to remove mesotympanic cholesteatoma. Radical mastoidectomy is also indicated if middle ear ventilation is impossible owing to complete inadequacy of eustachian tube function.

Mastoid Cavity Obliteration

The mastoid cavity created by a radical or modified radical mastoidectomy is at risk for chronic infection and persistent drainage. In the setting of a potentially large cavity, some surgeons elect to perform a mastoid obliteration procedure using materials such as bone pate, cartilage, acrylic, and HA cement. Alternatives include free abdominal fat grafts and regional soft tissue flaps. The major disadvantage associated with obliteration of the mastoid is that recurrent disease can remain hidden within the cavity. A CT scan may be required to evaluate patients for recurrent disease.

COMPLICATIONS OF CHRONIC OTITIS MEDIA

Complications of COM range from mild hearing loss to life-threatening intracranial infections. Intratemporal complications include facial nerve paralysis, labyrinthitis, labyrinthine fistula, coalescent mastoiditis, subperiosteal abscess, postauricular fistula, and petrositis. If infection spreads beyond the confines of the temporal bone, intracranial complications such as epidural abscess, subdural abscess, lateral sinus thrombophlebitis, meningitis, and brain abscess may result.

Electromyographic facial nerve monitoring is recommended in congenital temporal bone anomalies and revision operations if the surgeon is uncertain of prior anatomic modifications and when the canal of the facial nerve is known to be dehiscent. Some surgeons advocate the routine use of facial nerve monitoring in every chronic ear operation. All agree that monitoring is no substitute for detailed knowledge of temporal bone anatomy and adherence to principles such as adequate irrigation during drilling, drilling with a diamond bur near the canal of the facial nerve, and, most importantly, drilling parallel to the course of the facial nerve.

6

CRANIAL AND INTRACRANIAL COMPLICATIONS OF ACUTE AND CHRONIC OTITIS MEDIA

Lee A. Harker, MD

Complications of acute and chronic otitis media are uncommon but are serious and potentially lethal. Cranial complications occur within the temporal bone portion of the cranium, and intracranial complications occur when infection has spread toward the brain beyond the temporal bone. These complications can occur in individuals of any age, but 75% of them occur in the first two decades of life. For unexplained reasons, males are affected nearly twice as frequently as females. The highest incidences of these complications are found in people who are poor and live in overcrowded surroundings; have poor personal hygiene, poor health, decreased resistance to infection; and have inadequate health education or limited access to medical care. It is not uncommon for two or three complications of otitis media to be present at the same time. The pathophysiology, bacteriology, treatment, and complications are different for acute otitis media than they are for chronic otitis media, and the two diseases affect different age groups.

After the first several weeks of life, three principal microorganisms, *Streptococcus pneumoniae, Haemophilus influenzae,* and *Branhamella catarrhalis,* are responsible for most cases of acute otitis media and its complications. Acute otitis media arises from a previously normal middle ear to become an acute infection with hyperemia, mucosal edema, and exudation but without granulation tissue formation or bone erosion. The mechanisms by which acute otitis media causes complications include hematogenous dissemination during bacteremia, direct extension, and, less commonly, phlebitis and periphlebitis of the veins of the infected contiguous mastoid. A particularly virulent microorganism, decreased host resistance, and anatomic factors within the temporal bone can facilitate both the progression of an infection into a subacute or chronic state and the development of a complication by direct extension or phlebitis.

The usual mechanism by which acute otitis media causes complications is by direct extension through preformed pathways leading to the labyrinth or the cerebrospinal fluid (CSF). If bacterial infection follows preformed pathways into the labyrinth, it will result in suppurative labyrinthitis. If it reaches the CSF, it will result in meningitis. The preformed pathways can be congenital or acquired. Congenital pathways are found in enlarged vestibular aqueducts and Mondini's deformity, in which defects in the medial aspects of the labyrinth allow free passage of CSF into the labyrinth. These two congenital conditions also predispose to fistulous communications between the labyrinth and the middle ear, which allow bacteria to penetrate from the infected middle ear to the labyrinth and subsequently to the meninges.

Acquired preformed pathways include encephalocele with or without CSF leakage, temporal bone fractures (because they are not healed by bony union), semicircular canal fistulae, perilymphatic fistulae, and defects created by surgery. In all of these conditions, acute otitis media can initiate complications by direct extension.

Whereas acute otitis media is primarily a middle ear infection that extends into the contiguous mastoid, chronic otitis media frequently expresses the dominant portion of the infection within the mastoid rather than the middle ear. The term "chronic" is used when the infection has persisted for more than 8 weeks. Chronic otitis media may occur with a cholesteatoma or with chronic otorrhea from a tympanic membrane perforation without a cholesteatoma. It also occurs in children with indwelling ventilating tubes who develop otorrhea that persists and leads to chronic mastoiditis. Acute otitis media that does not resolve may develop into acute coalescent mastoiditis, the type of mastoiditis seen so frequently in the preantibiotic era.

The dominant pathologic features of chronic mastoiditis without cholesteatoma are granulation tissue formation and bone erosion. The mastoiditis with an indwelling ventilating tube infection will exhibit less bone erosion and granulation tissue. Cholesteatoma erodes bone even without active infection, but it usually produces a combination of infection, granulation tissue, and cholesteatomatous debris.

Chronic otitis media usually does not result in bacteremia and hematogenous complications. Direct extension of disease to adjacent structures can occur along preformed pathways as it does in acute otitis media, but this is relatively uncommon. Usually, patients with chronic otitis media and mastoiditis develop complications because bone erosion and infected granulation tissue have allowed the suppuration to spread to adjacent areas. The other common mechanism by which chronic otitis media causes complications is propagation of infection inside and along the veins of the mastoid. These veins connect with all of the areas surrounding the mastoid, providing abundant opportunities for phlebitis and periphlebitis to spread infection.

The bacteriology of chronic otitis media is markedly different than that of acute otitis media. Cholesteatoma and chronic mastoiditis without cholesteatoma most often have multiple bacteria involved with the infection, and, in the majority of these infected ears, anaerobic microorganisms are present as well. The most common pathogens are *Pseudomonas aeruginosa* and *Bacteroides* species. The microorganisms cultured from ears with chronic otitis media in patients with indwelling ventilating tubes are often resistant to antibiotics because the patients have already received many topical and systemic drugs. *Pseudomonas aeruginosa, Achromobacter xylosoxidans,* methicillin-resistant *Staphylococcus aureus,* and fungi are often found.

In evaluating patients who have complications of acute and chronic otitis media, the physician must answer two questions: (1) What complication or complications are present? and (2) From what form of otitis did these complications arise? The history and the physical examination provide most of the information for deciding which form of otitis media is present. Painless purulent drainage for several weeks to months indicates chronic otitis media, but the clinician must still determine whether this is secondary to cholesteatoma. Acute ear symptoms can represent an acute otitis media arising in a previously normal ear or a recrudescence of acute infection in an ear with chronic otitis media or chronic otitis media with effusion. The difference has great clinical significance. To help differentiate between the two clinical conditions, the clinician must obtain an accurate chronology of the current ear symptoms and a complete past history of the involved ear. The physician should formulate impressions about the type of otitis media and complications after performing the history and physical examination but before obtaining further studies.

Examining the ear provides the best clues to the type of otitis media responsible for the complication. The author recommends making a drawing of the tympanic membrane to clarify and record what is seen at the initial examination. The areas around the ear must be examined carefully and findings noted. This can establish the diagnosis of a postauricular, Bezold's, or temporal abscess. The neurologic examination provides the information necessary for the diagnosis of suppurative labyrinthitis, facial paralysis, and intracranial complications. In addition to examining cranial nerve function, the physician must assess the patient's sensorium and level of consciousness, determine if the patient has positive meningeal signs, and evaluate the patient for functional deficits in the cerebellum or cerebrum. Meningeal signs are the hallmark of meningitis, but they are also seen in intra-parenchymal abscess, subdural empyema, and sometimes epidural abscess and lateral sinus thrombosis. Focal neurologic deficits are most common in subdural empyema and temporal lobe cerebritis or abscess.

Computed tomography (CT) is the preferred imaging technique for assessing any bone involvement with acute or chronic otitis media. It will demonstrate opacification of the normal mastoid air cells in cases of acute otitis media and uncomplicated chronic otitis media and the breakdown and dissolution of the delicate mastoid septae so characteristic of coalescent mastoiditis. Erosion of the scutum, smooth-walled expansion of the attic and antrum, and areas of localized bone erosion are typical CT findings in cholesteatoma.

Magnetic resonance imaging (MRI) is a far more sensitive imaging technique than CT scanning for diagnosing intra-parenchymal brain infection or abscess, epidural abscess, lateral sinus thrombosis, or subdural empyema. If the condition of the patient permits, the physician should obtain both CT and enhanced MRI scans when intracranial complications are suspected.

To establish the diagnosis of meningitis, the physician must perform lumbar puncture and take the appropriate measurements of the CSF. To avoid herniation of the cerebellar tonsils during or after lumbar puncture, the physician must first obtain a CT scan to document that there is no evidence of increased intracranial pressure.

When complications are caused by acute otitis media, antibiotic therapy without mastoidectomy is adequate treatment for the otitis, although the physician should document complete resolution by CT scan following treatment. When complications result from chronic otitis media and mastoid-itis, the physician should institute aggressive broad-spectrum antibiotic therapy directed against both aerobic and anaerobic microorganisms. Mastoidectomy will be required. When a neurosurgical operation is necessary for an intracranial complication, it is performed first followed immediately by the mastoidectomy if the patient's condition permits. In general, the surgeon should remove the canal wall and perform an open cavity mastoidectomy technique when complications are secondary to cholesteatoma. If visualization of the pathology is adequate, it is not necessary to remove the canal wall when there is no cholesteatoma.

Postoperative follow-up is essential for patients who have experienced life-threatening complications of acute and chronic otitis media. Enhanced MRI scans should be obtained 2 to 4 weeks after treatment in these patients.

CRANIAL COMPLICATIONS

Mastoiditis

Coalescent mastoiditis is an acute bone-destroying infection in the mastoid that develops 2 to 4 weeks after a bout of acute otitis media. Typically, the symptoms of the otitis persist, worsen, or recur in a child who has very little history of previous ear disease. Coalescent mastoiditis runs an acute course of 1 to 3 weeks and frequently is associated with other complications, most commonly postauricular abscesses. Bezold's abscesses and intracranial complications also occur. If there are no additional complications, coalescent mastoiditis can be treated surgically or medically, but if antibiotics alone are used, a follow-up CT scan that documents a complete resolution is necessary.

Cholesteatoma can result in complications even without active suppuration because pathogenic bacteria are present in cholesteatoma matrix, and the cholesteatoma erodes bone and exposes adjacent structures to those bacteria. Most cholesteatomas exhibit active infection with granulation tissue, facilitating the development of complications. Cholesteatoma is responsible for most of the intracranial complications of chronic otitis media in patients over age 15 years.

Mastoiditis can occur with an intact tympanic membrane without otorrhea. "Masked mastoiditis" occurs when antibiotic therapy has completely cured the otitis media, but a blocked aditus has allowed the mastoiditis to continue. In other situations, the tympanic membrane may be abnormal but without the usual evidence of perforation or cholesteatoma. Mastoiditis in these situations can result in complications in the same way it would if otorrhea were present.

Abscess

Postauricular abscess is the most common complication of mastoiditis and usually develops from coalescent mastoiditis in young children. Cholesteatoma is the most common cause in older children and adults. Because only the superior portion of the mastoid is pneumatized in young children, subperiosteal abscesses begin above and behind the ear canal rather than directly behind it. When the abscess enlarges, soft tissue swelling displaces the auricle downward, outward, and forward, and the posterior superior external auditory canal skin becomes edematous. In most situations, the diagnosis is obvious because of the presence of postauricular swelling, erythema, tenderness, and fluctuance. The preferred treatment is surgical drainage by complete mastoidectomy combined with antibiotics.

Infection can also spread outside the mastoid into the upper neck and present as a Bezold's abscess. The abscess forms medial to the mastoid tip and sternocleidomastoid muscle by eroding bone medial to the digastric ridge in the inferior part of the mastoid or by extension to soft tissue through phlebitis. Sometimes it is difficult to establish that the tender swelling in the upper neck is secondary to mastoid disease because the skin overlying the mastoid appears normal. This is especially true when the tympanic membrane is intact. Tenderness to percussion of the mastoid will suggest the diagnosis that should be confirmed on CT scan. Complete mastoidectomy with incision and drainage of the abscess plus appropriate antibiotics is necessary.

Petrous Apicitis

The petrous apex may be pneumatized like the mastoid and is subject to the same types of infection as the mastoid. Petrous apicitis is uncommon, and the majority of cases occur in the 30% of individuals in whom the petrous pyramids of the temporal bones are pneumatized. The infection is either analogous to acute coalescent mastoiditis or chronic mastoiditis with granulation tissue formation without cholesteatoma. Only rarely does cholesteatoma involve the petrous apex. The symptoms of petrous apicitis are caused by irritation of the cranial nerves that pass through or adjacent to the petrous pyramid. Retro-orbital pain, diplopia, facial nerve paresis or paralysis, and otorrhea are the most common symptoms. The clinician should obtain both CT and enhanced MRI scans to prevent incorrectly interpreting differences in development between the two petrous apices and making an incorrect diagnosis of petrous apicitis. A sclerotic or marrow-containing apex on one side can be erroneously interpreted to be infected when compared with a normally pneumatized opposite side. Surgical treatment of infection in the petrous apex is more difficult than in the mastoid because there is limited exposure and poor access to the disease at surgery. In acute infections analogous to coalescent mastoiditis, surgical drainage, carried out through the best available routes of pneumatization shown on CT, is essential. Because surgical excision of infected tissue may be incomplete, appropriate antibiotic therapy is usually continued for at least 3 weeks.

Labyrinthine Fistula

One of the most common complications of cholesteatoma is erosion of the endochondral bone covering the lateral semicircular canal, and only rarely do fistulae develop in other parts of the labyrinth. When the overlying protective bone is lost, pressure can be transmitted from the external auditory canal to the endolymphatic compartment, evoking vestibular and sometimes auditory symptoms. The most common symptom is brief imbalance, unsteadiness, or vertigo initiated by pressure or temperature changes in the ear canal. The fistula test is positive in 55 to 70% of patients with lateral semicircular canal erosion, and the CT scan can also suggest the diagnosis.

The cholesteatoma is treated surgically, and the fistula is managed at the end of the operation with soft tissue grafting or exteriorization of the cholesteatoma. The surgeon should prepare to encounter erosion of the fallopian canal with facial nerve exposure in the middle ear, which is commonly associated with cholesteatomas that cause labyrinthine fistulae.

Facial Nerve Paralysis

Most cases of facial nerve paralysis occur in childhood and are secondary to acute otitis media. The bacterial infection reaches the facial nerve in the middle ear near the stapes, where the bony fallopian canal is frequently congenitally dehiscent. The inflammatory pressure has direct access to the nerve and inhibits nerve conduction. These pareses are self-limited, but patients with them should be treated with both antibiotics and tympanocentesis. Chronic suppurative otitis media without cholesteatoma most commonly affects the same area of the facial nerve (presumably in the same way). Surgery is indicated because of the chronic mastoiditis. Cholesteatomatous facial nerve paralysis can involve the nerve in any portion of the temporal bone but preferentially attacks the middle ear segment, where the fallopian canal is thin. The prognosis for recovery of facial nerve function is good unless suppurative neuritis has occurred or the paralysis has been of long duration and electroneurography reveals extensive degeneration.

Acute Suppurative Labyrinthitis

When bacterial infection involves the labyrinth, there is sudden complete loss of all vestibular and auditory function. Tinnitus and dizziness are rapidly followed by whirling vertigo, pallor, diaphoresis, nausea, and vomiting. These symptoms reach maximum intensity within 30 to 60 minutes. All affected patients are bedridden and unable to function for 1 to 3 days, and recovery takes 2 to 3 weeks. Surgery is necessary only if chronic mastoiditis is present.

Encephalocele and Cerebrospinal Fluid Leakage

Encephalocele and CSF leakage can occur when brain contents and meninges herniate into the mastoid through a defect in the tegmen or the posterior fossa dural plate. Encephalocele can occur without CSF leakage if the meningeal investment remains intact, and CSF leakage can occur in the absence of an encephalocele if there is a bony and dural defect without brain prolapse. Meningitis will commonly result when these conditions coexist with acute or chronic otitis media and mastoiditis. Mastoid surgery and the pathologic conditions that necessitate it are responsible for creating the great majority of these cases. Erosion of portions of the tegmen or the cerebellar plate by the mastoid infection or the surgical removal of that infection places the dura at the mercy of repeated sudden increases of intracranial pressure without any support. Thinning or irritation of the dura by the disease or the surgery facilitates prolapse, further dural thinning, rupture, and CSF leakage. Chronic mastoiditis with or without cholesteatoma can cause the same outcome without surgery but is much less common. Unless meningitis has already occurred, the physician may not suspect encephalocele and CSF leakage before mastoid surgery. Careful preoperative review of the CT scans to evaluate the tegmen and cerebellar plates in revision mastoid surgery is necessary to identify this difficult clinical situation preoperatively.

Middle-aged and older adults occasionally present with spontaneous CSF leakage from defects in the tegmen tympani that are usually associated with an encephalocele. These individuals have not experienced previous ear disease or undergone otologic surgery. They frequently present with an apparent serous middle ear effusion (which proves on analysis to be CSF), a conductive hearing loss, or repeated bouts of meningitis.

The risk of meningitis is exceedingly high when encephalocele and CSF leakage exist in the presence of acute or chronic otitis media and mastoiditis. After the physician stabilizes the meningitis, he or she must repair the defects. In some situations, the problem can be corrected entirely through the mastoid. In others, an extradural or intradural middle cranial fossa approach is necessary. These procedures require considerable skill and judgment.

INTRACRANIAL COMPLICATIONS

Meningitis

Meningitis is the most common complication of both acute and chronic otitis media and in the majority of cases results from hematogenous dissemination by bacteremia in very young children with acute otitis media. Acute otitis media also causes meningitis in patients who have congenital or acquired preformed pathways that give bacteria access to the meninges directly or give indirect access via the labyrinth. Chronic otitis media with or without cholesteatoma can also cause meningitis by direct extension from bone erosion or preformed pathways or by phlebitis and periphlebitis.

The predominant symptom of meningitis is a severe generalized headache in a febrile patient who prefers to lie quietly in a dark room. Vomiting is common. The sensorium is often depressed, and the patient may be totally unresponsive. Attempted flexion of the neck causes pain and nuchal rigidity, and Kernig's and Brudzinski's signs are positive. These meningeal signs so strongly suggest the presence of meningitis that when they are present, the physician must continue the investigation until he or she can rule it out.

The diagnosis is made by lumbar puncture but only after CT scan and funduscopic evaluation verify that lumbar puncture is safe. Appropriate antibiotics are given in consultation with neurologic opinion. Meningitis has a higher likelihood of mortality when it develops as a consequence of direct extension of infection and phlebitis or periphlebitis as opposed to when it is a hematogenous complication. Therefore, when chronic infection and preformed pathways coexist in a patient with meningitis, the chronic infection should be excised and the preformed pathways obliterated to prevent recurrences.

Brain Abscess

Suppurative ear disease is the third most common cause of brain abscess after cyanotic congenital heart disease and abscesses secondary to head injury or surgery. Males are affected 75% of the time, and nearly 50% of cases occur in the second decade of life, almost always affecting individuals in the lower socioeconomic classes. Otogenic brain abscesses occur on the same side as the otitis, equally divided between the adjacent temporal lobe and cerebellum. Almost three-fourths are secondary to cholesteatoma.

The patient often exhibits meningeal signs, toxicity, and obtundation in addition to signs and symptoms of the underlying ear disease. Temporal lobe abscesses may cause homonymous visual field defects, contralateral hemiparesis, aphasia, or seizures. Cerebellar abscesses are often accompanied by coarse horizontal nystagmus, dysmetria, dysdiadochokinesia, or action tremor.

Optimum evaluation includes CT of the temporal bone and enhanced MRI of the brain. If an intraparenchymal brain abscess is identified on MRI, it is critical to evaluate the patient and the imaging studies thoroughly for the presence of other intracranial complications. Brain abscess is a bona fide neurosurgical emergency, and broad-spectrum antibiotics effective against both aerobic and anaerobic microorganisms are immediately given intravenously. The neurosurgeon, the otologic surgeon, and the anesthesiologist should carefully plan the operation. First, the neurosurgeon drains the brain abscess. Then the otologist performs the mastoidectomy and manages any additional complications, such as epidural abscess or lateral sinus thrombosis, through a separate incision and a sterile field. A brain abscess is never evacuated through the mastoid. Overall, the likelihood of mortality from otogenic brain abscesses has decreased to approximately 10%, but it correlates with the patient's level of consciousness on admission.

Subdural Empyema

This fulminating purulent infection is located between the dura and the pia-arachnoid membranes and is among the most emergent of neurosurgical conditions. It is an uncommon type of intracranial bacterial infection, and relatively few cases result from acute or chronic otitis media. It presents a dramatic and even frightening clinical picture that begins with a severe headache and a marked rise in temperature. Nuchal rigidity and obtundation are quickly followed by focal neurologic deficits. Infection on the left side causes aphasia and progressive contralateral hemiparesis. Frequently, paralysis of conjugate gaze to the contralateral side or deviation of the eyes toward the side of the lesion is seen, and jacksonian seizures develop. Subdural empyema in the posterior fossa causes marked neck stiffness and papilledema, but the patient may exhibit few or no localizing signs. The entire clinical picture may evolve in as little as a few hours.

Imaging studies taken early in the disease do not always confirm the clinical impression, but studies that show a crescent-shaped low-density collection of pus displacing the brain from the inner table of the skull with enhancement of the adjacent cortex are diagnostic. Immediate neurosurgical drainage with appropriate antibiotic therapy is essential.

Epidural Abscess

An epidural abscess is a collection of pus between the temporal bone and the dura mater. Intense infection with granulation tissue, suppuration, and bone erosion usually begin the process and cause thickening of the dura (pachymeningitis). This type of abscess is frequently associated with other intracranial complications including lateral sinus thrombosis, meningitis, and intraparenchymal cellulitis or abscess. There are no signs and symptoms specifically attributable to epidural abscess, and many of the cases are only discovered at surgery. Enhanced CT scan or MRIs can detect both the dural enhancement and the abscess cavity between the temporal bone and the dura. The treatment is surgical, and the surgeon should enlarge the area of the bone erosion so that the entire abscess cavity is exposed and evacuated. If the epidural abscess involves the posterior fossa dura, the surgeon should also carefully inspect the sigmoid sinus and document that it is not occluded.

Lateral Sinus Thrombosis

Thrombosis of the lateral sinus usually starts because bone overlying the posterior fossa dura becomes eroded by granulation tissue, cholesteatoma, or coalescence. A perisinus abscess develops and exerts pressure on the outer dural wall of the sinus, resulting in necrosis. The necrosis extends to the intima and initiates thrombus formation. The thrombus can propagate posteriorly to the mastoid emissary vein and the transverse sinus or extend in the opposite direction to the jugular bulb and internal jugular vein. Lateral sinus thrombosis is most common in adults and older children in whom the cholesteatoma has eroded the bone overlying the sinus. It can also result from osteothrombophlebitis during mastoiditis associated with acute or chronic otitis media. In this situation, the bony plate overlying the lateral sinus is intact at the time of surgical exploration.

Symptoms of lateral sinus thrombosis include fever, headache, and neck stiffness. A repeated diurnal high spiking fever strongly suggests lateral sinus thrombosis and results from the hematogenous dissemination of bacteria and infected clot. The patient's headache mirrors the degree of venous obstruction that the clot has caused. The headache will be severe when the obstruction is sudden, and inadequate collateral venous drainage gives rise to increased intracranial pressure. In most cases, the mild increased intracranial pressure is tolerated as collateral venous drainage increases, and the headache and increased pressure slowly resolve over a few days. A CT scan can establish the diagnosis. Enhancement of the lateral sinus wall has a characteristic pattern called the "delta sign." Enhanced MRI can show the same enhancement and demonstrate abscess formation within the sinus as well.

In rare instances, the headache and intracranial pressure continue to increase, and venous drainage does not keep up with the arterial inflow. This results in cerebral edema that leads to progressive obtundation and death unless there is immediate aggressive medical and surgical management. Anticoagulation may be used as part of this comprehensive aggressive management but, ordinarily, is not part of the treatment of lateral sinus thrombosis. Likewise, ligation of the internal jugular vein is not a routine part of therapy but can be considered when the clot extends into the neck.

Otitic Hydrocephalus

Otitic hydrocephalus is still surrounded by confusion and controversy 70 years after it was first described. Some authors believe that it is a distinct clinical entity consisting of intracranial hypertension and resolved or resolving otitis media that has no relationship to lateral sinus thrombophlebitis and obstruction. Others believe that it represents a pathophysiologic consequence of inadequate collateral venous drainage secondary to lateral sinus thrombosis from any cause.

The principal symptom of otitic hydrocephalus is a diffuse severe headache that reflects increased intracranial pressure. In assessing any patient suspected of having otitic hydrocephalus, the physician must make three determinations: (1) whether the patient has increased intracranial pressure, (2) whether the patient has active acute or chronic mastoid infection, and (3) whether there is free flow of blood through the involved lateral sinus. The physical examination and the imaging studies are paramount in making these determinations. The results of these inquiries will allow the physician to formulate the appropriate treatment for the mastoid, the lateral sinus, and the increased intracranial pressure.

POTENTIAL ERRORS IN MANAGING PATIENTS WITH COMPLICATIONS OF ACUTE OR CHRONIC OTITIS MEDIA

* Failure to consider the presence of central nervous system complications
  a. Inadequate history
  b. Incomplete physical examination
  c. Inadequate imaging studies

- Inadequate antibiotics
- Performing lumbar puncture without a previous CT scan
- Failing to act rapidly enough in the face of an emergency
- Failing to consider the possibility of multiple complications
- Failure to consult with radiology, neurosurgery, pediatrics, and infectious disease specialists
- Failure to understand the appropriate surgical techniques to manage otogenic complications

7

OTOSCLEROSIS

Herman A. Jenkins, MD
Omid Abbassi, MD, PhD

The term otosclerosis is derived from the Greek words for "hardening of the ear." Otosclerosis is recognized as an alteration in bony metabolism of the endochondral bone of the otic capsule. The ongoing process of resorption and redeposition of bone results in fixation of the ossicular chain and conductive hearing loss. Otosclerosis occurs most commonly among Caucasians with an incidence of 1%, followed by Asians at 0.5%. It is far less common in African Americans. Guild, in postmortem examinations of temporal bones, found evidence of a higher prevalence rate histologically, with 8.3% of Caucasians and 1% of African Americans manifesting the disease. Although encountered in all age groups, usually the clinical presentation occurs between the second and fifth decades of life. The disease process has a female predominance of 2:1, and its progression tends to accelerate with hormonal changes, particularly during pregnancy or the use of birth control pills. Bilateral disease is present in 80% of patients.

The otosclerotic process is divided into two phases histologically. Bone resorption and increased vascularity characterize the early phase. As the mature collagen content diminishes, the bone acquires a spongy appearance (otospongiosis). In the late stage, the reabsorbed bone is replaced with dense sclerotic bone, thus the name otosclerosis. When involving the stapes, otosclerosis often starts from the fissula ante fenestram, although focal lesions involving the posterior annular ligament are also seen. In general, it progresses from an anterior focal lesion to complete footplate involvement and, in more advanced cases, may fill the oval window niche entirely with new bone (obliterative otosclerosis). In contrast, the round window is less frequently involved, and complete obliteration is a rare finding. Involvement of the cochlea can result in sensorineural hearing loss.

ETIOLOGY

A genetic component has long been recognized, and transmission has generally been accepted to be autosomal dominant with incomplete penetrance. The gene for otosclerosis has not been clearly identified, but authors in one study have narrowed its location to chromosome 15q25-26. Others have related otosclerosis to the *COL1A1* gene, which encodes for type 1 collagen. Investigators have noted its similarities to osteogenesis imperfecta and Paget's disease, both sharing lesions in the otic capsule nearly identical to that of otosclerosis.

Recent investigations on the role of infectious agents have implicated the measles virus as having, at least, an inciting role in patients with a genetic predisposition for otosclerosis. Elevated titers of immunoglobulin G specific for measles virus antigens have been found in the perilymph of patients with otosclerosis. Immunohistochemical evidence of measles antigen has also been demonstrated in active otosclerotic foci, using reverse transcriptase polymerase chain reaction amplification of measles virus ribonucleic acid. However, the actual role of the virus in producing the disease is not established.

CLINICAL PRESENTATION

The clinical presentation of otosclerosis is a progressive conductive hearing loss in an adult. Some patients report improved speech understanding in a noisy environment (known as paracusis of Willis). Tinnitus is the second most common complaint reported. Vestibular symptoms are uncommon. Sensorineural hearing loss may be associated with the conductive changes in the disease. However, an isolated sensorineural hearing loss caused by otosclerosis is rare.

Physical examination shows a normal appearance of the external auditory canal and tympanic membrane. Schwartze's sign, a reddish hue over the promontory caused by increased vascularity of the bone immediately under the periosteum, may be seen in the early stages of the disease but is not present in all patients.

LABORATORY TESTING

Depending on the stage of the disease, audiometric studies typically show a mild to moderate conductive hearing loss. The air–bone gap is wider at the lower frequencies. Carhart's notch is characteristic of otosclerosis and appears as a sensorineural hearing loss at 2 kHz that is spurious since the bone conduction in the midfrequency range is not reliable. Stapes fixation interferes with the bone conduction of the acoustic signal, and up to 15 dB of the apparent sensorineural hearing loss disappear after surgery for otosclerosis. With progression of the conductive loss, the Rinne test demonstrates greater bone conduction than air conduction, and Weber's test lateralizes to the affected side. The tympanogram is either depressed (A_S) or normal. The stapedial reflex may be normal in the early stages but cannot be elicited as stapes fixation proceeds. Speech discrimination is often normal, except in patients with cochlear involvement.

MEDICAL MANAGEMENT

Medical management of otosclerosis remains controversial and is primarily directed at maturing the involved bone and decreasing osteoclastic activity. Shambaugh and Scott introduced use of sodium fluoride as treatment, based on its success in osteoporosis. However, this required high doses, and the efficacy has not been clearly established. Bisphosphonates that inhibit osteoclastic activity and cytokine antagonists that inhibit bone resorption may offer hope for the future. Hearing aids, however, do offer an effective means of nonsurgical management of hearing loss in otosclerosis.

SURGICAL MANAGEMENT

The history of surgery for otosclerosis dates back to Kessel in 1877, with early attempts at mobilization and extraction of the stapes. Other otologists subsequently attempted similar procedures, notably Miot in 1890, who described an extensive experience with surgery and suggested various surgical techniques. His successes were many. However, the report by Seibenmann at the turn of the twentieth century was less encouraging and condemned the surgery. This effectively ended these early ventures into stapes surgery for conductive hearing loss.

Interest in this field of ear surgery lay dormant until 1938, when Lempert described the fenestration procedure that became popular with otologists of the era, rekindling interest in surgery for otosclerosis. The focus returned to the stapes with Rosen's report of stapes mobilization and the restoration of hearing. Shea introduced the stapedectomy, a technique of stapes extraction with tissue coverage of the oval window and polyethylene strut reconstruction of the stapes, in the 1950s, ushering in the modern approach to stapes surgery

The surgical goal in otosclerosis is restoration of the transmission mechanism for sound from the tympanic membrane, going through the ossicular chain to the oval window, bypassing the resistance of the fixed stapes footplate. Today, a variety of techniques are used to correct for stapes footplate fixation. Generally, the stapes arch is removed, and either a perforation or a partial to complete removal of the footplate is performed. A prosthetic implant is employed to connect the incus to the oval window.

Selection of patients for operation is based on audiologic findings and physical examination. Preferred are patients with normal middle ear aeration, free of any infection or tympanic membrane perforation and with a Rinne test that demonstrates bone conduction to be greater than air conduction. When bilateral disease presents, the worse hearing ear is treated first followed by the other ear several months later. Experienced otologists should perform surgery on the only hearing ear, exclusively and with great trepidation.

Preoperative consent is obtained, informing the patient of the risks of loss of hearing, vertigo, injury to the facial nerve, loss or alteration of taste, tympanic membrane perforation, prosthesis extrusion, prosthesis mobilization, and residual conductive hearing loss. Singers and musicians are informed of a possible change in the quality of sound perception that may affect their professional performance. Individuals who are exposed to or plan to be involved in activities associated with rapid and/or considerable change in pressure, such as scuba diving and piloting nonpressurized airplanes, are advised to refrain from stapedectomy.

Perioperative Treatment

The operation may be performed under either general or local anesthesia. With improvements in anesthesia, more otologists are now performing the operation under general anesthesia. Use of any anticoagulants during the 2 weeks prior to the operation should be avoided, including anti-inflammatory agents. Muscle relaxants in conjunction with anesthetic agents are not recommended because of their effect on facial nerve activity. Perioperative antibiotics are at the surgeon's discretion, but antiemetic agents are recommended.

Whether a general or local technique is employed, injections of local anesthetics should be administered in such a manner as to avoid unintentional involvement of the facial nerve medial to the mastoid tip. Sterility of the operative field is of paramount importance since a direct connection to the labyrinth is established during parts of the operation. Routine operative site scrub technique, including instillation of an antibacterial preparation solution into the external auditory canal, is recommended. Facial nerve activity is monitored by direct vision of the face through a transparent occlusive drape.

Surgical Technique

Stapes surgery may be performed via an endaural or anterior incisural incision. The endaural incision requires use of a speculum held stationary with the left hand or a speculum holder assembly. In contrast, the anterior incisura incision is held open using one or two self-retaining retractors, eliminating the need to operate through a speculum. The cosmetic result of the incision is rarely noticeable. The latter also provides direct access to the tragal cartilage if a perichondrial graft is desired.

Regardless of the approach, a tympanomeatal flap is raised, the annulus identified, and hemostasis established prior to entering the middle ear space. A 1% lidocaine with 1:100,000 epinephrine or an 1:1,000 epinephrine-soaked piece of Gelfoam is used in this step. The tympanomeatal flap is elevated anteriorly, and the chorda tympani nerve is dissected free toward the malleus. A portion of the scutum should be curetted to expose the incus and the incudostapedial joint. Fixation of the stapes is determined by palpation of the malleus while viewing the suprastructure and footplate of the stapes.

The distance between the midshaft of the long process of the incus and the footplate is measured. The incudostapedial joint is separated, and the stapedial tendon is severed. The stapes suprastructure is fractured inferiorly and removed from the middle ear.

Establishing contact with the perilymphatic space may be done in several ways. The trend within the last decade has moved to smaller fenestra to protect the inner ear as much as possible. Typically, a small fenestra is created, or the footplate is partially removed. When the surgeon removes the footplate, a stapedectomy is performed. In a partial stapedectomy, the footplate is fractured in half, with the posterior portion being removed. A perichondrial graft from the tragus or a vein graft is placed over the defect, and the prosthesis is positioned over it and secured to the incus.

In the stapedotomy technique, a perforation in the footplate is made, just large enough to allow passage of the prosthesis. Fisch popularized the technique in which a perforation is gradually enlarged with a handheld drill to 0.6 mm in diameter. The stapes replacement prosthesis of choice is placed in the perforation and attached to the incus. The length of the prosthesis used is longer (by 0.25 mm) than the distance between the medial aspect of the long process of the incus and footplate, measured earlier, since the tip of the prosthesis has to go through the footplate. The addition of fresh clotted blood to the area also helps reduce the risk of a perilymphatic fistula.

Many otologists have advocated use of a laser in performing a stapedotomy. The advantage of the laser is decreased manipulation of the suprastructure and footplate. The thermal effect is negligible. The disadvantages are the extra time, expense, and instrumentation needed.

Postoperative Management

Postoperatively, the patient is sent home to bed and to remain on light activity for several days. Pain management requires mild oral medication, and antibiotics are not necessary. Postoperative vertigo is treated with ondansetron (Zofran) or promethazine (Phenergan). Stool softeners help reduce straining and decrease the chance of a perilymphatic fistula formation. Patients are cautioned against blowing their noses and sneezing with their mouths closed.

Postoperative follow-up is scheduled in 1 week to remove the suture and packing and assess the integrity of the tympanic membrane. Hearing testing is done 4 to 6 weeks following the operation.

Pitfalls

The pitfalls of the surgery include inadequate exposure and anatomic variations. The endaural incision and speculum produce a narrower opening when compared with the anterior incisura approach. The scutum can cover the long process of the incus and the posterior half of the stapes. Adequate removal of the scutum ensures proper visualization of the footplate in the crucial stage of footplate perforation and prosthesis placement. An aberrant facial nerve may prohibit a stapedectomy, and relocation of the nerve, which carries a risk of facial weakness and paralysis, is not recommended. A dehiscent nerve has a higher chance of facial nerve injury.

Advanced otosclerosis with obliteration of the oval window requires drilling of the footplate and significant experience with temporal bone anatomy. Sclerotic obstruction of the round window is of less importance since only a small opening over the round window is necessary to allow proper cochlear function. Drilling out the round window often results in a severe hearing loss and is avoided.

If the footplate should drop into the vestibule, attempts should be made to remove it. However, this should be done only if one can easily grasp the edge and gently remove it. Never go fishing for bony fragments that descend into the vestibule, away from the annular rim.

During the stapedectomy, the protective function of the stapedius muscle is destroyed. A new technique in which the stapedius muscle is left in place and the posterior crus of the fractured suprastructure is shaped and used as an autologous stapes replacement graft has been proposed and used. The efficacy of this technique in preserving the acoustic reflex is controversial.

Results

Otosclerosis surgery has withstood the test of time since its reinstitution in the 1950s. Shea, in his review of 40 years of stapes surgery, reported closure to within 10 dB of the preoperative bone conduction level in over 95% of patients. Glasscock and colleagues reported over 91% closure to within 5 dB. Both groups reported significantly less success in revision surgery. Persson and colleagues contrasted stapedectomy and stapedotomy in the review of their series and demonstrated that partial and total stapedectomy had better results at all frequencies with the exception of 4 kHz. However, the hearing results in this group tended to deteriorate more quickly than in the stapedotomy patients. Others have reported similar preservation of high frequencies with stapedotomy. Outcome in the training situation demonstrates significantly poorer results. A definite learning curve in stapes surgery is present after training. The accepted overall rate of anacusis following stapes surgery is in the range of 1 to 2%.

Complications

The complications of the stapes surgery are immediate and delayed in nature. Immediate complications are those occurring during the operation, such as facial nerve paralysis secondary to infusion of the local anesthetic or injury, vertigo and/or hearing loss caused by suctioning of the perilymphatic fluid from the oval window during the operation, or persistent postoperative perilymphatic leakage from the oval window. Bed rest and light activities are recommended for vertiginous patients, and most recover shortly after the operation. Metallic taste and loss of taste caused by manipulation of or injury to the chorda tympani nerve are not uncommon. Labyrinthitis, although possible, occurs rarely under sterile conditions.

Delayed postoperative complications, including perilymphatic fistula, granuloma, and prosthesis dislocation, have been reported. Immediate treatment with antibiotics and rest is recommended. Re-exploration should be entertained to correct for the fistula should persistent vertigo occur. Granuloma formation can occur for totally unknown reasons and in the best of settings. Keeping all foreign material, such as the talcum powder of the glove and bone dust, away from the footplate area may decrease the chances of granulomas. A dislocated prosthesis requires re-exploration and revision.

8

HEREDITARY HEARING IMPAIRMENT

Richard J. H. Smith, MD
Stephen W. Hone, MD

Hearing impairment may be classified by mode of acquisition as inherited or acquired and by time of onset as prelingual (congenital) or postlingual (late onset). Approximately 50% of congenital deafness is inherited, and by the time children begin school, about 1 child in 650 to 2,000 has some form of hereditary hearing loss. As the incidence of deafness owing to infectious and iatrogenic causes diminishes and as our ability to diagnose genetic abnormalities improves, the relative importance of hereditary factors as causes of deafness increases.

Patterns of Inheritance

Genetic information is passed from one generation to the next encoded in the human genome. The human genome is composed of 46 chromosomes, 22 pairs of autosomes, and the sex chromosomes, XY in males and XX in females. Individuals inherit half of their chromosomes from their fathers and half from their mothers, meaning that every autosomal gene exists as a pair of alleles, one of paternal origin and the other of maternal origin. The alleles of a gene pair may be identical or subtle differences may be present. If they are identical, an individual is said to be homozygous for that gene pair; alternatively, if they are different, an individual is said to be heterozygous. For example, if a gene has two possible allele variants, A and A′, and an AA′ by AA′ mating occurs, the progeny will have genotypes AA, AA′, or A′A′. If normal function of this gene is essential for normal hearing, and A′ encodes an allele of the gene that is associated with hearing impairment, deafness could result. If progeny with genotypes AA′ or A′A′ are hearing impaired, one can infer that A′ is dominant over A. Alternatively, if all progeny have normal hearing except those with genotypes A′A′, one can infer that A′ is recessive with respect to A. In the first case, both parents will be hearing impaired, whereas in the second case, only A′A′ progeny will be hearing impaired. These patterns of allele segregation are referred to as autosomal dominant and autosomal recessive inheritance, respectively.

Deafness caused by genes on the X chromosome is inherited in an X-linked fashion and is usually recessive. The deafness is rarely penetrant in female carriers; however, of the progeny of a female carrier, half of the sons will be affected and half of the daughters will be carriers. Of the progeny of an affected male, all sons will be normal and all daughters will be carriers. Mitochondrial mutations associated with hearing impairment are inherited only through the mother; both sexes are affected equally.

Sixty to 70% of cases of hereditary deafness are autosomal recessive, 20 to 30% of cases are autosomal dominant, and 2% are X-linked. In nearly one-third of cases, other phenotypic characteristics cosegregate with the hearing loss, and these hearing impairments are labeled "syndromic." Typically, a wide range of phenotypic variation occurs, even in individuals carrying the same deafness-causing genetic mutation. In the absence of cosegregating physical findings, inherited deafness is said to be "nonsyndromic" and is subclassified by mode of inheritance as DFNA, DFNB, or DFN for dominant, recessive, or X-linked, respectively (DFN for *deafn*ess). Loci are ordered by appended integers to reflect the date of discovery. Mitochondrial deafness is designated by mutation type.

SYNDROMIC HEARING IMPAIRMENT

Hearing loss has been described in over 400 syndromes. Although there are many classifications for these syndromes, one of the more useful is based on the involved organ system. Some of the more common forms of syndromic hearing impairment are discussed below.

Autosomal Dominant Syndromic Hearing Impairment

Branchio-Oto-Renal Syndrome

The association of branchial arch anomalies with hearing impairment has long been recognized and designated as branchio-oto-renal syndrome (BOR). Persons with the BOR syndrome have branchial clefts or fistulae, otologic abnormalities, and renal anomalies. Disease prevalence approximates 1 in 40,000 in the general population. Hearing impairment, which is found in over 90% of affected individuals, is attributable to conductive, sensorineural, or mixed loss, with differences occurring even within families. Both stable hearing and progressive deterioration of hearing have been reported, the progressive loss reflecting associated temporal bone abnormalities such as dilated vestibular aqueduct (DVA). Renal anomalies are also common and occur in up to 75% of cases.

In the early 1990s, the BOR gene was mapped to chromosome 8q, and in 1997, the causative gene *EYA1* was cloned. However, in about 70% of persons with a BOR phenotype, *EYA1* mutations cannot be found. This finding, together with marked phenotypic variability, has suggested to some investigators that BOR is a heterogeneous disease, a hypothesis recently confirmed with the identification of a second BOR locus on chromosome 1p31.

Stickler's Syndrome

Stickler's syndrome (STL), also known as hereditary arthro-ophthalmopathy, is characterized by marfanoid features, spondyloepiphyseal dysplasia, joint hypermobility, midface hypoplasia, severe myopia, and varying degrees of Robin sequence (cleft palate, micrognathia, and glossoptosis). Because of the possibility of retinal detachment, ophthalmologic assessment is mandatory. Gene linkage studies have demonstrated considerable genetic heterogeneity, with mutations in *COL2A1*, *COL11A2*, and *COL11A1* implicated in STL1, STL2, and STL3, respectively. Because *COL11A2* is not expressed in the eye, persons affected with STL2 do not have myopia.

Treacher Collins Syndrome

Treacher Collins syndrome (TCS) is a disorder of craniofacial development affecting structures derived from the first branchial arch. It is characterized by midface hypoplasia, micrognathia, macrostomia, colobomas of the lower eyelids, downward slanting palpebral fissures, cleft palate, and conductive hearing loss owing to external and middle ear abnormalities. The reported incidence of TCS is about 1 in 50,000 live births. The causative gene *TCOF1* encodes a protein called treacle that is structurally related to nucleolar phosphoproteins and may play a role in nucleolar-cytoplasmic transport.

Waardenburg's Syndrome

Waardenburg's syndrome (WS), an auditory-pigmentary syndrome characterized by premature graying, a white forelock, synophrys, heterochromia iridis, hearing loss, and dystopia canthorum, was first described by Petrus Waardenburg in 1951. The prevalence of this syndrome in the general population is 1 in 42,000, and among the congenitally deaf, it is 1.43%. Four clinical types of WS are recognized. Waardenburg's syndrome type 1 is distinguished from WS2 by the presence of dystopia canthorum in the former, a condition that results from medial fusion of the eyelids leading to a reduction in the visible sclera medial to the iris. Hearing loss, which occurs in 60% of cases of WS1 and in 80% of cases of WS2, is typically sensorineural, prelingual, and nonprogressive and varies from mild to profound; profound bilateral loss is most common. Waardenburg's syndrome type 3 or Klein-Waardenburg syndrome is a severe variant of WS1 with associated limb and skeletal abnormalities. Waardenburg's syndrome 4 or Shah-Waardenburg syndrome combines the features of WS2 with Hirschsprung's disease. Both WS1 and WS3 are caused by mutations in *PAX3*, some cases of WS2 are caused by mutations in the microphthalmia gene (*MITF*), and the WS4 phenotype results from mutations in *EDNRB*, its ligand *EDN3*, or *SOX10*.

Autosomal Recessive Syndromic Hearing Impairment

Jervell and Lange-Nielsen Syndrome

Jervell and Lange-Nielsen syndrome (JLNS) is characterized by profound prelingual sensorineural hearing loss, syncope, and sudden death owing to a prolonged Q–Tc interval. Diagnostic criteria include a Q–Tc > 440 ms in males and > 460 ms in females. Syncopal attacks are usually associated with exertion or emotion; with prompt diagnosis and antiarrhythmic treatment, the high mortality rate can be significantly reduced. Mutations in *KCNQ1* and *KCNE1*, which encode subunits of a voltage-gated potassium channel protein, have been shown to cause JLNS. Some heterozygous individuals may have a prolonged Q–Tc interval in the absence of hearing loss and are prone to life-threatening arrhythmias.

Pendred's Syndrome

Pendred's syndrome (PS) is characterized by congenital sensorineural hearing loss and goiter and may account for up to 7.5% of all cases of childhood deafness. Hearing loss is most frequently profound and is associated with temporal bone abnormalities ranging from DVA to Mondini's dysplasia. Goiter may be apparent at birth but typically presents in midchildhood. The thyroid defect can be diagnosed by administering perchlorate, which releases unbound iodide from thyroid follicular cells. Despite this abnormality, affected individuals usually remain euthyroid. The disease is caused by mutations in *PDS*, a member of the solute carrier 26 gene family. The encoded protein, pendrin, transports chloride and iodide and mediates the exchange of chloride and formate, properties that suggest tissue-specific functions.

Usher's Syndrome

Usher's syndrome (USH) is the most common autosomal recessive syndromic form of hearing impairment. Characterized by blindness caused by retinitis pigmentosa and sensorineural hearing loss, it is responsible for half of all deaf-blindness in the United States and an estimated 3 to 10% of all congenital deafness. It can be classified into three different types based on clinical presentation. Usher's syndrome types 1 and 2 are most common, whereas USH3 is quite rare, accounting for only 5 to 15% of all USH.

Vestibular dysfunction differentiates USH1 from USH2. Hearing loss and vestibular areflexia are typically profound in the former, and hearing aids are frequently ineffectual. Persons with USH2, in contrast, have normal vestibular function and usually have a moderate-to-severe hearing loss. They use hearing aids effectively and communicate orally. Persons with USH3 have progressive vestibular and auditory dysfunction.

Initial visual problems with USH begin as nyctalopia or night blindness. This problem can occur in the preschool years, although visual acuity usually remains good until the third decade. Studies of multiplex families have documented considerable intrafamilial variation in the rate and degree of visual deterioration. Electroretinography may uncover early retinitis pigmentosa.

Usher's syndrome demonstrates considerable genetic heterogeneity. To date, seven USH1 loci (USH1A–G), three USH2 (USH2A–C) loci, and one USH3 locus have been identified.

Five of the relevant genes have been cloned, *MYO7A*, *USH1C*, *USH2A*, *CDH23* and *PCDH15*, mutations that cause USH1B, USH1C, USH2A, USH1D, and USH1F, respectively.

X-Linked Syndromic Hearing Impairment

Alport's Syndrome

Progressive glomerulonephritis, sensorineural hearing loss, and specific eye findings characterize Alport's syndrome (AS), which can be inherited as an X-linked or autosomal disorder. To facilitate diagnosis, four clinical criteria were established in 1988. In the presence of unexplained hematuria, a person can be considered affected if three of the following criteria are met: (1) a positive family history of hematuria or chronic renal failure, (2) electron microscopic renal biopsy evidence of AS, (3) characteristic eye signs of anterior lenticonus or white macular flecks or both, and (4) high-frequency sensorineural hearing loss. The characteristic eye findings are rarely noted in childhood and may become apparent only with renal failure; hearing loss is postlingual, progressive, and sensorineural.

The typical male with X-linked AS presents with hematuria at age 3 to 4 years, often following an upper respiratory tract infection. Toward the end of the first decade, hearing loss is detectable, and in the midteens, hypertension develops. By 25 years of age, over 90% of affected males have abnormal renal function. The clinical course in female carriers is much more variable. Most are clinically asymptomatic through life, although nearly all have evidence of microscopic hematuria and about one-third develop macroscopic hematuria. X-linked AS is caused by mutations in *COL4A5*, a member of the type IV collagen gene family.

Mitochondrial Syndromic Hearing Impairment

Hearing loss may be associated with a number of syndromic mitochondrial diseases. Most frequent are the acquired mitochondrial neuromuscular syndromes, such as MELAS (mitochondrial encephalopathy, lactic acidosis, and stroke-like episodes) and MERRF (myoclonus epilepsy and with ragged red fibers), and maternally inherited diabetes mellitus associated with deafness.

NONSYNDROMIC HEARING IMPAIRMENT

Over 70 different nonsyndromic hearing impairment loci have been mapped, and a number of the relevant genes have been cloned. The protein products of these genes include ion channels, membrane proteins, transcription factors, and structural proteins.

Autosomal Dominant Nonsyndromic Hearing Impairment

Autosomal dominant modes of inheritance account for 15% of cases of nonsyndromic hearing impairment (ADNSHI). The typical phenotype is one of postlingual hearing loss. The hearing loss starts in the second to third decades of life and progresses until it is moderate to severe in degree. However, the frequencies that are initially affected vary. For example, DFNA1, DFNA6, and DFN14 are characterized by a low-frequency hearing loss that progresses to involve the remaining frequencies. With other loci, hearing loss starts in the mid- or high frequencies before progressing. The DFNA3, DFNA12, DFNA13, DFNA23, and DFNA24 phenotypes are exceptional as they are congenital hearing losses on which age-related changes become superimposed.

Autosomal Recessive Nonsyndromic Hearing Impairment

Up to 85% of cases of nonsyndromic hearing loss are inherited in a recessive mendelian fashion. The typical phenotype is more severe than in ADNSHI and accounts for the majority of cases of congenital profound deafness. The first locus, DFNB1, was reported in 1994, and, 3 years later, the gene responsible for DFNB1, *GJB2* (gap junction beta 2), was cloned. This gene encodes connexin 26 (Cx26), one of a class of proteins involved in gap junction formation. It is postulated that gap junctions allow potassium ions that enter hair cells' stereocilia during mechanoelectrical transduction to be recirculated into the stria vascularis.

The most significant discovery in the field of genetic deafness to date has been the finding that mutations in Cx26 are responsible for over half of moderate-to-profound congenital deafness in many world populations. Numerous different deafness-causing allele variants of *GJB2* have been identified, and in the United States and much of northern Europe, the most prevalent mutation is the 35delG mutation. In the midwestern United States, the carrier rate for this mutation is 2.5%, whereas the carrier rate for all deafness-causing Cx26 mutations is 3%. Other "common" mutations are found in different populations, such as the 167delT mutation in Ashkenazi Jews.

These discoveries have had immediate application to clinical practice. In many populations, a definitive diagnosis can now be made in 50% of cases of congenital hereditary hearing loss. The ability to establish causality affects recurrence chance estimates and makes genetic counseling an important part of the evaluation of hereditary deafness. However, the degree of hearing loss in a child with Cx26-related deafness cannot be used to predict the degree of hearing impairment in a sibling as there can be considerable intrafamilial variability.

X-linked Nonsyndromic Hearing Impairment

X-linked nonsyndromic hearing impairment is rare and makes up only 1 to 3% of nonsyndromic hearing loss. It exhibits considerable phenotypic heterogeneity, but most affected males have a congenital hearing loss, which can vary from severe to profound. Hearing loss is mild to moderate in carrier females.

Mitochondrial Nonsyndromic Hearing Impairment

Mitochondrial mutations may play a role in age-related hearing loss and have been implicated in a type of nonsyndromic deafness associated with increased susceptibility to aminoglycoside ototoxicity.

Age-Related Hearing Loss

Mitochondrial mutations may be a contributing factor to age-related hearing loss. The number of mutation-carrying mitochondria per cell increases with age, resulting in a progressive reduction in oxidative phosphorylation capacity, the impact of which is tissue dependent. High rates of mitochondrial DNA deletions in the lymphocytes of persons with idiopathic sensorineural hearing loss have been detected. Temporal bone studies also have shown an increased load of mitochondrial mutations in persons with age-related hearing loss when compared with controls.

Familial Aminoglycoside Ototoxicity

A point mutation at base pair 1555 (adenine to guanine) in the 12S ribosomal ribonucleic acid causes both maternally inherited nonsyndromic hearing loss and maternally inherited susceptibility to aminoglycoside ototoxicity. In the United States, over 15% of persons with aminoglycoside-induced hearing loss carry this mutation, a point of major clinical relevance for the prevention of aminoglycoside hearing loss. Accordingly, it is prudent to inquire about any family history of aminoglycoside ototoxicity prior to drug administration. Individuals who develop ototoxicity should be tested for the 1555 mutation and offered family counseling if the mutation is detected.

CLINICAL DIAGNOSIS OF HEARING IMPAIRMENT

A complete history is an important element in the diagnosis of hereditary hearing impairment. Directed questions should focus on prenatal, perinatal, and postnatal history. A record of speech and language milestones can establish whether the hearing loss is pre- or postlingual; however, even deaf infants coo and babble naturally up to the age of 6 months. A history of poor motor development may indicate vestibular dysfunction. Consanguinity or common origins from ethically isolated areas should increase suspicion of hereditary hearing impairment. If there are a number of family members with hearing loss, constructing a pedigree may delineate the mode of inheritance. Since most cases of hereditary hearing impairment are nonsyndromic, abnormal physical findings are absent. However, even in cases of syndromic hearing impairment, these cosegregating traits may be subtle, so the physical examination should include a systematic evaluation of all systems.

The hearing test of choice for infants and young children with suspected hearing impairment is the auditory brainstem response, which gives accurate hearing thresholds from 1 to 4 kHz. In older children or adults, a standard audiogram can be obtained. Specific laboratory tests should be ordered on the basis of the history, physical examination, and age of the patient. For example, if PS is suspected, a perchlorate challenge test can be obtained to detect a defect in iodide uptake by the thyroid gland. If AS is being considered, urinalysis should be performed. Serology can be used to rule out acquired causes of early deafness, such as cytomegalovirus infection, toxoplasmosis, and congenital rubella. Temporal bone computed tomography is the single best radiologic test for the evaluation of deafness, with a reported incidence of anatomic abnormalities ranging from 6.8 to 28.4%. If BOR syndrome is being considered, renal ultrasonography also should be performed. An ophthalmology opinion should be obtained in all children with severe-to-profound deafness as half will have ocular abnormalities. Chromosomal karyotyping is indicated in a child born to parents with a history of miscarriages, when the constellation of anomalies in a child is not recognizable as a previously reported syndrome, or if there are associated central nervous system or cardiac defects.

Referral to a clinical geneticist should be requested to ensure that parents and patients adequately understand issues such as recurrence chance. Genetic testing for most of the types of deafness discussed in this chapter is not yet clinically available; however, it is likely that in the next 5 years, many genetically based tests will be offered, making some older tests obsolete.

MANAGEMENT

Early identification of hearing impairment in infants and young children and early rehabilitation are essential for development of age-appropriate speech and language skills. To achieve this goal, newborn hearing screening programs have been implemented in most states and linked to rehabilitative programs. The level of habilitative intervention required depends on the degree of hearing impairment. Counseling of the family, proper hearing aid selection, hearing aid fitting, and continued audiologic assessment are important. Schools that teach sign language, oral-aural communication, and a combination of both may be necessary. Cochlear implantation may be an option in persons with severe and profound hearing impairment. A variety of support systems exist, particularly on the World Wide Web. In the United States, the National Institute on Deafness and Other Communication Disorders established the Hereditary Hearing Impairment Resource Registry (HHIRR) <www.boystown.org/hhirr> to disseminate information on hearing impairment to professionals and families.

FUTURE DEVELOPMENTS

The rapid advances in the genetics and molecular biology of hearing and deafness that occurred during the last decade of the twentieth century are continuing at pace. Inexpensive genetic tests are becoming available for early detection of hearing impairment, and the use of these tests will ultimately impact management decisions by better defining therapeutic and habilitative options. In the next decades, it is likely that physicians will be able to offer patients new, practical, and effective treatments for sensorineural hearing impairment.

9

TRAUMA TO THE MIDDLE EAR, INNER EAR, AND TEMPORAL BONE

Mitchell K. Schwaber, MD

Two types of injury are likely to involve the external auditory canal: blunt and penetrating trauma and thermal and caustic burns. Isolated blunt trauma to the ear canal is most often caused by the insertion of a foreign object into the ear to scratch the skin or to remove wax. The skin of the canal is easily abraded. Infection may develop, and pain, hearing loss, or infected drainage causes the patient to seek help. The canal should be gently cleaned using a microscopic technique, and blood clots, debris, and wax should be removed. The tympanic membrane should be inspected to determine the extent of injury. Ciprofloxacin and hydrocortisone otic drops are prescribed to control the infection.

Mandibular injuries, particularly those that drive the mandible posteriorly into the jaw joint, will occasionally fracture the anterior wall of the ear canal, resulting in laceration of the skin and exposure of bone. If exposed bone is found, it should not be débrided at this point but rather assessed later when the canal has healed. Squamous cell epithelium can be entrapped by the fracture fragments, leading to the development of a canal cholesteatoma. Débridement, grafting, reconstruction, or meatoplasty may be required to ensure a healthy, open ear canal.

Penetrating injuries of the external auditory canal are usually caused by gunshot or stab wounds. Facial nerve injury, tympanic membrane perforation, and ossicular dislocation can result from gunshot wounds of the external auditory canal. The facial nerve is most likely to be injured at the stylomastoid foramen, apparently because it is relatively fixed at that point. In the absence of any of these specific injuries, gunshot wounds of the ear canal require cleaning, a light dressing, and prophylactic antibiotics.

Burns and caustic injuries of the ear canal, if severe, can cause circumferential scarring and stenosis of the canal. Most of these injuries are caused by a thermal burn, a caustic burn, or a welding injury. Most thermal burns of the ear canal are caused by flash injuries, fires, lightning strikes, or hot liquids such as oil. Superficial thermal burns of the ear canal are usually treated with the application of antibiotic ointment. If more than one half of the ear canal is involved or has third-degree burns, in addition to the application of antibiotic ointment, the canal is stented with soft Silastic tubing to prevent stenosis. Stenosis of the canal is treated aggressively with corticosteroid injections, frequent dilations, and, in some cases, skin grafting or meatoplasty.

Caustic burns are usually caused by a chemical spill or a foreign object such as an alkaline battery. In the latter case, otic drops must be withheld as they provide an external electrolyte bath for the battery, enhancing leakage and generation of an external current with subsequent tissue electrolysis and hydroxide formation. The foreign body should be removed as soon as possible, under general anesthesia if needed.

TYMPANIC MEMBRANE AND THE MIDDLE EAR

Trauma to the tympanic membrane and the middle ear can be caused by (1) overpressure, (2) thermal or caustic burns, (3) blunt or penetrating injuries, and (4) barotrauma. *Overpressure* is by far the most common mechanism of trauma to the tympanic membrane. The major causes of overpressure include slap injuries and blast injuries. Slap injuries are extremely common and can be a result of either a hand or water slap. Slap injuries usually result in a triangular or linear tear of the tympanic membrane. Most of these perforations cause mild hearing loss, aural fullness, and mild tinnitus. Blast injuries, although much less common, are potentially much more serious. Blast injuries may be caused by bomb explosions, gasoline explosions, and air bag deployment in automobile accidents. Blast injuries from bomb explosions not only disrupt the tympanic membrane but also can cause temporal bone fracture, ossicular discontinuity, perilymphatic fistula (PLF), or high-frequency sensorineural hearing loss owing to cochlear injury.

Following an overpressure injury, blood, purulent secretions, and debris should be carefully suctioned from the ear canal, and the perforation size and location should be recorded. An audiogram should be obtained as soon as the patient's condition allows. The status of the cranial nerves, including the facial nerve and the vestibular nerve, as well as the central nervous system, should be determined. If the tympanic membrane perforation is dry, it should be observed (ie, drops are not indicated). If there is drainage through the tympanic membrane perforation, the clinician should determine and note if the drainage is consistent with cerebrospinal fluid (CSF). If a CSF leak is suspected, an immediate computed tomography (CT) scan of the temporal bone should be obtained to rule out a fracture. If the drainage is not consistent with CSF, oral antibiotics and ciprofloxacin and hydrocortisone otic drops should be prescribed. A history of vertigo or nausea and vomiting and an audiogram showing a conductive hearing loss of more than 30 dB suggest disruption of the ossicular chain. Profound sensorineural loss may signify oval window or cochlear damage.

Thermal injuries to the tympanic membrane include welding and lightning injuries. Welding injuries occur when hot slag enters the ear canal and passes through the tympanic membrane. Welding injuries often result in nonhealing perforations, either as a result of infection or possibly because the slag acts to cauterize or devascularize the tympanic membrane as it passes through it. If infection occurs, the patient is treated with ciprofloxacin and hydrocortisone otic drops and an oral antibiotic. If the perforation is dry, it should be observed for a period of 12 weeks for spontaneous healing. If the drumhead does not heal, tympanoplasty should be performed.

Lightning and electrocution injuries are not rare, and the most frequent ear injury is perforation of the tympanic membrane. The most common vestibular disturbance is transient vertigo. Other clinical findings include sensorineural hearing impairment, conductive hearing loss, tinnitus, temporal bone fracture, avulsion of the mastoid process, burns of the ear canal, and facial nerve paralysis. The initial management of the patient struck by lightning consists of life support measures. Thereafter, the patient should have a thorough audiovestibular assessment. Tympanic membrane perforations caused by lightning injury often do not heal. Tympanoplasty should be delayed in these patients for 12 weeks because spontaneous healing may take that long.

Caustic injuries to the tympanic membrane can cause a perforation. The middle ear can develop an extensive granulation reaction with scarification, ossicular fixation, and a chronic infection. Caustic injuries also can lead to canal blunting as the raw surfaces that surround the canal form a cicatrix, leading to narrowing of the ear canal and loss of the vibratory surface of the tympanic membrane. Similarly, following a caustic injury, chronic myringitis can develop, creating a raw, weeping surface. Caustic injuries are initially treated with ciprofloxacin and hydrocortisone otic drops, oral antibiotics, and analgesics. When the ear has stabilized, and preferably when drainage has diminished, the middle ear and tympanic membrane can be reconstructed.

Tympanic membrane perforations historically have a healing rate that approaches 80%. Perforations produced by heat or corrosives, foreign objects, lightning and welding injuries, and water pressure are less likely to heal, perhaps because they are larger or more likely to be infected. Good hearing results regardless of the method of tympanoplasty, although spontaneous healing results in the best hearing outcome.

Regardless of the method used, successful tympanoplasty requires adequate exposure, débridement of middle ear granulation and scar tissue, de-epithelialization of the perforation, and careful graft placement, including support of the graft until healing occurs.

Penetrating trauma to the middle ear can, of course, result in perforation of the tympanic membrane, but unlike overpressure and thermal injury, the incidence of ossicular disruption and facial nerve and other middle ear injuries is much greater. The most common causes are low-velocity gunshots followed by injury with a foreign object such as a stick or instrument. This type of injury should be suspected in patients with a tympanic membrane perforation, blood in the middle ear or ear canal, and the presence of vertigo or dizziness, a conductive loss greater than 25 dB, a sensorineural hearing loss, or a facial paralysis. In these patients, the ear canal should be gently cleaned under microscopic vision, and the tympanic membrane and middle ear should be carefully inspected. A complete neurotologic examination, including facial nerve evaluation and examination for nystagmus, gait stability, fistula test, Romberg's test, and Dix-Hallpike test, should be performed. Imaging studies including CT scans of the temporal bone and magnetic resonance imaging (MRI) scans and even arteriography may be indicated depending on the type of injury suspected.

TEMPORAL BONE FRACTURES

Fractures of the temporal bone are caused by blunt injuries, and depending on the force and direction of the blow delivered, different types of fractures occur. Blunt trauma can be delivered by an object striking the head or by the head being thrown against a solid object. Traditionally, temporal bone fractures are classified as either longitudinal (extracapsular) or transverse (capsular) with respect to the long axis of the petrous portion of the temporal bone. Both are basal skull fractures and are associated with ecchymosis of the postauricular skin (Battle's sign).

Longitudinal fractures are, by far, the most common, accounting for 70 to 90% of temporal bone fractures, and typically result from a direct lateral blow to the temporal or parietal aspect of the head. The longitudinal fracture begins in the external auditory canal and extends through the middle ear and along the long axis of the petrous pyramid. Characteristically, there is bleeding from the ear canal owing to laceration of its skin and from blood coming through the perforated tympanic membrane. Facial paralysis occurs in 15%, and sensorineural hearing loss occurs in 35%.

Transverse fractures typically result from deceleration impacts in the occipital area. The fracture line traverses the long axis of the petrous portion of the temporal bone and usually extends through the cochlea and fallopian canal, resulting in sensorineural hearing loss and facial paralysis in most cases. There is bleeding into the middle ear, but the tympanic membrane remains intact and becomes blue-black owing to the hemotympanum.

POST-TRAUMATIC OSSICULAR CHAIN DISRUPTION

Post-traumatic ossicular chain abnormalities include incudostapedial joint separation, dislocation of the incus, fracture and dislocation of the stapes, massive dislocation of the entire chain, and ossicular fixation caused by scarring or ossification. Incudostapedial joint separation is the most common ossicular abnormality and is more often seen with penetrating trauma and longitudinal temporal bone fractures. The forces that cause this type of fracture tend to displace the malleus and incus medially and inferiorly. As a consequence, incudostapedial joint separation is most common with longitudinal fractures followed by dislocation of the incus. In patients in whom significant conductive hearing loss (ie, greater than 25 dB) is found, incudostapedial joint separation or incus dislocation should be suspected. In patients in whom mixed hearing loss is found or significant vertigo occurs, a fracture or dislocation of the stapes should be suspected. In this situation, the force may have sheared the crura off the footplate or the entire stapes may be dislocated. This distinction is important in management in that incus subluxation or incudostapedial joint separation cannot be observed until the hemotympanum and swelling have resolved. In most cases, because of the tendency of the drumhead to adhere to the stapes, the residual conductive hearing loss is minimal after healing and requires no surgery. On the other hand, stapes dislocation with vertigo and/or progression of the sensorineural hearing loss is an indication for timely surgical exploration and repair to prevent anacusis.

One of four procedures is used to repair the ossicular abnormality. In the vast majority of patients, the incus is so displaced that it cannot be used efficiently. In these patients, the surgeon may choose to place a partial ossicular replacement prosthesis (PORP), linking the stapes directly to the drumhead. The PORP is attached to the stapes capitulum and is then covered with a thin wafer of cartilage. Alternatively, the surgeon may choose to link the stapes to the malleus, using either a commercially available prosthesis or a sculpted incus. These two techniques give comparable results, usually resulting in a 15 to 20 dB air–bone gap. In some cases, the surgeon may choose to place a total ossicular replacement prosthesis (TORP) with an intact stapes.

This type of placement offers greater stability for the prosthesis, which can be placed between the tympanic portion of the facial nerve canal and the superstructure of the stapes. A small perichondrial graft placed on the footplate between the crura further stabilizes this assembly, as does linking the prosthesis to the malleus. Like the PORP technique, a thin wafer of cartilage should be placed over the TORP to link it to the drumhead. Of course, a TORP can be used in patients in whom the stapes superstructure is disrupted or fractured. The stapes footplate should be covered with a perichondrial graft to stabilize the TORP and to ensure that any footplate fractures are covered. In some patients, the stapes superstructure is damaged or the footplate is disrupted in the presence of an otherwise normal malleus and incus. In these patients, a stapes prosthesis can be used. The first step in this circumstance is to ensure that a depressed stapes is carefully elevated out of the vestibule. Once the stapes footplate is in a satisfactory position, it is covered with perichondrium, and a stapes prosthesis can be linked from the incus or malleus to the footplate.

POST-TRAUMATIC PERILYMPHATIC FISTULA

Severe head trauma, whether blunt or penetrating, is associated with a high incidence of sensorineural hearing loss. Nearly one-third of these patients develop a high-frequency hearing loss, which is thought to arise from a cochlear concussion, shearing of the basilar membrane, hair cell degeneration, and avulsion of auditory nerve fibers. Excessive stapes footplate excursion can also cause this same pathophysiologic consequence, so differentiating a concussion from a PLF can be difficult. Traumatic PLFs can result from penetrating trauma with resultant fracture or subluxation of the stapes, from an overpressure injury such as a blast or a severe barotrauma event, or from a fracture of the temporal bone.

A PLF is a persistent, abnormal communication between the inner ear and the middle ear air space. In most cases, this communication occurs through the oval or round windows, although, occasionally, a fistula through a semicircular canal is discovered. As opposed to a cochlear concussion, the hearing threshold in PLF cases continues to fluctuate or to deteriorate. Tinnitus and fullness are also common complaints of these patients. However, the features that differentiate a PLF from a labyrinthine concussion are episodic vertigo, movement-triggered vertigo, persistent unsteadiness, and often nausea. In the setting of trauma, with progressive hearing loss and episodic vertigo, a PLF should be suspected. Special attention should be given to the evaluation for spontaneous nystagmus, an abnormal Romberg's test, a positive fistula sign, a positive Dix-Hallpike sign, an unsteady gait, or an abnormal step test. Audiometric assessment may show a mixed hearing loss or a pure sensorineural hearing loss.

If a PLF is suspected, bed rest, corticosteroids, and even diuretics can be tried for a period of 2 to 3 days to determine if spontaneous healing might occur. If symptoms persist, the middle ear should be explored. A subluxed stapes should be carefully elevated and secured in position using perichondrium and fibrin glue. If the oval window is indeed intact, the surgeon should carefully inspect the round window niche and membrane. At this point, several maneuvers are performed to visualize a PLF, including Trendelenburg's positioning, neck compression, and a Valsalva-like maneuver administered by the anesthesiologist. A PLF is likely present if fluid emanates from the oval window or pools in the round window niche with these maneuvers. Whether PLF is found or not, most authors apply a soft tissue patch to the round and oval windows at this point. Following PLF repair, the episodic vertigo significantly improves in the vast majority of patients. However, the hearing results are much less predictable as only 15 to 20% of patients demonstrate substantial hearing improvement. The hearing threshold is usually stabilized, however.

POST-TRAUMATIC VESTIBULAR DYSFUNCTION

The most common type of post-traumatic vestibular dysfunction, by far, is benign paroxysmal positional vertigo (BPPV). This occurs in 50% of patients with temporal bone fractures and in 25% of patients with a head injury without fracture. In this circumstance, the dizziness begins usually within a few days of the injury, although it can be delayed for several months. Post-traumatic BPPV is thought to occur because deceleration forces disrupt the macula of the utricle, with release of the otoconia that ordinarily rest in a gel layer that covers the surface of the macula. The otoconia float into a dependent canal, most often the posterior semicircular canal, but the problem has been described in other canals. The shifting of the mass of otoconia actually displaces the fluid in the canal on head tilting. As a consequence, a short burst of vertigo occurs, with a typical 5- to 7-second delay, lasting 20 to 30 seconds. Typically, post-traumatic BPPV is unilateral and is triggered by placing the affected ear in the down position. This condition can be diagnosed by performing a Nylen-Bárány or Dix-Hallpike maneuver and observing the nystagmus that is triggered. Typically in this maneuver, the nystagmus has a rotary motion, either clockwise or counterclockwise, toward the down and affected ear. Untreated, this condition usually lasts 3 to 4 months and gradually resolves. Treatment consists of vestibular rehabilitation or physical therapy, specifically using particle-repositioning maneuvers such as the modified Epley or Semont maneuvers. In approximately 80% of patients, the symptoms are immediately alleviated by this method of treatment.

Post-traumatic vestibular dysfunction can also be caused by shearing of labyrinthine membranes as a result of concussive forces. In this circumstance, the patient may complain of chronic unsteadiness rather than true vertigo. In cases of chronic unsteadiness, a program of vestibular rehabilitation therapy can be helpful.

Post-traumatic vestibular dysfunction also occurs after transverse temporal bone fractures. With a transverse fracture, a severe episode of vertigo occurs, which gradually improves, much like a patient who has undergone a labyrinthectomy. In symptomatic patients, caloric excitability and positional nystagmus indicate residual function in the traumatized labyrinth. In these rare patients, a case can be made for a transmastoid labyrinthectomy to eliminate all vestibular function.

Post-traumatic vestibular dysfunction can also occur if the central portion of the vestibular system is injured, such as that seen with cerebellar injury, brainstem nuclei injury, or even vestibular nerve avulsion. Careful audiovestibular testing can determine if a predominantly central vestibular injury has occurred, as might be suggested by eye tracking abnormalities on electronystagmography in the presence of normal symmetric caloric tests or abnormal auditory brainstem testing with normal otoacoustic emissions. Treatment considerations in these patients might include vestibular rehabilitation therapy, special glasses, and antinauseants.

POST-TRAUMATIC COCHLEAR DYSFUNCTION

In addition to PLF, sensorineural hearing loss following trauma can be attributable to a variety of mechanisms including fracture of the otic capsule, concussion of the inner ear without fracture, noise- or blast-induced injury, and central auditory pathway injury. Transverse fractures of the temporal bone usually cross the vestibule or the basal turn of the cochlea, resulting in total sudden sensorineural hearing loss.

It is common to find high-frequency sensorineural hearing loss following head injury with or without fracture, blast injuries, and extreme noise exposure (ie, transient noise louder than 120 dB). These mechanisms affect the cochlea in a similar fashion. Most often the hearing loss centers around 4 kHz, although more severe injuries can certainly affect all of the frequencies. According to Schuknecht, concussive forces on the cochlea result in a pressure wave that damages the outer hair cells in the basal turn, features identical to those seen with noise-induced hearing loss. Alternatively, deceleration, blast injuries, and extreme noise transmit forces to the stapes footplate that result in disruption of the basilar membrane and the organ of Corti, with resultant degeneration of the spiral ganglion of the cochlea. In some patients, improvement in thresholds is observed 2 weeks after the onset. If not, these patients should receive auditory rehabilitation, including use of a hearing aid.

Post-traumatic hearing loss can also be found in injuries of the auditory nerve, brainstem, and temporal cortex. In patients with temporal lobe injury following head trauma, typically there are complaints of difficulty understanding speech in noisy environments. In the few documented cases, speech understanding is diminished as measured with hearing-in-noise tests or synthetic sentence intelligibility testing. Rehabilitation in these circumstances includes special listening devices and auditory training using neuroplasticity techniques (ie, fast-forward therapy to improve temporal processing).

10

OCCUPATIONAL HEARING LOSS

Peter W. Alberti, MB, PhD

Exposure to excessive sound is worldwide the most common cause of acquired adult sensorineural hearing loss. In the United States, it is estimated that 30 million individuals are exposed to damaging levels of noise in the workplace. This chapter discusses the effect of noise on the ear, noise-induced hearing loss (NIHL), and its prevention.

EFFECT OF SOUND ON THE EAR

Sound, depending on its intensity, may produce (1) adaptation, (2) temporary threshold shift (TTS), and (3) permanent threshold shift (PTS) in hearing. Adaptation, which occurs whenever the ear is stimulated by sound, is a physiologic phenomenon, and for sounds of 70 dB sound pressure level (SPL) or less, recovery occurs within half a second. Temporary threshold shift is a short-term effect usually measured in minutes and hours rather than seconds or days, in which the hearing threshold elevates temporarily after exposure to noise. It occurs following intense sound stimulation. Tones of higher frequency cause more TTS than lower-frequency tones of similar intensity. The amount of TTS increases for the duration and intensity of the sound exposure.

Most TTSs recover in a few hours. If the noise exposure is sufficiently intense, however, TTS may last for several days or weeks. This is pathologic TTS, almost always accompanied by some residual PTS. The cutoff point seems to be a TTS of approximately 40 dB. Below this, recovery is swift; above this, it is delayed. One mechanism for TTS that has been demonstrated is that glutamate oversecretion at the synapses between hair cells and the auditory nerve fibers leads to synaptic overload, swelling of synaptic terminals, and damage to both the primary auditory nerve fibers and hair cells.

One of the practical problems of TTS is its effect on accurate quantification of hearing loss, in both audiometric screening and pension evaluation. Permanent threshold shift is a permanent elevation of the hearing threshold; the term is usually confined to post–noise exposure elevation of hearing threshold.

HAIR CELL INJURY

Intense sound damages the hair cells. Outer hair cells are more susceptible than inner hair cells to damage from sound. The degree and type of damage to hair cells are related to the amount of noise exposure. The first sign is shortening of the cilial rootlet. This acute finding, produced by the least damaging noise, is associated with floppy cilia and is partly reversible. The resistance of cilia to deformation after noise stress is reduced. The first signs of an irreversible change are damage to the intercilial connections and actual fracture of the rootlet at the level of the cuticular plate. The cilia fall over and ultimately are absorbed. With these greater degrees of damage, intracellular changes also occur, including damage to lysosome granules, mitochondria, and the nucleus. As with other tissues in the body, there is a process of damage and repair. The repair with mild degrees of injury is within the cell itself; with greater degrees of injury, healing and scar formation occur by migration of other cells.

It appears that oxidative stress is a major cause of hair cell damage both in NIHL and antibiotic ototoxicity. Excessive stimulation by noise produces reactive oxygen species (ROS), which damage phospholipids in cell and nuclear membranes and DNA; they increase intracellular Ca^{++} and up-regulate cell death genes. There may be ways of preventing or diminishing the formation of ROS, for example, by increasing endogenous antioxidant systems by administering substances such as *N*-acetylcysteine. The administration of glutathione, a powerful antioxidant, to guinea pigs prior to noise exposure leads to less cochlear damage and hearing loss than in matched noise-exposed animals that are not protected. Antioxidants also protect the inner ear of chinchillas from the damaging effects of impulse noise. Glial cell line–derived neurotrophic factor also provides protection from noise. It and heat shock protein (which protects hair cells against excessive stimulation) are produced when the ear is exposed to mild noise and may account for "toughening" of the ear to noise by prior sound exposure. Although promising, none of these mechanisms have yet any practical application in humans. Prior toughening appears to work by up-regulating the production of antioxidants such as glutathione.

Damage from noise and aminoglycosides affects nerves as well as hair cells. Therefore, protective strategies, although so far mainly based on hair cell protection from ROS, also include protection of axons by neurotrophins.

It is also becoming evident that the development of NIHL is also related to feedback from the central nervous system. The nerve supply of the outer hair cells is by efferent fibers. There is an active feedback system, which may be responsible for depressing the contractile activity of outer hair cells, thereby diminishing the stimulus to the associated inner hair cells. This may function to sharpen frequency discrimination and perhaps to eliminate the effect of low masking sound. This can alter the sensitivity of the cochlea by 20 or 30 dB. In other words, the outer hair cells have a tuning effect on the inner hair cells.

The contractions produce audible sounds detected as otoacoustic emissions (OAEs). These have been intensively studied to see if alteration of OAE after sound exposure can be used to predict susceptibility to noise exposure. To date, there are no definite outcomes.

NOISE-INDUCED HEARING LOSS

Intense acoustic overstimulation, whether acute or chronic, can produce TTS and PTS. Acoustic damage can also occur from a single intense sound such as an explosion or even a single gunshot. Typically, the first audiometric change in both TTS and PTS is a drop in hearing at 3, 4, or 6 kHz, with normal hearing below and above these levels. This is known as an acoustic notch. In the early phases, the ear usually recovers.

Most recovery takes place within the first 12 hours after noise exposure and is overwhelmingly complete within 48 hours. However, after a single massive insult such as an explosion, recovery may continue for many weeks until the hearing loss is stable. This is usually accompanied by some PTS.

Noise-induced PTS is overwhelmingly caused by chronic exposure to excessive sound levels in the workplace, whether civilian or military, and may be potentiated by additional social and recreational noise exposure. The speed of onset and the degree of loss are related to the total quantity of noise exposure, that is, its intensity and duration, and to the individual's susceptibility to damage by the noise. In general terms, industrial noise exposure is less intense but more prolonged than military noise exposure.

There are remarkably few long-term longitudinal studies equating hearing loss with noise exposure.

NATURAL HISTORY OF NOISE-INDUCED PERMANENT THRESHOLD SHIFT

It is unlikely that PTS will occur without TTS, and it is also unlikely that PTS will be greater than TTS. Other than that, there is little relationship between the two, and attempts to predict PTS from TTS have not been successful. Permanent threshold shift usually starts in the higher frequencies characteristically at 4 or perhaps 3 or 6 kHz and gradually spreads into neighboring frequencies. To begin with, the hearing loss is asymptomatic, and only when it spreads to 2 kHz does it give rise to complaints. As time goes on, the notch disappears as the hearing in the higher frequencies worsens (as a result of aging), so that the audiogram becomes indistinguishable from many other sensorineural hearing losses. It is stated, probably correctly, that after 10 years of exposure to a given noise, the loss in the higher frequencies stops worsening, but gradually the loss spreads into the lower frequencies. The major part of the loss may occur quite early in the first 2 or 3 years. The rate of spread and the degree of loss are related to both the intensity of sound and the individual's susceptibility to noise. In mice, there is a genetic susceptibility to hearing loss from noise, and a recessive gene (*Ahl*) that is responsible for premature age-related hearing loss is also implicated in excessive susceptibility to NIHL. If this is also true in humans, it may help explain some of the variability noted in response to sound exposure.

DAMAGE RISK CRITERIA

It is currently accepted that, within a significant range with a lower boundary of safe sound and an upper boundary of sound so intense that it produces acute permanent damage, equal amounts of sound exposure produce equal amounts of damage. Thus, a given sound experienced for 8 hours does as much harm as twice that sound experienced for 4 hours or half that sound experienced for 16 hours. Doubling sound intensity is equivalent to a 3 dB increase in SPL. Thus, a 93 dB sound is twice as intense as a 90 dB sound, and a 103 dB sound is twice as intense as a 100 dB sound. However, it is suggested that if noise exposure is intermittent, as is usually the case in industry, the ear has time to recover, and the 3 dB rule may be too strict. The appropriate technique of evaluating the harmful effects of impact sound is still debated. It is suggested that impulse noise is more damaging than steady-state noise of the same intensity.

TINNITUS

Tinnitus is a distressing and frequent concomitant of NIHL. Transient tinnitus is experienced commonly after exposure to intense sound and almost invariably after a blast injury, but it usually clears. After years of exposure, however, it may become permanent and is present permanently in 50 to 60% of those with NIHL.

COMBINED EFFECTS OF OTOTRAUMATIC AGENTS

Many things are known to injure the inner ear, for example, drugs, infections, trauma, age, and noise. Most of these agents have a final common pathway: they damage the hair cells and other structures of the cochlea. There is great interest about how they interact. Aminogylcoside antibiotics and excessive sound exposure both exert their effect on hearing by releasing ROS, which explains their synergy; this common pathway also suggests ways of protection by exposing the hair cells to antioxidants.

Certain industrial solvents and chemicals are ototoxic. Toluene is the most commonly used, most studied, and probably the most ototoxic industrial chemical. It produces hearing loss and potentiates the effect of noise exposure. Carbon disulfide and heavy metals have also been implicated. Noise and vibration act synergistically in those who suffer from white hand and work in the cold such as foresters using chain saws or shipbuilders.

The interaction between noise exposure and aging is debated. It appears that presbycusis is additive to noise change, but in later years, aging is a much more dominant cause of worsening hearing than further noise exposure.

SOCIOACUSIS

The noise levels of everyday life are steadily increasing. Transportation is the main cause—automobiles, particularly on thruways, motorcycles, trains, planes, and the substitution of diesel for gasoline. In some cities, for example Bangkok, sound levels exceed 100 dB in the city center. At home, too, the blender, vacuum cleaner, and lawnmower all add to noise. Noise levels within public transportation are high; some subway systems have sound levels above 90 dBA (dB on the A-weighted scale). Environmental noise is a particular hazard in the megacities of Asia, with transportation noise being the dominant hazard. The combination of two-stroke engine noise from motorcycles and motorized rickshaws (frequently unsilenced), old, poorly maintained diesel-powered trucks and buses, air horns, bazaar noise, and sounds from small roadside metal-forming shops produce a cacophony that not only makes living unpleasant, it also puts hearing at risk.

Recreational noise also is hazardous. Firecrackers can produce sudden deafness in children, and their use in public festivities, such as national day celebrations or religious ceremonies, may produce permanent hearing loss.

There is much concern about the use of personal radios and cassette and compact disc players and the potential effect of pop, rock, and disco music, although it would appear that they are not harmful. The sound output of power tools and horticultural equipment are real hazards, and children from rural areas appear particularly at risk. Indeed, farm workers are a major at-risk group for occupational hearing loss.

NONAUDITORY EFFECTS OF NOISE

There is great controversy about noise as a cause of hypertension. Certainly, sound may precipitate acute cardiovascular changes, but these are almost certainly normal physiologic responses to warning signals. If there is a real effect, it is extremely small. The effect of noise on sleep deprivation is also a matter of concern.

SOCIAL ANTHROPOLOGY OF HEARING LOSS

The interaction between individuals with hearing impairment and the general population is currently much studied. One aspect is the impact on the lives of those with occupational hearing loss and their families. The middle-aged man with NIHL is isolated from his family, his children may become alienated as they feel that their father is disinterested in their activities, and he, in turn, feels that he is being excluded from family conversation. There may be considerable stress between husband and wife; communication becomes more difficult, producing anger, fatigue, and feelings of guilt on both sides.

CLINICAL FEATURES OF NOISE-INDUCED HEARING LOSS

There are no clear-cut clinical features that distinguish NIHL from several other causes of sensorineural hearing impairment. The diagnosis is based on history, physical examination, and appropriate laboratory investigation, including full hearing tests. Although there are audiometric configurations suggestive of the diagnosis, they may have many variations, and no one configuration fits all cases or excludes a case. To compound matters, NIHL, like any other chronic disorder, may coexist with other lesions. The diagnosis, which is circumstantial, is largely based on a careful history and is frequently made by exclusion, that is, if other causes of hearing loss have been excluded, noise exposure has been adequate, and there is an appropriate hearing loss, it is customary to attribute the loss to that cause. The diagnosis must be made individually, and one should avoid the epidemiologic error of believing that noise exposure and hearing loss are necessarily causally related. Noise-induced hearing loss may be superimposed on other diseases.

If physical signs or symptoms suggest other ear disease, this should be followed through, and, in particular, causes of asymmetric hearing loss should be investigated. It is possible to have an asymmetric hearing loss from noise exposure such as, for example, individuals who fire guns off one shoulder, concert violinists, workers who use certain industrial equipment such as rock drills, and people who drive farm tractors with one ear to the engine and the head constantly turned over the shoulder, protecting the other ear.

The audiogram quantifies the hearing loss. Where indicated, further investigation should be initiated, including imaging. When noise exposure is believed to be the cause of the hearing loss, various causes of loss must be sought, for example, recreational, military, and occupational. Ultimately, it may become a matter of clinical skill and exquisite judgment to establish both the cause of the hearing loss and the proportion that should be attributed to any given employer.

HEARING TESTS

Diagnostic hearing tests used in occupational hearing loss are of greater accuracy than routine clinical diagnostic audiology; it cannot be overemphasized that the tester must be experienced in this type of work. The basis for most pension and compensation awards is the pure-tone audiogram. At the time of testing, there should be no TTS. Authorities have legislated different time periods out of noise for this, ranging from 48 hours to 6 months. It is the author's view that if the claimant has been subjected to chronic noise exposure, a period of 48 hours free of noise is adequate for compensation assessment. The situation is different after a major blast accident or head injury, in which recovery may continue for a period of many weeks, and a compensation assessment should not be undertaken for a minimum of 3 months after the episode.

The types of test to be undertaken vary by local use. They must be undertaken with properly calibrated equipment and in appropriately calibrated soundproof enclosures. A test to quantify hearing loss accurately requires standard behavioral audiometry: air conduction, bone conduction, and speech reception thresholds. Further tests are undertaken as indicated.

Quantification for compensation purposes must be frequency-specific and parallel tonal audiometry. In unilateral hearing loss, the Stenger test is effective. In bilateral hearing loss, electric response testing is necessary, and in this group of patients, slow vertex response audiometry is the most effective. Auditory brainstem responses usually provide only a click threshold, which gives a general idea of the level of hearing but not a simulacrum of an audiogram. The probability of a hearing loss of 40 dB or greater at 500 Hz being caused by something other than noise is high. These patients produce a high yield of other ear disease and of nonorganic hearing loss.

HEARING CONSERVATION PROGRAMS

Noise-induced hearing loss is incurable but largely preventable. A hearing conservation program has the following features: (1) noise hazard identification, (2) engineering controls, (3) personal hearing protection, (4) monitoring, (5) record keeping, (6) health education, (7) enforcement, and

(8) program evaluation. It is multidisciplinary, involving the industrial hygienist, engineer, nurse, audiometric technician, and, frequently, supervisory audiologist and otologist.

11

OTOTOXICITY

Leonard P. Rybak, MD, PhD
John Touliatos, MD

Ototoxicity is defined as damage to the auditory or vestibular system caused by a drug or chemical. The ototoxic effect may be reversible or permanent. Various drugs and chemicals may affect either the auditory or the vestibular system or both. Various cells in the inner ear may be damaged by specific ototoxic agents. This chapter describes the ototoxic effect of the more commonly used drugs. These agents include the aminoglycoside antibiotics, the antineoplastic drugs cisplatin and carboplatin, the loop diuretics, and the salicylates.

AMINOGLYCOSIDE ANTIBIOTICS

The aminoglycoside antibiotics are important drugs used to treat tuberculosis and life-threatening gram-negative bacterial infections. This family of drugs includes streptomycin, neomycin, kanamycin, amikacin, gentamicin, tobramycin, netilmicin, sisomicin, and lividomycin. Of these, kanamycin and amikacin tend to cause greater damage to the cochlea than to the vestibular system, whereas streptomycin and gentamicin are more likely to damage the vestibular system. This explains why the latter two drugs have been employed to ablate vestibular function in patients with Meniere's disease. In the case of unilateral Meniere's disease, streptomycin and gentamicin have been administered by the transtympanic route. In patients with bilateral Meniere's disease, titration with systemic streptomycin has been employed in some cases. Since aminoglycosides are poorly absorbed from the gastrointestinal tract (and intact skin), these drugs are usually given parenterally. The concentration of aminoglycosides in the body is determined by the dose magnitude and frequency of administration as well as the function of the kidneys. With renal failure, the amount of drug in the body tends to accumulate with repeated dosing. Therefore, the dose magnitude and the time interval between doses should be adjusted to compensate for a reduced rate of renal elimination.

Damage to the cochlea begins with the outer hair cells in the basal turn. Thus, the high-frequency hearing is adversely affected first. The mechanisms involved in causing injury to the cochlea appear to include the formation of free radicals in the cochlea following chelation of iron by the aminoglycoside antibiotic. Animal studies have shown that treatment with iron chelators such as salicylates reduces the ototoxicity caused by aminoglycosides by removing iron before it can be chelated by the aminoglycoside, thus preventing the formation of free radicals.

The free radicals generated by aminoglycosides may be prevented from causing damage to the inner ear by various protective agents. Without protective molecules, the free radicals produced may trigger apoptosis in the cochlea. Inhibitors of the enzyme caspase may prevent this enzyme from acting in the apoptotic cascade, protecting against hair cell death. Neurotrophins or growth factors may also protect the inner ear from damage. Free radical scavengers prevent the free radicals from interacting with membrane lipids and prevent the formation of toxic products of this interaction, which would otherwise damage the hair cells of the cochlea.

A recently identified risk factor for aminoglycoside-induced hearing loss is a genetic susceptibility. Mothers can transmit, as a genetic trait, the hypersensitivity to aminoglycoside ototoxicity. A mitochondrial deoxyribonucleic acid

(DNA) mutation has been associated with aminoglycoside-induced hearing loss. Individuals with this trait can suffer severe hearing loss after receiving only a few doses of an aminoglycoside antibiotic.

In some cases, reversible vestibular damage occurs. However, permanent damage may be more common. Compensation for the deficit may occur over time. Oscillopsia is a severe symptom of vestibular toxicity that can be caused by aminoglycosides. Oscillopsia is a peculiar form of dysequilibrium demonstrated as a perception of vertical movement or "jiggling" of stationary objects as the patient walks. Patients with this symptom may have an ataxic gait and a total absence of caloric response.

Patients do not usually complain about hearing loss until they have at least a 30 dB change in hearing at frequencies as low as 3,000 to 4,000 Hz. This makes the detection of ototoxicity difficult unless audiometric monitoring is performed. This is especially important in high-risk patients, such as those with renal failure, those receiving higher than usual drug doses, those with persistently elevated drug levels in the serum despite dosage adjustments, or those with some baseline hearing or balance disorder. When audiometric measurements are made, the usual definition of ototoxicity is a hearing loss of 10 dB bilaterally at any frequency. However, some authors recommend using 20 dB as the threshold amount of hearing loss. By the time the patient complains of hearing loss, there will usually be at least a 30 dB hearing loss measured audiometrically.

CISPLATIN AND CARBOPLATIN

Cisplatin is one of the most frequently used antitumor agents. A high percentage of patients undergoing treatment with cisplatin have been found to have hearing loss. The likelihood of hearing loss appears to be greater when cisplatin is administered in higher doses and when it is injected rapidly intravenously. The dose of cisplatin has been increased to achieve better cancer remission and cure rates. Unfortunately, the probability of hearing loss following cisplatin treatment is greater when it is accompanied by cranial irradiation. Other risk factors include a low serum albumin and anemia. Symptoms that suggest ototoxicity from cisplatin include ear pain, tinnitus, and a subjective decrease in hearing acuity. Hearing loss from cisplatin is usually bilateral and begins in the high frequencies. Hearing loss may start after the first dose of cisplatin or may not become manifest until multiple doses have been administered. Thus, the hearing loss may be sudden, gradual, or progressive and cumulative. Children who are treated with high doses of cisplatin have a high incidence of hearing loss that appears to be cumulative and dose dependent. Hearing loss in children may be detected more readily with measurement of otoacoustic emissions.

It appears that the probability of cisplatin ototoxicity is reduced or eliminated when cisplatin is administered locally into tumors. Cisplatin administered in a gel of collagen containing epinephrine has been used to treat accessible tumors of the head and neck, esophagus, and trunk without causing hearing loss. Presumably, this dosage form causes the drug to remain in high concentrations within the tumor, and little drug gains access to the systemic circulation to affect the cochlea or the nervous system or to damage the kidney.

Carboplatin is a member of the next generation of platinum antitumor agents. It is less likely to damage the kidney than cisplatin. Like cisplatin, carboplatin causes bone marrow suppression, and the latter seems to be the dose-limiting toxicity of carboplatin. Although it was initially hoped to be much less ototoxic than cisplatin, carboplatin does cause significant hearing loss.

This drug has been used to treat malignant brain tumors. The blood-brain barrier is first opened pharmacologically with mannitol. This allows carboplatin to pass the blood-brain barrier and to penetrate the brain tumor in high concentrations. However, this type of therapy is associated with a high incidence of hearing loss. Fortunately, this type of hearing loss can be prevented by administration of sodium thiosulfate. This latter drug prevents the ototoxic effect of carboplatin apparently without reducing the antineoplastic effect on the brain tumor since sodium thiosulfate does not cross the blood-brain barrier.

Although most ototoxic agents, including cisplatin, damage the outer hair cells first, carboplatin has been shown to damage selectively the inner hair cells in the chinchilla. This raises interesting questions about why the inner hair cells appear to be targeted by carboplatin.

LOOP DIURETICS

Loop diuretics are powerful drugs that act on the loop of Henle of the kidney to inhibit the reabsorption of sodium, potassium, and chloride by a specific ion transporter mechanism. This results in the loss of a large volume of water and electrolytes in the urine. These drugs are very effective in the treatment of congestive heart failure and other diseases characterized by an excess of fluid in the body. Since these drugs are excreted in the urine, the rate of excretion is reduced in the presence of renal failure. The half-life of furosemide in the body can be prolonged by a factor of 10 to 20 in patients with advanced renal failure.

Animal and human temporal bone studies have shown that ototoxic doses of loop diuretics can produce severe edema in the stria vascularis and can alter the normal electrolyte composition of endolymph in experimental animals. Treatment of experimental animals with ototoxic doses of furosemide can cause a significant reduction in the concentration of potassium in the endolymph.

The incidence of hearing loss with furosemide, the most commonly used loop diuretic, has been reported to be about 6%. Most of these hearing losses are reversible. Permanent hearing loss has been reported in high-risk premature neonates treated with furosemide, and profound permanent hearing loss has been reported after ethacrynic acid administration in transplant patients.

SALICYLATES

Salicylates, such as aspirin, are taken by many adults and some children. Salicylates are rapidly absorbed from the gastro-intestinal tract after oral administration. Absorption of salicylates is influenced significantly by gastric emptying time and whether food is present in the stomach. With food in the stomach, the absorption of aspirin may be slowed by a factor of two. Aspirin is metabolized in the body to salicylic acid, which has a biologic half-life of only 15 to 20 minutes. Salicylates are distributed in extracellular water compartments and are rapidly excreted by the kidneys. They tend to concentrate in the liver and kidney, whereas the concentration in the brain tends to be much lower. Salicylates quickly enter the perilymph after systemic administration.

Salicylate poisoning produces the syndrome of salicylism. This condition is marked by severe acid-base imbalance, hyperventilation, nausea, vomiting, tinnitus, and coagulation abnormalities.

Hearing loss caused by salicylates is correlated with the concentration in the blood. Tinnitus occurs at lower concentrations of salicylates in the blood and may warn the physician that increasing the dose may cause hearing loss. Salicylates may temporarily reduce the stiffness of the lateral membrane of the outer hair cells, which may correlate with the cochlear pattern on audiometric site of lesion testing.

Temporal bone studies of patients with audiometrically documented salicylate-induced hearing loss showed no significant cellular alterations at the light microscopic level beyond those expected for the age of the patients.

It is incumbent on the physician to be aware that many drugs and chemicals can cause hearing loss so that appropriate action to minimize the damage to the inner ear can be taken if the clinical situation permits doing so.

12

IDIOPATHIC SUDDEN SENSORINEURAL HEARING LOSS

Robert A. Dobie, MD

EPIDEMIOLOGY

Idiopathic sudden sensorineural hearing loss (ISSNHL) develops over a period of less than 3 days, with a threshold change for the worse of at least 30 dB in at least three contiguous audiometric frequencies. Idiopathic sudden sensorineural hearing loss is almost always unilateral. According to Byl, ISSNHL affects about 1 person per 10,000 per year; this would correspond to over 25,000 cases per year in the United States. In contrast, Hughes and colleagues estimate only 4,000 cases per year in the United States. All ages and both sexes are affected; the peak ages are 30 to 60 years.

Tinnitus is usually present. Vertigo is frequent, either spontaneous (as in acute vestibular neuronitis) or as isolated positional vertigo. Sixty-five percent of patients recover completely with or without treatment, most within 2 weeks. Low-frequency losses have a better prognosis than high-frequency losses; of course, this is true of all types of rapidly progressive or fluctuating sensorineural hearing loss, not just ISSNHL.

ETIOLOGY

There has been considerable speculation about viral and vascular causes, with rather more evidence for the former than the latter. The evidence that viral infection (or reactivation of latent viruses) is the most important cause of ISSNHL is mostly circumstantial: viruses are known to cause sensorineural hearing loss (SNHL) with cochlear pathology similar to that seen after ISSNHL, and patients with ISSNHL often demonstrate immunologic evidence of viral infection. The rubella (German measles) virus caused thousands of cases of congenital deafness during a 1964–1965 epidemic; most were associated with a syndrome that included eye, heart, and brain abnormalities. Since the introduction of the mumps-measles-rubella (MMR) vaccine, the congenital rubella syndrome has virtually disappeared in the United States.

At present, the most important viral cause of congenital deafness is cytomegalovirus (CMV), a member of the herpes virus family. Cytomegalovirus has been cultured from the inner ear and causes cochlear lesions in experimentally infected animals. Congenital CMV syndrome includes deafness as well as lesions of the eye, brain, liver, and spleen. Most CMV-infected neonates do not demonstrate the full-blown CMV syndrome. Indeed, "asymptomatic" CMV causes more hearing loss than "symptomatic" (syndromic) CMV infection. Neonatal CMV screening has shown an infection rate (virus cultured from urine) of 1.3%; 10% of these neonates had either congenital or progressive hearing loss. No vaccine is yet available to reduce or eliminate hearing loss from CMV.

Neonatal herpes simplex virus (HSV) infection is associated with hearing loss in about 10% of cases. Rare since the widespread use of the MMR vaccine, mumps deafness occurred in about 5 of every 10,000 mumps cases and was usually unilateral. Like CMV, the mumps virus has been cultured from the inner ear and causes cochlear lesions in experimental animals. Measles (rubeola) virus accounted for 3 to 10% of bilateral deafness in children prior to the MMR vaccine. The varicella-zoster (or herpes zoster) virus causes chickenpox in children and shingles in adults. When the geniculate ganglion is involved, with facial paralysis plus auricular bullae, it is called herpes zoster oticus (HZO) or Ramsay Hunt syndrome. About 6% of HZO cases exhibit sensorineural hearing loss. Herpes zoster viral deoxyribonucleic acid (DNA) has been identified in temporal bone tissue taken from a patient with HZO and sudden hearing loss. Human immunodeficiency virus (HIV) may cause hearing loss directly but more commonly makes the host more susceptible to other viruses, many of which (CMV, HSV, adenovirus) have been cultured from the HIV-infected inner ear, as well as to other infectious agents.

Schuknecht and Donovan first showed that ears from patients who had suffered ISSNHL demonstrated atrophy of the organ of Corti and tectorial membrane and spiral ganglion cell losses; these findings were similar to those seen in cases (mumps, measles) known to be caused by viral infections and different from the cochlear pathology (fibrous and osseous proliferation) seen after ischemic deafness.

Veltri and colleagues showed that patients with ISSNHL frequently had seroconversion (increasing antibody levels) for several viruses, including mumps, influenza, measles, HSV, rubella, and CMV. Wilson focused specifically on HSV, noting that 16% of ISSNHL patients showed seroconversion compared with only 4% of controls. The identification of DNA from HSV in human spiral ganglion and the development of an animal model for HSV neurolabyrinthitis have added to the suspicion that this virus may be an important cause of ISSNHL. Pitkaranta and colleagues noted that there are many negative serologic studies, failing to implicate HSV or other viruses, but also noted that long-dormant neurotropic viruses can reactivate and cause localized disease without triggering changes in systemic immunoglobulin levels.

Since no organ can survive without adequate blood supply and since vascular disease affects so many different organ systems, it is natural that investigators have looked for evidence that SNHL is linked to vascular disease (or to its risk factors). Given the intensity of their efforts, the evidence is extremely weak.

In other organ systems, vascular disease may cause either gradual (eg, congestive heart failure) or sudden/stepwise (eg, stroke) deterioration of function. If vascular disease is important for the cochlea, one should expect it to cause hearing loss of both sudden and gradual onset. After excluding common causes (noise, head injury, etc), the vast majority of cases of adult-onset SNHL cannot be labeled any more precisely than to call them age related. If vascular disease was an important component of age-related hearing loss (ARHL), we might expect patients (and longitudinal studies of ARHL) to describe stepwise progression, with substantial asymmetry as one ear suffers ischemic events while the other escapes, at least for awhile. The rarity of such reports in ARHL should cast doubt on the vascular hypothesis. Are vascular disease and its risk factors (eg, diabetes) correlated with ARHL? The extensive literature addressing this issue has been reviewed and can best be described as inconclusive.

Focusing on patients presenting with ISSNHL, are some of these cases attributable to "vascular accidents" (thrombosis, embolism, or hemorrhage) affecting the cochlea? If so, the incidence of ISSNHL would be expected to be much higher in men than in women and to rise sharply with age; neither is true. Frequent recurrences and (over time) bilaterality would also be expected, yet most people who suffer ISSNHL have only one event, affecting only one ear. Studies of vascular disease and risk factors have shown only that diabetics with ISSNHL have a poorer prognosis, not that any of these factors predict the likelihood of suffering ISSNHL. None of this proves that vascular disease is totally irrelevant to ISSNHL. Inner ear hemorrhages with sudden deafness do occur rarely in patients with leukemia, sickle cell disease, and thalassemia. Until otologists are able to assess cochlear blood flow, we will probably never know much about the role of vascular disease in ISSNHL; at this point, it appears to be somewhere between small and negligible.

Simmons postulated that double inner ear membrane breaks, including perilymph fistulae, could be responsible for some cases of ISSNHL. Today, most otologists believe that perilymph fistulae do occur, causing SNHL and dizziness, but almost exclusively in the context of identifiable barotrauma: after scuba diving, violent nose blowing, or extreme exertion during breath holding.

DIFFERENTIAL DIAGNOSIS

Dozens of otologic and systemic disorders have been associated with sudden SNHL. The more important identifiable causes of sudden SNHL (by definition, these are not "idiopathic") are clinically easy to diagnose (eg, meningitis, acoustic trauma, head injury). Others, such as multiple sclerosis, are usually missed when sudden SNHL is the first manifestation. In areas where Lyme disease is endemic, it is probably wise to ask patients with sudden SNHL about a recent rash or arthralgia.

MANAGEMENT

A minimum workup includes a careful otologic history and examination, as well as an audiogram (including the Stenger test). Otoacoustic emissions are sometimes present (implying sparing of outer hair cells) in ISSNHL, but it is unclear whether otoacoustic testing is clinically useful. Routine blood testing in ISSNHL is of dubious value. Children with ISSNHL (rare!) should receive a complete blood count as a screening test for leukemia. If there are clinical clues pointing toward Lyme disease, confirmatory testing is indicated. If corticosteroid therapy is being considered in a patient who has not been tested for diabetes in recent years, a blood glucose test is in order.

About 1% of patients presenting with sudden SNHL have acoustic tumors, and even complete recovery does not completely rule out this diagnosis. When hearing in the affected ear is poor, magnetic resonance imaging (MRI) with gadolinium contrast injection is the most appropriate study. For patients with better hearing, either MRI or auditory brainstem response testing may be appropriate.

Wilson and colleagues (1980) showed, in a randomized clinical trial, that patients receiving oral corticosteroids achieved substantial recovery more frequently than patients receiving placebo. This benefit was apparent only for "moderate" degrees of loss; 78% of patients in this category who received corticosteroids recovered compared with 38% of those who received placebo. A nonrandomized study by Moskowitz and colleagues (1984) showed benefits similar to those seen in the Wilson and colleagues study (89% recovery with corticosteroids, 44% recovery without treatment). Many, if not most, otologists offer oral corticosteroids to patients with ISSNHL who have no contraindications (eg, diabetes, active duodenal ulcer, tuberculosis). Useful oral antiviral drugs have been available in recent years but have yet to be found helpful for patients with ISSNHL.

The vascular hypothesis is extremely popular in Europe, where treatments such as oral pentoxifylline and intravenous dextran (intended to reduce blood viscosity), apheresis (intended to remove low-density lipoprotein cholesterol from the blood), and carbogen (a mixture of 10% carbon dioxide and 90% oxygen) and papaverine (intended to dilate blood vessels) are often used. None of these has been shown to be superior to placebo.

13

PERILYMPHATIC FISTULAE

Robert I. Kohut, MD

The cochlear and vestibular phenomena caused by a peri-lymphatic fistula (PLF) have been observed for over 100 years. Surgery was even performed by expert surgeons look-ing for the labyrinthine capsule defect in patients with a pos-itive fistula test. No defects were found. Thoughts developed that the fistula symptoms were caused by a hypermobile stapes. The operating microscope was not available; there-fore, minute quantities of fluid escaped surgical identifica-tion. The recognition of PLF with surgical documentation awaited the advent of stapes surgery in which a sudden sig-nificant change in sensory hearing loss after surgery some-times occurred. This caused the surgeon to conjecture that there was an incomplete seal by the grafting material of the oval window. This was confirmed both at re-exploration and by patient response.

Later, nonsurgical cases with similar PLF symptoms were proven to be PLF by surgical exploration and patient response. Yet the phenomenon of PLF was not fully accepted. It forced the thought in the skeptical that if the phenomenon were accepted as an entity, previous incomplete diagnostic or inadequate surgical observations had occurred. Rejection of the possible presence of PLF continued to be the rule for the most skeptical. The implications regarding misdiagnosis loomed ever greater.

The reliance on endoscopic middle ear exploration for evidence of fluid collection (perilymph) appears to have the possibility of a false-negative result. This is probably owing to the heat produced by the instrument (patients complain of heat) potentially causing the evaporation of minute quantities of fluid (a few microliters). Also, there is the inability to identify, as is necessary in surgical cases, the presence of fluid using sharp pick placement on the areas in question looking for changes in reflected light. Another testing paradigm appeared to be needed.

Unrelated to the above assumptions and examination techniques, the predictive temporal bone histologic studies of the author and his colleagues allowed a test of clinical diagnostic criteria, which were found to be extremely accurate ($p < .001$, sensitivity 59%, specificity 91%). However, the sensitivity of 59% suggests that many with this disorder go undiagnosed. The sites of the fistula(e) are the fissula ante fenestram (FAF) and the fissure of the round window niche (RWF), and, infrequently, the fossula post fenestram (FPF) and the center of the stapes footplate are identified as sites of patencies.

DIAGNOSTIC EXCLUSIONARY CRITERIA

The diagnostic criteria tested require first the exclusion of the presence of inflammation, granuloma, neoplasia, or anatomically related neurologic abnormalities.

CLINICAL DIAGNOSTIC CRITERIA

The clinical diagnostic criteria for PLF, in the absence of the above exclusionary criteria, are for *hearing*, sudden or rapidly progressive sensory hearing loss, and for *balance*, (1) constant dysequilibrium (however mild), (2) positional nystagmus/vertigo, and (3) a positive Hennebert's symptom or sign.

The diagnostic criteria may not all be present at the time of the initial examination, although this is usually the case if fine testing methods are used. For greater sensitivity, the fistula test may be performed with the patient standing with the eyes closed and feet close together to elicit the vestibulospinal response. A positive response is body sway (sign) or the sensation of sway or loss of balance (symptom). For the vestibulo-ocular response, infrared observation techniques are used for fine nystagmic eye movements or Hennebert's sign in the fistula test. This also serves to support the validity of an observed vestibulospinal response to fistula testing or the patient's report of Hennebert's symptom in response to fistula testing.

Further, nystagmic responses to positional changes can also be missed unless these infrared observation techniques are used. However, even with special methods, because of response fatigue (or adaptation) on repeat testing at one session, repeat testing at a second examination session may be necessary. How short this interval can be has not been determined, but a 1-day interval appears adequate.

In a temporal bone histologic study, the prevalence of patencies of the FAF and RWF was 24%. Therefore, the mere histologic presence of these patencies seems not to predict symptoms during life. On the other hand, when hearing and balance symptoms had been present during life, the presence of the patencies predicts the specific set of symptoms and signs related to the PLF. One explanation to this seeming dilemma seems plausible: there is another variable, perhaps distinguishable only with special histologic techniques. The author and his colleagues are engaged in an investigation testing the following hypothesis: "Some patencies are permeable to fluid, some are not, and only those permeable to fluid are related to clinical manifestestations." So far, in preliminary studies, differences in proteoglycans (extracellular mucopolysaccharides bound to protein chains in covalent complexes) appear to be so related.

THE POSSIBILITY OF A PERILYMPHATIC FISTULA: ELEMENTS THAT HEIGHTEN ONE'S AWARENESS (ABSENCE NOT AN EXCLUDING FACTOR)

For either hearing loss (sudden sensory or rapidly progressive) or vestibular symptoms, there is often a precipitating factor related to barometric pressure change—sometimes severe, as with scuba diving, or as mild as travel in the mountains or an airplane flight.

CLINICAL MANAGEMENT

Clinical management requires 6 weeks of modified posture/activity for all but sudden hearing loss, for which modified bed rest for 5 days is required. Surgical management only follows an unsuccessful period of modified activity. During modified activity, the patient is to keep the head higher than the heart, lift no more than 10 pounds, avoid straining at stool or other forms of straining, and have the head of the bed (not pillows alone) elevated 4 to 8 inches. If there is no improvement of vestibular symptoms or signs at 6 weeks, surgery is recommended. With improvement, continued modified activity is advised.

For sudden hearing loss, hospitalization for 5 days at modified bed rest with the head of the bed elevated 30 degrees and bathroom privileges with help only. Daily audiograms (bedside) are performed. If there is no improvement at 5 days, surgery is performed on the sixth day. If there is significant improvement in hearing at 5 days, the patient is discharged on the above modified-activity regimen. Should the hearing get worse, as indicated by the audiogram, earlier surgery should be considered. The use of corticosteroids or other medications has not been tested as a variable in this regimen. Their use remains at the discretion of the otologist.

Surgical Management

The patient's surgery is performed under local anesthesia without premedication if at all possible. This avoids the masking of the symptoms (occurrence or resolution) that the patient may report and the physical straining that not uncommonly occurs with general anesthesia. If necessary, anesthesia "standby" for the administration of a nonvestibular quelling sedative can be employed.

The areas of the FAF, RWF, and FPF, as well as the stapes footplate, are examined using a standard tympanomeatal flap. At times, mucosal reflection from these areas or laser desiccation is necessary. The field must be made bloodless before observation for perilymph can be undertaken, and except for removal of gross blood, a 26-gauge suction tip is used.

The areas in question are meticulously cleared of any debris, and clear fluid is aspirated if present. Repeated reaccumulation is diagnostic of a PLF.

The RWF is located on the floor of the round window niche extending anteriorly, often initially obscured by mucosal bands (not to be confused with the round window membrane or a rupture of the round window membrane). Fluid escaping from the round window niche has been seen to reaccumulate on repeated aspiration from the fissure area in the presence of an intact round window membrane.

Grafting material (loose fibrous tissue overlying the temporalis fascia is previously obtained and finely minced) is placed piece by piece, the finest piece first buttressed by following pieces, over the area where the PLF is observed. Some surgeons graft all sites of potential leakage. This practice has not been tested against the efficacy of selective grafting. Sometimes identification of the transparent fluid (perilymph) requires touching the area in question with a sharp pick and watching for a change in reflected light (a sparkle) followed by 26-gauge aspiration and retouch for determining recurrence.

Postoperative hospitalization with modified bed rest for 5 days and house confinement with modified activity for 6 weeks appears to allow the best results. Continued modified activity is advisable.

An alternate surgical method is the injection of autologous blood into the middle ear through the tympanic membrane. It has been reported as effective in post-stapedectomy PLF. Presumably, a fibrous seal results because of the sterile inflammatory response to the blood.

14

AUTOIMMUNE INNER EAR DISEASE

Jeffrey P. Harris, MD, PhD
Elizabeth M. Keithley, PhD

In 1979, McCabe first brought attention to a possible discrete clinical entity when he presented a series of patients with bilateral, progressive hearing loss showing improvement following treatment with corticosteroids. Whereas others had described patients with ear-related illnesses associated with systemic immune disorders, none had collected such a large series or speculated that these patients might have an organ-specific illness. Since then, autoimmunity has been proposed as a cause of other inner ear disorders, including Meniere's disease, sudden sensorineural hearing loss (SNHL), and acute vertigo. There is also a relationship between inner ear disorders and systemic autoimmune diseases such as polyarteritis nodosa, systemic lupus erythematosus (SLE), relapsing polychondritis, ulcerative colitis, and Wegener's granulomatosis, which often include auditory and vestibular symptoms. Moreover, some patients with suspected autoimmune inner ear disease (AIED) have either presented with or later developed systemic autoimmune disease.

Unlike other organs and tissues, the inner ear is not amenable for biopsy. What little histopathology has been published from patients with suspected AIED shows fibrosis and/or bone deposition in the labyrinth, consistent with the late sequelae of inflammation. Specific immune reactivity against inner ear antigens is often detected in patients with suspected AIED, but the results vary. Lymphocyte migration assays using inner ear tissue as a target have been disappointing, providing at best very low stimulation indexes. More promising results have been obtained with Western blotting. Significantly more patients with suspected AIED show reactivity against a 68 kD antigen than do matched normal-hearing or rheumatologic controls. Autoimmune inner ear disease has also been associated with reactivity against 45 to 50 kD, 30 kD, and 20 kD antigens. Although the reactivity of patient sera against tissue sections of the inner ear has shown reproducible labeling, it is not a practical diagnostic technique.

ETIOLOGY

Because of the relative rarity of this condition and its recent recognition, very few temporal bones with a diagnosis of AIED have been evaluated. More studies have assessed the inner ears of patients with systemic autoimmune disorders. Sone and colleagues assessed 14 temporal bones from seven individuals with SLE. The duration of disease and ages varied widely. The most consistent findings were hair cell and spiral ganglion cell loss. Unusual accretions were also observed in the stria vascularis of 6 of 14 temporal bones.

Animal models have been valuable adjuncts in the study of AIED since the antigen and immunization history can be controlled, and histopathology is available. Immunization of guinea pigs with bovine or swine inner ear extracts results in the development of a modest hearing loss and mild inner ear inflammation in a subset of animals. Declines in compound action potentials, but not the cochlear microphonic, suggest that the hearing loss occurred at the level of the inner hair cell and/or spiral ganglion neuron rather than at the level of the outer hair cell. Hearing losses were associated with increased Western blot reactivity to 68 kD and other antigens.

Immunization with specific proteins has also resulted in hearing loss. Based on the observation that myelin protein P0 was associated with immunoreactivity against a 30 kD inner ear protein in patients with AIED, Matsuoka and colleagues immunized mice with purified bovine P0. They observed an approximately 10 dB hearing loss and a monocellular infiltrate in the eighth nerve. Experimental autoimmune encephalomyelitis can be induced by immunization with the neuronal S-100β calcium-binding protein and by passive transfer of T cells sensitized to this antigen. Based on this finding, Gloddek and colleagues found that passive transfer of S-100β-reactive T cells produced a 10 dB hearing loss in rats, as well as a cellular infiltrate into perilymph. A monoclonal antibody raised against cochlear tissues of approximately 68 kD that specifically reacts with supporting cells in the organ of Corti has been shown to produce high-frequency hearing loss in mice carrying the hybridoma. Infusion of this antibody into the cochlear perilymph with an osmotic minipump induced a 20 dB hearing loss and minor hair cell losses.

To explore the reaction of T cells to self-antigens in the inner ear, Iwai and colleagues used a model of graft-versus-host disease. T cells from C57BL/6 mice injected into the systemic circulation of BALB/c mice infiltrated and proliferated in the perisaccular region surrounding the endolymphatic sac but not in the inner ear. These findings confirm the role of the endolymphatic sac in mediating immunity in the inner ear, as well as the communication of the normal sac with circulating lymphocytes. This provides an additional foundation for autoimmunity as an etiology in disorders involving the sac, such as Meniere's disease.

Animal models have also been used to study the relationship between systemic autoimmune disease and the inner ear. The MRL-Fas[lpr] mouse, a model of SLE, because of the accumulation of autoreactive T cells normally eliminated by

Fas-mediated apoptosis, displays progressive hearing loss. The most striking inner ear pathology involves the stria vascularis, with progressive, hydropic degeneration of intermediate cells, consistent with the strial pathology observed in human SLE temporal bones. Ruckenstein and Hu observed the deposition of both complement-fixing and non–complement-fixing antibodies in the stria vascularis bound to the capillary walls but not associated with inflammation. Systemic treatment with dexamethasone suppressed antibody deposition but failed to suppress strial degeneration and hearing loss. It seems that the hearing loss has a genetic basis. In contrast to this result, Wobig and colleagues found that systemic prednisolone treatment protected hearing in MRL-Fas^{lpr} mice. The Palmerston-North mouse, also a model of SLE with hearing loss, develops abnormal mineralization of connective tissue in the eighth nerve root within the modiolus. However, there is no deposition of antibody or cellular infiltration of the cochlea.

As better imaging becomes available, the identification of inflammation in the inner ear should become possible. Having this information will certainly improve our diagnostic capability as well as our knowledge of the basic pathogenesis of this disorder.

DIAGNOSIS

Diagnosis of AIED is still problematic. There is no universally accepted set of diagnostic criteria or tests for a condition that appears to have several independent causes. In general, in all cases of idiopathic, rapidly progressive, bilateral hearing loss, AIED should be suspected. However, involvement of the second ear may occur months or even years after presentation of symptoms in the first ear. Hearing loss may be manifested as either diminished hearing acuity, decreased discrimination, or both and may involve significant fluctuations over time. In bilateral Meniere's disease, with its triad of vestibular dysfunction, low-tone, fluctuant hearing loss, and tinnitus, AIED should also be suspected, especially when the second ear becomes involved shortly after the first.

Aside from an empiric trial with high-dose corticosteroids showing improved inner ear function, Western blot assays are currently the most widely used diagnostic test for AIED. Reactivity to an approximately 68 kD inner ear antigen is detected in a significant proportion of patients with AIED and Meniere's disease. This, or an antigen with shared epitopes, is also present in kidney and is a member of the heat shock protein (HSP) family. Reactivity against inner ear antigens of other molecular weights, especially in the 45, 30, and 20kD ranges, has also been reported. Few of these other antigens have been characterized or found to be present in statistically significant proportions of hearing loss versus control populations. Preabsorption with bovine HSP (bHSP) 70 does not remove all reactivity to the 68 kD inner ear antigen, and immunization of animals with HSP 70 does not appear to produce hearing loss. Immunoreactivity to a 30 kD antigen has been associated with myelin protein P0. The 68 kD antigen has been associated with HSP 70, and immunoreactivity against bHSP 70 has been found to be correlated with AIED. Other specific antigenic targets have also been studied. Modugno and colleagues observed antithyroid antibodies in 27% of cases of benign paroxysmal positional vertigo, significantly more than were observed in a group of normal controls. Using immunoblotting and enzyme-linked immunosorbent assay, Yamawaki and colleagues observed antibodies against the sulfoglucuronosyl glycolipid, but not sulfoglucuronosyl paragloboside, in 37 of 74 patients with AIED as compared with only 3 of 56 pathologic and 2 of 28 healthy controls.

In a prospective study to determine the relationship of the results of the 68 kD antigen Western blot assay with response to treatment, Moscicki and colleagues found that a positive result was associated with a 75% rate of hearing improvement with corticosteroids compared with 18% of patients who were Western blot negative. In this study, activity of disease was an important predictor of a positive antibody response and response to treatment. Eighty-nine percent of patients with active bilateral progressive hearing loss had a positive 68 kD antibody, whereas patients with inactive disease were uniformly negative.

A number of other recent studies have focused on the diagnostic utility of antibodies against HSP 70. In a retrospective case series, Hirose and colleagues evaluated a variety of assays for systemic autoimmune disease, as well as a Western blot assay against bHSP 70, for their utility in predicting responsiveness of hearing loss to corticosteroids. Again in this study, positivity in the HSP 70 Western blot assay was the best predictor of corticosteroid responsiveness in AIED. Although the sensitivity was low (42%), the specificity was 90%, and the positive predictive value was 91%. Bloch and colleagues tested the serum of 52 patients with bilateral, progressive, idiopathic hearing loss or Meniere's disease in Western blot assays to recombinant bHSP 70 (rbHSP 70) and recombinant human HSP 70. Reactivity against rbHSP 70 was observed in 40 of 52 patients. Only 12 patients also reacted to recombinant human HSP 70. They also tested the positive sera against a panel of recombinant peptide fragments of bHSP 70. Reactivity was observed to widely separate epitopes. However, most positive patients reacted preferentially or only to an amino acid segment from the carboxy terminus of rbHSP, aa 427–461. Within this dominant epitope, the bovine peptide differs from the corresponding human peptide by only one amino acid.

Western blotting has also been used to explore the possibility that a subset of patients with Meniere's disease have an immunologic basis. Gottschlich and colleagues demonstrated that 32% of patients with Meniere's disease were anti–68 kD positive. Rauch and colleagues reported that anti–HSP 70 antibodies were found in 47% of patients with Meniere's disease, and that the level increased to 58% when the disease was bilateral. Recently, however, Rauch and colleagues had a similar level of sensitivity in 134 patients with Meniere's disease but a much lower level of specificity owing to a relatively high level of reactivity in blood donor control sera. This high rate of positivity in the control serum was unexplained and contradicts their previously low level of positives in control sera as well as those reported by others. Serial serum samples revealed no correlation between antibody level and clinical course of disease. These observations led them to question the clinical utility of the HSP 70 assay in Meniere's disease. The answer to whether a subset of patients with classic Meniere's disease is immune mediated is currently unclear.

A number of investigators have reacted sera of patients with AIED against tissue sections to detect immunoreactivity against inner ear antigens. Bachor and colleagues detected immunoreactivity to rat cochlear sections in 14 of 15 patients showing hearing loss in the cochlea opposite an ear deafened by trauma or inflammation. Using rat cryosections of the inner ear, Arbusow and colleagues detected antibodies against vestibular sensory epithelia in 8 of 12 patients with idiopathic bilateral vestibular pathology as compared with 1 of 22 healthy controls and 0 of 6 patients with systemic autoimmune disease. Ottaviani and colleagues detected immunoreactivity against endothelial cells using sections of rat kidney tissue in 8 of 15 patients with sudden hearing loss as compared with 2 of 14 normal controls. Helmchen and colleagues observed positive but low levels of immunoreactivity against inner ear sections using serum from patients with Cogan's syndrome. However, unlike anticorneal antibodies, the anticochlear immunoreactivity levels were not correlated with disease stage.

CLASSIFICATION OF AUTOIMMUNE INNER EAR DISEASE

Over the past two decades since McCabe's published article on AIED, many patients have been diagnosed and treated for rapidly progressive SNHL, and many have had their hearing maintained or even improved with treatment. As a result of the growing experience with patients with corticosteroid-sensitive hearing loss, a pattern has begun to emerge that warrants a classification scheme to sort out patients better as they present with such a broad category of inner ear dysfunction. Although the following classification scheme is intended specifically for that purpose, it is likely that over the next few years it will be further refined:

Type 1   Organ (Ear) Specific
- Rapidly progressive bilateral SNHL
- All age ranges, although middle age most common
- No other clinical evidence of systemic autoimmune disease
- Positive otoblot (Western blot 68 kD or HSP 70)
- Negative serologic studies (antinuclear antibody, erythrocyte sedimentation rate, rheumatoid factor, C1q binding assay, etc)
- Greater than 50% response rate to high-dose corticosteroids

Type 2   Rapidly Progressive Bilateral Sensorineural Hearing Loss with Systemic Autoimmune Disease
- Rapidly progressive bilateral SNHL
- Hearing loss often worst with flare of autoimmune condition
- Other autoimmune condition is present (SLE, ulcerative colitis, polyarteritis nodosa, vasculitis, rheumatoid arthritis, Sjögren's syndrome)

- Otoblot may be positive or negative
- Serologic studies will be positive in accordance with the illness (ie, antinuclear antibody–high titers, rheumatoid factor positive, circulating immune complexes)
- Corticosteroid responsive and may be managed with targeted therapies for underlying illness

Type 3 Immune-Mediated Meniere's Disease
- Bilateral, fluctuating SNHL with vestibular symptoms that may predominate
- Subset of patients with delayed contralateral endolymphatic hydrops or recent instability of better hearing ear in a patient with burned out Meniere's disease
- Otoblot positive 37 to 58%; may show presence of circulating immune complexes
- Corticosteroid responsive and may require long-term immunosuppression owing to relapses

Type 4 Rapidly Progressive Bilateral Sensorineural Hearing Loss with Associated Inflammatory Disease (Chronic Otitis Media, Lyme Disease, Otosyphilis, Serum Sickness*)
- Evidence of a profound drop in hearing with long-standing chronic otitis media
- May show inflammation of the tympanic membrane and perforations
- Hearing loss progresses despite treatment of the infectious agent (treponemal or rickettsial)
- Otoblot negative; serologic tests for the underlying disease may be positive; should be evaluated for granulomatous disease and vasculitis by biopsy if tissue is available
- Corticosteroid responsive and may require long-term immunosuppression

---

* Has been reported after vaccinations, although anecdotally.

Type 5 Cogan's Syndrome
- Sudden onset of interstitial keratitis and severe vestibulo-auditory dysfunction
- Otoblot negative for 68 kD but positive for 55 kD antigen
- Responds to high-dose corticosteroids, although it becomes resistant over the long term

Type 6 Autoimmune Ear Disease Like
- Young patients with idiopathic rapidly progressive bilateral SNHL leading to deafness
- Severe ear pain, pressure, and tinnitus
- Otoblot and all serology negative
- May have an unrelated, nonspecific inflammatory event that initiates ear disease
- Not responsive to immunosuppressive drugs, although they are tried

TREATMENT

Once a diagnosis of AIED is established or considered highly presumptive, high-dose prednisone is the mainstay of treatment. Early institution of 60 mg of prednisone daily for a month is now widely used since short-term or lower-dose long-term therapy and has either been ineffective or fraught with the risk of relapse. Prednisone is then tapered slowly if a positive response to therapy is obtained. If during the taper hearing suddenly falls, reinstitution of high-dose prednisone is indicated. One sensitive predictor of imminent relapse can be the appearance of loud tinnitus in one or both ears. If patients show corticosteroid responsiveness but attempts at taper result in relapse, the addition of a cytotoxic drug should be considered.

Methotrexate (MTX) and cyclophosphamide (Cytoxan) are the most widely used cytotoxic drugs. The former has the advantage of being less toxic and has fewer long-term hematopoietic risks, such as the development of neoplasia. If MTX is used, it should be given as an oral dose 7.5 to 20 mg weekly with folic acid. The patient should be monitored closely for toxicity with complete blood count, platelets, blood urea nitrogen, creatinine, liver function tests, and urinalysis. It should be noted that the prednisone-sparing effects of MTX may take 1 to 2 months to achieve; therefore, prednisone should be maintained until such effects are obtained. Also, if high-dose prednisone has not been effective in restoring hearing, it is unlikely that MTX will offer additional efficacy. Therefore, for patients with severe hearing losses, positive 68 kD Western blots, and nonresponsiveness to prednisone or MTX therapy, consideration should be given to a trial of cyclophosphamide. At oral doses of 1 to 2 mg per day taken each morning with liberal amounts of fluid, the risk of hemorrhagic cystitis or drug effects on the bladder can be minimized. Again, appropriate monitoring of peripheral blood counts is required. Cyclophosphamide should not be administered to children, and the risk of permanent sterility should be outlined. If, on the other hand, no response to high-dose prednisone is achieved and the patient is 68 kD Western blot negative, it may be futile to continue potentially toxic drugs with little evidence for AIED as the cause. There are, however, no hard and fast rules, and a practitioner may be justified in trying cytotoxic drugs on an empiric basis because unrelenting progressive deafness is a serious handicap for a previously normal-hearing person. Luetje recommended plasmapheresis for difficult to manage patients, and this can be a useful adjunct to the above-mentioned immunosuppressive drugs. At the time of writing, a multi-institutional clinical trial is under way to compare the efficacy of MTX and prednisone versus prednisone alone for the management of AIED. The results of this trial should help to delineate appropriate therapy for suspected AIED.

Parnes and colleagues noted that local corticosteroids appear to be more effective in the treatment of other autoimmune disorders, such as corneal inflammation owing to Cogan's syndrome. They therefore investigated the pharmacokinetics of hydrocortisone, methylprednisone, and dexamethasone in perilymph and endolymph after oral, intravenous, or intratympanic administration. Dexamethasone was found to be largely excluded from the cochlea. Both methylprednisone and hydrocortisone reached inner ear fluid after systemic administration, attenuated presumably by the blood-labyrinthine barrier. Much higher levels of all three drugs were observed in cochlear fluid after intratympanic administration, with rapid declines over a 6- to 24-hour period. Similar results were noted by Chandrasekhar and colleagues. Parnes and colleagues also reported that repeated intratympanic administration of corticosteroids in a small series of patients with hearing loss of diverse origins was followed by improvement in some cases, but no control group was included. In contrast, Yang and colleagues found that local immunosuppression had no effect on experimental immune-mediated SNHL in an animal model. It should be noted that local effects are not, of course, the only basis for the therapeutic efficacy of immunosuppressants. By decreasing peripheral blood leukocytes, these agents reduce the population of cells that can be recruited to the inner ear to participate in immune and inflammatory damage. An experiment designed to prevent entry of cells into the cochlea using antibodies to intercellular adhesion molecule 1 did show a reduced number of infiltrated inflammatory cells in the cochlea following antigen challenge. Although the inflammation was not entirely prevented, such a strategy may be worth pursuing. An analogous situation exists for ocular immunologic disorders such as uveitis. Despite the greater accessibility of the eye to topical drugs than the inner ear, ophthalmologists would never consider local therapy in lieu of high-dose corticosteroids for these disorders. Perhaps a lesson taken from their experience might lessen the enthusiasm that currently exists for treatment solely by local middle ear corticosteroid instillation.

DISCUSSION

Debate continues as to whether AIED exists as a separate entity. Some authors prefer to refer to this condition as immune-mediated inner ear disease. Clearly, the evidence for specific autoimmunity is indirect. Hearing and vestibular problems that are diagnosed as autoimmune in origin are often responsive to corticosteroids. Although this suggests that the condition involves inflammation, one cannot infer the involvement of specific immunity. The fact that inner ear disease is often present in systemic autoimmune disorders provides strong evidence that autoimmune processes can damage the labyrinth but does not speak to the issue of organ-specific disease. Animal models of hearing loss and/or vestibular dysfunction secondary to immunization with inner ear antigens provide stronger evidence of specific autoimmunity.

Autoimmune inner ear disease is difficult to diagnose. Although it is generally agreed that the condition should be bilateral and rapidly progressive, the involvement of the second ear may take months or even years to manifest. Although rapidly progressing conditions are more readily held to be autoimmune, AIED is increasingly considered as a potential cause of Meniere's disease and as a less likely cause of sudden hearing loss.

Improved diagnostic tests are clearly required. No one test appears to be positive in more than 30 to 40% of patients who otherwise fit the criteria for autoimmune disease. One possible explanation for this is that rapidly progressive SNHL has a number of different causes, including autoimmune, viral, genetic, developmental, vascular, and perhaps metabolic. Many of these cannot be separated by their presentation; therefore, it would not be unusual or unexpected for many of these patients to have negative antibody testing, and some might even improve with corticosteroids (viral for example) who were not autoimmune. Another possibility is that autoimmunity exists to a variety of inner ear antigens. Given the variety of autoimmune disorders that can affect the inner ear, the variety of antigens with which sera from patients with AIED will react, and the fact that immunization with a variety of proteins can lead to hearing loss in animal models, this would appear to be a strong possibility.

The usefulness of Western blotting for antibodies directed against the 68 kD antigen or HSP 70 as a diagnostic assay seems clear, although there is little evidence to support an etiologic role for HSP 70. It is possible that HSP 70 shares one or more epitopes with an inner ear antigen, although reactivity to widely variable epitopes of HSP 70 argues against this. Alternatively, HSP 70 immunoreactivity may all be a well-correlated epiphenomenon, perhaps produced by immunization of self-proteins during inflammatory responses arising from other causes. Lastly, initial Western blot assays were tested with serum against inner ear tissue containing a 68 kD antigen. After the recognition that HSP 70 showed results similar to 68 kD, a number of groups adopted HSP 70 as the target antigen. This may, however, be the wrong approach if HSP 70 merely shares epitopes but is not the actual antigen in 68 kD inner ear immunoreactivity. Future studies will certainly improve our knowledge of the actual antigenic target(s) involved in AIED.

Despite uncertainty over etiology and difficulties in diagnosis, this condition is frequently responsive to treatment with immunosuppressive drugs. Since there are few forms of SNHL that can be treated other than symptomatically, AIED represents a unique opportunity to reverse SNHL and vestibular disorders. For this reason alone, the diagnosis should be considered when symptoms are appropriate. Both clinical and basic research on this condition is warranted.

15

MENIERE'S DISEASE, VESTIBULAR NEURONITIS, BENIGN PAROXYSMAL POSITIONAL VERTIGO, AND CEREBELLOPONTINE ANGLE TUMORS

Jacob Johnson, MD
Anil K. Lalwani, MD

This chapter discusses the common disorders that affect the vestibular system. The common disorders affecting the peripheral vestibular system include benign paroxysmal positional vertigo (BPPV), Meniere's disease, and vestibular neuronitis. The most common disorder of the vestibular nerve is a vestibular schwannoma (VS). Vestibular schwannomas account for 80% of all cerebellopontine angle (CPA) lesions. Other common CPA tumors that often present by injuring the auditory and vestibular systems include meningiomas and epidermoids.

COMMON PERIPHERAL VESTIBULAR DISORDERS

Benign Paroxysmal Positional Vertigo

Benign paroxysmal positional vertigo was first recognized by Bárány in 1921 and was further characterized by Dix and Hallpike in 1952. It is one of the most common peripheral causes of vertigo. The incidence may range from 10 to 100 per 100,000 individuals per year. The average age of onset is in the fifth decade, and there is no gender bias. Twenty percent have a history of head or ear injury including surgery. The patients complain of the sudden onset of vertigo lasting 10 to 20 seconds when in certain positions with no associated hearing loss. Triggering movements include rolling over in bed into a lateral position, getting out of bed, looking up and back, and bending over. Patients have normal hearing, no spontaneous nystagmus, and a normal neurologic evaluation. Remissions usually occur over several months, although 30% of patients have symptoms for more than 1 year. Benign paroxysmal positional vertigo occurs because the posterior semicircular duct has debris attached to the cupula (cupulolithiasis) or free floating in the endolymph (canalolithiasis). The semicircular duct becomes stimulated by the movement of these particles in response to gravity. The semicircular ducts normally sense angular acceleration, not gravity. The diagnosis is made by noting a characteristic nystagmus (latency of 1 to 2 seconds, downbeat, rotatory nystagmus that is fatigable) when the patient is placed into the Dix-Hallpike position (while moving from the seated to the supine position, the head is turned 45 degrees to the right or left, toward the affected ear, and brought over the edge of the examining table so that the head hangs slightly, although still supported by the examiner). The use of specific maneuvers (Epley, Brandt, Semont) to reposition the debris into the utricle provides relief for the majority of patients. Patients may have unpredictable recurrences and remissions, and the rate of recurrence may be 10 to 15% per year. For resistant patients, the primary surgical option is posterior semicircular canal occlusion.

Meniere's Disease

History and Pathogenesis

Meniere's disease or endolymphatic hydrops is an idiopathic inner ear disorder characterized by attacks of vertigo, fluctuating hearing loss, tinnitus, and aural fullness. The recognition that vertigo was linked to the inner ear rather than only to central sources was first clearly described by Prosper Meniere in 1861. In 1938, Charles Hallpike and Hugh Cairns made the most significant advance in understanding the pathogenesis of Meniere's disease by describing dilation of the saccule and scala media with obliteration of the perilymph spaces of the vestibule and scala vestibuli.

The cause of the endolymphatic hydrops continues to elude us. The cause of Meniere's disease has been attributed to anatomic, infectious, immune, and allergic factors. The focus of most studies has been the endolymphatic duct and sac (ES), with the basic premise being that there is increased endolymphatic fluid owing to impaired reabsorption of the endolymphatic fluid in the endolymphatic duct and ES. There has been no conclusive proof of an infectious agent related to Meniere's disease. The role of immune and allergic factors in Meniere's disease is under active investigation. The ES is able to process antigens and mount a local antibody response. The ES may be vulnerable to immune injury because of the hyperosmolarity of its contents and due to the fenestrations in its vasculature. A significant percentage (50%) of patients with Meniere's disease have concomitant inhalant and/or food allergy, and treating these allergies with immunotherapy and diet modification has improved the manifestations of their allergy and their Meniere's disease.

Epidemiology and Natural History
The incidence of Meniere's disease ranges from 10 to 150 in 100,000 persons per year. There is no gender bias, and patients typically present in the fifth decade of life. Meniere's disease is characterized by remissions and exacerbations. Longitudinal studies have shown that after 10 to 20 years, the vertigo attacks subside in most patients, and the hearing loss stabilizes to a moderate to severe level (50 dB HL).

Meniere's disease usually affects one ear initially, but the cumulative risk of developing Meniere's disease in the other ear appears to be linear with time.

Diagnostic Evaluation

Meniere's disease is a clinical diagnosis. Audiologic assessment initially shows a low-frequency or low- and high-frequency (inverted V) sensorineural hearing loss. As the disease progresses, there is a flat sensorineural hearing loss. With electrocochleography, the cochlear microphonic, summating potential (SP), and eighth nerve action potential (AP) can be measured. In Meniere's disease, the SP to AP ratio is often increased but lacks the specificity or sensitivity to diagnose Meniere's disease consistently or predict its clinical course. Vestibular testing (electronystagmography with caloric testing) shows peripheral vestibular dysfunction.

Management

The primary management of patients with Meniere's disease is a low-salt diet (1,500 mg/d) and diuretics (hydrochlorothiazide) if needed. Acute attacks are managed with vestibular suppressants (meclizine, diazepam) and antiemetic medications (prochloperazine suppository). The majority of patients are controlled with conservative management. Medically refractory patients with serviceable hearing may undergo intratympanic gentamicin therapy, ES surgery, or vestibular nerve section. Patients without serviceable hearing may undergo intratympanic gentamicin therapy or transmastoid labyrinthectomy.

Vestibular Neuronitis

Vestibular neuronitis is the third most common cause of peripheral vestibular vertigo following BPPV and Meniere's disease. The natural history of vestibular neuronitis includes an acute attack of vertigo that lasts a few days with complete or at least partial recovery within a few weeks to months. The patient has normal hearing and a normal neurologic examination. Like Meniere's disease, the pathogenesis is not known, but the majority of patients recover with no sequelae. Some patients may later develop BPPV. The proposed causes for vestibular neuronitis include viral infection, vascular occlusion, and immune mechanisms. The primary role of the physician is to rule out a central cause of the acute vertigo. Magnetic resonance imaging (MRI) with emphasis on identification of both infarction and hemorrhage in the brainstem and cerebellum is obtained in patients with risk factors for stroke, patients with additional neurologic abnormalities, and patients who do not show improvement within 48 hours. The treatment is primarily supportive care, including antiemetics and vestibular suppressants that are withdrawn as soon as possible to not interfere with central vestibular compensation. Patients with persisting vestibular symptoms should receive vestibular rehabilitation therapy including habituation, postural control, and gait and general conditioning exercises.

COMMON CEREBELLOPONTINE ANGLE TUMORS

Anatomy

The CPA consists of a potential cerebrospinal fluid (CSF)-filled space in the posterior cranial fossa bounded by the temporal bone, cerebellum, and brainstem. The CPA is traversed by cranial nerves V to XI, and the facial (VII) and vestibulocochlear (VIII) nerves are most prominent. The vestibulocochlear nerve divides into three nerves: the cochlear nerve and the superior and inferior vestibular nerves in the lateral extent of the CPA or medial part of the internal auditory canal (IAC). The lateral aspect of the IAC is divided into four quadrants by a vertical crest, called Bill's bar, and a transverse crest. Cranial nerve VII comes to lie in the anterior-superior quadrant and is anterior to the superior vestibular nerve and superior to the cochlear nerve, whereas the inferior vestibular nerve lies in the posterior-inferior quadrant and is inferior to the superior vestibular nerve and posterior to the cochlear nerve. The superior vestibular nerve carries sensation from the utricle and the superior and lateral semicircular ducts, and the inferior vestibular nerve innervates the saccule and the posterior semicircular duct.

Cerebellopontine angle tumors account for 10% of all intracranial tumors. Nearly 90% of all CPA tumors are VSs, meningiomas, and epidermoids. Cerebellopontine angle lesions become clinically symptomatic by causing compression of the neurovascular structures in and around the CPA. The classic description of these symptoms by Harvey Cushing includes initially unilateral hearing loss, vertigo, nystagmus, altered facial sensation, facial pain that later progresses to facial palsy, vocal cord palsy, dysphagia, diplopia, respiratory compromise, and death. This description highlights the untreated natural history of CPA tumors. The treatment of CPA tumors includes surgical removal, observation, and irradiation.

Natural History

Each of these CPA tumors has a similar clinical presentation and is primarily differentiated by its imaging characteristics. The natural history of most CPA tumors includes a slow rate of growth. Studies show that periods of growth are intermixed with periods of quiescence. The average growth rate is 1.8 mm/year for VSs. This slow growth causes progressive and often insidious symptoms and signs as there is displacement, distortion, and compression of the structures in the IAC and the CPA. Occasionally, the tumor may undergo rapid expansion owing to cystic degeneration or hemorrhage into the tumor. A rapid expansion causes rapid movement along the subsequently described phases of CPA symptoms and may cause rapid neurologic deterioration. Intracanalicular growth affects the vestibulocochlear nerve in the rigid IAC and causes unilateral hearing loss, tinnitus, and vertigo or dysequilibrium. These three symptoms are the typical presenting complaints of most patients with CPA tumors. Intial tumor growth into the CPA cistern does not cause significant new symptoms because structures in the CPA are initially displaced without injury. As the tumor approaches 3 cm, the tumor abuts the boundaries of the CPA and results in a new set of symptoms and signs. Compression of cranial nerve V causes corneal and midface numbness or pain. Further distortion of cranial nerve VIII and now VII causes further hearing loss and dysequilibrium and also facial weakness or spasms. Brainstem distortion leads to narrowing of the fourth ventricle. Further growth leads to the final clinical spectrum described by Cushing of hydrocephalus, lower cranial neuropathies, respiratory compromise, and death.

Symptoms and Signs

Hearing loss is present in 95% of patients with VSs and the primary complaint in all CPA tumors. Tinnitus is present in 65% of patients with VSs. The tinnitus is most often constant with a high buzzing pitch. Owing to the central compensation from the slowly evolving vestibular injury, patients tolerate and adapt well to the dysequilibrium. The majority of patients will have self-limiting episodes of vertigo. Facial and trigeminal nerve dysfunction occurs after the auditory and vestibular impairments and usually causes midface (V2) numbness and loss of the corneal reflex.

Diagnostic Evaluation

The diagnostic evaluation includes a complete audiologic assessment, possibly a vestibular evaluation, auditory brainstem response (ABR), and imaging. Pure-tone audiometry in patients with VSs shows asymmetric, down-sloping, high-frequency sensorineural hearing loss in almost 70% of patients. The hearing may also be normal or may involve only the low frequencies or have a flat, trough, or peak configuration. Twenty percent will have an episode of sudden hearing loss. Retrocochlear hearing loss causes speech discrimination scores to be lower than would be predicted by the pure-tone thresholds. If the audiologic evaluation suggests a retrocochlear lesion, imaging of the CPA is performed to rule out a retrocochlear lesion. Vestibular testing lacks specificity in terms of diagnosing CPA tumors. As the detection limits and costs of imaging studies have improved, the role of ABR in the diagnosis of VSs has declined.

Vestibular Schwannomas

Vestibular schwannomas originate from the Schwann cells of the superior or inferior vestibular nerves. They arise in the medial part of the IAC or lateral part of the CPA. Various epidemiologic studies have shown an incidence of 10 per 1 million individuals per year. There is no gender bias. The age of presentation is 40 to 60 years. Ninety-five percent of VSs occur in a sporadic fashion. The remaining 5% of patients have neurofibromatosis 2 or familial VSs. The age of presentation is earlier in nonsporadic VSs, and patients usually present in the second or third decades of life. Vestibular schwannomas occur owing to mutations in the gene for the tumor suppressor protein merlin, located on chromosome 22q12. Merlin is a cytoskeletal protein and may have a role in cell–cell contact inhibition. The classic histologic findings include areas of densely packed cells with spindle-shaped nuclei and fibrillar cytoplasm intermixed with hypocellular areas containing vacuolated, pleomorphic cells. These dense regions are called Antoni A areas, and the hypocellular regions are called Antoni B areas. Within the Antoni A areas, the palisades of the nuclei are termed Verocay bodies.

Imaging

Magnetic resonance imaging with gadolinium contrast provides the gold standard for VS diagnosis or exclusion. The MRI characteristics of a VS include a hypointense globular mass centered over the IAC on T_1-weighted images with enhancement when gadolinium is added. Vestibular schwannomas are iso- to hypointense on T_2-weighted images. In situations in which MRI scans cannot be used or are not accessible, a computed tomographic (CT) scan with iodine contrast or an ABR offers a reasonable alternate screening modality. A CT scan with contrast provides consistent identification of CPA tumors over 1.5 cm or CPA tumors that have at least a 5 mm CPA component. Vestibular schwannomas appear as ovoid masses centered over the IAC with nonhomogeneous enhancement. Computed tomographic scans with contrast can miss intracanalicular tumors unless there is bony expansion of the IAC.

Management

The primary management for VSs is surgical removal. The roles of observation and radiotherapy are currently for patients who cannot tolerate a surgical procedure or who have a life span of less than 5 years. The surgical approaches to the CPA include translabyrinthine, retrosigmoid, and middle fossa craniotomies. The appropriate approach for a particular patient is based on the hearing status, size of the tumor, extent of IAC involvement, and experience of the surgeon. The approaches are either hearing preserving or hearing ablating. The retrosigmoid and middle fossa approaches are hearing preserving. They, however, have limitations of exposure to all aspects of the CPA and IAC. The middle fossa approach is well suited for patients with good hearing and a less than 2 cm tumor. The retrosigmoid approach is well suited for patients with good hearing and a tumor less than 4 cm and not involving the lateral part of the IAC. The lateral part of the

IAC is usually only directly accessible via a retrosigmoid approach by removing the posterior semicircular canal. The violation of the posterior semicircular canal will lead to hearing loss. The translabyrinthine approach causes total hearing loss and so is appropriate for patients with poor hearing (pure-tone average > 30) or patients with good hearing and tumors not accessible by the hearing-preserving approaches.

Operative and Postoperative Complications

The intraoperative complications for all three approaches include vascular injury, air embolism, parenchymal brain injury, and cranial nerve injury. Postoperative complications include hemorrhage, stroke, venous thromboembolism, syndrome of inappropriate antidiuretic hormone, CSF leak, and meningitis. The most common complication is CSF leak, which occurs in 10 to 15% of patients either via the wound or via a pneumatic pathway to the eustachian tube. The majority of these leaks resolve with conservative care, which includes placing wound sutures at the leak site, replacing the mastoid dressing, decreasing intracranial pressure with acetazolamide, restricting fluid intake, and resting in bed. Some patients will also require a lumbar subarachnoid drain, and very few patients will need surgical re-exploration. A related complication is meningitis. Meningitis occurs in 2 to 10% of patients and may be aseptic, bacterial, or lipoid owing to irritation from the fat graft.

Prognosis and Rehabilitation

Patients are most concerned about deafness, imbalance, and facial nerve weakness. The most important factors for hearing preservation are tumor size and preoperative hearing level. Hearing preservation ranges from 20 to 70%. Almost half of the patients will have vertigo or imbalance beyond the postoperative period, but these symptoms have minimal impact on daily activities. The rapidity of vestibular compensation after unilateral vestibular loss is determined by the patient's efforts to exercise and challenge the vestibular system. Facial nerve function is also best predicted by tumor size. In smaller tumors, over 90% of patients will have House-Brackmann grade 1 or 2 function (grade 1 is normal and grade 6 is complete paralysis). If all sizes are considered, approximately 80% of patients will have grade 1 or 2 function.

In summary, all three approaches have mortality rates of less than 1%, with over a 90% rate of tumor removal and facial nerve preservation. The translabyrinthine approach has facial nerve preservation rates as high as 98%. The retrosigmoid approach allows 50% hearing preservation, and the middle fossa approach allows up to 70% hearing preservation. The recurrence rate is less than 1.5%, and the majority of patients feel that they can return to full preoperative activities by 3 months. These three approaches allow the management of most CPA tumors. A small subset of patients will not be surgical candidates and will require observation or radiation therapy.

Observation

The predictable correlation between VS size and significant neurologic symptoms and the relative slow growth of VS allow observation to be a management option for VSs. Patients may be observed if their life expectancy is shorter than the growth time required for the VS to cause significant neurologic symptoms. The growth pattern of the VS should be assessed in these patients with a second radiologic evaluation in 6 months and then yearly radiologic evaluations. Studies have shown that 15 to 24% of patients undergoing conservative management will require surgery or stereotactic radiation. If the growth rate in the first year exceeds 2 to 3 mm/yr, the patient will likely need treatment for the VS. The patient should understand that the costs of conservative management include having to treat a tumor that is larger and less amenable to hearing preservation procedures and/or stereotactic radiation.

Stereotactic Radiation

The goal of stereotactic radiation is to prevent further growth of the VS while preserving hearing and facial nerve function. This goal directly differs from the goal of complete tumor removal in microsurgical therapy. The mechanism of stereotactic radiation relies on delivering radiation to a specific intracranial target by using several precisely collimated beams of ionizing radiation. The beams take various pathways to the target tissue, therefore creating a sharp dose gradient between the target tissue and the surrounding tissue. The ionizing radiation causes necrosis and vascular fibrosis, and the time course of effect is over 1 to 2 years. There is an expected transient swelling of the tumor for 1 to 2 years. The practical aspects include that the patient wears a stereotactic head frame, computer-assisted radiation planning using an MRI scan, and a single treatment for delivery of the radiation.

The success of stereotactic radiation to arrest tumor growth depends on the dose of radiation delivered. However, the rate of cranial neuropathies, including hearing loss, is decreased by lowering the radiation dose. The current trend has been to lower the marginal radiation dose, and the long-term tumor control with these current dosing plans is under investigation. Since VSs have a slow growth rate, these studies will require 5- to 10-year follow-ups to be confident about tumor control. Studies have shown control rates from 85 to over 95%. The hearing preservation rate decreases each year after radiation and stabilizes after 3 years at 50%. The rate of facial nerve dysfunction varies from 3 to 50% based on the radiation dose at the margin of the tumor and the length of the facial nerve in the radiation field. As the long-term effectiveness and sequelae of stereotactic radiation are further defined, the indications for radiation therapy will become further defined.

Meningioma

Meningiomas are the second most common CPA tumors and account for 3 to 10% of tumors at this location. Compared with schwannomas, meningiomas are a more heterogeneous group of tumors in regard to pathology, anatomic location, and treatment outcome. The majority of these tumors are benign and slow growing, and 1% will become symptomatic. Meningiomas differ in pathogenesis, anatomic location, and imaging characteristics from VSs but are nearly indistinguishable in terms of clinical presentation and audiovestibular testing. Symptoms and signs more common with meningiomas relative to VSs include trigeminal neuralgia (7 to 22%), facial paresis (11 to 36%), lower cranial nerve deficits (5 to 10%), and visual disturbances (8%). Meningiomas arise from arachnoid villi cap cells and are located along dura, venous sinuses, and neurovascular foramina. Molecular studies have shown deletions in chromosome 22 in nearly 75% of meningiomas. Meningiomas are primarily managed by surgical excision.

Imaging

Imaging provides the diagnosis of meningioma and allows the differentiation between meningioma and VS. A CT scan without contrast shows an iso- or hyperdense mass with areas of calcification in 10 to 26% and provides information regarding hyperostosis or bony invasion. Meningiomas enhance homogeneously with CT contrast, and 90% of meningiomas can be detected by contrast-enhanced CT. Magnetic resonance imaging is the study of choice for the diagnosis of meningiomas. Meningiomas are hypo- to isointense on T_1-weighted MRIs and have a variable intensity on T_2-weighted images. Areas of calcification appear dark on both T_1- and T_2-weighted images. Unlike VSs, meningiomas are broad based (sessile) and usually not centered over the porus acusticus internus. The broad-base attachment to the petrous wall leads to an obtuse bone-tumor angle. There is no widening of the IAC. Also unlike VSs, meningiomas more commonly herniate into the middle fossa. T_1-weighted enhanced images can show an enhancing dural tail (meningeal sign) adjacent to the bulk of the tumor in 50 to 70% of meningiomas.

Management

The two primary management options are observation and surgery. Surgical treatment ideally consists of total meningioma removal, excision of a cuff of surrounding dura, and drilling of the underlying bone. The surgical approach is based on the tumor location and the patient's hearing status. In contrast to VSs, the anatomic location of posterior fossa meningiomas is varied. The site of the meningioma is a major determinant of types of morbidity from the tumor and the success of treatment. Meningiomas commonly arise along the inferior petrosal sinus and may involve the petrous apex, lateral part of the clivus, Meckel's cave, sigmoid sinus, jugular bulb, and superior petrosal sinus. Sixty percent of CPA meningiomas involve the middle fossa and may require a combined middle and posterior fossa craniotomy. The type of posterior fossa craniotomy in the combined approach will depend on the need for hearing preservation and the extent of surgical exposure required. Total tumor removal is accomplished in 70 to 85% of patients with meningiomas. The long-term recurrence after total tumor removal is between 10 and 30%, whereas that of subtotal removal is over 50%. Hearing preservation is more likely than in VSs and approaches 70%. The facial nerve function has a 17% rate of deterioration from preoperative levels. The mortality is between 1 and 9%.

Epidermoids

Epidermoids are much less common than VSs or meningiomas. They account for approximately 5% of CPA lesions.

Epidermoids likely develop from ectodermal inclusions that become trapped during embryogenesis. These ectodermal inclusions lead to a keratinizing squamous cell epithelium in the CPA. Epidermoids are slow growing and often grow to a significant size before causing CPA symptoms because they initially grow around structures via paths of least resistance rather than cause compression. Epidermoids have a higher rate of preoperative facial (40%) and trigeminal (50%) nerve involvement relative to VSs. On CT, epidermoids are hypodense compared to brain. A distinguishing characteristic relative to VSs and meningiomas is that epidermoids show no enhancement with intravenous contrast. Epidermoids have irregular borders, are not centered on the IAC, and do not usually widen the IAC. Epidermoids have similar imaging characteristics as CSF on MRI (hypointense on T_1-weighted images and hyperintense on T_2-weighted images). Epidermoids are treated by surgical excision, but total removal is more difficult than it is with VSs because they become adherent to normal structures.

16

PRESBYACUSIS

John H. Mills, PhD
Paul R. Lambert, MD

Presbyacusis is defined generally as the hearing loss associated with increasing chronologic age. By the year 2030, according to the National Center for Health Statistics, 32% of the population will be elderly, and 75% of them will have clinically significant hearing loss.

BACKGROUND

Although Toynbee in 1849 was perhaps the first to write about age-related hearing loss and to prescribe a treatment (application of solutions of silver nitrate or mercurous chloride to the external auditory canal), Zwaardemaker in 1891 is credited with the first accurate description of presbyacusis. With the use of Dalton whistles, Zwaardemaker demonstrated that older persons had more difficulty detecting high-pitched sounds than younger persons. By the use of bone-conduction testing, he considered age-related hearing loss to be of cochlear origin. Since the 1930s, age-related changes have been observed at nearly every location in the aging auditory system, from the external ear with collapsing canals to neural degeneration extending from the auditory nerve to the auditory brainstem and temporal lobe.

TERMINOLOGY

Although there are several definitions of the term presbyacusis, most of the confusion can be eliminated by the use of the terms presbyacusis, socioacusis, and nosoacusis. A generic definition of presbyacusis is age-related hearing loss that is the effect of aging in combination with lifelong exposures to nonoccupational noise, ototoxic agents, diet, drugs, and other factors. A more precise definition of presbyacusis is hearing loss that increases as a function of age and is attributable to "aging" per se. This "purely aging" hearing loss probably has a genetic basis. Socioacusis is defined as the hearing loss produced by exposure to nonoccupational noise in combination with lifestyle factors such as diet and exercise. Nosoacusis is the hearing loss attributable to diseases with ototoxic effects. It is important for medical and legal reasons to differentiate presbyacusis from socioacusis, nosoacusis, and occupational hearing loss.

Most studies indicate that hearing losses caused by exposure to noise are additive (in decibels), with the hearing loss attributed to presbyacusis. A small sensorineural hearing loss (SNHL) of 25 dB at age 25, for example, seemingly has little social or medical relevance; however, by age 70, a hearing loss of 25 dB caused by the aging process is added to the existing SNHL. The result is a hearing loss of 50 dB. Thus, a seemingly minor hearing loss at a young age becomes a severe loss when the effects of presbyacusis become evident. Rules for combining hearing losses attributable to presbyacusis, nosoacusis, and socioacusis are not always straightforward. In medical-legal assessment, it is assumed that presbyacusic effects add in decibels to the hearing loss produced by noise. As stated above, this approach is supported by data for groups of subjects under a limited set of conditions; however, for individuals and complicated noise exposures, the procedures for allocation of hearing loss into different components are controversial.

EPIDEMIOLOGY

There has been a significant effort to describe hearing levels as a function of age, and there is now an international standard for men and women, International Standards Organization (ISO) 1999: "Acoustics: Determination of Occupational Noise Exposure and Estimation of Noise-Induced Hearing Impairment." Two databases have been developed: A and B. The subjects in Data Base A are highly screened and represent "pure aging" effects as well as socioacusis. The subjects in Data Base B are considered to reflect "pure aging" effects, socioacusis, some nosoacusis, and some effects attributable to occupational hearing loss. Hearing loss in the higher frequencies is measurable by age 30, increases systematically to age 60 (and beyond), is largest at 4 and 6 kHz, and is larger in males than in females. There are also significant differences between Data Base A and Data Base B, presumably owing to differences in subject selection. Significant debate exists about the appropriateness and validity of Data Bases A and B, particularly in a medical-legal context involving the assessment of occupational noise-induced hearing loss.

The data have been replotted to show the average hearing loss at 0.5, 1, 2, and 3 kHz as a function of chronologic age. Hearing loss at these particular audiometric test frequencies is used in the computation of hearing handicap as recommended by the American Academy of Otolaryngology-Head and Neck Surgery (AAO-HNS). Hearing loss increases systematically from age 20 through age 75. There are at least two remarkable findings. One is that the largest difference between the worst case (males, Data Base B) and the best case (females, Data Base A) is only about 5 dB. Second, even at age 75, the hearing loss is only about 20 dB. According to the AAO-HNS definitions of hearing handicap, the average hearing loss at 0.5, 1, 2, and 3 kHz must exceed 25 dB to be considered a hearing handicap. According to the AAO-HNS definition of hearing handicap, substantially less than 50% of the population, male or female, have a hearing handicap even at age 75. Other less selective epidemiologic data suggest that the prevalence of a hearing handicap among older persons is substantially higher than that indicated by the epidemiologic data used in the ISO 1999 standard. Using 1,662 subjects from the famous Framingham study of cardiovascular disease, Gates and colleagues reported that 55% met or exceeded the AAO-HNS definition of hearing handicap. The difference between the results of Gates and colleagues and those of ISO 1999 reflect sampling differences and the inclusion of subjects older than age 75 in the Gates and colleagues sample.

One dramatic feature of age-related hearing loss is the decline of hearing levels at frequencies higher than 3 kHz. By age 50 to 59, the hearing loss at 16 kHz is greater than 60 dB. Hearing levels at 4 and 8 kHz exceed 50 dB by age 70 and exceed 70 dB at 8 kHz by age 79. Hearing loss at frequencies above 8 kHz is even more pronounced and is not predictable by hearing levels in the 1 to 4 kHz range.

The interpretation of epidemiologic data is not straightforward. One point of view is that these age-related changes in hearing thresholds are genetically determined, age-dependent events that are totally endogenous. They are largely independent of socioacusis and nosoacusis. Gates and colleagues have estimated the role of genetics in age-related hearing loss. Their heritability estimates suggest that as much as 55% of the variance associated with age-related hearing loss is attributable to the effect of genes. These heritability estimates are similar to those reported for hypertension and hyperlipidemia, are much stronger in women than in men, and can be used to support the point of view that age-related changes in hearing reflect the combined effect of genetics, socioacusis, and nosoacusis. In some views of presbyacusis, socioacusis is given a major role, almost surely because of the famous Mabaan study.

A hearing survey of Mabaans, a tribe located in a remote and undeveloped part of Africa, showed exceptionally good thresholds for males and females in their sixth to ninth decades. In addition to the lack of exposure to noise, the Mabaans were reported to lead a low-stress lifestyle, have a low-fat diet, and have a low prevalence of cardiovascular disease. This study became the scientific basis for the thesis that persons in Western industrialized societies were at risk of hearing loss because of socioacusis. Later analysis of the Mabaan data indicated very few differences between hearing levels of Mabaans and hearing levels of well-screened individuals from industrialized societies. One possible exception was that the hearing levels of Mabaan males over the age of 60 were slightly better in the high frequencies than their Western male counterparts.

LABORATORY STUDIES: HUMANS AND ANIMALS

The most extensive source of histopathologic data is the temporal bone studies of Schuknecht and colleagues, who have identified four types or categories of presbycusis: (1) sensory, characterized by atrophy and degeneration of the sensory and supporting cells; (2) neural, typified by loss of neurons in the cochlea and central nervous system (CNS); (3) metabolic, characterized by atrophy of the lateral wall of the cochlea, especially the stria vascularis; and (4) mechanical, where the inner ear changes its properties with a resulting inner ear conductive hearing loss. Each of these categories was hypothesized to have a characteristic audiometric configuration (ie, flat, sloping) and to be audiometrically identifiable. In subsequent studies, difficulty was encountered in correlating the audiometric configuration with anatomic data and in differentiating one type of presbycusis from another on the basis of the audiometric configuration.

In 1993, Schuknecht and Gacek revised the categories of presbycusis as follows: "1) sensory cell losses are the least important type of loss in the aged; 2) neuronal losses are constant and predictable expressions of aging; 3) atrophy of the stria vascularis is the predominant lesion of the aging ear; 4) no anatomical correlates for a gradual descending hearing loss ... reflect a cochlear conductive loss; 5) 25% cannot be classified using light microscopy." These conclusions are important for at least two reasons. One is that the significance of sensory cell losses is de-emphasized. The second is that the dominance of strial degeneration is emphasized. These two points bring a consensus to human temporal bone results and those obtained from experiments with animals.

Many of the histopathologic observations made on human temporal bones have been confirmed and extended in experimental animals. In aging rodents, there is usually a small loss of sensory (outer) hair cells in the most basal and most apical regions of the cochlea. Nerve loss (spiral ganglion cells) occurs throughout the cochlea. The lateral wall of the cochlea, including the stria vascularis, shows degeneration originating in both the base and apex and extending to midcochlear regions as the animal ages. As with humans, the most prominent type of presbyacusis in laboratory animals (exception is mice like C57) is the metabolic category that, in addition to strial degeneration, is characterized by a loss of the protein Na^+,K^+-adenosine triphosphatase. Sometimes the loss of this protein occurs when the stria vascularis appears normal under microscopic examination. Accordingly, the prevalence of "metabolic presbyacusis" may prove to be substantially higher in humans when the appropriate immunohistochemical techniques are applied to human temporal bones.

The stria vascularis and underlying spiral ligament have a prominent role in generating electrochemical gradients and regulating fluid and ion homeostasis. Histopathologic studies have provided strong evidence for vascular involvement in age-related hearing loss. Morphometric analyses of lateral wall preparations stained to contrast blood vessels have revealed losses of the strial capillary area in aged animals. The vascular pathology first presented as small focal lesions mainly in the apical and lower basal turns and progressed with age to encompass large regions at both ends of the cochlea. Remaining strial areas were highly correlated with normal microvasculature and with the endocochlear potential. Not surpisingly, areas of complete capillary loss invariably correlated with regions of strial atrophy. Thus, considerable support exists for the major involvement of the strial microvasculature in age-related degeneration of the stria vascularis; however, the question of what constitutes the initial injury remains unanswered. Although it is tempting to speculate that atrophy of the stria vascularis occurs secondarily to vascular insufficiency resulting from capillary necrosis, the reverse could be true.

The most prominent changes in the physiologic properties of the aging ear are losses of auditory nerve function as indicated by increased thresholds and reduced slopes of input-output functions of the compound action potential (CAP) of the auditory nerve. Slopes of input-output functions of the CAP and the auditory brainstem response (ABR) are decreased even when the increase in thresholds is only 5 to 10 dB. Thus, what appears to be an abnormal function of the auditory brainstem in older animals reflects only the abnormal output of the auditory nerve. The reduced amplitudes of evoked potentials in aging ears are probably reflective of asynchronous neural activity in the auditory nerve as well as spiral ganglion cell loss.

The endolymphatic potential (ie, the 80 to 90 mV DC resting potential in the scala media of the cochlea) often is reduced significantly and proportionally to degeneration of the stria vascularis. In animals, hearing losses can be reduced by introducing a DC current into the scala media and raising a low endolymphatic potential (ie, 15 mV) to a value approaching 60 to 70 mV. Degeneration of the stria vascularis with the resultant decline in the endocochlear potential has given rise to the "dead battery theory" of presbyacusis.

Cochlear nonlinearities are preserved in aging animals as indicated by two-tone rate suppression (ie, activity of the auditory nerve elicited by one tone is suppressed or eliminated by the addition of a second tone of different frequency). In aging animals, the mechanism of two-tone rate suppression appears to remain intact, whereas in noise- or drug-induced injury of the cochlea, a reduction or complete loss of two-tone rate suppression may be the first indicator of injury of the cochlea, usually outer hair cells. These data are an excellent indicator that the pathologic basis of age-related hearing loss is fundamentally different from the pathologic basis of noise- or drug-induced hearing loss.

Otoacoustic emissions, both transient evoked and distortion product, are nonlinear phenomena that are assumed to reflect the integrity of sensory cells, especially outer hair cells. Given this assumption, one would expect to find very high correlations between loss of outer hair cells and changes in otoacoustic emissions; however, inconsistent relations among distortion products and sensory cell pathology have been reported, including normal emissions in the presence of missing outer hair cells as well as reduced emissions in the presence of a complete complement of outer hair cells. In aging animals with a minimal loss of outer hair cells, distortion-product emissions are reduced in amplitude but are clearly present and robust. In aging human ears, transient emissions are present in about 80% of persons with a pure-tone average (PTA) hearing level better than 10 dB, present in about 50% with a PTA of 11 to 26 dB, and absent in about 80% with a PTA greater than 26 dB. Thus, the presence of a transient otoacoustic emission suggests excellent hearing levels for most persons, whereas its absence reveals very little.

A recent development is the association of mitochondrial deoxyribonucleic acid (mtDNA) deletions with SNHL and age-related hearing loss. Ueda and colleagues, using DNA specimens extracted from peripheral blood leukocytes, found a higher rate of mtDNA deletions in patients with SNHL than in controls. Seidman tied mtDNA to presbyacusis and mtDNA to reactive oxygen metabolites (ROMs). Reactive oxygen metabolites are highly toxic molecules that can damage mtDNA resulting in the production of specific mtDNA deletions. Thus, compounds that block or scavenge ROM should attenuate age-related hearing loss. Rats were assigned to treatment groups including controls, caloric restriction, and treatment with several antioxidants, including vitamins E and C, and were allowed to age in a controlled environment. The calorie-restricted groups maintained the best hearing, lowest quantity of mtDNA deletions, and least amount of outer hair cell loss. The antioxidant-treated subjects had better hearing than the controls and a slight trend for fewer mtDNA deletions. The controls had the poorest hearing, most mtDNA deletions, and most hair cell loss. These data suggest that nutritional and pharmacologic strategies may prove to be an effective treatment that would limit age-related increases in ROM production, reduce mtDNA deletions, and thus reduce age-related hearing loss. Reactive oxygen metabolites and oxidative stress have been implicated in noise-induced hearing loss, ototoxic hearing loss, and cumulative injury that presents as age-related hearing loss. It is speculated that there is a genetic impairment of antioxidant protection that leads to the production of both age-related and noise-induced hearing loss by placing the cochlea into a state of vulnerability. Although an age-related hearing loss gene has been identified, the murine Ahl mutation, the discovery of the molecular/genetic basis of presbyacusis, noise-induced hearing loss, and SNHL in general is truly just beginning.

PERCEPTION OF AUDITORY
SIGNALS AND SPEECH

There are age-related declines in differential sensitivity for intensity, frequency, and time. Until recently, these age-related declines in the basic properties of the ear and hearing were almost always measured in older persons with significant hearing losses. Thus, it was nearly impossible to separate the effects of a hearing loss from the effects of aging. Recently, however, discrimination for both intensity and frequency has been shown to decline with age only at low frequencies and independently of any hearing loss. These results are important because they are negative effects measured in the presence of normal hearing and may very well represent age-related declines in information-processing capability. It remains unclear whether these age-related declines represent age-related effects of the auditory periphery, CNS, or both.

In a study of speech discrimination as a function using data from 2,162 patients, Jerger showed that speech discrimination declined systematically as a function of age; however, the decline with age is mirrored by changes in thresholds. For subjects with moderate-to-severe hearing losses, the decline with age was significant for persons between the ages of 45 and 85 with hearing losses of 40 to 60 dB. In contrast, persons over the age range of 50 to 80 performed as well as 25 year olds as long as their average hearing loss at 0.5, 1, and 2 kHz was less than 35 dB. This fact runs counter to the stereotype of 70- to 80-year-old persons.

When subjects were placed into three age groups over the range from 55 to 84 years in whom hearing levels were nearly identical ($\pm$ 3 dB), there were no age-related declines. In an additional analysis using partial correlations, significant gender effects were observed (ie, significant declines with age for males but not for females).

There are many additional studies of speech discrimination using background noises, degraded speech signals, reverberation, and other variations. Many of these studies show age-related effects; however, the interpretation is not straightforward. Some believe that there is a large CNS component to presbycusis, whereas others have shown that speech discrimination is predictable given the audiometric hearing loss and the audibility of the speech material. Indeed, as much as 95% of the variance in speech discrimination results can be accounted for on the basis of the audiogram. There are many age-related declines in auditory behavior that are not strongly associated with auditory thresholds; however, it remains difficult to separate central processing disorders from disorders initiated by a pathologic input from the aging cochlea.

AUDITORY-EVOKED POTENTIALS

In regard to the ABR, most studies show age-related declines in the amplitude of wave V that should be interpreted to reflect peripheral hearing loss rather than changes in the brainstem. Even in older persons with excellent hearing levels, ABR waveforms are of "poor quality" and reduced amplitude, reflecting pathology of the cochlea and auditory nerve and a reduction in synchronized neural activity. For young subjects with normal and abnormal hearing, thresholds measured behaviorally are about 10 dB better than thresholds estimated from the ABR. For aging subjects, this behavioral/ABR disparity is 20 dB. Whereas CAP and ABR are decreased in amplitude in older subjects, potentials produced at higher levels in the CNS by long-duration signals may be unaffected or even increased in amplitude. Age-related increases could reflect a number of factors, including efforts by the CNS to compensate for peripheral deficits or changes in the excitatory/inhibitory balance of the auditory CNS.

ALLEVIATION/TREATMENT

Assuming that any problems with the external and middle ear are diagnosed and treated, assuming that other medical issues are under control, and assuming a diagnosis of presbyacusis, in the general sense, the best treatment currently available is a hearing aid. The results from surveys indicate that as few as 10 to 30% of the older population who would clearly benefit from an aid do not use an aid and may have never even tried one. The reasons for not using an aid or being a dissatisfied user include cost, the stigma of a hearing handicap and of being old, difficulty in manipulating controls, and too little benefit, particularly in the presence of background noise. Every older person with a hearing loss should be considered a potential candidate for a hearing aid.

ACKNOWLEDGMENT

Preparation of this chapter was supported by the National Institutes of Health (P01 DC00422). Nancy Smythe assisted in preparation of the final document.

17

TINNITUS AND HYPERACUSIS

Pawel J. Jastreboff, PhD, ScD
Margaret M. Jastreboff, PhD

There is no precise, short, and distinctive definition of tinnitus. A patient experience–oriented definition describes tinnitus as ringing, buzzing, the sound of escaping steam, hissing, humming, cricket-like, or a noise in the ears. Tinnitus as "a phantom auditory perception" represents a physiologic definition of tinnitus, pointing out a lack of a physical acoustic stimulus related to tinnitus. There is also the definition proposed by the Committee on Hearing, Bioacoustics and Biomechanics of the US National Research Council, which describes tinnitus as "a conscious experience of sound that originates in the head of its owner."

Six to 17% of the general population experience tinnitus lasting for a period of at least 5 minutes. About 3 to 7% of people seek help for their tinnitus, and 0.5 to 2.5% report severe effects of tinnitus in their lives. People of all ages experience tinnitus, including children, and the prevalence of tinnitus increases significantly with aging. Hearing loss and noise exposure have been correlated with increased prevalence of tinnitus as well. There is no clear effect of gender. Neither smoking, coffee, nor alcohol has been shown to increase the prevalence of tinnitus directly.

The mechanisms of tinnitus generation involve structures of the auditory system (periphery, central auditory pathways) and the central nervous system. Proposed mechanisms responsible for the emergence of tinnitus-related neuronal activity include abnormal coupling between neurons, local decrease of spontaneous activity enhanced by lateral inhibition, discordant damage/dysfunction of outer and inner hair cells, unbalanced activation of type I and type II auditory nerve fibers, abnormal neurotransmitter release from inner hair cells, decreased activity of the efferent system, mechanical displacement within the organ of Corti, abnormalities in transduction processes, various aspects of calcium function, physical/biochemical stress on the auditory nerve, and enhanced sensitivity of the auditory pathways after decreased auditory input.

Tinnitus may be part of more complex medical conditions, such as conductive hearing loss (otitis media, cerumen impaction, ossicular stiffness/discontinuity, otosclerosis), sensorineural hearing loss (Meniere's disease, presbyacusis, cochlear otosclerosis, vestibular schwannoma, sudden hearing loss), and hormonal changes (pregnancy, menopause, thyroid dysfunction). Tinnitus can be induced by some medications or withdrawal from them.

Somatosounds (sometimes considered as objective tinnitus) are the sounds produced by structures adjacent to the ear (neoplasm, arterial, venous, myoclonus), structures in the ear (eg, spontaneous otoacoustic emissions), or joint abnormalities (temporomandibular joint disorders).

We do not have an objective method to detect and measure tinnitus. Therefore, interview, psychoacoustic characterization (perceptual location, pitch, loudness, maskability, postmasking effects), and physiologic evaluation (otoacoustic emissions, efferent mediated suppression of otoacoustic emissions, spontaneous auditory nerve activity, auditory brainstem responses, late cortical potentials, positron emission tomography, single-photon emission computed tomography, functional magnetic resonance imaging, magnetoencephalography) are typical approaches in clinical practice.

Tinnitus is a symptom that can cause significant emotional and somatic distress and significantly influence patients' quality of life, particularly if allowed to become a chronic problem. The list of reported complaints is long and includes emotional problems such as irritation, annoyance, anxiety, and depression; hearing problems such as difficulty with speech comprehension; and somatic problems such as headache, neck pain, and jaw pain. Tinnitus can be very intrusive and may cause difficulty with sleep and concentration and a decreased ability to participate in everyday activities and social events; it may also create problems in relationships. A detailed interview, aimed at characterizing the specifics and degree of tinnitus impact on patients, coupled with otolaryngologic evaluation, provides the most thorough assessment and allows the practitioner to address all of the issues that need to be considered, including the potential intervention of a psychologist/psychiatrist to accompany the commencement of specific tinnitus-oriented treatment.

Tinnitus is frequently accompanied by decreased sound tolerance (oversensitivity to sound), which, in many cases, is a sum of hyperacusis and misophobia. Approximately 40% of tinnitus patients exhibit decreased sound tolerance. There is no generally accepted definition for decreased sound tolerance to suprathreshold sounds. According to *Stedman's Medical Dictionary*, hyperacusis is defined as "Abnormal acuteness of hearing due to increased irritability of the sensory neural mechanism." Based on neurophysiology, hyperacusis can be defined as abnormally strong reactions to sound occurring within the auditory pathways. At the behavioral level, it is manifested by a subject experiencing physical discomfort as a result of exposure to moderate/weak sound, which would not evoke such a reaction in the average population. Misophonia can be defined as abnormally strong responses to sound of the autonomic and limbic systems without abnormally high activation of the auditory system, resulting from enhanced connections between the auditory and limbic systems. At the behavioral level, patients are afraid (phobic reaction) or have a negative attitude to sound (misophonia). Hyperacusis can lead people to avoid louder environments and therefore preclude them from working and interacting socially. In extreme cases of decreased sound tolerance, patients' lives are totally controlled by the problem. It is inevitable in all cases with significant hyperacusis that misophonia and/or phonophobia will be present and further enhance the effects of hyperacusis.

Hyperacusis has been linked to a number of medical conditions, such as tinnitus, Bell's palsy, Lyme disease, Williams syndrome, Ramsay Hunt syndrome, poststapedectomy, perilymph fistula, head injury, migraine, medications, withdrawal from benzodiazepines, high pressure of the cerebrospinal fluid, Addison's disease, and hyperthyroidism. The etiology of hyperacusis includes sound exposure, head injury, stress, and medications.

The mechanisms of hyperacusis are unproven. At the peripheral level, it is possible to speculate that the abnormal enhancement of vibratory signals within the cochlea by the outer hair cells might result in overstimulation of the inner hair cells and subsequently results in hyperacusis. Damage to the cochlea or a decrease in auditory input results in a decrease in the threshold of response in about 25% of neurons in the ventral cochlear nucleus and inferior colliculus, and studies with evoked potentials indicated an abnormal increase in the gain in the auditory pathways after such manipulations. Some of the medical conditions can be linked to the central processing of signals and modification of the level of neuromodulators as possible factors inducing or enhancing hyperacusis. Evaluation of loudness discomfort levels provides a good estimation of hyperacusis and misophonia.

The most common treatments for tinnitus include the following:

- *Antireassurance*. Telling tinnitus patients that "Nothing can be done; go home and learn to live with it" enhances patients' feeling of hopelessness.
- *Pharmacology*. All studied drugs for tinnitus (such as lidocaine, tocainide, diazepam, alprazolam, nortriptyline, carbamazepine, clonazepam, baclofen, niacin, nimodipine, betahistine, caroverine, furosemide, and ginkgo biloba) have failed to prove their efficacy in a significant proportion of patients. Still, various local anesthetics, sedatives, antidepressants, anticonvulsants, vasodilators, calcium channel blockers, and other drugs are frequently prescribed. Lidocaine administered intravenously is the only substance proven to abolish subjective tinnitus for a short period of time, but there is no practical way to use this drug in clinical practice.
- *Surgery*. Surgery can offer help for some patients with somatosounds, conductive hearing loss, and Meniere's disease. Neither transection nor microvascular decompression of the auditory nerve, promoted in the past, has proven to be effective.
- *Electric suppression*. Electrical suppression of tinnitus has been tried since 1855, with mixed results. Only intracochlear (or with electrode on the promontory) stimulation has shown consistent and positive results in approximately 50% of cases. Other approaches were less effective. Two new variants of electrical stimulation for tinnitus have been introduced recently: deep brain stimulation and high-frequency electrical stimulation of the cochlea performed by placing an electrode on the promontory or via cochlear implant. Both approaches are at a very initial stage of investigation.
- *Masking*. Masking includes the use of an external sound to cover tinnitus and bring immediate relief to some patients. In practice, the approach did not withstand the test of time.

- *Psychological approaches.* Psychological management of chronic tinnitus, such as cognitive therapies, behavioral modifications, coping strategies, and minimizing distress protocols, can be helpful for some patients. They are improving patients' well-being and minimizing tinnitus-caused emotional discomfort.

Treatments of hyperacusis include advising patients to avoid sound (use ear protection) or the desensitization of patients by exposure to a variety of sounds. The first approach actually makes the auditory system even more sensitive and further exacerbates hyperacusis. The desensitization approach includes the recommendation of using sound with certain frequencies removed or short exposures to moderately loud sound. The newest approach to tinnitus and hyperacusis involves continuous, prolonged exposure to a gradually increased level of sound.

Presented during the last decade, the neurophysiologic model of tinnitus and hyperacusis offers the basis for a new approach, known as tinnitus retraining therapy (TRT), to help patients with tinnitus, hyperacusis, and somatosounds. Several observations led to this model. It is known that tinnitus induces distress in only about 25% of those who perceive it. There is no correlation among the psychoacoustic characterization of tinnitus, tinnitus-induced distress, and treatment outcome. The experiment by Heller and Bergman showed that the perception of tinnitus cannot be pathologic since essentially everyone (tinnitus emerged in 94% of people without prior tinnitus when isolated for several minutes in an anechoic chamber) experiences it when put in a sufficiently quiet environment. These observations strongly argue that the auditory system plays a secondary role and other systems in the brain are dominant in clinically relevant tinnitus (ie, tinnitus that creates discomfort and annoyance and requires intervention).

Analysis of the problems reported by tinnitus patients, who exhibit a strong emotional reaction to its presence, a high level of anxiety, and psychosomatic problems, indicates that the limbic and autonomic nervous systems are crucial in individuals with clinically relevant tinnitus. Sustained activation of the limbic and autonomic nervous systems is essential in creating distress and therefore clinically relevant tinnitus.

Tinnitus-related neuronal activity is processed by different parts of the central nervous system and involves the conscious and subconscious processing loops working in a dynamic balance scenario. A continuous presence of tinnitus, combined with attention given to it, results in plastic modifications of synaptic connections, yielding the modification of receptive fields corresponding to the tinnitus signal and its subsequent enhancement.

Although the initial signal provided by the auditory system is needed to start the cascade of events, its strength is irrelevant as the extent of activation of the limbic and autonomic nervous systems depends on the strength of negative associations linked to tinnitus and the susceptibility of the feedback loops to further modifications. It appears that tinnitus-related neuronal activity may result from compensatory processes that occur within the cochlea and the auditory pathways to minor dysfunction at the periphery.

The neurophysiologic model includes several systems of the brain involved in analysis of clinically relevant tinnitus. All levels of the auditory pathways, starting from the cochlea through the subcortical centers and ending at the auditory cortex, are essential in creating the perception of tinnitus. When subjects are not bothered or annoyed by tinnitus, auditory pathways are the only pathways involved, and tinnitus-related neuronal activity is constrained within the auditory system. Therefore, although subjects are perceiving tinnitus, they are not disturbed by it.

In approximately 25% of those with tinnitus, strong negative emotions are induced, which, in turn, evoke a variety of physiologic defense mechanisms of the brain, mediated by the limbic and autonomic nervous systems. Improper activation of these systems by tinnitus-related neuronal activity results, at the behavioral level, in the problems described by tinnitus patients. Activation of both systems can be achieved through two routes. The first includes stimulation of the autonomic and limbic systems from higher level cortical areas, which are involved in our awareness, verbalization, and beliefs. The second arises from the subconscious level and provides stimulation from the lower auditory centers. The activation going through these two routes changes the strength of synaptic connections, enhancing the stimulation of the limbic and autonomic nervous systems by the tinnitus-related neuronal activity during the process when tinnitus becomes a clinical problem.

The question of how the neutral signal of tinnitus can evoke persistent strong distress can be explained by the principles of conditioned reflexes linking sensory information with reactions. To create a conditioned reflex, the temporal coincidence of sensory stimuli with negative (or positive) reinforcement is sufficient. These types of associations of sensory stimuli are constantly created in normal life. As long as the sensory stimulus is limited in time and there is no functional link between stimulus and reinforcement, this conditioned reaction will gradually disappear (habituate) owing to passive extinction of the reflex. There are two different types of habituation: habituation of reaction and habituation of perception. Habituation is a crucial characteristic of brain function necessitated by the brain's inability to perform two tasks requiring complete attention simultaneously.

The central nervous system screens and categorizes all stimuli at the subconscious level. If the stimulus is new and unknown, it is passed to a higher cortical level, where it is perceived and evaluated. However, in the case of a stimulus to which we have previously been exposed, the stimulus is compared with patterns stored in memory. If the stimulus was classified as nonimportant and does not require action, it is blocked at the subconscious level of the auditory pathways and does not produce any reactions or reach the level of awareness. The reaction to this stimulus and its perception is habituated. In everyday life, habituation occurs to the majority of sensory stimuli surrounding us.

However, if a specific stimulus was once classified as important and, on the basis of comparison with the patterns stored in memory, was linked to something unpleasant or dangerous, this stimulus is perceived and attracts attention. Furthermore, the sympathetic part of the autonomic nervous system is activated, inducing reaction that further reinforces memory patterns associated with this stimulus.

In the case of tinnitus, it is impossible to remove the reactions induced by the excitation of the sympathetic autonomic nervous system or even change them in a substantial manner. The solution to achieve the passive extinction of conditioned reflex, in which both stimulus (tinnitus) and negative reinforcement are continuously present, is to decrease the magnitude of this negative reinforcement over a period of time. Once activation of the autonomic nervous system is lowered, this decreases negative reinforcement to a signal that is continuously present, gradually decreases the strength of the conditioned reflex, and further decreases the reaction. Once tinnitus has achieved a neutral status, its habituation is inevitable.

Tinnitus retraining therapy is a clinical implementation of the neurophysiologic model of tinnitus. It consists of counseling and sound therapy. Retraining counseling (teaching session) in TRT is oriented toward removal of the patient's negative associations with tinnitus and reclassification of tinnitus into a category of neutral stimuli. By activating a naturally occurring mechanism of brain function, habituation, and the plasticity underlying it, it is possible to achieve over time primarily habituation of the tinnitus-induced reaction of the brain and the body and secondarily habituation of the tinnitus perception. The clear goal of achieving an active and selective block of tinnitus-induced reactions is set for the patients.

In addition to decreasing the strength of the activation of the limbic and autonomic nervous systems, initiated during the counseling session, the second component of TRT is sound therapy. By increasing background neuronal activity, we can effectively decrease the strength of the tinnitus signal, which activates the limbic and autonomic nervous systems; achieve a decrease of reactions induced by tinnitus; and, through this, facilitate extinction of the conditioned reflex.

Five principles influence relationships between the physical intensity of sound and its effectiveness on tinnitus habituation: (1) stochastic resonance (enhancement of the signal by adding low-level noise); (2) dependence of the signal's strength on its contrast with the background; (3) total suppression of the signal, preventing any retraining and consequently habituation; (4) partial suppression ("partial masking"), which does not prevent retraining but does make it more difficult as the training is performed on a different stimulus than the original; and (5) activation of limbic and autonomic nervous systems by too loud or unpleasant sounds, yielding an increase in tinnitus and contracting habituation.

In most tinnitus patients, the sound level used should blend/mix with the tinnitus signal, but both sounds should still be clearly identifiable (below the level of partial suppression or "partial masking"). By decreasing the difference between the tinnitus-related neuronal activity and the background ongoing neuronal activity, the apparent strength of the tinnitus signal decreases, and this weaker signal is passed to the higher level cortical areas and, most importantly, to the limbic and autonomic nervous systems. This helps in initiating and sustaining the process of passive extinction of conditioned reflexes that link tinnitus to negative reactions.

Enriched sound background is provided by a number of means. Sound generators are frequently used to provide patients with stable, low-level, broad-band noise. The optimal setting of the sound level is different when hyperacusis is the dominant or only problem. Patients start with a sound level, disregarding the effect of stochastic resonance, closer to their threshold but as high as their sound sensitivity allows without inducing annoyance.

In the normal acoustic environment, there is a high proportion of low-frequency sounds, below 200 Hz, which provide constant stimulation of the auditory pathways. This yields a strong recommendation for people who have relatively normal low-frequency hearing to be provided with sound generators or hearing aids with fittings as open as possible to preserve stimulation in the low-frequency range. Blocking the ear canal with closed ear molds decreases the auditory input, and many patients experience enhancement of tinnitus when their ears are occluded. Hearing aids for tinnitus patients are used primarily as a part of sound therapy to provide extra amplification of background sounds and only secondarily for communicative purposes. To enrich the auditory background, nature sounds, neutral music, or tabletop sound generators may be used.

Typically, patients in the TRT protocol may see improvement in about 3 months, with clear changes in about 6 months. Many patients achieve a high level of control of their tinnitus by about 12 months. Improvement in hyperacusis is typically faster and the success rate higher than that of tinnitus without hyperacusis. The results from other centers and ours using TRT show satisfactory results in over 80% of patients.

In conclusion, tinnitus and hyperacusis are still challenging topics to study and symptoms to treat. Many questions remain unanswered. The mechanisms of tinnitus and hyperacusis are speculative and not proven yet. We do not have objective methods for detection and evaluation of tinnitus. We believe that the neurophysiologic model of tinnitus and TRT provide a promising approach that may ultimately result in a better understanding of tinnitus and in providing greater help to patients with tinnitus and hyperacusis.

18

COCHLEAR IMPLANTS

Richard T. Miyamoto, MD
Karen Iler Kirk, PhD

Hearing loss poses a monumental obstacle to the acquisition and maintenance of effective communication skills. The perception as well as the production of speech is highly dependent on the ability to process auditory information. Early identification of hearing loss is an important first step in managing the effects of hearing impairment. Once identified, the level of residual hearing, if any, must be determined and an appropriate sensory aid recommended. Conventional amplification is usually the initial procedure of choice. If little or no benefit is realized with hearing aids, cochlear implants become therapeutic options. Communication skills and needs must be assessed and a communication mode selected. A sophisticated multidisciplinary team approach that addresses the varied needs of the deaf recipient is required. Essential components of the aural/oral (re)habilitation program include listening skill development, speech therapy, speech-reading training, and language instruction.

Cochlear implants seek to replace a nonfunctional inner ear hair cell transducer system by converting mechanical sound energy into electrical signals that can be delivered to the cochlear nerve in profoundly deaf patients. The essential components of a cochlear implant system are a microphone, which picks up acoustic information and converts it to electrical signals; an externally worn speech processor that processes the signal according to a predefined strategy; and a surgically implanted electrode array that is in the cochlea near the auditory nerve. Transmission of the electrical signal across the skin from the external unit to the implanted electrode array is most commonly accomplished by the use of electromagnetic induction. The critical residual neural elements stimulated appear to be the spiral ganglion cells or axons. Damaged or missing hair cells of the cochlea are bypassed.

COCHLEAR IMPLANT SYSTEMS

Multichannel, multielectrode cochlear implant systems are designed to take advantage of the tonotopic organization of the cochlea. The incoming speech signal is filtered into a number of frequency bands, each corresponding to a given electrode in the array. Thus, multichannel cochlear implant systems use place coding to transfer spectral information in the speech signal as well as encode the durational and intensity cues of speech.

Nucleus Cochlear Implant Systems

The Nucleus 22-channel cochlear implant manufactured by Cochlear Ltd. of Australia was the first multichannel cochlear implant to receive US Food and Drug Administration (FDA) approval for use in adults and children, and it has been used in more patients than any other cochlear implant system worldwide. The Nucleus CI24M cochlear implant received FDA approval for adults and children in 1998.

Three processing strategies are currently available for use with the Nucleus cochlear implants. Two of the strategies use the *n-of-m* approach, in which the speech signal is filtered into *m* bandpass channels and the *n* highest envelope signals are selected for each cycle of stimulation. The spectral peak, or SPEAK, strategy is the most widely used with the Nucleus 22-channel cochlear implant and is available to users of either the Nucleus 22-channel or the Nucleus CI24M system. This strategy filters the incoming speech signal into 20 frequency bands; on each stimulation cycle, an average of six electrodes is stimulated at a rate that varies adaptively from 180 to 300 pulses per second. An *n-of-m* strategy using much higher rates of stimulation, known as advanced combined encoder (ACE) strategy, can be implemented in the new Nucleus CI24M device. The third processing strategy available with the Nucleus CI24M system is the continuous interleaved sampling (CIS) strategy. The CIS strategy filters the speech signal into a fixed number of bands, obtains the speech envelope, and then compresses the signal for each channel. On each cycle of stimulation, a series of interleaved digital pulses rapidly stimulates consecutive electrodes in the array. The CIS strategy is designed to preserve fine temporal details in the speech signal by using high-rate, pulsatile stimuli.

Clarion Cochlear Implant System

The Clarion multichannel cochlear implant system is manufactured by the Advanced Bionics Corporation. This device has been approved by the FDA for use in adults (1996) and children (1997). The Clarion multichannel cochlear implant has an eight-channel electrode array. Two processing strategies can be implemented through a body-worn processor. The first is CIS, described above, which is used to stimulate monopolar electrodes. The second strategy, simultaneous analog stimulation (SAS), filters and then compresses the incoming speech signal for simultaneous presentation to the corresponding enhanced bipolar electrodes. The relative amplitudes of information in each channel and the temporal details of the waveforms in each channel convey speech information.

Medical Electronic (Med-El) Cochlear Implant System

The Combi 40+ cochlear implant system manufactured by the Med-El Corporation in Innsbruck, Austria, is currently undergoing clinical trials in the United States. The Med-El cochlear implant has 12 electrode pairs and has the capability of deep electrode insertion into the apical regions of the cochlea. This device uses the CIS processing strategy and has the capacity to provide the most rapid stimulation rate of any of the cochlear implant systems currently available. Both body-worn and ear-level speech processors (the CIS Pro+ and Tempo+, respectively) are available for the Med-El cochlear implant.

PATIENT SELECTION

The selection of cochlear implant candidates is a complex process that requires careful consideration of many factors. Current selection considerations are as follows:

Adults

Cochlear implantation was initially limited to postlingually deafened adults who received no benefit from hearing aids and had no possibility of worsening residual hearing. This population, particularly those with a recent onset of deafness, has been the most readily identifiable beneficiary of cochlear implants. A period of auditory experience adequate to develop normal speech perception, speech production, and language skills before the onset of deafness is an invaluable prerequisite. Experience gained with this initial cochlear implant population served to establish expected performance limits.

Adult candidacy criteria are based primarily on aided speech recognition abilities. No upper age limit is used in the selection process as long as the patient's health will permit an elective surgical procedure under general anesthesia. Elderly cochlear implant patients obtain benefits that are similar to those obtained by younger adult patients with the same device.

Adult candidacy criteria recently have been broadened to include adults with severe-to-profound hearing loss who derive some limited benefit from conventional hearing aids (sentence recognition scores < 40 to 50% correct in the best aided condition). Implantation of an ear with any residual, aidable hearing carries the risk that the implanted ear could be made worse than that ear with a hearing aid. Current investigations are testing the hypotheses that an ear with some residual hearing may have a better neuronal population, increasing the likelihood of superior performance with a cochlear implant, especially with more complex multi-channel stimulation.

Adults with prelingual hearing loss are generally not considered good candidates for cochlear implantation. However, prelinguistically deafened adults who have followed an aural/oral educational approach may receive significant benefit.

Children

Cochlear implant technology complicates the already challenging management of the deaf child. The general selection guidelines applied to adults are applicable to children; however, the selection of pediatric cochlear implant candidates is a far more complex and ever-evolving process that requires careful consideration of many factors. In contrast to adults, both pre- and postlingually deafened children are candidates for cochlear implantation.

A trend toward earlier cochlear implantation in children has emerged in an attempt to ameliorate the devastating effects of early auditory deprivation. Electrical stimulation appears to be capable of preventing at least some of the degenerative changes in the central auditory pathways.

Implanting very young children remains controversial because the audiologic assessment, surgical intervention, and postimplant management in this population are challenging. Profound deafness must be substantiated and the inability to benefit from conventional hearing aids demonstrated. This can be difficult to determine in young children with limited language abilities. For very young children, parental questionnaires are commonly used to assess amplification benefit.

Until recently, the youngest age at which children could be implanted under FDA clinical trials was 2 years. In 1998, the age limit was dropped to 18 months, and the most recently initiated clinical trials of new cochlear implant systems permit implantation of children as young as 12 months of age. Because the development of speech perception, speech production, and language competence normally begins at a very early age, implantation in very young congenitally or neonatally deafened children may have substantial advantages. Early implantation may be particularly important when the etiology of deafness is meningitis as progressive intracochlear ossification can occur and preclude standard electrode insertion. A relatively short window of time exists during which this advancing process can be circumvented.

AUDIOLOGIC ASSESSMENT

The audiologic evaluation is the primary means of determining suitability for cochlear implantation. Audiologic evaluations should be conducted in both an unaided condition and with appropriately fit conventional amplification. Thus, all potential candidates must have completed a period of experience with a properly fit hearing aid, preferably coupled with training in an appropriate aural re(habilitation) program. The audiologic evaluation includes measurement of pure-tone thresholds along with word and sentence recognition testing. Aided speech recognition scores are the primary audiologic determinant of cochlear implant candidacy. For very young children or those with limited language abilities, parent questionnaires are used to determine hearing aid benefit.

word and sentence recognition scores of 36 and 74%, respectively, for adults with the SPEAK strategy. Similar performance levels have been reported for adults who use either the Clarion or the Med-El cochlear implant system. Compared with the results obtained with previous generations of cochlear implants, adults who use the current devices achieve higher word recognition skills and acquire those skills at a faster rate. As Wilson and his colleagues pointed out, a number of within-subject factors also contribute to successful cochlear implant use. Two such factors are age at implantation and duration of deafness. Specifically, patients who are implanted at a young age and have a shorter period of auditory deprivation are more likely to achieve good outcomes. The findings regarding other predictive factors have been less conclusive. For example, Gantz and colleagues found that measures of cognitive ability were not associated with patient performance, whereas Cohen and colleagues reported that measures of IQ were significantly associated with good speech perception skills. Other factors that have been found to correlate significantly with adult outcomes include speech-reading ability and degree of residual hearing.

Performance Results in Children

Postlingually deafened adults and children use the information transmitted by a cochlear implant to make comparisons to previously stored representations of spoken language. However the majority of children who receive cochlear implants h congenital or prelingually acquired hearing loss. Thes dren must use the sound provided by a cochlear in acquire speech perception, speech production, and s guage skills. Furthermore, because young child ited linguistic skills and attention spans, the performance in this population can be quit evaluate the communication benefits of c in children effectively, a battery of tests tally and linguistically appropriate should b

Speech Perception Outcomes

In early investigations, children who used the Nucleus cochlear implant with a feature extraction strategy demonstrated significant improvement in closed-set word identification (ie, the ability to identify words from a limited set of alternatives) but very limited open-set word recognition. The introduction of newer processing strategies yielded greater speech perception benefits in children, just as in adults. Many children with current cochlear implant devices achieve at least moderate levels of open-set word recognition. For example, Cohen and colleagues reported word recognition scores for a group of 19 children that ranged from 4 to 76% words correct, with a mean of 44%. Similarly, Zwolan and colleagues reported average scores of approximately 30% correct on a more difficult measure of isolated word recognition in children. The development rate of postimplant auditory skills seems to be increasing as cochlear implant technology improves and as children are implanted at a younger age. Furthermore, comparison studies have shown that the speech perception abilities of pediatric cochlear implant recipients meet or exceed those of their peers with unaided pure-tone average thresholds $\geq$ 90 dB hearing loss (HL) who use hearing aids.

A number of demographic factors have been shown to influence performance results in children with cochlear implants. Early results suggested better speech perception performance in children deafened at an older age with a corresponding shorter period of deafness. However, when only children with prelingual deafness (ie, < 3 years) were considered, age at onset of hearing loss was no longer a significant factor. It is evident that earlier implantation yields superior cochlear implant performance in children. Finally, variables of communication mode and/or unaided residual hearing also influence speech perception performance. children, and those who have more residual hearing prior to implantation, typically demonstrate superior speech understanding.

Speech Intelligibility and Language

Improvements in speech perception are the most direct benefit of cochlear implantation. However, if children with cochlear implants are to succeed in the hearing world, they must also acquire intelligible speech and their surrounding linguistic system. The speech intelligibility and language abilities of children with cochlear implants improve significantly over time. Although a great deal of variability exists, the best pediatric cochlear implant users demonstrate highly intelligible speech and age-appropriate language skills. These superior performers are usually implanted at a young age and are educated in an oral/aural modality.

19

FACIAL PARALYSIS

Phillip A. Wackym, MD
John S. Rhee, MD

FACIAL NERVE ABNORMALITIES

Congenital

Möbius' Syndrome (Congenital Facial Diplegia)

Möbius' syndrome is a rare congenital disorder, which usually includes bilateral seventh nerve paralysis and unilateral or bilateral sixth nerve paralysis. It is considered to have an autosomal dominant inheritance pattern with variable expressivity. The etiology of Möbius' syndrome is unclear. The clinical observation of congenital extraocular muscle paralysis and facial paralysis is the typical presentation of this disorder.

Hemifacial Microsomia

The term hemifacial microsomia refers to patients with unilateral microtia, macrostomia, and mandibular hypoplasia. Goldenhar's syndrome (oculoauriculovertebral dysplasia) is considered to be a variant of this complex and is characterized by vertebral anomalies and epibulbar dermoids. Approximately 25% of patients with hemifacial microsomia have facial nerve weakness.

Osteopetrosis

Osteopetrosis is a generalized dysplasia of bone, which may have an autosomal dominant or recessive inheritance pattern.

Optic atrophy, facial paralysis, sensorineural hearing loss, and mental retardation are common in the recessive form, and death usually occurs by the second decade. The dominant form causes progressive enlargement of the cranium and mandible and clubbing of the long bones.

Acquired

Trauma

Approximately 90% of all congenital peripheral facial nerve paralysis improve spontaneously, and most can be attributed to difficult deliveries, cephalopelvic disproportion, high forceps delivery, or intrauterine trauma. These types of congenital facial paralysis are often unilateral and partial, especially involving the lower division of the facial nerve.

Blunt trauma resulting in temporal bone fracture is best evaluated with high-resolution temporal bone computed tomographic (CT) scans. Longitudinal fractures are the most common type (approximately 90%) and are also the most common type of fracture associated with facial nerve injury. The geniculate ganglion region of the facial nerve is most frequently injured.

Frontal and particularly occipital blows to the head tend to result in transverse fractures of the temporal bone. Since they often extend through the internal auditory canal or across the otic capsule, hearing loss and vertigo commonly result. Although only 10 to 20% of temporal bone fractures are transverse in orientation, they cause facial nerve injury in approximately 50% of patients. The anatomic region of the facial nerve most commonly injured is the labyrinthine segment.

Penetrating injuries to the extratemporal facial nerve should be explored urgently to facilitate identification of the transected distal branches using a facial nerve stimulator. If primary repair is not possible, the principles of facial nerve repair using cable grafts should be followed. In infected wounds, urgent exploration and tagging of identified distal branches should precede control of the infection and granulation. Subsequent repair usually requires the use of cable grafts.

Facial nerve injury may occur with otologic surgery. The risk of injury of the facial nerve is particularly high in children with congenital ear malformations. Additional groups at higher risk for injury to the facial nerve include infants who are undergoing mastoid surgery.

Infection

Bacterial Facial paralysis as a complication of otitis media has become rare in children owing to ready access to medical care and antibiotics. Temporal bone CT should be performed in all patients to eliminate the diagnosis of coalescent mastoiditis. Intravenous antibiotics in combination with myringotomy and tympanostomy tube placement remain the initial management algorithm for bacterial acute otitis media complicated by facial paralysis.

Facial paralysis complicating mastoiditis or cholesteatoma is also rare. The surgical management of these patients includes mastoidectomy, excision of the cholesteatoma, and appropriate antibiotic therapy.

Infection with the spirochete *Borrelia burgdorferi* (Lyme disease) can result in facial paralysis. As is the case with other spirochete infections, the clinical manifestations of this tick-borne infection are protean. Serologic diagnosis should be followed by antibiotic therapy. Tetracycline is considered to be the agent of choice; however, erythromycin and penicillin have been successfully used.

Viral Herpes zoster oticus (Ramsay Hunt syndrome) is the cause of 2 to 10% of facial paralysis, including 3 to 12% in adults and approximately 5% in children. The recrudescence of herpes varicella-zoster virus in the geniculate ganglion is postulated as the etiology for this syndrome. Patients may experience paresis or complete paralysis, with the poorest prognosis for recovery in the latter group. The most common site of vesicular eruption is in the concha of the auricle, followed by the posteromesial surface of the auricle, the mucosa on the palate, and the anterior two-thirds of the tongue.

Antiviral agents such as valacyclovir (Valtrex) (1 g orally three times a day for 10 to 14 days) or famciclovir (Famvir) (500 mg orally three times a day for 10 days), which achieve adequate levels by an oral route, are now available as an alternative to intravenous acyclovir (Zovirax) for the treatment of patients with Ramsay Hunt syndrome. Likewise, oral corticosteroids have been advocated for patients with Ramsay Hunt syndrome.

Bell's palsy is responsible for 60 to 75% of all cases of facial paralysis. In the past, Bell's palsy was defined as an "idiopathic facial paralysis" or as a mononeuropathy of undetermined origin. Recent observations have linked the cause to latent herpes simplex virus 1 in the geniculate ganglion.

Bell's palsy is an acute, unilateral paresis or paralysis of the facial nerve in a pattern consistent with peripheral nerve dysfunction. The onset and evolution are typically rapid, less than 48 hours, and the onset of paralysis may be preceded by a viral prodrome. The symptoms during the early phase of facial paralysis include facial numbness, epiphora, pain, dysgeusia, hyperacusis (dysacusis), and decreased tearing. The pain is usually retroauricular and sometimes radiates to the face, pharynx, or shoulder. Physical findings of this subtle polyneuritis include hypoesthesia or dysesthesia of the fifth and ninth cranial nerves and of the second cervical nerve. Motor paralysis of branches of the tenth cranial nerve is seen as a unilateral shift of the palate or vocal cord paresis/paralysis. Recurrence of Bell's palsy occurs in 7.1 to 12% of patients.

A 10-day course of oral antiviral medication along with prednisone is recommended for treatment. Criteria for surgical decompression include electroneuronography (ENoG) degeneration greater than 90% relative to the unaffected side, no voluntary facial electromyographic (EMG) activity on the affected side, and the operation within 14 days of onset. Decompression is limited to the meatal and labyrinthine segment through a middle cranial fossa approach.

Other viral infections such as primary chickenpox, mononucleosis, mumps, and poliomyelitis can result in facial paralysis that may or may not resolve spontaneously. For these specific viral infections, immunization, when available, is the most effective preventive measure, and supportive care is required during the active infection.

Benign or Malignant Neoplasms

Tumor involvement of the facial nerve should be considered in facial paralysis if one or more of the following clinical features are present: facial paralysis that progresses slowly over 3 weeks, recurrent ipsilateral facial paralysis, facial weakness associated with muscle twitching, long-standing facial paralysis (greater than 6 months), facial paralysis associated with other cranial nerve deficits, or evidence of malignancy elsewhere in the body.

Several benign and malignant tumors can involve the facial nerve along its intracranial, intratemporal, or extracranial course. Schwannoma is the most common primary tumor of the facial nerve. It is benign and usually involves the labyrinthine, tympanic, and mastoid segments of the facial nerve. Nerve resection and interpositional nerve grafting may initially be necessary for restoration of continuity; however, decompression will often give patients many years of facial nerve function before resection and grafting must be completed.

Tumors may arise in the vicinity of the facial nerve and cause facial weakness either by compression or direct invasion. When the tumor is benign, the continuity of the facial nerve should be preserved at all costs by sharp dissection and mobilization techniques. A malignant process with direct invasion of the nerve usually mandates resection of the involved portion of the nerve with immediate interpositional nerve grafting.

Hemifacial Spasm

Hemifacial spasm is typically a disorder of the fourth and fifth decades of life and occurs twice as often in women as it does in men. Electrophysiologic and surgical observations indicate that the facial nerve hyperactivity in hemifacial spasm is caused by a vascular compression of the facial nerve. Microvascular decompression operations involve separating the compressive vessel from its point of contact with the cranial nerve root entry or exit zone and interposition of a prosthesis (usually Teflon felt) to prevent further nerve compression. The absence of a clear site of arterial compression has been associated with high recurrence rates.

Miscellaneous Disorders

The onset of simultaneous bilateral facial paralysis suggests Guillain-Barré syndrome, sarcoidosis, sickle cell disease, or some other systemic disorder. Guillain-Barré syndrome is a relatively common neurologic disorder and is an acute inflammatory polyradiculoneuropathy that progresses to varying degrees of paralysis. The etiology remains unknown; however, autoimmune or viral mechanisms have been considered. The facial paralysis is typically bilateral and often resolves spontaneously after a prolonged course of paralysis.

Melkersson-Rosenthal Syndrome Melkersson-Rosenthal syndrome is a neuromucocutaneous disease with a classic triad of recurrent facial (labial) edema and recurrent facial paralysis associated with a fissured tongue. The underlying etiologic factor has been thought to be a neurotropic edema causing compression and paralysis of the facial nerve as it passes through the fallopian canal. Recurrent paralysis over a prolonged period of time usually results in increasing residual dysfunction. If evidence of residual paresis exists, facial nerve decompression of the labyrinthine segment and geniculate ganglion through a middle cranial fossa exposure is recommended at the time of the next episode of paralysis.

NEURODIAGNOSTIC TESTS

Electroneuronography and Electromyography

Electroneuronography uses supramaximal electrical stimulation of the facial nerve at the level of the stylomastoid foramen to produce a compound muscle action potential. This evoked electromyogenic response is recorded with surface electrodes placed over the perioral (nasolabial) muscles. Both the normal and affected sides are tested and the amplitude of the responses are compared. The percentage of degenerated fibers is calculated arithmetically. Electroneuronography can be used to differentiate nerve fibers that have minor conduction blocks (neurapraxia) from those that have undergone wallerian degeneration; however, ENoG cannot differentiate the type of wallerian degeneration (axonotmesis versus neurotmesis). The severity of the injury can be inferred from the rate of degeneration after injury.

The timing for performing ENoG should take into consideration the time course of wallerian degeneration. With a known complete transection of the facial nerve (eg, traumatic injury), 100% wallerian degeneration occurs over 3 to 5 days as the distal axon slowly degenerates. Therefore, early testing, within 3 days of paralysis, may not be representative of the degree of injury.

Electromyography

Facial EMG is important to use as an adjunctive tool when making decisions regarding surgery. Electromyography is the more useful single diagnostic study after 3 weeks of facial paralysis and is also important when deciding whether to perform nerve substitution procedures and other reanimation procedures.

FACIAL NERVE SURGERY

Middle Cranial Fossa (Transtemporal) Approach for Decompression from the Porus of the Internal Auditory Canal to the Tympanic Segment

The middle cranial fossa exposure is used to expose the internal auditory canal (IAC) and labyrinthine segments of the facial nerve when preserving existing auditory function is desirable. The geniculate ganglion and tympanic portions of the nerve can also be decompressed from this approach. The middle cranial fossa route is the only method that can be used to expose the entire IAC and labyrinthine segment with preservation of hearing. This, in combination with the retrolabyrinthine and transmastoid approaches, enables visualization of the entire course of the facial nerve and still preserves the function of the inner ear. The middle cranial fossa technique is the most commonly used for decompression of the facial nerve in Bell's palsy and longitudinal temporal bone fractures.

NERVE REPAIR

Whenever the continuity of the facial nerve has been disrupted by trauma, iatrogenic injury, or tumor invasion, every effort should be made to restore its continuity. In some instances, an end-to-end reapproximation can be accomplished, but if any tension occurs at the anastomotic site, an interposition nerve graft has a better chance of providing facial movement. All nerve repair techniques produce synkinesis, but sphincteric function of the mouth and eye is usually restored. If the epineurium is cleaned from the end of the nerve for approximately only 0.5 mm, sutures can still be placed in the epineurium for reapproximating the nerve segments.

When an interposition graft is required, the greater auricular and sural nerves are the preferred graft donor sources. The nerve graft should be 10 to 20% larger in diameter than the facial nerve and long enough to ensure tension-free anastomosis.

FACIAL REANIMATION PROCEDURES

Management of the Upper Third of the Face

Eye Care

Protection of the eye is paramount. It is necessary to protect the cornea from foreign bodies and drying. Dark glasses should be worn during the day, artificial tears instilled at the slightest evidence of drying, and a bland eye ointment used during sleep. Patients who demonstrate a poor Bell's phenomenon or have trigeminal nerve deficits are particularly at risk for corneal damage. Taping the eye closed is not usually recommended, but early exposure keratitis may require patching or, rarely, a tarsorraphy. A formal ophthalmologic examination is recommended prior to any surgical intervention.

Eyebrow

Ptosis of the eyebrow can have functional and cosmetic consequences. In the elderly patient, the functional loss of the frontalis and orbicularis oculi muscle is compounded by the loss of tissue elasticity and decrease in the bulk of the subcutaneous tissue. This can lead to significant brow ptosis and hooding of the upper eyelid, which may cause lateral visual field compromise.

The two most commonly used procedures to correct brow ptosis are the midforehead lift and the direct brow lift. Both procedures require direct skin and subcutaneous tissue excision, followed by suspension of the orbicularis oculi muscle to the frontal bone periosteum.

Upper Eyelid

Today, tarsorraphy should be reserved for only those patients with a severe risk for exposure keratitis or those who have failed upper eyelid reanimation procedures. The most commonly used procedure is the insertion of a prosthetic, specifically a gold weight implant or a palpebral wire spring. In experienced hands, the palpebral wire spring can produce excellent results, affording the capability of mimicking, to some extent, the spontaneous blink. However, insertion of the palpebral wire spring is technically more difficult with a higher reported extrusion and infection rate. Gold weight implantation is a relatively simple procedure that is highly successful, well tolerated by patients, and easily reversible if facial muscle function returns. Prefabricated gold weight implants come in weights ranging from 0.8 to 1.6 g. The largest weight allowing eyelid closure without causing more than slight lid ptosis should be chosen.

Lower Eyelid

The goals for lower lid management are to improve lower lid margin approximation to the globe, correct ectropion, and maximize the efficiency of the tear drainage system. Lower lid–tightening procedures include the Bick procedure, tarsal strip, and midlid wedge resection. Lid-tightening procedures must not disturb the delicate interface between the lacrimal punctum and the globe. As a general rule, up to one-eighth of the lid can be resected without disturbing the relationship of the inferior punctum to the globe.

Management of the Lower Two-Thirds of the Face

The ultimate goal in treatment of the lower two-thirds of the face is to create symmetric, mimetic movement of the facial musculature. The best chance for this outcome is with primary repair of the facial nerve, with or without nerve interposition grafting. However, primary nerve repair is not always possible, and alternative procedures must be entertained.

Role of Electromyography in Planning Facial Reanimation Procedures

The degree of motor end plate degeneration and prognosis for spontaneous recovery of the facial nerve can be assessed with EMG. The presence of normal or polyphasic action potentials at 1 year following facial nerve injury portends a favorable outcome, and no reanimation procedures are indicated. If fibrillation potentials are found, this indicates intact motor end plates but no evidence of reinnervation. This finding supports the use of a nerve substitution procedure to take advantage of the potential neurotized tone and movement of the intrinsic facial musculature. Electrical silence obtained from EMG indicates complete denervation and atrophy of the motor end plates. Neurotized reanimation procedures are contraindicated, and other reanimation procedures should be entertained.

Nerve Substitution Procedures

Nerve substitution procedures are indicated when primary facial nerve repair is not possible. The most commonly described nerve substitution procedures are the XI–VII crossover, VII–VII cross-facial, XII–VII crossover, and XII–VII jump graft. The VII–VII cross-facial grafting involves linking a functional branch of the facial nerve on the nonparalyzed side to a division of the facial nerve on the paralyzed side by using a long interpositional nerve graft (sural or medial antebrachial cutaneous). The disadvantages of this procedure include the sacrifice of a portion of the normal facial function on the contralateral side, a long interval for innervation (9 to 12 months), and a lack of substantial neural "firepower" owing to the relatively few number of axons grafted. Theoretically, the advantage of this technique is the possibility of symmetric mimetic movement.

Hypoglossal-facial (XII–VII) crossover is most appropriately performed for complete and permanent facial paralysis up to 2 years after injury. Poor candidates for the XII–VII crossover include patients with multiple lower cranial nerve deficits. Sacrifice of the hypoglossal nerve may not be well tolerated and compensated for in the presence of other cranial neuropathies. Improved facial tone and symmetry occurs in 90% of patients following XII–VII anastomosis. The results are more impressive in the midface and less in the frontalis and lower portions of the face. The return of muscle tone is seen within 4 to 6 months following neurorrhapy, with better results seen in earlier repairs. Voluntary facial movements follow with progressive improvements over the next 1 to 2 years. True spontaneous facial expressions are rare, although, through motor sensory re-education, patients may develop spontaneous animation with speech. Synkinesis, hypertonia, and hemilingual atrophy are all noted deficiencies of the classic XII–VII crossover.

The XII–VII jump graft technique was devised to offset some of the above-noted disadvantages of the classic XII–VII crossover. The procedure entails placing an interpositional nerve graft between a partially transected hypoglossal nerve trunk, distal to the hypoglossal descendens, and the distal facial nerve trunk. Several authors have reported comparable functional results to the XII–VII crossover, and the problems of hypertonia and mass facial movements have not been encountered.

Muscle Transposition Procedures (Dynamic)

Regional muscle transposition can provide dynamic reanimation of the mouth in patients with long-standing facial paralysis (over 2 years). It is indicated for patients with congenital facial paralysis (Möbius' syndrome) or when facial nerve grafting or nerve substitution techniques are contraindicated. It can also be performed in conjunction with a facial nerve grafting or nerve substitution procedure in select cases to augment results. The temporalis muscle is most commonly used because of its length, contractility, and favorable vector of pull. Masseter muscle transposition can be useful following radical parotid surgery or when the temporalis muscle is not available.

The results of the transposition should be evident by 4 to 6 weeks, with the patient able to produce a broad smile by tensing the temporalis muscle. Complications include infection, hematoma, and seroma. The most common reasons for failure of the procedure are inadequate overcorrection and suture dehiscence at the orbicularis oris–temporalis muscle interface.

Suspension Procedures (Static)

Static suspension procedures are indicated for those patients who are not candidates for nerve substitution or dynamic reanimation procedures. These procedures can provide permanent support, or, in cases for which reinnervation of the facial muscles is expected, static procedures can provide temporary or additional support until reinnervation of the facial muscles is complete. A variety of materials are available for static suspension procedures, ranging from autografts (palmaris longus tendon, fascia lata tendon) to alloplasts.

Innervated Free Muscle Transfer

The ideal indication for innervated free muscle transfer is in the patient with Möbius' syndrome, in whom both facial nerve and musculature are not available. It is also indicated as an alternative to regional muscle transfers or static procedures in patients with long-standing facial paralysis (> 2 years). It is usually performed as a two-stage procedure in which an initial cross-facial nerve graft is combined with a subsequent free muscle transfer (most commonly the gracilis or serratus anterior). Alternatively, the innervated free flap may be grafted to the hypoglossal nerve, performed as a single-stage procedure.

In select patients, this procedure provides the possibility for dynamic, mimetic movement that cannot be achieved by static procedures. The disadvantages, however, are manifold, including donor site morbidity, risk for vascular thrombosis, lengthy operative time, long interval for reinnervation, and muscle bulkiness.

NEUROMUSCULAR FACIAL RETRAINING TECHNIQUES

For patients who have experienced some recovery of facial nerve function and also for those patients who experience synkinesis, neuromuscular facial retraining therapy is an important treatment modality. These techniques can be applied before and after reanimation procedures to optimize outcome. In general, these techniques can be used to address loss of strength, loss of isolated motor control, muscle tension hypertonicity, and/or synkinesis. This method combines techniques such as patient education in basic facial anatomy, physiology, and kinesiology; relaxation training; sensory stimulation; EMG biofeedback; voluntary facial exercises with mirror feedback; and spontaneously elicited facial movements. Botulinum toxin injections may be used to augment the results of neuromuscular facial retraining when dealing with synkinesis and hypertonicity.

20

OLFACTION AND GUSTATION

Richard L. Doty, PhD
Steven M. Bromley, MD

The senses of smell and taste determine the flavor of foods and beverages and provide, among other things, early warning of such dangerous environmental chemicals as leaking natural gas, spoiled food, and air pollution. Causes of olfactory dysfunction can range from relatively benign factors (eg, the common cold) to serious brain diseases and disorders, often at their earliest stages, including Alzheimer's disease, idiopathic Parkinson's disease, and schizophrenia. Early detection of such disorders allows for optimal early medical or surgical intervention.

OLFACTORY SYSTEM

The olfactory receptors are located high in the nasal vault, within a pseudostratified sensory epithelium lining the cribriform plate and sectors of the superior turbinate, middle turbinate, and superior part of the septum. The olfactory neuroepithelium is not a homogeneous structure, exhibiting metaplastic islands of respiratory-like epithelium that accumulate over a lifetime, presumably as a result of insults from viruses, bacterial agents, and toxins. Six general classes of cells are found within this structure: ciliated bipolar sensory receptor cells, supporting or sustentacular cells, microvillar cells, Bowman's glands and duct cells, globose basal cells, and horizontal basal cells. The *receptor cells*, which harbor the receptors on their cilia, are derived embryologically from the olfactory placode and hence are of central nervous system (CNS) origin. The axons of these ~ 6 million cells converge into 50 or so "fila" ensheathed by glia that traverse the cribriform plate to form the outermost layer of the olfactory bulb. The *sustentacular cells* serve to insulate the receptor cells from one another, aid in the regulation of mucous composition, and help to deactivate odorants and xenobiotics. The function of the bell-shaped ciliated *microvillar cells* located at the epithelial surface is unknown. *Bowman's glands* serve as the source of most of the mucus in the olfactory region, whereas the *globose and horizontal basal cells* are the progenitor cells of the other cell types within the epithelium.

The olfactory bulb is composed of six concentric layers: the olfactory nerve layer on the surface, glomerular layer, external plexiform layer, mitral cell layer, internal plexiform layer, and granule cell layer. The unmyelinated axons of the olfactory nerve cells enter the glomerular layer, where they synapse with the second-order neurons, primarily mitral and tufted cells. These second-order neurons, in turn, send collaterals that synapse within the periglomerular and external plexiform layers of the bulb, in some cases resulting in self-inhibition of the second-order neurons and in others facilitating or inhibiting the firing of neighboring cells. The mitral and tufted cell axons project via the lateral olfactory tract to the ipsilateral primary olfactory cortex, which is comprised of the anterior olfactory nucleus, piriform cortex, olfactory tubercle, entorhinal area, periamygdaloid cortex, and corticomedial amygdala. Some projections occur, via the anterior commissure, from pyramidal cells of the anterior olfactory nucleus to contralateral elements of the primary olfactory cortex. A number of projections from the primary to secondary (ie, orbitofrontal) cortex are direct, whereas others relay within the thalamus.

After traversing the largely aqueous phase of the olfactory mucus, odorants bind to receptor cell cilia, initiating G protein– and cyclic adenosine monophosphate–mediated transduction cascades. Most olfactory receptors are representatives of a large (~ 1,000) multigene family of G protein–coupled seven-transmembrane receptors. Each olfactory receptor neuron expresses only one type of receptor, and neurons expressing the same gene appear to be randomly distributed within a few segregated strip-like "spatial zones" of the neuroepithelium, at least in the rodent. Each receptor binds many different molecules, although selectivity exists such that not all odorant molecules activate all receptors. Since olfactory neurons that express a given receptor gene project to the same glomeruli, the glomeruli can be considered functional units and the pattern across them as the proximal code for odorant quality.

The olfactory neuroepithelium has the ability to regenerate, although in cases in which significant damage to the basement membrane has occurred, regeneration is nonexistent or incomplete. Under normal circumstances, relatively continuous neurogenesis occurs within basal segments of the epithelium; however, many receptor cells are relatively long-lived and appear to be replaced only after they are damaged. Receptor cell death, as well as replenishment from progenitor cells, is determined by both endogenous and exogenous factors. Apoptotic cell death occurs in cells representing all stages of regeneration, implying multiple levels of biochemical regulation of neuronal numbers.

Smell dysfunction can be classified as follows: *anosmia*: inability to detect qualitative olfactory sensations (ie, absence of smell function); *partial anosmia*: ability to perceive some, but not all, odors; *hyposmia* or *microsmia*: decreased sensitivity to odors; *hyperosmia*: abnormally acute smell function; *dysosmia* (sometimes termed cacosmia or parosmia): distorted or perverted smell perception to odor stimulation; *phantosmia*: a dysosmic sensation perceived in the absence of an odor stimulus (ie, an olfactory hallucination); and *olfactory agnosia*: inability to recognize an odor sensation, even though olfactory processing, language, and general intellectual functions are essentially intact, as in some stroke patients. Olfactory dysfunction can be either bilateral (binasal) or, less commonly, unilateral (uninasal).

Three steps are involved in assessing a patient with chemosensory dysfunction: (1) a detailed clinical history, (2) quantitative olfactory testing, and (3) a thorough physical examination emphasizing the head and neck and employing appropriate brain and rhinosinus imaging. The clinical history should establish precipitating events, search for underlying medical or neurologic disorders, and evaluate all of the medications and prior treatments the patient has undergone. For example, *sudden olfactory loss* suggests the possibility of head trauma, infection, or ischemia. *Gradual loss* can reflect the development of degenerative processes or progressive obstructive lesions or tumors within the olfactory receptor region or central neural structures. *Intermittent loss* can be indicative of an intranasal inflammatory process. Quantitative olfactory testing using modern standardized tests with normative data (eg, the widely employed University of Pennsylvania Smell Identification Test or UPSIT) should be used to (1) establish the validity of the patient's complaint, (2) characterize the exact nature of the problem, (3) accurately monitor changes in function over time (including those resulting from therapeutic interventions), (4) detect malingering, and (5) accurately establish compensation for disability. As documented by the UPSIT, about one half of the population between 65 and 80 years of age experiences significant decrements in the ability to smell. Over 80 years of age, this figure rises to nearly 75%.

For most patients complaining of olfactory problems, careful otolaryngologic and neurologic assessment is warranted. Visual acuity, visual field, and optic disk examinations are of value in detecting possible intracranial mass lesions that produce increased intracranial pressure with papilledema and optic

atrophy (eg, Foster Kennedy syndrome, which consists of ipsilateral anosmia, ipsilateral optic atrophy, and contralateral
papilledema owing to a meningioma near the ipsilateral optic
nerve). A thorough nasal endoscopic evaluation should be performed using both flexible and rigid endoscopes, paying specific attention to the olfactory meatal area. Medical imaging
can be invaluable in understanding the basis of a number of
smell and taste disturbances. Magnetic resonance imaging
(MRI) is the method of choice for evaluating soft tissue (eg,
olfactory bulbs, tracts, and cortical parenchyma). Computed
tomography (CT) is the most useful and cost-effective technique to assess sinonasal tract inflammatory disorders and is
superior to MRI in the evaluation of bony structures adjacent
to the olfactory pathways (eg, ethmoid, cribriform plate).

Most cases of chronic anosmia or hyposmia are attributable to prior upper respiratory infections, head trauma, or
nasal and paranasal sinus disease, typically reflecting long-
lasting or permanent damage to the olfactory neuroepithelium. Of these causes, viral upper respiratory infections are
most common. Other causes include intranasal neoplasms
(eg, inverted papilloma, hemangioma, and esthesioneuroblastoma), intracranial tumors or lesions (eg, olfactory
groove meningiomas, frontal lobe gliomas), neurologic
diseases (eg, Alzheimer's disease, idiopathic Parkinson's
disease, multiple sclerosis, schizophrenia), exposure to airborne toxins, therapeutic interventions (eg, septoplasty,
rhinoplasty, turbinectomy, radiation therapy, medications),
epilepsy, psychiatric disorders, and various endocrine and
metabolic disorders. Depression, progressive supranuclear
palsy, MPTP(1-methyl-4-phenyl-1,2,3,6-tetrahydropyri-
dine)-induced parkinsonism, and multiple system atrophy
appear not to be accompanied by significant decrements in
the ability to smell. Smell loss, in some cases only dis-
cernible by quantitative testing, can aid in some instances in
the identification of persons at risk for later significant cog-

nitive decline, as well as differentiating among some neurologic disorders (eg, Parkinson's disease and progressive
supranuclear palsy). Most dysosmias reflect dynamic elements usually associated with degeneration of the olfactory
neuroepithelium and remit over time, although some can
reflect central factors (eg, in temporal lobe epilepsy).
Usually, some smell function is present in dysosmic patients.
Meaningful treatments are available for some olfactory
disorders owing to blockage of airflow to the olfactory
neuroepithelium (eg, rhinosinusitis, polyposis, intranasal
tumors, and distorted intranasal architecture). Central
lesions, such as CNS tumors that impinge on olfactory bulbs
and tracts and epileptogenic foci within the medial part of
the temporal lobe that result in olfactory seizures, can, in
some cases, be resected in a manner that allows for some
restoration of olfactory function. Discontinuance, dose
changes, or substitution of other modes of therapy can be
effective for some medications that induce distortions or
losses of olfaction. Some cases of extremely debilitating
chronic dysosmia (usually of a number of years duration
and often unilateral), in which weight loss is marked or
daily functioning is markedly impaired, are amenable to
surgical intervention (eg, ablation of regions of the olfactory
epithelium or olfactory bulb removal). There is no compelling evidence that zinc and vitamin therapies are beneficial except in rare cases in which frank deficiencies exist.

THE GUSTATORY SYSTEM

Sensations such as sweet, sour, bitter, and salty, as well as
"metallic" (iron salts), "umami" (monosodium glutamate, disodium gluanylate, disodium inosinate), and "chalky" (calcium
salts), are mediated via the taste buds of the gustatory system.
Unlike olfaction, taste sensations are carried by several cranial
nerves (ie, CN VII, IX, and X). Intraoral CN V free nerve end-

ings are also stimulated by some foods and beverages (eg, carbonated or spicy foods), contributing to the overall gestalt of flavor. Hence, a piece of chocolate in the mouth is not only sweet but has texture and temperature. The sensation of "chocolate," however, is dependent on retronasal stimulation of the olfactory receptors. Unfortunately, many patients and their physicians fail to distinguish between "taste" sensations mediated by the taste buds from CN I–mediated "taste" sensations (eg, lemon, strawberry, meat sauce, etc).

The taste receptors are located within the goblet-shaped taste buds distributed over the dorsal surface of the tongue, margin of the tongue, base of the tongue, soft palate, pharynx, larynx, epiglottis, uvula, and first third of the esophagus. Most taste buds are found on the lingual surface within the fungiform, foliate, and circumvallate papillae. Taste buds are continually bathed in secretions from the salivary glands and nearby lingual glands. Ebner's glands discharge into the troughs surrounding the vallate papillae, and lingual glands empty into the long fissures between the folds of the elongated foliate papillae on the posterior aspect of the margin of the tongue. On average, the human tongue contains around 4,600 taste buds.

Tastants initiate the transduction process via one of two mechanisms: (1) directly gating apical ion channels on the microvilli within the taste bud (a process that probably occurs with sour- and salty-tasting stimuli) and (2) activating receptors coupled to G proteins that, in turn, activate second-messenger systems (a process that probably occurs with sweet- and bitter-tasting stimuli). Taste threshold sensitivity is directly related to the number of taste papillae and hence taste buds that are actively stimulated.

Cranial nerve VII conveys taste sensations from (1) the taste buds of the fungiform papillae on the anterior two-thirds of the tongue via its chorda tympani branch and (2) the taste buds of the soft palate, which are innervated by its greater superficial petrosal branch via the lesser palatine nerve.

All circumvallate and most, if not all, foliate taste buds within the posterior third of the tongue are innervated by the lingual-tonsillar branch of the glossopharyngeal nerve (CN IX). The pharyngeal branch of CN IX supplies the taste buds in the region of the nasopharynx. The taste buds on the epiglottis, aryepiglottal folds, and esophagus are innervated by the vagus nerve (CN X) via the internal portion of its superior laryngeal branch. After CN VII, IX, and X enter the brainstem, they synapse, respectively, in descending (and overlapping) order within the nucleus tractus solitarius (NTS) of the medulla. Cells from the NTS also make reflexive connections, via the reticular formation, with cranial motor nuclei that control (1) such taste-related behaviors as chewing, licking, salivation, and swallowing; (2) preabsorptive insulin release; and (3) muscles of facial expression. The major gustatory projections from the NTS ultimately lead to activation of cortical gustatory structures. In primates, these occur via the thalamic taste nucleus; namely, the parvicellular division of the ventroposteromedial thalamic nucleus. From the thalamic taste nucleus, fibers project to the primary taste cortex located deep in the parietal operculum and adjacent parainsular cortex. A secondary cortical taste region is present within the caudomedial/caudolateral orbitofrontal cortex, several millimeters anterior to the primary taste cortex.

Gustatory disorders can be classified in a manner similar to olfactory disorders: *ageusia*: inability to detect qualitative gustatory sensations from all (total ageusia) or some (partial ageusia) tastants; *hypogeusia*: decreased sensitivity to tastants; *dysgeusia*: distortion in the perception of a normal taste (ie, an unpleasant taste when a stimulus that would normally be perceived as pleasant is presented) or the presence of a taste in the absence of a stimulus (sometimes termed phantogeusia); *gustatory agnosia*: inability to recognize a taste sensation, even though gustatory processing, language, and general intellectual functions are essentially intact. Some patients complain of oral sensations of burning or numbness, which may or may not have their genesis in gustatory afferents. An extreme example is *burning mouth syndrome*, in which the patient experiences the sensation of "burning" within the mouth without obvious physical cause.

Total ageusia is rare and, when present, is usually produced by central (eg, ischemia, pharmacologic intervention) events since regeneration of taste buds can occur and peripheral damage would have to involve multiple pathways to induce taste loss. Hence, regional deficits are much more common, reflecting local changes on the surface of the tongue, as well as damage to single taste nerves. However, most patients are unaware of regional deficits. Indeed, patients rarely recognize their loss of taste sensation on one half of the anterior part of the tongue following unilateral sectioning of the chorda tympani nerve in middle ear surgery.

A history similar to that described earlier for patients complaining of olfactory disturbance should be obtained from patients complaining of gustatory disturbance. Specific consideration as to the type of stimuli that can or cannot be detected by the patient is essential to distinguish between retronasal CN I flavor loss and true taste bud–mediated gustatory loss. One should specifically inquire whether the patient can detect the saltiness of potato chips, pretzels, or salted nuts; the sourness of vinegar, pickles, or lemons; the sweetness of sugar, soda, cookies, or ice cream; and the bitterness of coffee, beer, or tonic water. If the patient indicates that there is a problem in such detection, the possibility of a true taste bud–mediated dysfunction exists. Care in assessing prior or current auditory and vestibular problems is essential to uncover possible alterations in chorda tympani function within the middle ear. Importantly, the physical examination should not only look for local causes of dysfunction (eg, candidiasis, scarring, gingivitis, inflammation, burning from gastric reflux, gingivitis, etc) but also for nongustatory deficits in CN VII, IX, and X that may reflect overall damage responsible for producing a taste disorder (eg, abnormal facial motion, swallowing, salivation, gag reflex, voice production).

Other common causes of taste dysfunction are Bell's palsy, Ramsay Hunt syndrome, head and neck trauma (eg, basilar temporal bone fractures), various tumors and lesions (eg, acoustic neuromas, tumors of the hypophysis with marked extrasellar growth, facial nerve schwannomas extending into the middle cranial fossa, and cerebellopontine angle lesions), and brainstem, thalamic, or other infarcts.

Numerous surgical interventions can induce taste dysfunction. Cranial nerve IX is susceptible to damage during tonsillectomy, bronchoscopy, or laryngoscopy. Surgical or surgery-related procedures such as uvulopalatoplasty, endotracheal intubation (owing to injury of the lingual nerve), and the employment of a laryngeal mask have all been associated with taste loss or alteration. The chorda tympani nerve fibers are at particular risk from surgical procedures that involve the middle ear. One study, for example, found that 78% of patients with bilateral section and 32% of patients with unilateral section of the chorda tympani had persistent adverse gustatory symptoms. Third molar surgery also can produce long-lasting taste loss that is correlated with the depth of impaction. Most importantly, medications commonly produce taste disturbances. Such side effects can be very debilitating and, in rare instances, have contributed to extreme weight loss and even suicide. Among offending agents are antiproliferative drugs, lipid-reducing drugs, antihypertensive agents, diuretics, antifungal agents, antirheumatic drugs, antibiotic drugs, and drugs with sulfhydryl groups, such as penicillamine and captopril. Onset of taste dysfunction following the use of some agents can take weeks or even months. Drug cessation does not immediately resolve such problems. It is noteworthy that approximately one-fourth of all cardiac medicines (including antilipemic agents, adrenergic blockers, angiotensin-converting enzyme inhibitors, angiotensin II antagonists, calcium channel blockers, vasodilators, anticoagulants, antiarrhymics, and various diuretics) are listed in the *Physicians' Desk Reference* as having potential side effects of "altered," "bad," "bitter," or "metallic taste."

Radio- or chemotherapy for head and neck cancer can induce taste loss and dysgeusia, as well as salivary dysfunction. Symptoms usually begin early in the course of treatment, and post-treatment recovery can take several months and, in rare instances, much longer. Aversions to certain foods appear during the course of treatment in a significant number of cancer patients undergoing such treatments. Although typically idiosyncratic and transient, some taste aversions can be long-lasting and can produce generalized anorexia and cachexia. A means for mitigating such aversions is to have the patient consume a novel food immediately before the first course of therapy. This simple maneuver somehow interferes with the formation of conditioned aversions to preferred dietary items, focusing the aversion primarily on the novel food.

Among other causes of taste dysfunction are hypothyroidism, renal disease, liver disease, myasthenia gravis, Guillain-Barré syndrome, numerous neoplasms, and familial dysautonomia (a genetic disorder with a lack of taste buds and papillae). Idiopathic dysgeusia has been associated with blood transfusions. Complaints of taste loss or distortion are reported in many carcinomas and mass lesions. For instance, whereas squamous cell carcinoma of the mucous membranes of the upper aerodigestive tract can interfere with taste by direct destruction of receptors, mass lesions along the course of CN VII, IX, and X may cause impairment through neural compression. Malnutrition associated with these tumors can also lead to ageusia. Significant increases in recognition thresholds for sour in breast cancer patients have been reported.

Gustatory symptoms have been reported in association with epileptic seizures. Examples of taste sensations that have been reported in such cases include "peculiar," "rotten," "sweet," "like a cigarette," "like rotten apples," and "like vomitus." Some of these "tastes," however, likely represent smell sensations that are miscategorized as tastes by both the patients and their physicians.

Hypergeusia and some forms of dysgeusia may arise from selective taste nerve damage or alterations. Hence, anesthetizing one chorda tympani nerve has been reported to increase the perceived intensity of bitter substances, such as quinine, applied to taste fields innervated by the contralateral glossopharyngeal nerve. In contrast, perceived intensity of NaCl applied to an area innervated by the ipsilateral glossopharyngeal nerve appears decreased. When both chorda tympani nerves are anesthetized, the taste of quinine is intensified and the taste of NaCl is diminished in CN IX taste fields on both sides of the tongue.

Quantitative taste testing is rarely performed in the clinic, largely because of issues of practicality (eg, time and expense of presenting and preparing limited shelf-life taste stimuli). Although a number of chemical taste tests have been described in the literature, electrogustometry (applying microamp currents by battery to the taste fields) is much more practical in assessing dysfunction. Imaging studies of the gustatory pathways can be useful in explaining the gustatory symptoms of some patients; thus, in addition to detecting large central lesions and tumors, modern MRI techniques can detect subtle lesions (eg, infarcts) within brain structures that correlate both with patient complaints and with the results of sensory testing.

As with other sensory systems, prognosis in cases of taste dysfunction is inversely related to the degree of neural or structural damage, although, clinically, such damage can rarely be assessed. Fortunately, the taste nerves and buds are relatively resilient, and many cases of taste loss or distortion spontaneously resolve, at least to some degree, over time. In some dysgeusic cases, antifungal and antibiotic treatments have been reported to be useful, although double-blind studies of the efficacy of such treatments are lacking. Chlorhexidine employed in a mouthwash has been suggested as having efficacy for some salty or bitter dysgeusias, possibly as a result of its strong positive charge. In the case of neural damage from viruses, presumably the damaged taste afferents regenerate. In cases of taste loss secondary to hypothyroidism, thyroxine replacement therapy reportedly brings back taste sensitivity to normal levels. Taste disorders that reflect side effects of pharmacologic agents can, in some instances, be reversed by discontinuance of the offending drug, by employing alternative medications, or by changing drug dosage. It should be kept in mind, however, that a number of pharmacologic agents appear to induce long-term alterations in taste that may take many months to disappear after drug discontinuance.

ACKNOWLEDGMENT

This work was supported, in part, by Grants PO1 DC 00161, RO1 DC 04278, RO1 DC 02974, and RO1 AG 27496 from the National Institutes of Health (R. L. Doty, Principal Investigator).

21

ACQUIRED IMMUNE DEFICIENCY SYNDROME

Frank E. Lucente, MD
Samir Shah, MD
Jeffrey Vierra, MD

Acquired immune deficiency syndrome (AIDS) has had a significant impact on the practice of otolaryngology. The fact that many patients originally presented with physical findings in the head and neck region, especially during the 1980s, required a high level of vigilance for detecting these findings as manifestations of human immunodeficiency virus (HIV) infection. New measures for handling instruments in the office and operating room emerged as part of the universal precautions that were promulgated as a way of controlling spread of the infection. The mechanisms of transmission of infection also caused otolaryngologists and all physicians to become familiar with certain social and sexual practices among their patients and to evaluate the need for blood transfusions. Finally, the awareness that HIV infection occurred in the health care worker population at the same rate as in the general population led to the development of measures for recognizing and dealing with risks of transmission and management of AIDS-related impairment.

EPIDEMIOLOGY

More than 600,000 cases of AIDS have been reported in the United States since 1981, and as many as 900,000 Americans were estimated in the year 2000 to be living with HIV infection. The epidemic is growing most rapidly among minority populations. The prevalence is six times higher in African Americans and three times higher in Hispanics than among Whites. In the United States and Europe, transmission is primarily homosexual or via blood. Most patients are 20- to 49-year-old men in high-risk groups (eg, homosexual or bisexual men with unsafe sexual practices, intravenous drug users who share needles, and recipients of transfused blood or blood components who sometimes transmit HIV to women heterosexually). In the United States, women are an increasing proportion of all AIDS cases and currently constitute about 20% of all cases.

In Africa, South America, and Southern Asia, transmission is primarily heterosexual. In these areas, men and women are nearly equally affected. Mixtures of the two patterns have been found in countries such as Brazil and Thailand. Typically, diseases follow routes of transportation and trade to cities and secondarily to rural areas. Recent statistics from sub-Saharan Africa show 25 to 30% prevalence of HIV positivity.

Currently, the blood supply in developed countries is safe from HIV contamination by virtue of donor deferral and routine screening for HIV antibodies. In the United States, the risk of acquiring HIV from screened blood is estimated as 1 in 225,000 units; the rare infection would be caused by blood from an infected individual who had not seroconverted at the time of donation.

TRANSMISSION

The AIDS virus is a retrovirus, meaning that the virus possesses a single strand of ribonucleic acid (RNA) as its genetic material, which it can then convert to a double strand of deoxyribonucleic acid (DNA) for incorporation into the genome of the cell that it infects. This synthesis of DNA from an RNA template is accomplished by the enzyme reverse transcriptase (RNA-dependent DNA polymerase). The spherical virus attaches to the CD4 receptor on T helper cells with high affinity. Other cells have a few CD4 receptors and serve as targets for infection. These include circulating and fixed macrophages, gut epithelial cells, and perhaps glial cells.

The known routes of transfer of HIV are blood, blood products, unsafe sexual activity, and transmission from mother to child perinatally. Scientists also have found no evidence that HIV is spread through sweat, tears, urine, or feces unless contaminated with blood.

CLINICAL COURSE

The median time from infection with HIV to the development of AIDS-related symptoms has been approximately 10 years. However, there has been wide variation in disease progression. Approximately 10% of HIV-infected persons progress to AIDS within the first 2 to 3 years following infection. Recent studies show that people with high levels of HIV in their bloodstream are more likely to develop new AIDS-related symptoms or to die than individuals with lower levels of virus. New anti-HIV drug combinations that reduce a person's "viral burden" to very low levels may delay the progression of HIV disease, but it remains to be seen if these drugs will have a prolonged benefit. Other drugs that fight the infections associated with AIDS have improved and prolonged the lives of HIV-infected people by preventing or treating conditions such as *Pneumocystis carinii* pneumonia.

OPPORTUNISTIC INFECTIONS

Opportunistic infections have remained the proximate cause of death for nearly all AIDS patients. Advances in prophylaxis have decreased the incidence of *Pneumocystis, Toxoplasma, Mycobacterium avium* complex (MAC), *Cryptococcus,* and other opportunistic infections and consequently their contribution to morbidity and mortality.

Patterns of specific opportunistic infections vary geographically, among risk groups, and as a result of medical interventions. In the United States and Europe, over 90% of AIDS patients with Kaposi's sarcoma are homosexual or bisexual men, probably because they are co-infected with human herpesvirus 8, a newly identified viral cofactor (with HIV), for Kaposi's sarcoma. Toxoplasmosis and tuberculosis (TB) are more common in tropical areas, where the prevalence of latent infections with *Toxoplasma gondii* and *Mycobacterium tuberculosis* in the general population is high. Even in developed countries, where background levels of TB are low, HIV has caused increased rates and atypical presentations of TB. Widespread use of effective prophylaxis against such agents as *P. carinii* and MAC has reduced the risk of these infections in developed countries.

ANTIRETROVIRAL THERAPY

Recommendations regarding the use of antiviral drugs in HIV are in flux. When and what to initiate, when to change regimens, and how to minimize the development of resistance and cross-resistance are continually being re-evaluated. Clearly, monotherapy results in resistance and loss of efficacy as a result of the huge viral burden, short viral half-life, and propensity to mutate.

The classes of anti-HIV drugs include reverse transcriptase inhibitors (nucleoside and non-nucleoside) and protease inhibitors. The protease inhibitors are the most potent antiviral drugs. Inhibition of viral protease prevents cleavage of an important structural polyprotein that results in noninfectious viral particles.

Viral loads are critical in determining efficacy of regimens; the goal is to make all viral loads undetectable because high loads drive CD4 loss and ultimately produce immune suppression. The current recommendation is to initiate a three-drug regimen in patients with a detectable viral load of over 5,000 to 10,000 HIV RNA copies per milliliter, regardless of CD4 count. This regimen offers sustained viral suppression compared with double- and single-drug regimens.

Triple combinations containing a protease inhibitor are considered the most potent of all regimens. The difficulty with multidrug therapy is that the patient may not fully comply because of the number of pills and adverse effects. Even minimal noncompliance causes drug resistance and loss of efficacy. When changing a failing regimen, two new drugs (preferably three new drugs) should be started. All regimens must be individualized; and occasionally, when patients are unable to comply with the rigors of three drugs, double therapy is preferable to no therapy.

OTORHINOLARYNGOLOGIC MANIFESTATIONS

Patients who are HIV positive can acquire otorhinolaryngologic diseases similar to those experienced by patients without HIV infection. In most instances, these conditions are treated in a manner similar to the treatment of HIV-negative patients, but it is often prudent to involve the patient's primary care physician or infectious disease specialist in the therapeutic team.

Patients who are HIV positive can develop otorhinolaryngologic conditions that are more specifically related to their HIV status, and it has been estimated that approximately 50% of patients with AIDS present with a symptom or physical finding in the head and neck region, including the tracheobronchial tree.

Ear

One of the most common findings in HIV patients is acute and serous otitis media. Patients present with aural fullness, hearing loss, and/or otorrhea. Patients with CD4 counts over 200 often respond with oral antibiotics and local care; however, patients with low CD4 counts often need placement of tympanostomy tubes to relieve symptoms.

Otitis externa is also a common presentation. However, the otitis externa can be complicated by Kaposi's sarcoma, molluscum contagiosum, herpes simplex, and seborrheic dermatitis involving the auricle or pinna. Treatment must include any special care in addition to local care.

Sensorineural hearing loss can occur in up to 69% of AIDS patients; cytomegalovirus (CMV) is often implicated because CMV inclusion-bearing cells can sometimes be found in cranial nerve VIII in the internal auditory canal, cochlea, or vestibular endolymphatic epithelium. Other causes of the hearing loss may include primary cochlear effects of HIV, ototoxic drugs, or demyelination in the auditory tract. Facial paralysis is common in patients with HIV and is probably a reflection of the higher incidence of viral infections.

Skin

Dermatologic involvement in the head and neck also occurs quite commonly. Seborrheic dermatitis tends to be more floric than in seronegative patients. It is treated with topical corticosteroid creams. If secondary infection occurs, topical antibiotics and occasionally systemic antibodies are added to the regimen. Herpes zoster presents more aggressively than in the non–HIV-infected patient; there is greater postherpetic neuralgia that is prolonged and more resistant to treatment. Herpes simplex virus (HSV) requires early culture for diagnosis and usually responds well to oral therapy with acyclovir. Molluscum contagiosum, a skin disease caused by a pox virus, causes crops of round lesions with central umbilication in th periorbital and eyelid areas that are often much larger and more difficult to manage than in the non-HIV patient.

Nose

Chronic rhinitis with nasal crusting and dryness is particularly common among patients with HIV infection. Although no specific treatment has been routinely successful, administration of guaifenesin (1,200 mg bid) has proved efficacious. Supportive care and humidification are useful.

Externally, herpes simplex can often be seen involving the nasal vestibule. The infection presents as a chronic nonhealing inflammatory process that extends onto the septum, the nasal alae, and, ultimately, the upper lip and face. Again, early culture for diagnosis and treatment with appropriate antiviral agents will show substantial improvement.

Sinusitis occurs with increasing frequency as the CD4 cell count decreases. Acute sinusitis in patients with a CD4 count greater than 200 is usually caused by bacteria similar to those found in non-HIV patients. However, patients with low CD4 counts have *Pseudomonas aeurginosa, Staphylococcus aureus,* and fungal and other opportunistic agents causing the sinusitis. Treatment requires broad-spectrum antimicrobial agents.

Allergic rhinitis has been shown to occur secondary to eosinophilia and an increase in immunoglobulin E levels from HIV. Treatment with topical nasal corticosteroids and second-generation antihistamines can alleviate these symptoms. Nasal obstruction is common and is often caused by enlarged adenoids because the virus replicates in this lymphoid organ.

Oral Cavity and Oropharynx

Oral candidiasis is one of the most common head and neck problems in HIV-infected patients. It can take either the usual form, with white patches easily detachable from a hyperemic base, or a purely erythematous form, with the mucosa appearing uniformly smooth and inflamed. Treatment with topical agents is usually effective; however, when immune deficiency becomes profound, systemic therapy with drugs such as fluconazole and occasionally amphotericin may be indicated. The possibility of candidal esophagitis should be investigated in patients with persistent and significant dysphagia, odynophagia, and dehydration.

Angular cheilitis, giant herpetic ulcers, and gingivitis are also common. Giant oral ulcers can be as large as 2 to 3 cm. Because of the severe pain and anorexia that can result, these lesions should be treated with topical and systemic corticosteroids and antibiotics in severe cases. Gingivitis and gingival atrophy are very common conditions, and necrotizing infections of the periodontal region can occur despite aggressive local and systemic therapy. For this reason, HIV-infected patients should develop good oral hygiene and have frequent follow-up with their dentist.

Epstein-Barr virus seems to cause an oral finding unique to AIDS called hairy leukoplakia. This consists of white patches along the lateral borders of the tongue and occurs early in the course of HIV infections, sometimes being the first clue that the patient may be HIV infected. Since hairy leukoplakia is asymptomatic, it does not usually require treatment; but it does alert the clinician to suspect HIV infection.

Larynx

The larynx is an often difficult area to evaluate and diagnose accurately. Viral (HSV, CMV) and fungal infections (histoplasmosis, coccidioidomycosis, aspergillosis, and candidiasis) have been described in the larynx of HIV-infected patients. Diagnosis is often made after laryngoscopy with biopsies and cultures.

Esophagus

In esophageal candidiasis, the patient often presents with worsening dysphagia that is not always associated with oral candidiasis. Other causes include HSV, CMV, and aphthous ulcerations. Esophageal examination may reveal thick, erythematous, whitish mucosa. The diagnosis is made with a potassium hydroxide (KOH) smear. Treatment is with topical (nystatin or clotrimazole troches) or systemic antifungal medication (fluconazole, amphotericin).

Neck

Neck masses are common in HIV-infected patients. Most commonly, this finding represents cervical lymphadenopathy, but parotid gland cysts and infectious processes can also occur. In the early stages of HIV disease, lymph node enlargement occurs throughout the body. When the lymphadenopathy is symmetric and otherwise asymptomatic, there is usually no indication for biopsy. If a lymph node grows out of proportion to the other lymph nodes or is associated with systemic symptoms, biopsy is indicated.

Salivary glands, especially the parotid glands, develop cysts that often have bilateral involvement termed benign lymphoepithelial cysts. These lesions typically arise from the intraparotid lymph nodes rather than the parotid salivary gland tissue. Computed tomography shows multiple cystic lesions, and the diagnosis can be confirmed with fine-needle aspiration. No treatment is required if the patient is asymptomatic. Aspiration of these cysts may be warranted for cosmetic reasons. However, the fluid is likely to recur, and it is important for the patient to understand the limitation of such treatment. Surgical excision of the cysts is not recommended owing to the possibility of facial nerve damage.

Neoplasms

Kaposi's sarcoma has a predisposition for the mucous membranes as well as for the skin of the face. The primary treatment for Kaposi's sarcoma has been radiation therapy. This is done at low dosage levels ranging from 1.5 to 2.5 Gy. For localized disease, other treatment options may include laser therapy, cryotherapy, and intralesional injection with chemotherapeutic agents.

Non-Hodgkin's lymphoma is the second most common malignancy seen in HIV patients. It presents in extranodal locations, usually of B-cell origin, and can be fairly aggressive with rapid onset and progression. This malignancy is treated with a combination of chemotherapy and radiation therapy.

Squamous cell carcinoma of the head and neck in the HIV-infected patient presents at a more advanced stage, has an aggressive tumor growth rate, and tends to occur in younger patients. Treatment plans should take into account the adverse response HIV patients can have to radiation therapy. Surgical management should be considered based on the underlying health and immune status of the patient.

CONCLUSION

Over 50% of patients with HIV and AIDS present with a symptom or physical finding in the head and neck region. The most common findings include otitis media, seborrheic dermatitis, chronic rhinitis, oral candidiasis, and lymphoid hyperplasia. Treatment should be individualized and requires a team approach for management.

22

ETIOLOGY OF INFECTIOUS DISEASES OF THE UPPER RESPIRATORY TRACT

John L. Boone, MD

Common Cold

More than 200 viruses have been associated with the common cold. Approximately 50% of colds are caused by rhinoviruses, of which there are over 100 serotypes. Coronaviruses account for about 10% of infections. Other viruses known to cause common colds include parainfluenza viruses, respiratory syncytial viruses, influenza viruses, and adenoviruses. Specific serotypes of adenovirus are associated with pharyngoconjunctival fever and epidemic keratoconjunctivitis.

Pharyngitis

Approximately 70% of acute sore throats are caused by viruses. Most of these occur as part of common cold or influenza syndromes. The most common viral agents are rhinovirus, coronavirus, adenovirus, influenza, and parainfluenza viruses. Other associated viruses include respiratory syncytial virus, herpes simplex virus (types 1 and 2), coxsackievirus, Epstein-Barr virus (EBV), cytomegalovirus (CMV), and human immunodeficiency virus (HIV).

Adenoviruses are common agents of acute pharyngitis. Specific serotypes are also the cause of pharyngoconjunctival fever, a syndrome characterized by fever, pharyngitis, and follicular conjunctivitis. Community epidemics of this infection often center around contaminated public swimming pools.

Herpangina is a vesicular and ulcerative pharyngitis most often caused by coxsackievirus. It is seen primarily in children ages 3 to 10 years. Mucosal vesicles and ulcers surrounded by erythematous rings form over 2 to 3 days. Lesions are most commonly noted on the anterior tonsillar pillars, as well as soft palate, tonsils, pharyngeal walls, and posterior aspects of the buccal mucosa. Fever and sore throat are sometimes accompanied by anorexia and abdominal pain. Most cases are mild and resolve in 3 to 6 days.

Vincent's angina is an acute oropharyngeal ulcerative condition caused by a combination of anaerobic gram-negative and fusobacterial microorganisms. Infection typically manifests as unilateral pseudomembranous tonsillar ulceration with pain, fetid breath, and cervical lymphadenopathy. Acute necrotizing ulcerative gingivitis, or "trench mouth," is a similar process of the gingiva. Treatment is with penicillin and metronidazole.

Neisseria gonorrhoeae should be considered as a cause of pharyngitis in sexually active patients, especially those with known orogenital contact. Gonococcal pharyngitis can occur without associated urethritis.

Acute Epiglottitis (Supraglottitis)

Formerly, *Haemophilus influenzae* type b (Hib) was the etiologic agent in almost all cases of supraglottitis in children. However, with the advent of the Hib vaccine, the rates of disease caused by this microorganism have dramatically decreased. Although *H. influenzae* is still identified in areas where the vaccine is available, group A streptococcus has been recovered more frequently in more recent studies. Other causes of acute supraglottitis in children are uncommon and include other streptococci, *Staphylococcus aureus, H. influenzae* non–type b, and *H. parainfluenzae*. Immunocompromised patients are more likely to have these or other more unusual pathogens.

Acute supraglottitis is increasingly recognized in adults. In most cases, no etiologic agent is found. *Haemophilus influenzae* type b and *Streptococcus pneumoniae* have been most frequently identified.

Acute Laryngotracheobronchitis (Croup)

Acute laryngotracheobronchitis, or croup, produces inflammation of the subglottic area that results in stridor and respiratory distress. Most patients are between the ages of 3 months and 3 years. Parainfluenza viruses (types 1, 2, and 3) are the most frequent etiologic agents, accounting for almost 75% of isolated viral agents. Influenza A virus, respiratory syncytial virus, adenoviruses, enteroviruses, and rhinoviruses are less commonly isolated. Rarely, bacterial agents such as *Mycoplasma pneumoniae, S. pneumoniae, S. aureus,* and *Moraxella catarrhalis* have been associated with croup. They likely represent superinfection of a preceding viral disease.

Sinusitis

Acute community-acquired sinusitis in adults is most frequently associated with *S. pneumoniae* and nontypable *H. influenzae*. To these pathogens, in children, may be added *M. catarrhalis*. Anaerobic bacteria are recovered in about 5 to 10% of cases of acute sinusitis in adults, usually in the presence of dental disease. In isolated sphenoid sinusitis, *S. aureus*, alpha-hemolytic streptococci, and *S. pneumoniae* were reported to be the primary pathogens.

In studies of chronic sinusitis, the most common microorganisms identified were those seen in acute sinusitis plus *S. aureus*, coagulase-negative *Staphylococcus*, and anaerobic bacteria. Infection is often polymicrobial, and anaerobic bacteria play a far greater role than in acute sinusitis.

Nosocomial sinusitis is commonly polymicrobial and has a high incidence of *S. aureus*, anaerobes, and gram-negative bacteria such as *Pseudomonas aeruginosa, Escherichia coli, Klebsiella pneumoniae, Proteus mirabilis,* and *Enterobacter* species. In cystic fibrosis patients with acute sinusitis, *P. aeruginosa* and *H. influenzae* were the most frequently isolated pathogens.

Otitis Media

In children with acute otitis media, *S. pneumoniae, H. influenzae,* and *M. catarrhalis* are the microorganisms most commonly isolated. Most cases of *H. influenzae* are attributable to nontypable strains. The most notable recent trends in the bacteriology of acute otitis media have been the rise in the proportion of patients infected with drug-resistant *S. pneumoniae* and an overall increase in β-lactamase-producing *H. influenzae* and *M. catarrhalis.* In adults, *S. pneumoniae* and *H. influenzae* are the most frequently isolated bacterial pathogens. Neonatal otitis media is most frequently associated with pathogens similar to those seen in children; however, gram-negative enteric microorganisms and *S. aureus* are more frequently identified.

Bacteria isolated in cases of chronic otitis media are seldom those seen in the initial acute otitis media. Polymicrobial infections are common. *Pseudomonas aeruginosa* and *S. aureus* are seen more frequently. Anaerobes are present in 50% of cases. In chronic suppurative otitis media with cholesteatoma, *P. aeruginosa, S. aureus*, and anaerobes predominate.

SPECIFIC VIRUSES

Epstein-Barr Virus

Epstein-Barr virus, a member of the herpesvirus family, is a double-stranded deoxyribonucleic acid (DNA) virus. Infection by EBV is largely limited to epithelial cells of the pharynx and to B lymphocytes. Primary infection is initiated in the oropharyngeal epithelium. Adjacent B lymphocytes are infected and disseminate the virus to local and distant lymphoid tissue. Within B lymphocytes, the virus establishes a latent infection. In infants and small children, the host immune response is weak, and symptoms of infection are mild. The immune systems of adolescents and young adults respond more vigorously and cause the symptoms of infectious mononucleosis.

Epstein-Barr virus is the predominant cause of infectious mononucleosis, which is characterized by fever, fatigue, pharyngitis, and lymphadenopathy. Splenomegaly, mild hepatitis, and cerebritis may also occur. The diagnosis is suggested by the clinical features. Abnormal laboratory findings include the presence of atypical lymphocytes in the peripheral blood, elevation of hepatic enzymes, and the presence of positive heterophile antibodies (the "Monospot" test).

Epstein-Barr virus is closely linked to nonkeratinizing nasopharyngeal carcinoma and to Burkitt's lymphoma, a tumor of B lymphocytes limited largely to children in tropical Africa and New Guinea. Epstein-Barr virus genomes are also found in about one-third of the non-Hodgkin's B-cell lymphoma found in patients with acquired immune deficiency syndrome (AIDS).

Cytomegalovirus

Cytomegalovirus is the largest member of the herpesvirus family. The virus is ubiquitous, and serologic evidence suggests that up to 80% of adults have been infected. In infants and children, CMV infection generally causes few symptoms. In young adults, however, CMV can produce a mononucleosis syndrome with fever, fatigue, pharyngitis, lymphadenopathy, and relative lymphocytosis. It is estimated that 20% of infectious mononucleosis is caused by acute CMV infection. Symptoms are generally less severe than seen with EBV infection, and the heterophil antibody test will remain negative.

Primary or reactivated CMV infections commonly cause disease in immunosuppressed hosts, such as persons with HIV infection or transplantation patients. Clinical features include encephalitis, chorioretinitis, hepatitis, pneumonitis, colitis, esophagitis, and oral ulcers. Cytomegalovirus is among the most common viral pathogens causing congenital abnormalities. Clinical features of fetal involvement include mental retardation, hearing loss, jaundice, chorioretinitis, microcephaly, and pneumonitis.

Human Immunodeficiency Virus

Human immunodeficiency virus is a retrovirus. It is able to convert its own single-stranded ribonucleic acid to double-stranded DNA for incorporation into a host cell genome. The principal targets are T helper (CD4) cells, which are central to the function of cell-mediated immunity. Impairment of these cells renders a patient susceptible to a variety of opportunistic infections and unusual malignant diseases.

The prevalence of specific pathogens in acute and chronic sinusitis of HIV-infected patients with a CD4 count of greater than 200 cells/mm^3 is similar to that of non–HIV-infected patients. Patients infected with HIV with CD4 counts less than 200 cells/mm^3 are more susceptible to unusual pathogens. Infections with *P. aeruginosa* are more frequent. Patients with AIDS are at increased risk for invasive fungal sinusitis. *Aspergillus fumigatus* has been most frequently reported.

Children with HIV infection have an increased incidence of otitis media. Causative microorganisms do not seem to differ from those found in immunocompetent hosts. Unusual pathogens, however, should be suspected when a patient has a severely depressed immune system or responds poorly to standard antibiotic therapy.

Pneumocystis carinii is a common cause of pneumonia in AIDS patients. Otitic involvement may present with aural discharge and the presence of a polyp in the middle ear or external canal. Diagnosis is made by biopsy of the polyp. The infection responds well to trimethoprim-sulfamethoxazole.

Oral candidiasis is a common feature of HIV infection. Oral hairy leukoplakia is caused by EBV. The lesion is most frequently located on the lateral surface of the tongue and has a white corrugated or filiform appearance. Herpes simplex viral infections are more common in HIV-infected patients. Lesions are generally more severe, numerous, and persistent than in immunocompetent hosts. Herpes labialis is frequent and may extend onto the face to form a giant herpetic lesion.

SPECIFIC BACTERIA

Group A Beta-Hemolytic Streptococcus (*Streptococcus pyogenes*)

Group A beta-hemolytic streptococcus (GABHS) is a chain-forming, gram-positive coccus. It secretes certain toxins and enzymes that have clinical effects or cause antibodies to be produced that may be used for serologic identification. Streptolysin O is antigenic and is the basis of the antistreptolysin O (ASO) antibody assay, the most widely used streptococcal antibody test.

Group A beta-hemolytic streptococcus is a leading cause of pharyngitis. The greater significance of these microorganisms lies in their capacity to cause complications. Toxin-mediated complications of GABHS include scarlet fever and streptococcal toxic shock-like syndrome. Both are thought to be associated with the release of streptococcal pyogenic exotoxins by certain M protein serotypes. Poststreptococcal acute glomerulonephritis (AGN) is a delayed, nonsuppurative complication resulting in inflammation of the renal glomeruli. The pathogenesis of AGN is unclear. Acute rheumatic fever (ARF) is a nonsuppurative complication of GABHS characterized by inflammatory lesions of the heart, joints, subcutaneous tissues, and central nervous system. The pathogenesis of ARF is poorly understood. The Jones criteria remain useful in making the diagnosis of ARF.

Corynebacterium diphtheriae

Diphtheria is caused by toxin-producing strains of *Corynebacterium diphtheriae,* a nonmotile, pleomorphic, unencapsulated, gram-positive bacillus. The virulence of *C. diphtheriae* results from the action of a potent exotoxin. Local action of the exotoxin in the upper respiratory tract induces a characteristic pseudomembrane. Systemically, the exotoxin has a predilection for the heart (myocarditis), nerves (demyelination), and kidneys (tubular necrosis).

The posterior structures of the mouth and proximal parts of the pharynx are the most common sites for respiratory tract diphtheria. Onset is abrupt and involves sore throat, malaise, and fever. Initial erythema progresses to development of an adherent pseudomembrane typically on one or both tonsils with extension to the soft palate, oropharynx, and nasopharynx. Cervical lymph nodes are usually enlarged, and severely ill patients may have a bull-neck appearance. Laryngeal and tracheobronchial involvement usually results from direct spread from the pharynx.

Diagnosis is confirmed by culture on Loeffler medium. Toxin production is demonstrated by immunodiffusion (Elek test), monoclonal enzyme immunoassay, or polymerase chain reaction. Treatment involves the use of antitoxin, antibiotics (penicillin, erythromycin), and protection of a compromised airway.

Klebsiella rhinoscleromatis **(Rhinoscleroma, Scleroma)**

Klebsiella rhinoscleromatis is a capsulated gram-negative coccobacillus endemic to tropical and subtropical areas of Africa, America, and Asia. It causes a chronic granulomatous disease of the upper respiratory tract. The nose is almost always involved. The initial catarrhal stage is manifested by purulent rhinorrhea, crusting, and obstruction. In the granulomatous stage, multiple nodules form and coalesce to form blue-red or pale granulomas. Severe cases can progress to local destruction and cosmetic deformity. Broadening of the nose produces the characteristic Hebra nose. The final fibrotic stage causes cicatrix formation. Less commonly, the larynx and trachea are affected. Stenosis at these sites can cause airway obstruction.

Diagnosis is made by clinical findings and biopsy. Treatment is with prolonged antibiotics (tetracycline, ciprofloxacin, streptomycin). Surgery may be required for laryngeal stenosis.

Mycobacterium tuberculosis

Mycobacterium tuberculosis, an acid-fast bacillus, is the most common cause of granulomatous disease of the larynx. Symptoms of laryngeal tuberculosis include hoarseness, odynophagia, and dysphagia. Examination may show edema, submucosal nodules, and shallow ulcerations. The posterior part of the larynx is more commonly involved. The diagnosis is made by biopsy. Laryngeal tuberculosis responds well to antitubercular chemotherapy. Fibrotic disease from advanced disease may require surgical reconstruction.

Tuberculous otitis media may cause otorrhea, granulation tissue, aural polyps, tympanic perforations, or facial weakness. Biopsy secures the diagnosis. Treatment is with antitubercular chemotherapy. Surgical intervention may be indicated in the presence of facial paralysis, subperiosteal abscess, labyrinthitis, or extension of the infection into the central nervous system.

Mycobacterium leprae

Mycobacterium leprae is a gram-positive, acid-fast bacillus. The nose is by far the most frequently involved site in the upper respiratory tract. Lesions begin as a pale, nodular, plaque-like thickening of the mucosa. Untreated lesions progress to ulceration, septal perforation, and saddle-nose deformity. The larynx is less commonly involved. Involvement nearly always begins at the tip of the epiglottis. Diagnosis of leprosy is most reliably made by biopsy. Rifampin, dapsone, and clofazimine are the most widely used antileprosy drugs.

Actinomyces

Actinomyces israelii is an anaerobic gram-positive bacterium. It is an inhabitant of the normal oral flora that takes advantage of infection, trauma, or surgical injury to penetrate mucosa and invade adjacent tissue. Cervicofacial actinomycosis may vary from an indolent infection to a more rapidly progressive, tender, fluctuant infection. Infection spreads without regard to tissue planes. Progression leads to formation of a hard, board-like lesion ("lumpy jaw"), suppuration, draining fistulae, and the presence of "sulfur granules."

Diagnosis is by clinical features, biopsy, and culture. Treatment consists of prolonged antibiotics (penicillin) and surgical débridement.

SPECIFIC FUNGAL INFECTIONS

Candidiasis

Candida albicans is the most frequent of several species that cause candidiasis. It is a commensal of the oral cavity. Infection usually only follows changes in the local bacterial flora, mucosal integrity, or host immunity. Oral candidiasis ("thrush") can vary greatly in appearance. Erythematous and hyperplastic variants have been described. Candidiasis may also be responsible for median rhomboid glossitis and angular cheilitis. Candidiasis less commonly infects the larynx and pharynx. Diagnosis is made by direct laryngoscopy and biopsy.

Aspergillosis and the Phaeohyphomycoses

Aspergillus is the most common cause of fungal sinusitis. Infections take one of four forms: acute invasive fungal sinusitis, chronic invasive fungal sinusitis, "fungus ball," and allergic fungal sinusitis. The presence of *Aspergillus* or other fungi must be suspected in cases of sinusitis that do not respond to the usual medical treatment. Often the proper diagnosis is suggested only at surgery. Diagnosis is confirmed by histology and culture. Treatment of acute and chronic invasive forms requires surgical drainage, débridement, and the use of systemic antifungal agents. Treatment for a fungus ball requires only surgical removal and aeration of the involved sinus. Allergic fungal sinusitis is treated by surgical débridement and aeration of the involved sinuses followed by the use of systemic and topical corticosteroids. Immunotherapy may decrease the incidence of recurrence.

The phaeohyphomycoses (dematiaceous fungi) cause disease in a manner similar to *Aspergillus*. Examples include *Drechslera, Bipolaris, Curvularia, Alternaria, Cladosporium*, and other species.

Mucormycosis

Nearly all cases of mucormycosis occur in immunocompromised patients. Craniofacial disease usually originates in the nose or sinuses. Vascular invasion by hyphae leads to thrombosis with resultant ischemic infarction and necrosis. The lateral nasal wall and turbinates are the most frequent site of initial involvement. Edema and erythema are followed by cyanosis and necrosis. Spread may be very rapid into the orbit, cranium, palate, or face. Prompt diagnosis requires a high index of suspicion and is confirmed by biopsy. A computed tomography scan delineates the extent of infection. Treatment requires surgical débridement of all nonviable tissue as well as the prolonged use of amphotericin B.

Histoplasmosis

Histoplasma capsulatum is found throughout the world and in the United States is especially prevalent in the Mississippi and Ohio River valleys. Disseminated histoplasmosis occurs most frequently in patients with impaired cell-mediated immunity, such as AIDS. The larynx is the most common upper respiratory site of infection, with preference for the anterior part of the larynx and epiglottis. Lesions may appear nodular or ulcerative. Diagnosis is made by biopsy. Amphotericin B is the drug of choice for severe disease. An oral antifungal azole may be used for milder infections or suppressive therapy.

Blastomycosis

Blastomyces dermatitidis is most prevalent in the eastern portion of North America and over a wide area of Africa. The skin is frequently involved. Involvement of the nose, sinuses, larynx, or mouth may cause well-circumscribed, indurated lesions of the mucosa. Diagnosis is made by biopsy. Many patients with indolent upper respiratory infections can be treated with a prolonged course of oral azoles. Amphotericin B is used in more severe infections.

Cryptococcosis

Cryptococcus neoformans is distributed worldwide. A common natural source is avian droppings. Many patients with cryptococcosis are immunosuppressed (ie, AIDS). The upper respiratory tract is rarely involved. Laryngeal lesions have been described as edematous, exudative, or verrucous. Diagnosis is made by biopsy. The antifungal azoles and amphotericin B are used for treament.

Coccidioidomycosis

Coccidioides immitis is endemic to arid portions of the southwestern United States and northern Mexico, as well as scattered areas of Central and South America. In the upper respiratory tract, the larynx is most frequently involved. Lesions may be nodular or ulcerative. Diagnosis is made by biopsy. Antifungal azoles may be used for indolent disease, but amphotericin B is required for severe infections.

Paracoccidioidomycosis

Paracoccidioides brasiliensis is endemic to those areas of Latin America with hot, humid summers and dry, temperate winters. Lesions of the mucosa of the oral cavity, nose, pharynx, and larynx are painful and manifest as well-defined areas of hyperemic granulation tissue and ulceration. Diagnosis is made by biopsy. Treatment is with antifungal azoles, amphotericin B, and sulfonamides.

MISCELLANEOUS INFECTIONS

Rhinosporidiosis

Rhinosporidium seeberi has been difficult to classify. Recent studies have demonstrated it to be an aquatic protistan fish parasite near the animal-fungal divergence. Rhinosporidiosis is endemic to South Asia and occasionally seen in tropical Africa and America. It is a chronic inflammatory disease that most frequently involves the nasal mucosa, manifesting as a friable, painless, bleeding, polypoid growth. Diagnosis is made by biopsy. Surgical excision is the preferred treatment. No effective medical treatment as yet exists.

23

ALLERGIC RHINITIS

Jayant M. Pinto, MD
Robert M. Naclerio, MD

Allergic rhinitis affects up to 20% of the adult population in the United States, and its prevalence is increasing. Quality-of-life studies demonstrate that allergic rhinitis causes significant impairment of function. In the United States, approximately $1.5 billion is spent annually on office visits and medications. This burden is augmented when one considers related disorders such as asthma and sinusitis thought to be affected by allergic rhinitis.

Symptoms of allergic rhinitis can begin at any age but are most frequently first reported in adolescence or young adulthood. The rates of prevalence are similar for males and females, and no racial or ethnic variations are reported. The incidence of developing an allergic diathesis is higher in children whose parents suffer from allergic rhinitis. If one parent has allergies, the chances of the child's having rhinitis are 29% and increase to 47% when both parents have the disease. The rate of loss of allergic rhinitis symptoms has been estimated to be about 10%, which occurs in patients with the mildest form of the disease.

Part of the clinical importance of allergic rhinitis lies in its association with complications related to chronic nasal obstruction. Total nasal obstruction regardless of cause can result in sleep disturbances, hyposmia, and sinusitis. Whether nasal polyps result from allergic rhinitis remains an open question. The contribution of allergic rhinitis to middle ear disease is debated. Allergic rhinitis occurs in 80% of asthmatic subjects, and 40% of allergic rhinitic patients have asthma, suggesting a close link between the two diseases.

There has been an apparent increase in the prevalence of allergic rhinitis. One explanation of this increase is the hygiene theory, which purports that a decrease in infections in early childhood may increase the prevalence of atopic diseases. The decreasing prevalence of early childhood infections can be explained by the lower risk of exposure to infectious agents in early life as a result of increased immunization, improved sanitary conditions, and smaller family size.

PATHOPHYSIOLOGY

After sensitization of the nasal mucosa to an allergen, subsequent exposure leads to cross-linking of specific immunoglobulin (Ig)E receptors on mast cells that results in degranulation of the mast cells, with the release of inflammatory mediators that are responsible for allergic symptoms. Proinflammatory substances produced by other inflammatory cells are also generated after antigen exposure, most prominent among which are eosinophil products and cytokines. Cytokines generated by lymphocytes, mast cells, and other cells are found in both resting and stimulated nasal mucosa. Cytokines can upregulate adhesion molecules on the vascular endothelium and possibly on marginating leukocytes, leading to the migration of these cells into tissues. Other cytokines also promote chemotaxis and survival of recruited inflammatory cells. Chemokines are chemoattractant cytokines. Some of these inflammatory cells elaborate substances that cause local damage and mucosal modifications. Another important player is the nervous system, which amplifies the allergic reaction by both central and peripheral reflexes that result in changes at sites distant from those of antigen deposition. All of these changes lower the threshold of mucosal responsiveness and amplify it to a variety of specific and nonspecific stimuli, making allergic individuals more responsive to stimuli to which they are exposed in daily life.

Allergic rhinitis and asthma often coexist. Treatment of allergic rhinitis with intranasal corticosteroids can improve symptoms of asthma and reduce bronchial hyperresponsiveness. Asthmatics have a reduced ability to warm and humidfy cold, dry air, and subjects with seasonal allergic rhinitis also have a reduced ability to condition air, possibly with adverse implications for the lower airways.

ALLERGENS

Allergens are foreign substances capable of provoking an IgE-mediated response. Allergens are often categorized into indoor and outdoor types. Pollens causing allergy in temperate climates are released into the air from plants, trees, weeds, and grasses and are carried great distances. About 75% of patients with seasonal allergens have symptoms attributable to ragweed, 40% have them to grasses, and 5% to trees alone. Approximately 25% have allergies to both grass and ragweed, and 5% have allergies to all three pollens. Trees clearly have geographic variations. Pollination, and hence the allergy season, occurs in a predictable annual pattern for different regions of the country. The pattern, however, varies throughout the country. In the traditionally arid Southwest, previously a haven for allergy sufferers, increased urbanization and irrigation have contributed to increasing the pollen load. Humans tend to bring their allergens with them.

The most frequent perennial allergens are animal danders, dust mites, cockroaches, and molds. Dust mites are microscopic organisms and are the major allergens in "house dust." These mites feed on human epithelial scales and thrive in warm, humid environments (60 to 70% relative humidity, temperature 65° to 80°F). Bedding provides an ideal environment for proliferation of dust mites. Dust mite feces, the source of the allergen, are relatively large particles that remain airborne for short periods, unlike outdoor pollen. They settle from the air rapidly, and air filtration systems cannot effectively remove them. Lowering the indoor relative humidity to less than 50% during the summer months has a profound effect on the mite population throughout the year.

Cat and dog danders are the most frequent, but mice, guinea pigs, and horses can all be important sources of indoor allergens. The cockroach is an important source of allergen in inner-city populations. Allergenicity occurs to body parts and to feces. Molds, although less well studied, are sources of allergens, particularly in warm, humid environments. They tend to be found inside older homes in areas of decreased ventilation or increased dampness. Although a phenomenal variety of molds exist, *Alternaria* and *Cladosporium* are principally responsible for symptoms attributable to outdoor exposure, and *Aspergillus* and *Penicillium* are most prevalent indoors.

The patient's work environment may also be a source of allergens. Symptoms occurring only at work and subsiding on weekends may reflect an occupational disorder. At risk are flour handlers, workers in paint and plastic industries, woodworkers, fish and shellfish processors, and animal handlers. Unfortunately, few specific tests exist for the diagnosis of these disorders. Allergic reactions to natural rubber latex have increased, especially for health care workers who have high exposure by direct skin contact and inhalation of latex particles from powdered gloves.

CLINICAL PRESENTATION

History

Antigen exposure causes itching within seconds that is soon followed by sneezing. Rhinorrhea follows, and within about 15 minutes, nasal congestion peaks. Besides nasal symptoms, patients often complain about ocular pruritus, tearing, pharyngeal itching, throat clearing, cough, and ear popping. Other commonly reported symptoms include postnasal drip, increased lacrimation, dry cough, red eyes, headaches (pressure) over the paranasal sinus areas, and loss of smell or taste. These symptoms are nonspecific and have significant clinical overlap with other disorders. Itching of mucous membranes and repetitive sneezing, however, are the symptoms most suggestive of allergic disease. The relative importance of each symptom may vary among individuals, but nasal congestion tends to be the most bothersome, although each symptom is usually present, at least to some degree.

When obtaining the history, the physician should attempt to link exposure to allergens temporally with the occurrence of symptoms. This temporal correlation is the hallmark of allergic rhinitis. Patients with seasonal allergies complain only of recurrent symptoms at specific times of each year that coincide with pollination periods. In contrast, a history of year-round symptoms may indicate sensitivity to a perennial allergen or multiple seasonal allergens. Symptoms immediately following exposure to a potential source of allergen, such as a cat, strongly suggest an allergy to that allergen. Exposures to perennial allergens tend to be accentuated in winter in colder climates, when ventilation is reduced.

Additional considerations in history taking include the response to prior therapy and evidence of complications. Related effects of the pathophysiology must be addressed. For example, nasal obstruction may lead to mouth breathing. In children, this may be manifested as adenoid facies, with a high palatal arch and abnormal dental development. In adults, nasal obstruction may contribute to snoring and sleep-disordered breathing. Obstruction of sinus ostia may predispose to sinusitis.

A general medical history remains important. Past medical history may document systemic disorders that affect the nose, such as hypothyroidism. Pregnancy can produce nasal congestion and may require modification of treatment strategies. The presence of pulmonary disease such as asthma should be sought. Indeed, a significant percentage of patients with allergic rhinitis have asthma. Between 5 and 10% of asthmatic subjects may have intolerance to aspirin and nonsteroidal anti-inflammatory drugs. A family history of allergic rhinitis increases the chances of the patient's having an allergic disorder. Nasal symptoms might also be attributable to intake of medications such as beta blockers, which may contribute to nasal congestion through interference with the adrenergic mechanism. Tricyclic antidepressants may produce dryness of the nasal mucosa by virtue of their anticholinergic effects. Angiotensin-converting enzyme inhibitors can produce a chronic cough. Birth control pills can cause nasal congestion, and topical eyedrops can also induce nasal symptoms.

EXAMINATION

The classic description of allergic facies includes mouth breathing, allergic "shiners," and a transverse supratip nasal crease from long-term rubbing of the nose upward to relieve itching. These classic presentations occur more often in children, but absence of these signs does not exclude the disease.

Examination of the nose begins with observing the external appearance for gross deformities such as a deviation suggesting previous trauma or expansion of the nasal bridge, suggestive of nasal polyps. A nasal speculum permits evaluation of the anterior third of the internal nasal architecture and character of the nasal mucosa. Structural anomalies providing an anatomic basis for obstruction or recurrent infections such as septal deviations or spurs should be sought. The character and consistency of nasal secretions should be noted. These can vary from thin and clear to thick and whitish. The nasal mucosa may be swollen and pale bluish, although these signs are not pathognomonic of the disease. Ocular examination may demonstrate injection of the conjunctiva or swelling of the eyelids. The examination of allergic individuals often appears normal, and the primary importance of the physical examination is to rule out other causes of or contributors to the symptoms.

Decongestion of swollen nasal mucosa with a topical decongestant improves visualization and allows the differentiation of reversible from irreversible changes. Combining the vasoconstrictor with a topical anesthetic allows complete examination with an endoscope. The region of the middle meatus should be examined carefully because secretions there might be suggestive of acute or chronic sinusitis. Nasal polyps that were not visualized by anterior rhinoscopy may be seen during a careful endoscopic examination.

DIAGNOSIS

The identification of allergen(s) responsible for the patient's symptoms is important both for establishing the diagnosis and for the institution of avoidance measures. Symptoms occurring in temporal relation to allergen exposure suggest sensitization but are not diagnostic. Sensitization implies the presence of elevated levels of IgE directed against a specific allergen and can be demonstrated by a wheal and flare response to skin testing with allergen extracts or by measuring the level of antigen-specific IgE antibodies in the serum. However, individuals can show evidence of sensitization by a positive skin test or elevated specific antibody levels in the serum without having evidence of clinical disease. This emphasizes the importance of a good history in the evaluation of patients with suspected allergic disorders. In patients with a positive history, the magnitude of skin responses often corresponds with the severity of symptoms.

Skin Testing

Skin testing includes both puncture and intradermal testing. Negative puncture tests are usually confirmed by intradermal tests, which are more sensitive. The response is graded in comparison with a positive histamine or codeine response, and a negative control with the diluent for the allergen extracts is also included to control for nonspecific reactivity to the vehicle. Skin testing is valid in infants and young children, but the criteria for a positive reaction need to be adjusted because the reactions are smaller. Measurement of serum-specific IgE levels is also valid in this younger age group. Its advantages include greater sensitivity, the rapidity with which results are obtained, and low cost. Its disadvantages include inability to perform the test in patients with dermatographism or extensive eczema, poor tolerance of many children for multiple needle pricks, the need to maintain the potency of the allergen extracts, and possible systemic reactions. Drugs may interfere with skin test responses; therefore, careful instructions must be given to the patient in advance.

In Vitro Immunoglobulin E Measurements

Drawing blood for the measurement of specific IgE can circumvent some of the disadvantages of skin testing. Data from clinical studies comparing the results of skin testing and in vitro tests for specific IgE determination suggest a good correlation between the two, with a higher sensitivity for skin testing. Therefore, both determinations of specific IgE levels and skin testing are useful in the diagnosis of allergic disorders, but their results should always be interpreted in the context of clinical symptoms. The disadvantages of this form of allergy testing include cost, slightly lower sensitivity, and the time delay between drawing the blood and obtaining the results.

False-positive results may occur if patients have elevated IgE levels in their sera because of nonspecific binding.

Therefore, although IgE levels alone are of limited usefulness in the diagnosis of allergic rhinitis, and because elevated levels can also exist in patients with nonallergic conditions, these levels must be obtained in conjunction with a determination of specific IgE levels. False-negative results may also occur from inhibition by IgG antibodies with similar affinities as in patients receiving immunotherapy.

THERAPY

Prevention remains the mainstay of treatment of allergic rhinitis. If allergen exposure can be reduced, this should be part of long-term management. Short-term avoidance does not result in an instant resolution of symptoms and is rarely completely achievable. A number of interventions can be made to reduce allergen exposure, including removal of a pet and restriction of activities. For dust mites, replacing feather pillows and bedspreads with synthetic ones that can be washed in hot water (hotter than 130°F) and covering mattresses with commercially available plastic covers (< 10 μm) are helpful. Removing carpets and frequent vacuuming also help. Where carpets cannot be removed, acaricidal products can directly kill mites. Air conditioning can reduce exposure to outdoor allergens, but air conditioning and filter systems are not sufficient to reduce dust mite allergens. Rain reduces outdoor allergens. Humidifiers must be cleaned regularly to avoid becoming a source of mold allergens. Humidity should not exceed 40 to 50% because higher levels encourage the growth of dust mites and molds.

Pharmacotherapy provides the quickest relief. Antihistamines begin to take effect within 1 hour. They are excellent for the treatment of sneezing and watery rhinorrhea. When cost is not an issue, nonsedating antihistamines should always be prescribed. Sedating antihistamines may cause worse performance impairment than alcohol to the level of legal intoxication. To minimize cost, a long-acting, sedating antihistamine can be administered around bedtime and its efficacy allowed to persist into the next day without its sedative side effect, although adverse central nervous system effects may still occur. Decongestants, such as pseudoephedrine, can be added to antihistamines in fixed combinations or as separate agents to relieve nasal congestion. When taken in prescribed doses, they do not induce hypertension in normotensive patients, nor do they alter pharmacologic control of stable hypertensive patients. Decongestants should not be used in patients with uncontrolled hypertension, coronary artery disease, cardiac insufficiency, diabetes, hyperthyroidism, closed-angle glaucoma, prostatic hypertrophy, or urinary retention or in patients taking monoamine oxidase inhibitors. Cromolyn sodium is an alternative to antihistamines as an initial treatment, but the need for frequent dosing, with the resultant reduction in compliance, should be kept in mind. Leukotriene modifiers may be used for effects against congestion in asthmatic or refractory cases and may be used in combination with antihistamines in patients who do not tolerate other therapies.

Topical intranasal corticosteroids are the mainstay of therapy. These have been shown to be more effective than antihistamines when used regularly or on an as-needed basis. They are highly effective in reducing all of the nasal symptoms of allergic rhinitis, including congestion. They are nonsedating, have few side effects, and are well tolerated by patients. The daily cost of treatment with nasal corticosteroids is less than that of the daily use of nonsedating antihistamines. Topical corticosteroids are initially given at the dose recommended in the *Physicians' Desk Reference*. Patients should be seen 2 weeks after initiating therapy to monitor for the development of local side effects. Superficial septal erosions can occur secondary to trauma from the nozzle, and the application technique should be carefully reviewed with these patients. The dosage is adjusted depending on the response: if a patient is better but continues to have breakthrough symptoms, the frequency of administration is increased; if excellent control is achieved, the frequency or the dose should be reduced. Furthermore, periods of exacerbations can be predicted, based on a patient's pattern of allergies; therefore, medication dosage can be varied accordingly. Ocular symptoms may not be controlled by intranasal corticosteroids but may be addressed by adding an ophthalmic preparation or an oral antihistamine. Anticholinergic agents play a limited role in the control of rhinorrhea.

In children, the long-term use of certain topical corticosteroids is approved in patients as young as age 3 years or greater. For most topical corticosteroids, it is recommended to reduce the dose by half in young children. Because of the small possibility that intranasal corticosteroids can interfere with growth, these medications should always be given in the lowest effective dose. Growth should be carefully and regularly monitored. Treatment with topical corticosteroids requires patient education. The physician must often reassure patients as to the safety of intranasal corticosteroids compared with oral preparations.

Initiation of immunotherapy depends on patient preference and the response to pharmacotherapy. Immunotherapy has not been shown to be more effective than intranasal corticosteroids. Patients who are taking beta blockers should not receive immunotherapy because, if anaphylaxis occurs, they cannot be resuscitated. Immunotherapy of symptomatic asthmatic patients should be administered with great caution because these patients have the greatest morbidity. Immunotherapy should not be started in pregnant women because of the risk of anaphylaxis and the resultant effect of hypotension on the fetus.

Novel therapies such as anti-IgE and third-generation antihistamines are in trials. A perhaps more elegant therapeutic strategy would be to effect long-lasting changes in immune responses away from an allergic phenotype. Such a strategy might alter the natural course of disease and allow discontinuation of medication. This type of immunotherapy may involve immunization with allergen, modified allergen, peptides of allergen, and complementary deoxyribonucleic acid (DNA) of allergen, with adjuvants, including immuno-stimulatory DNA sequences, cytokines, and bacterial products. These therapies will require further study but ultimately may prove useful in expanding the armamentarium against allergic rhinitis.

24

ACUTE AND CHRONIC NASAL DISORDERS

Valerie J. Lund, MS, FRCS, FRCS(Ed)

Nasal disorders may be broadly divided into allergic and non-allergic conditions, with the latter subdivided into infectious and noninfectious together with a differential diagnosis that includes polyps, mechanical factors, tumors, granulomas, and cerebrospinal fluid rhinorrhea. A long list of investigations is available, but the most important thing is to take a careful clinical history, combined with examination of the nose that must include rigid nasal endoscopy. Additional tests of mucociliary clearance, nasal airway assessment, olfaction, and various hematologic investigations may be indicated in individual patients.

MUCOCILIARY FUNCTION

Nasal Mucociliary Clearance

A simple test of mucociliary function can be performed by placing a 0.5 mm piece of saccharin on the anterior end of the inferior turbinate approximately 1 cm from the end to avoid areas of squamous metaplasia. The time taken to taste something sweet in the mouth is measured, which normally takes 30 minutes or less. If longer than an hour has elapsed, it is worth repeating the test in case the particle has fallen out and checking that the patient is capable of tasting saccharin.

Ciliary Beat Frequency

When the saccharin test is prolonged or if specific ciliary abnormalities are suspected, it is possible to examine the cilia directly by taking a sample with a small disposable, cupped spatula (Rhinoprobe) and observing cilia activity under a phase-contrast microscope with a photometric cell. The frequency can be measured with a real-time analyzer and expressed in hertz, the normal range from the inferior turbinate being 12 to 15 Hz. However, this technique is not available in every center.

Electron Microscopy

If the nasomucociliary clearance time and ciliary beat frequency are abnormal, samples may be obtained with the spatula or via direct biopsy for electron microscopy studies to diagnose conditions such as primary ciliary dyskinesia (PCD).

Nitric Oxide Measurement

The level in parts per million of nitric oxide present in the expired nasal and pulmonary air can be helpful in establishing normal mucociliary function. In PCD, the nitric oxide level that is an indirect marker of ciliary metabolism is much reduced to double figures or less in the nose and single figures from the chest. However, as nitric oxide is predominantly produced in the sinuses, conditions such as nasal polyposis that obstruct gas exchange from these areas can also result in a very low reading from the nasal gases. The level is commensurately elevated in the presence of inflammation.

NASAL AIRWAY ASSESSMENT

Nasal Expiratory or Inspiratory Peak Flow

Nasal expiratory or inspiratory peak flow, which uses a peak-flow meter, has the advantage of being inexpensive, quick, and easy to perform. It is useful for repeated examinations and compares well with active anterior rhinomanometry. Of the two methods, forced inspiration is preferred, although it can produce significant vestibular collapse in some individuals. Forced expiration inflates the eustachian tube, which may be uncomfortable and may also produce an unpleasant quantity of mucus in the mask.

Rhinomanometry

Rhinomanometry attempts to evaluate nasal airway resistance by making quantitative measurement of nasal flow and pressure. It employs the principle that air will flow through a tube only when there is a pressure differential passing from areas of high to low pressure. When the nasal mucosa is decongested, the reproducibility of rhinomanometry is good, but it requires some expertise to produce consistent results and has therefore remained primarily a research tool. Active anterior rhinomanometry is more commonly used as the posterior technique cannot be used in 20 to 25% of individuals owing to an inability to relax the soft palate.

Acoustic Rhinometry

In acoustic rhinometry, an audible sound pulse is electronically generated and is passed into the nose, where it is altered by variations in the cross-sectional area. The reflected signal is picked up by a microphone and analyzed allowing determination of area within the nasal cavity as a function of distance. From this, volumes may be derived, thus providing topographic information rather than a measure of airflow. It appears to be more reproducible and to have greater applicability than rhinomanometry but is still being evaluated as a clinical tool.

OLFACTION

Olfactory Thresholds

Estimation of olfactory thresholds may be established by presentation of serial dilutions of pure odorants such as carbinol.

The patient is presented with two bottles, one containing only the diluent solution as the control, the other the odorant in progressively increasing or decreasing concentrations. Each is sniffed in turn until a point is reached when the patient cannot distinguish between the control and test bottle. This indicates the minimum detectable odor.

Scratch and Sniff Tests

The University of Pennsylvania Smell Identification Test (UPSIT) uses patches impregnated with microencapsulated odorants. The patient is forced to choose among a number of options after scratching the patch to release the odor. The results are well validated for age and sex and take into account answers guessed correctly as well as give an indication of malingering.

Alternative identification tests include the Zurich Smell Test, in which eight odorants must be correctly identified. The test choices are offered pictorially as well as in English. The Sniffin' Sticks combine both a qualitative and quantitative assessment of olfaction.

INFECTIOUS RHINITIS

Infectious rhinitis or "rhinosinusitis," which better describes the pathophysiology, may be attributable to a long list of causative agents. These include viruses, bacteria, fungi, protozoa, and parasites. A number of congenital conditions may predispose patients to infection of the respiratory tract, including PCD, cystic fibrosis, and immune deficiency. The most common cause of infection in the upper respiratory tract is the common cold, caused by over 100 different types of rhinovirus. Most young adults suffer from two to three colds each year, and it is estimated that 0.5 to 2% of these will become bacterially infected. The virus is normally transported into the nose by direct contact with the fingers rather than by airborne contamination, and once the virus gains access to the respiratory epithelium, it will produce ciliary stasis and destruction. After 1 to 3 days' incubation, a prodromal or "dry phase" occurs followed by a catarrhal phase. This may be followed by resolution or secondary bacterial infection when the discharge becomes mucopurulent. Little other than symptomatic relief can be offered in the form of decongestants and antipyretics. Influenza in its various forms constitutes a more specific and potentially serious viral respiratory tract infection, resulting in pandemics with significant morbidity and mortality in susceptible populations. More permanent damage to both ciliated and olfactory epithelium may result, and although vaccines are available, their usefulness is limited by the potential for viral mutation.

Etiologic Factors

A number of congenital conditions may predispose patients to infection of the respiratory tract.

Primary Ciliary Dyskinesia

Some individuals are born with a congenital abnormality of the cilia that affects their motility. Electron microscopic examination reveals disorganized microtubules and the absence of dynein arms. In addition to nasal problems, patients usually exhibit lower respiratory tract infection, serous otitis media, and infertility problems. In full-blown Kartagener's syndrome, patients have bronchiectasis, sinus infection, and situs inversus in approximately 50% of cases.

Cystic Fibrosis

Cystic fibrosis is an autosomal recessive disease, the most common inherited fatal disease of White children, caused by a defective mucosal chloride transport gene. In its most severe form, it presents with malabsorption and progressive obstructive pulmonary disease, but approximately one-third of children and one-half of adults suffer from multiple bilateral nasal polyps, and the majority of patients have a chronic pansinusitis. The polyps have been attributed to an abnormality of sodium and water transport across membranes, and the histology of the polyps differs significantly from those in other conditions, having less eosinophils and more lymphocytes and plasma cells. *Pseudomonas aeruginosa* is commonly found in association with sinus disease and may be targeted specifically with appropriate antibiotics such as the quinolones. The majority of patients are managed by a combination of medical therapies with intranasal corticosteroids and surgery. The results of surgery are compromised by the condition, although are still regarded as worthwhile by patients. Other medical therapies have included intranasal furosemide, amiloride, and messenger ribonuclease.

Bacterial Folliculitis and Vestibulitis

Folliculitis and vestibulitis may result when *Staphylococcus aureus* invades a pilosebaceous follicle. The condition is exquisitely painful as the vestibular skin is tightly bound to the underlying cartilages. Local cleaning and systemic antibiotics such as floxacillin should be given and the possibility of a cavernous sinus thrombosis considered. This may result from retrograde venous spread of infection. The condition carries a serious morbidity, often with bilateral blindness and mortality. Initially, the patient complains of headache, and painful paresthesia is the distribution of the trigeminal nerve followed by other cranial neuropathy, resulting in ophthalmoplegia. Rapid institution of high-dose intravenous antibiotics has reduced the mortality to between 10 and 27%.

Erysipelas

Erysipelas is an acute beta-hemolytic streptococcal infection producing fever, erythema, and induration of involved skin often in a butterfly pattern across the nose, adjacent cheeks, and upper lip. The infection generally responds well to penicillin or erythromycin. Other specific infections in this region include diphtheria, rhinoscleroma, leprosy, tuberculosis, and syphilis.

NONINFECTIOUS RHINITIS

Idiopathic or vasomotor rhinitis is the most common form of nonallergic, noninfectious rhinitis. This is a diagnosis of exclusion manifest by an upper respiratory tract hyperresponsiveness to changes in temperature, humidity, and environmental irritants such as cigarette smoke. The perennial symptoms include nasal blockage, anterior rhinorrhea, and postnasal discharge, sometimes with sneezing in the absence of positive allergy tests. Therapy includes avoidance of obvious triggers together with topical medication such as corticosteroids and/or anticholinergic agents, with surgery playing a limited role. Occupational exposure to environmental irritants may produce similar symptoms that can be accompanied by asthma, conjunctivitis, and dermatitis.

A range of physiologic and pathologic endocrine conditions can affect the nose, for example, pregnancy, hypothyroidism, and acromegaly. In pregnancy, saline douche, topical nasal corticosteroids, and oral decongestants may be safely prescribed.

A range of medications may produce nasal symptoms. These include aspirin and other nonsteroidal anti-inflammatory agents, cardiovascular preparations, topical ophthalmic beta blockers, oral contraceptives, and recreational drugs such as cocaine. The long-term use of topical decongestants may result in rhinitis medicamentosa. This is caused by a rebound congestion ultimately followed by a significant mucosal atrophy. A short course of oral corticosteroids may be necessary to wean patients off their use. Certain foods and alcoholic beverages may also produce nasal reactions, as may emotional responses, for example, "honeymoon rhinitis."

Primary atrophic rhinitis attributed to *Klebsiella ozaenae* is relatively uncommon in the West, although secondary atrophy is not infrequently seen following excessive surgery, trauma, radiotherapy, and a chronic granulomatous condition. The foul-smelling crusts and capacious airway are distressing to the patient. Topical treatments and surgery, including closure of the nose, have been advocated.

Nonallergic rhinitis with eosinophilia should probably be regarded as a subgroup of idiopathic rhinitis characterized by nasal eosinophilia and perennial symptoms of sneezing, itching, rhinorrhea, and blockage. Topical corticosteroids usually offer the best symptomatic control.

MECHANICAL NASAL OBSTRUCTION

Mechanical nasal obstruction may be caused by septal deviation and/or turbinate enlargement, although the sensation of congestion may occur in the absence of reduced airflow, secondary to inflammation within the ostiomeatal complex. Septal deviation may be congenital or acquired, and if sufficient to impede airflow may be surgically corrected.

Complications of trauma and/or surgery include septal hematoma and septal perforation. Infection after nasal surgery is uncommon but, when it occurs, is very painful and may cause a significant elevation of body temperature. Cases of toxic shock syndrome have been described as a result of nasal packing. This condition is generally caused by a staphylococcus and is characterized by headache, pyrexia, tachycardia, changes in blood pressure, erythema of the skin, and subsequent desquamation of the skin of the hands. Treatment with systemic β-lactamase-resistant antistaphylococcal antibiotics should be instituted as soon as possible.

Enlargement of the turbinates, particularly of the inferior turbinate, may lead to alteration in airflow. If medical treatment fails with topical nasal corticosteroids, surgical reduction may be undertaken. A range of techniques, including lateral out-fracture, submucous diathermy, linear electric cautery, turbinectomy, submucous resection, laser turbinectomy, and intraturbinal corticosteroid injection, have been advocated.

Foreign bodies are occasionally the cause of nasal obstruction but are more often characterized by a unilateral foul-smelling discharge, and removal under a general anesthetic is usually recommended.

GRANULOMATOUS CONDITIONS

A range of systemic conditions including granulomas, vasculitides, and connective tissue disorders such as systemic lupus erythematosus may affect the nose. Sarcoidosis is a systemic condition of unknown cause characterized by noncaseating epithelioid granulomas. The upper respiratory tract is usually involved in association with the lower respiratory tract and produces obstruction, mucopurulent blood-stained discharge, and crusting. There may be septal perforation with saddling of the nasal bridge and lupus pernio. No one test is diagnostic, although the presence of a raised angiotensin-converting enzyme is strongly suggestive of the condition but to be followed by confirmatory histology. Local and systemic treatment with corticosteroids and oral cytotoxic agents is often required.

In Wegener's granulomatosis, the upper and lower respiratory tracts are usually involved and may be followed by a focal glomerulonephritis, which rapidly leads to renal failure and death. Any part of the body may be affected, although there is a particular predilection for the ears, nose, and throat. Nasal blockage, blood-stained discharge, and crusting, together with destruction of the septum and a characteristic implosion of the nasal bridge, may be observed. A positive antineutrophil cytoplasmic antigen (c-ANCA) is strongly supportive of the diagnosis. Medical therapy includes systemic corticosteroids and a variety of cytotoxic drugs, including cyclophosphamide and azathioprine.

Amyloid deposits have also been described in the skin of the vestibule.

EPISTAXIS

A range of conditions, both local and general, may produce nosebleeds of varying magnitude. Management includes the diagnosis of any underlying condition and will be largely determined by the severity of the bleed. This can range from first aid measures and cauterization to various forms of packing, arterial ligation, or embolization. Cauterization under endoscopic control and/or endoscopic ligation of the sphenopalatine artery has reduced the need for long-term packing.

Hereditary hemorrhagic telangiectasia is an autosomal dominant, non–sex-linked transmitted condition characterized by telangiectasias, which are deficient in muscle and/or elastic tissue. The majority of patients experience epistaxis of varying severity, although the lesions can be found anywhere in the body.

RHINOPHYMA

Rhinophyma is a disfiguring enlargement of the external nose caused by overgrowth of sebaceous tissue. This may be reduced by a variety of techniques, including laser therapy.

MALIGNANT SKIN TUMORS

Malignant tumors of the skin of the nose include basal cell and squamous cell carcinoma, both of which may be treated by radiotherapy and/or surgical excision.

25

SINUSITIS AND POLYPOSIS

Andrew P. Lane, MD
David W. Kennedy, MD

PATHOPHYSIOLOGY OF RHINOSINUSITIS

Rhinosinusitis is an extremely prevalent disorder that has a significant impact on the quality of life of affected individuals and places a large economic burden on the United States as a whole. The underlying causes of acute rhinosinusitis are multiple and include a variety of host and environmental factors. Ultimately, however, the common pathway of acute sinusitis is thought to be the presence of bacteria in a sinus cavity with an obstructed ostium. This requires not only blockage of the normal anatomic outflow of the sinus but also a failure of the mucociliary clearance function of the mucosa that would ordinarily remove the bacteria. Reversible ostial obstruction may occur in the setting of viral upper respiratory infection, allergy, environmental irritants, and barotrauma. Irreversible blockage caused by fixed anatomy may contribute to the problem or be the sole etiologic agent. Once the ostium becomes occluded, a local hypoxia develops in the sinus cavity and sinus secretions accumulate. This combination of low-oxygen tension and a rich culture medium of secretions allows exponential bacterial growth. Abnormalities of the epithelial cilia or the quality or quantity of the mucus also will hinder bacterial removal. Any systemic disease leading to an immunocompromised state will potentially predispose a patient to acute sinusitis. Chronic illness, such as diabetes or malnutrition, metabolic derangement, chemotherapy, or long-term corticosteroid therapy, will similarly increase the tendency to develop acute sinusitis.

Rhinosinusitis lasting longer than 12 weeks is classified as chronic. The underlying pathophysiology of chronic sinusitis is not necessarily infectious and is often a self-perpetuating inflammatory process. Whereas acute sinusitis is histologically an exudative process characterized by neutrophilic infiltration and necrosis, chronic sinusitis is a proliferative process remarkable for thickening of the mucosa. The predominant infiltrative cell in chronic sinusitis is the eosinophil, both in the allergic and the nonallergic patient. There is evidence that potent eosinophil-attracting chemokines are produced in the sinus mucosa, elaborated by a variety of cell types under the stimulation of cytokines produced largely by T cells. An increase in the levels of interleukin-4 and interleukin-5 in the sinonasal tract promotes the continued migration and prolonged life span of eosinophils. A number of proinflammatory cytokines are up-regulated and participate in the process of directing lymphocyte and granulocyte traffic while causing further production of cytokines in an autocrine fashion. Degranulation of eosinophils releases several destructive enzymes that damage the epithelium. This disrupts the normal barrier function and the mucociliary activity of the mucosa, allowing bacteria and fungi to colonize the sinus cavities. The damage to the epithelium irritates sensory nerve endings, causing pain and stimulating changes in mucus secretion and endothelial permeability via reflex pathways.

FUNGAL RHINOSINUSITIS

Some forms of sinusitis are caused by fungal microorganisms within the sinonasal tract. The fungal infection can be either invasive or noninvasive. The invasive forms can present in either an indolent, chronic form or a fulminant, acute form.

The latter frequently occurs in immunosuppressed patients, such as diabetics in ketoacidosis, transplant recipients, human immunodeficiency virus (HIV)-infected individuals, and patients undergoing chemotherapy. Without control of the underlying immunosuppression, the process is rapidly progressive and may extend into the orbits and intracranial space despite aggressive surgical and medical management. The mainstays of therapy are aggressive surgical débridement and intravenous antifungal agents. In contrast, chronic invasive sinusitis tends to occur in immunocompetent hosts and generally advances very slowly. Vascular invasion in the chronic form is minimal or nonexistent. There are two noninvasive types of fungal sinusitis, the first being a fungal ball growing within a sinus cavity. The other noninvasive form of fungal sinusitis is an entity known as allergic fungal rhinosinusitis, which is not caused by the abnormal presence of fungus in the nose but rather is an abnormal response to nonpathogenic fungi that exist in the environment. Therapy consists of surgical débridement and systemic corticosteroids.

POLYPOSIS

Nasal polyps are associated with a number of systemic diseases including aspirin intolerance, intrinsic asthma, primary ciliary dyskinesia, and cystic fibrosis. They are frequently observed in chronic rhinosinusitis, including allergic rhinosinusitis, and other chronic sinonasal inflammatory states. Overall, the mechanisms behind polyp formation are believed to be multifactorial. A variety of environmental and genetic factors play a role in the pathogenesis of inflammatory polyps, and the role of proinflammatory cytokines, chemokines, and chemotactic mediators is increasingly being appreciated. When significant intranasal polyposis is present, polyps can easily be seen by anterior rhinoscopy. Grossly, they are translucent to pale gray, pear shaped, smooth, soft, and freely mobile. Polyps arise from the lateral nasal wall and, in many cases, are limited to the middle meatus, where they can only be visualized endoscopically. The typical complaints associated with polyposis are nasal congestion, rhinorrhea, and olfactory dysfunction. Unilateral polyps should raise concern for allergic fungal sinusitis or inverted papilloma. A single, unilateral polyp originating high in the nasal cavity or with a stalk that is not clearly visible may represent an encephalocele or meningocele. As a rule, if the intranasal mass does not have the characteristic appearance of a polyp, is unilateral, bleeds easily, or has a stalk that is not clearly identified, imaging studies are indicated before proceeding with management.

The most important element in the treatment of nasal polyposis is medical therapy with corticosteroids. Both oral corticosteroids and topical nasal corticosteroids are effective in shrinking polyps and controlling their recurrence. Topical corticosteroids are first-line therapy that should be employed prior to considering surgical intervention. Unless there is a contraindication, a trial of a tapering course of oral corticosteroids is also frequently used prior to surgical resection. Should surgery eventually become necessary, topical corticosteroids and occasionally oral corticosteroids may be needed for long-term maintenance. Surgery for polyps is indicated when medical management fails to give symptomatic improvement or if complications develop. Successful treatment ultimately depends on a commitment by both the patient and the doctor to an intensive postoperative course, which may be quite prolonged and involve multiple débridements.

COMPLICATIONS OF RHINOSINUSITIS

The complications of sinusitis can be divided broadly into those involving the orbits and those that involve the intracranial space. In the antibiotic era, such complications have become less commonplace, but they still have the potential for serious morbidity or even mortality. Awareness and early recognition of complications are necessary to minimize adverse sequelae. Fortunately, improved diagnostic modalities and advances in medical and surgical techniques have significantly reduced the risk of blindness or life-threatening intracranial infections. Ethmoiditis most commonly leads to orbital involvement, followed by infections of the maxillary, frontal, and sphenoid sinuses. Infections of the ethmoid can directly erode the thin lamina papyracea or extend through suture lines or foramina into the orbit. Intracranial complications of sinusitis occur less frequently than orbital complications but are potentially life-threatening if not recognized and treated. Most intracranial infections arise from the frontal sinus, although extension from the other sinuses is possible. The most frequent route of spread is retrograde thrombophlebitis via valveless veins in the posterior table of the frontal sinus that communicate directly with dural veins. The types of complications that may develop include osteomyelitis of the frontal bone, meningitis, epidural abscess, subdural empyema, and intracerebral abscess. Pott's puffy tumor is a well-circumscribed swelling of the forehead caused by anterior extension of frontal sinusitis. The edema of the skin and soft tissue overlies a collection of pus under the periosteum of the anterior table of the frontal sinus.

In cases of orbital complications, the decision to proceed to surgery is made based on a number of factors and is individualized to the particular patient. Progressive visual loss demands aggressive management and drainage of the source of infection. Surgical intervention should be considered when there is disease progression after 24 hours of antibiotics or no improvement after 2 to 3 days of therapy. Ideally, surgery involves approaching both the orbital complication and underlying sinusitis simultaneously. The mainstay of therapy for suspected intracranial complications is intravenous antibiotics capable of crossing the blood-brain barrier. If cultures can be obtained from the affected sinuses, this will guide specific antibiotic choice. A neurosurgical consultation is sought when a procedure may be necessary to drain an intracranial collection. Corticosteroids are usually not used during an active infectious process; however, they are sometimes employed to reduce severe brain edema. Surgery should be directed at the involved sinuses as well as the intracranial process unless the patient's condition limits operative time, in which case, the neurosurgical procedure takes precedence.

DIAGNOSIS OF RHINOSINUSITIS

The most common complaints associated with rhinosinusitis are nasal obstruction and nasal congestion. These sensations likely result from the thickening of the sinus and nasal mucosa, along with reactive swelling of the inferior and middle turbinates. Postnasal discharge is also a common symptom reported by sinusitis patients. These symptoms, which largely reflect inflammation of the nasal cavities, are present in allergies and colds as well as sinusitis. Facial pain, pressure, or fullness can be a more localizing symptom of sinus disease that may help in its identification. Particularly in acute sinusitis, pain over the maxillary or frontal regions can be a prominent feature in the patient's history. Maxillary sinus pain may also be referred to the upper teeth and palate. Ethmoid sinusitis classically causes pain between or behind the eyes. Sphenoid inflammation or infection tends to cause more insidious pain that may be referred to the occipital, vertex, or bitemporal regions of the skull. Of course, there are many other causes of headache and dental pain besides sinusitis; thus, facial or head pain is not a specific finding. Also, pain is a less common finding once sinusitis becomes chronic, except when there is an acute exacerbation. Similarly, acute sinusitis is sometimes associated with systemic symptoms such as malaise, fever, and lethargy, whereas chronic sinusitis typically is not. A common symptom seen in chronic disease more often than in the acute situation is olfactory loss. Sore throat, cough, and fatigue may be present in either case.

The external findings in sinusitis may be limited and non-specific. Periorbital, forehead, or cheek swelling is sometimes apparent, and there may also be associated tenderness in these regions to palpation or percussion. The oral cavity and oropharynx should be examined for dental pathology and for the presence of postnasal discharge. Anterior rhinoscopy can reveal mucosal hyperemia and edema of the septum and inferior turbinate. It may be possible to discern mucopurulent discharge in this manner, although the site of origin is not likely to be visualized. In recent years, there has been a tremendous advance in the use of nasal endoscopes for the diagnosis of nasal and sinus disease. Such endoscopes may either be rigid or of a flexible fiberoptic design. With endoscopy, the middle meatus can be seen directly, and any purulent discharge may be traced either to the middle meatus or sphenoethmoidal recess. A swab can then be used to obtain this material under endoscopic control, yielding highly accurate cultures that may direct specific antibiotic therapy.

The imaging study of choice today for rhinosinusitis is computed tomography (CT) with fine coronal sections at the level of the ostiomeatal complex. This technique is excellent in assessing bony detail and thus provides an accurate road map for endoscopic sinus surgery. It also is sensitive in demonstrating mucosal thickening and revealing trapped secretions within the sinus cavities. Unfortunately, the mucosal changes seen by CT are not specific for sinusitis and thus should be interpreted cautiously. Viral respiratory tract infections and allergy will both cause mucosal thickening in the absence of infectious or chronic sinusitis. Magnetic resonance imaging is a complementary study that is more sensitive than CT in showing soft tissue detail. It can clearly demonstrate dural inflammation that would not be appreciable by CT and shows the communication of encephaloceles with the intracranial space.

MEDICAL TREATMENT OF RHINOSINUSITIS

Once the diagnosis of acute sinusitis is ensured, the goal of therapy is to prevent disease progression and the possibility of serious sequelae. Antibiotics should be instituted for all cases of acute sinusitis. Historically, there has been a dramatic reduction in the incidence of complications secondary to sinusitis since the introduction of antibiotics. The selection of first-line antibiotics for acute sinusitis is directed by the knowledge of the most common pathogens. The choice of a second-line antibiotic is dependent on a number of variables including patient allergies, dosing schedule, proven efficacy, physician experience, and the patient's previous response history, as well as resistance patterns in the community. Beta-lactam cephalosporins have long been the most common second-line agents, although macrolides and fluoroquinones have recently been increasing in popularity. The most relevant pharmacokinetic parameter of beta-lactamase-resistant antibiotics is the time above minimal inhibitory concentration, which has been shown to correlate with efficacy. Once antibiotics have been instituted, the duration of therapy is controversial. Symptoms should begin to improve within 48 to 72 hours, and it is important to maintain appropriate follow-up to ensure that the complete course of antibiotics is taken. A good guideline is a 10- to 14-day course of therapy, which can be lengthened for persistent symptoms.

A variety of therapeutic measures can augment the effectiveness of antibiotics in the treatment of acute sinusitis. The goal of these interventions is to restore proper nasal function through improvement in ciliary function and reduction of mucosal edema. Many simple, inexpensive supportive measures are effective because they help to clear crusts and thick mucus. Examples include nasal saline sprays, humidifiers (warm or cool), steam, hot soup, or tea. Mucolytic agents such as guaifenesin also are useful because they lead to thinning of the mucus, which promotes clearance and prevents stasis. Systemic and topical decongestants act on α-adrenergic receptors to cause vasoconstriction and reduction of edema and are therefore appropriate to relieve nasal obstruction, re-establish ostial patency, and ventilate the sinuses. Antihistamines have been used empirically in patients with sinusitis and allergy, although no studies show a clearly beneficial role for these medications. In the setting of acute infectious sinusitis, first-generation antihistamines may actually be counterproductive because of their anticholinergic side effects of mucosal dryness, crusting, and increased mucus viscosity. Systemic corticosteroids are potent anti-inflammatory agents that reduce tissue edema and inhibit inflammatory mediator production; thus, they can prove beneficial in the treatment of acute sinusitis. However, since a number of potential complications are associated with corticosteroids, the use of corticosteroids is not widely accepted for acute sinusitis. In general, the risk of adverse side effects when corticosteroids are used conservatively over short, tapered doses is minimal; therefore, these drugs are reasonable adjunctive therapy for acute sinusitis treated primarily with antibiotics.

In chronic sinusitis, the microorganisms primarily involved are coagulase-positive and coagulase-negative species of *Staphylococcus* and *Streptococcus*. Antibiotic therapy should therefore be directed at these pathogens, although resistance is a constant problem. The duration of antibiotic therapy in chronic sinusitis is not clearly defined but is typically on the order of 4 to 8 weeks. The goals of ancillary therapy for chronic sinus disease are similar to those in the acute situation; however, there are some important differences. When an underlying condition such as allergy, polyposis, fungal infection, or systemic disease is present, the treatment must first be directed toward controlling these processes. In the case of allergic rhinosinusitis, management with antihistamines, topical nasal corticosteroids, and immunotherapy will be of more value than it would in an acute infection. Likewise, systemic corticosteroids are indispensable for the treatment of polyps and sinus inflammation caused by systemic granulomatous or autoimmune diseases.

SURGICAL THERAPY FOR RHINOSINUSITIS

Endoscopic Sinus Surgery

The philosophy behind functional endoscopic sinus surgery (FESS) stems from an understanding of the relationship between the middle meatal anterior ethmoid complex, termed the ostiomeatal unit, and the pathogenesis of maxillary and frontal sinus disease. Messerklinger first described the surgical principles of FESS and demonstrated that relieving the ostiomeatal unit of obstruction and inflammation could reverse mucosal disease within the frontal and maxillary sinuses. Today FESS has become the standard operation for rhinosinusitis, supplanting a variety of open procedures that had previously been employed.

Functional endoscopic sinus surgery can be performed under local or general anesthesia. Local anesthesia with intravenous sedation may be preferable because sensory information remains intact along the periorbita and skull base. However, there has been a general tendency toward performing more endoscopic sinus surgery under general anesthesia in recent years.

The majority of the dissection in FESS is carried out using a 0-degree endoscope because the angulation of the other telescopes can be disorienting. The 30-degree endoscope is usually required for examination and manipulation of the maxillary sinus ostium and frontal recess.

An important principle in FESS is the preservation of mucosa wherever technically feasible. The extent of surgery is based on the preoperative assessment of the disease present; however, in most cases, a sickle knife is first used to perform an infundibulotomy, and the uncinate is removed. The bulla ethmoidalis is then entered and removed. Depending on the extent of disease, the posterior ethmoid may be entered through the inferior and medial area of the basal lamella. The skull base is most easily identified within the posterior ethmoidectomy and serves as the superior boundary for the dissection. The sphenoid ostium is located and, if necessary, widened beginning inferiorly and medially. At this point, the dissection is continued anteriorly along the skull base, with care not to injure the anterior and posterior ethmoid arteries. The mucosa along the skull base is also preserved. The frontal recess is dissected only if required because manipulation of this region can lead to stenosis of the frontal ostium. In addition, frontal recess surgery increases the requirement for postoperative care. Operating within the frontal recess is the most challenging segment of the operation. Finally, the natural ostium of the maxillary sinus is identified and enlarged.

The overall success of FESS is in large part owing to appropriate postoperative care. The goal during this period is to promote mucosal generation within the sinus cavities. Systemic antibiotics are used, and their use may be prolonged when severe, chronic inflammation is present. Patients may be instructed to irrigate the nose with saline solution twice daily. For the majority of patients with chronic sinusitis, surgery alone does not result in a permanent disease resolution. Long-term, culture-directed, systemic antibiotics and prolonged use of topical nasal corticosteroids are frequently required. It is critical to the ultimate success of endoscopic sinus surgery that meticulous, sometimes aggressive, débridement be performed in the weeks following the procedure to clear crusts, osteitic bone fragments, and forming scar tissue before these factors create persistent inflammation and disease recurrence. Endoscopic surveillance and proactive treatment of residual disease eliminate the need for most revision surgery and lead to long-term success.

Open Sinus Procedures

Although FESS can be used effectively for most medically recalcitrant sinus disease, there are still occasional circumstances under which open sinus procedures may be indicated.

Maxillary Sinus

In cases of symptomatic maxillary sinus mucoceles, antrochoanal polyps, mycetoma, or foreign bodies not accessible via an intranasal endoscopic approach, the traditional open procedure has long been the Caldwell-Luc procedure. This procedure begins with a gingivobuccal incision, made from the second molar to the ipsilateral canine tooth. Dissection proceeds sharply through the submucosal tissue and the maxillary periostium down to bone. A periostial elevator is used to raise the periosteum and overlying soft tissue superiorly to the level of the infraorbital foramen. Once adequate exposure is achieved, the maxillary sinus is entered through its anterior wall superior to the roots of the canine and premolar teeth using an osteotome or cutting bur. This approach gives good visualization of all portions of the maxillary sinus and allows complete removal of infectious material and masses that would not be easily reached through a middle meatus antrostomy. Stripping of the mucosa with forceps or curettes is to be condemned and will result in permanent sinus dysfunction. The most common complication of the Caldwell-Luc approach is paresthesia or anesthesia of the cheek, teeth, and gingiva secondary to traction on the infraorbital nerve.

Ethmoid Sinus

The external ethmoidectomy has been largely supplanted by

the endoscopic approach; however, there remain some situations in which this approach may prove useful. For example, excellent exposure may be provided externally for biopsies of certain orbital lesions or lesions of the ethmoid or frontal sinuses. Also, this approach may be employed for rapid and safe access for orbital complications of acute ethmoid or frontal sinusitis. The external ethmoidectomy incision generally begins at the inferior margin of the medial aspect of the eyebrow, curving gently downward midway between the medial canthus and the anterior aspect of the nasal bones. The incision is carried successively through the skin, subcutaneous tissues, and periosteum, which is then elevated posteriorly. Attention is given to protecting the trochlea and the attachment of the medial canthal ligament during periosteal elevation. The lacrimal sac is elevated atraumatically from the lacrimal fossa. Dissection proceeds in the subperiosteal plane beyond the posterior lacrimal crest, exposing the medial wall of the orbit. The anterior ethmoid neurovascular bundle is encountered approximately 24 mm posterior to the anterior lacrimal crest. The anterior ethmoid artery, found in the frontoethmoid suture line, is clipped or electrocoagulated and divided. Although it is not routinely necessary to dissect further posteriorly, the posterior ethmoid artery will be encountered approximately 12 mm posterior to the anterior ethmoid artery and approximately 6 mm anterior to the optic foramen. Once the lacrimal bone, frontal process of the maxilla, lamina papyracea, and orbital process of frontal bone have been widely exposed, the ethmoid is entered through the lacrimal fossa with a mallet and gouge or drill. The lamina papyracea is taken down to allow complete exenteration of the ethmoid cells.

Frontal Sinus
Open approaches to the frontal sinus are indicated for chronic, complicated frontal sinusitis that has not responded to trephination or conventional endoscopic sinus surgery.

Other indications include intracranial or orbital extension of disease, mucocele or mucopyocele, and osteomyelitis of the frontal bone. Frontal sinus trephination is an approach to the frontal sinus that is useful in the face of acute infection when mucosal bleeding may hamper an intranasal endoscopic approach. It is safe, is rapidly performed, and can decompress a pus-filled frontal sinus prior to a more definitive procedure. The procedure is also useful in conjunction with FESS to help locate the natural drainage pathway of the frontal sinus and to visualize the ostium from above and below. To perform a trephination, an incision is made beneath the medial portion of the eyebrow and carried through skin, subcutaneous tissue, and the periosteum over the frontal sinus floor. The wound is retracted superiorly and medially over the anterior table of the frontal sinus, and a drill is used to make a controlled hole into the sinus. If the hole is made with a diameter greater than 4 mm, an endoscope can be inserted to visualize the interior of the sinus. Purulence is removed for culture, and the sinus is irrigated.

Frontal sinus obliteration is an approach used in recalcitrant cases of frontal sinusitis. After endoscopic surgery, the frontal sinus ostium is sometimes very difficult to keep open from within the nose when osteoneogenesis is present. More extensive intranasal drill-out procedures may be successful in establishing long-term patency of a frontal sinus drainage pathway, but many times, it is not possible to maintain an opening into the sinus with any endoscopic or open surgical technique. In these patients, frontal sinus obliteration may be the only viable option. The technique has the advantage of unparalleled visualization of the entire frontal sinus and elimination of the need to reconstruct the nasofrontal drainage outflow. The negatives of the technique include the external scar, potential for forehead hypoesthesia, and loss of a connection between the nose and sinus through which endoscopic surveillance can be performed. The osteoplastic flap frontal sinus obliteration can be performed through either a gull-wing suprabrow incision or a bicoronal approach with the incision behind the hairline. With either approach, an oscillating saw is used to make bone cuts through the anterior table of the frontal sinus. The bone flap, with its periosteum attached superficially, is reflected inferiorly to expose the sinus. To perform an obliteration successfully, it is absolutely critical to remove all of the mucosa from within the sinus to prevent the development of a mucocele. The frontal ostium is occluded with pericranium or temporalis muscle to obliterate the connection to the nasal cavity. Abdominal fat is usually harvested through a periumbilical incision and cut to fit snugly within the confines of the sinus. When the graft is in place, the bone flap is replaced and fixed with small titanium plates to recreate the normal frontal contour.

The most significant disadvantage of a frontal sinus obliteration procedure is the loss of the ability to image the sinus following the procedure. This can make assessment of postoperative frontal sinus complaints difficult and delay detection of some late complications. Magnetic resonance imaging can differentiate fat from retained mucosa, secretions, and infection, whereas CT merely shows opacification of the sinus. Perioperative complications of the osteoplastic frontal sinus obliteration procedure include hematoma, infection or abscess of the bicoronal or abdominal wound, and dural injury from bone cuts outside the sinus. The major long-term complications of obliteration are pain or altered sensation, visible bony defects, and mucocele formation.

Sphenoid Sinus

Although the sphenoid sinus is readily accessible endoscopically through the nose, external approaches are frequently used to achieve wider exposure for resection of masses or for pituitary surgery. Most commonly, the open procedures involve operating through the septum to the face of the sphenoid. This can be accomplished via a transnasal septoplasty approach, an open rhinoplasty-type incision, or a sublabial incision. The transnasal approach has become more popular with the increased use of the endoscope; however, the technique requires a relatively large nose unless an alar incision is used. The external rhinoplasty incision gives unparalleled access and visualization but has the potential to leave a noticeable columellar scar. The sublabial approach is the one most often employed because it is easy, leaves no nasal scars, does not depend on nasal size, and allows the speculum to be placed in the midline. The drawbacks involve oral contamination of the wound and difficulties with oral incisions in denture wearers.

The nasal complications are typically related to the septoplasty portion of the procedure. These include septal perforation, saddle deformity, and tip deformity. Epistaxis and wound infection are also possible nasal problems postoperatively. There are potentially serious neurologic and vascular complications that may occur in sphenoid surgery since the carotid artery and optic nerves travel in the lateral wall of the sinus. Even if the optic nerve is not injured directly during surgery, overpacking of the sinus with fat can cause optic chiasmal compression and visual loss. Another possible complication is cerebrospinal fluid leak, which should be treated when it is recognized intraoperatively. During the postoperative period, patients must be closely monitored for evidence of change in mental status or signs of active bleeding. The cause of these findings will generally be discovered through radiologic evaluation, and proper intervention can be planned and undertaken by the operative team.

26

HEADACHE AND FACIAL PAIN

James M. Hartman, MD
Richard A. Chole, MD, PhD

The wide diversity of causes of craniofacial pain and the extreme overlap of historical features, coupled with nonspecific physical findings, serve to challenge the physician's ability to diagnose and ultimately relieve or control patients' craniofacial pain. However, an understanding of the different types of craniofacial pain lends a powerful tool to meet the challenge.

MIGRAINE-TYPE HEADACHES

Migraine-type headaches occur more commonly in women, with the peak age of onset in the second or third decades, but children and even infants may also be affected. They usually occur as recurrent episodes of severe, throbbing, unilateral head pain of sudden onset lasting 4 to 72 hours. However, 40% of migraineurs have bilateral pain. The headache often strikes after awakening in the morning. Routine activities of daily living exacerbate the symptoms. Coexisting symptoms with the headache are common, including nausea, vomiting, photophobia, and phonophobia. Stress is the usual precipitating factor. A family history of migraine is often present. Migraine without aura lacks any preheadache warning symptoms, whereas migraine with aura is also common, accounting for 20% of migraine sufferers. The typical aura lasts less than 1 hour and immediately precedes the onset of cephalalgia. It may be precipitated by menses, pregnancy, oral contraceptives, certain foods, or bright lights. Features of aura include focal neurologic symptoms, including visual changes such as scotomata or sensory and motor disturbances such as paresthesias, hemiparesis, or aphasia.

Treatment of migraine disorders includes initiation of supportive and educational measures, such as a headache diary to decrease the frequency of attacks. Specific measures prove useful, including the application of ice, isolation in a dark quiet room, using biofeedback or acupuncture, or inducing sleep, as well as avoiding known triggers such as cheese, alcohol, or chocolate. Medical therapy falls into two major categories: symptomatic treatment and preventive treatment. Symptomatic treatment must be individualized to provide adequate relief with minimal risk and side effects. Factors influencing choice of drugs should include the frequency that medications will be required, contraindications, route of administration, prior medication successes and failures, or need for breakthrough headache therapy. Nonspecific migraine therapy includes analgesics (acetaminophen, naproxen, ibuprofen, butalbital, isometheptene, dichloralphenazone [Midrin]; and indomethacin), and judicious use of opiates only for severe attacks. Specific therapy uses compounds that are known agonists of the 5-hydroxytryptamine$_1$ receptor and include ergot derivatives and synthetic triptan compounds. Often antiemetics or metoclopramide should be given first to avoid worsening or triggering nausea. To avoid chronic ergotamine-induced headache, it should not be taken more than 2 days a week. In addition to nausea, angina may be induced by these compounds; thus, their use in patients with risk of coronary artery disease is contraindicated. For children, the use of both acetaminophen and ibuprofen has been found effective, as have oral dihydroergotamine mesylate and sumatriptan in any form.

Prophylactic therapy is indicated when the frequency of episodes is greater than two per week. Prophylactic agents include antidepressants (amitriptyline, nortriptyline, doxepin, or trazodone); ergotamine in a sustained-release form (eg, Bellergal); beta blockers (metoprolol, atenolol, or propranolol); nonsteroidal anti-inflammatory drugs (NSAIDs) (naproxen, ibuprofen, or aspirin); calcium channel blockers (verapamil, nifedipine, nimodipine, or flunarizine); anticonvulsants (divalproex, valproic acid, gabapentin, or topiramate); and others (methysergide, fluoxetine, cyproheptadine, pizotifen, riboflavin, or lithium). Dosages should be titrated within recommended levels, and therapeutic trials of any agent should last at least 3 weeks. Among specific agents used for children, propranolol is most frequently used.

TENSION-TYPE HEADACHE

Tension-type headaches are more likely to occur in women, and usually a family history of headaches is present. The headaches are characteristically bilateral, with a tightening or band-like sensation in the frontotemporal region around the head spreading to the occipital region or trapezius muscles. The onset is gradual, whereas the quality is dull, nonthrobbing, and constant, sometimes lasting for weeks. The cephalalgia is triggered or exacerbated by stress or anxiety in most patients. Treatment of tension-type headaches uses nonpharmacologic and medical therapy. First, chronic medication overuse must be eliminated, a step that will improve many cephalalgia sufferers. Depression should be treated if present. Nonmedical remedies include reassurance, muscle relaxation, simple muscle exercises, stress management, biofeedback, and physical therapy. Most patients that suffer tension-type headache will respond to analgesics, such as aspirin or NSAIDs. Antidepressants, especially amitriptyline, have also proven effective. Agents capable of fostering dependence are best avoided. These include caffeine, opiates, and benzodiazepines. Some patients may require injection of local anesthetics into trigger points to provide sustained relief. Finally, injection of botulinum toxin (Botox) into pericranial muscles has recently been shown to be safe and effective.

CLUSTER HEADACHES

Cluster headaches are less common than tension-type or migraine headaches; however, the severity of the headaches is much greater. They affect men more often than women. They are unilateral, excruciating, and located around the eyes or in the maxilla and usually occur in middle age. The episodes typically last minutes to 3 hours. They tend to occur several times per day for several weeks, and then long headache-free periods occur; hence, they occur in clusters. No aura or nausea occurs, but the cephalalgia is associated with unilateral lacrimation, rhinorrhea, and nasal congestion. The headaches often wake a patient at the same time each night. Alcohol and histamine injections are capable of precipitating attacks, and attacks are more common in the spring or fall. Intracranial lesions, as well as viral meningitis, may produce cluster-like headaches that are more apt to be chronic.

Treatment of cluster headaches has abortive measures and prophylactic therapy. Episodes can be ended with inhalation of 100% oxygen for 10 minutes or administration of ergotamine or dihydroergotamine. Sumatriptan works best when given subcutaneously, taking about 10 minutes to take effect. Intranasal 4% lidocaine may also be effective. Prophylactic medications are the mainstay of treatment. In general, they should be used during the months when the cluster headaches are occurring and gradually discontinued after at least a 2-week headache-free period. The most frequently used treatment regimens include calcium channel blockers, such as nifedipine or verapamil. Invasive approaches for refractory cases include radiofrequency ablation of the trigeminal ganglion and blockade of the sphenopalatine ganglion.

HEADACHE ASSOCIATED WITH VASCULAR DISORDERS

Subarachnoid hemorrhage is typically experienced as the worst headache of the patient's life. Besides the severe intensity, the cephalalgia is sudden and may gradually worsen; it is bilateral and associated with neck stiffness, fever, transient loss of consciousness, diplopia, or seizures. A prodromal headache that is severe occurs in as many as 50% of patients several days or weeks before the major hemorrhage. Physical examination may reveal a changed mental status, restlessness, nuchal rigidity, retinal hemorrhages, papilledema, and focal or general neurologic signs such as cranial nerve III or VI palsy, aphasia, hemiparesis, or ataxia. The evaluation should begin with noncontrast head computed tomography (CT) with 3 mm cuts to find collections of blood. A lumbar puncture and evaluation of cerebrospinal fluid (CSF) should be performed next if the CT was negative for blood or mass effect. Abnormal findings include elevated CSF pressure, red blood cells in the CSF, or xanthochromia. If any test indicates that a subarachnoid hemorrhage has occurred, angiography and neurosurgical consultation are warranted urgently for treatment of the aneurysm.

Giant cell arteritis, often called temporal arteritis, mostly affects women over 50 years of age. It presents as a new-onset, daily, intermittent or continuous, temporal localized headache that is moderate to severe, burning sharp or throbbing, and unilateral or bilateral and lasts months to years. Patients with giant cell arteritis complain of aching of the jaw during chewing, weight loss, generalized fatigue, and low-grade fever and often have extremity pain. Visual symptoms include blurring, scotomata, and even sudden blindness. Physical findings consist of palpably thickened or tender scalp arteries that may have a diminished or absent pulse. An erythrocyte sedimentation rate (ESR) is almost always elevated over 50 mm per hour in patients with giant cell arteritis. If the diagnosis is suspected, a temporal artery biopsy is essential to confirm the diagnosis. Treatment should begin immediately to avoid sudden blindness, a complication found in up to 30% of untreated patients. This is secondary to involvement of the ophthalmic artery. Prednisone is the drug of choice and should be administered in high daily doses of 60 mg. Once the headache has gone into remission and the ESR corrects, the prednisone can be tapered over a period of weeks to a daily maintenance dose of 5 to 10 mg while continuing to check for a rise in the ESR. Often treatment must be continued several years to avoid the complication of blindness.

HEADACHE ASSOCIATED WITH NON-VASCULAR INTRACRANIAL DISORDERS

Benign intracranial hypertension is defined by the findings of papilledema; an otherwise normal neurologic examination (with a rare exception being abducens palsy); no intracranial mass, venous sinus thrombosis, or ventricular enlargement on head CT or magnetic resonance imaging (MRI); a normal protein, white cell count, and culture of the CSF; and, most importantly, an increased intracranial pressure of greater than 200 mm of water on lumbar puncture or intraventricular pressure monitor. The headache is intermittent and retro-orbital, gradually worsens, and is exacerbated by coughing or Valsalva's maneuver. Associated symptoms include visual dimming occurring for a minute or two at a time, eventual constriction of visual fields, and possible blindness, as well as unilateral or bilateral pulsatile tinnitus. It may be triggered by otitis media or mastoiditis, irregular menses, recent rapid weight gain, corticosteroid withdrawal, or ingestion of vitamin

A, tetracycline, or nalidixic acid. Treatment consists of weight reduction, a low-sodium diet, and diuretics, specifically aceta-zolamide or furosemide. Cerebrospinal fluid diversion by a ventriculoperitoneal shunt may be necessary for refractory cases or when visual fields fail to improve.

Primary or metastatic *intracranial neoplasms* present with discrete or generalized, intermittent or continuous, mild to moderate, unilateral, dull headache that worsens over time in 30% of patients. Early morning headache is a warning symptom, as is exacerbation by Valsalva's maneuver or cough. Sudden vomiting, cranial nerve dysfunction, and seizures may occur. Control of pain may be initially achieved with non-narcotic analgesics, but eventually, narcotics or neuralgia medications become necessary. Removal of the neoplasm when feasible is usually curative of the headache.

HEADACHE ASSOCIATED WITH SUBSTANCES OR THEIR WITHDRAWAL

Headache induced by chronic intake of some medicines is a common phenomenon. The cephalalgia occurs daily, often early in the morning, and is generalized, bilateral, dull, and of moderate severity. It may be associated with nausea and brought on with mild exertion. Tolerance to the offending analgesic seems to allow less and less relief to the patient, resulting in the use of increased dosages. Finally, headache-free intervals cease to exist. Both ergotamine and dihydroergotamine have been implicated, as have non-narcotic and narcotic analgesics. Common examples include aspirin, acetaminophen, NSAIDs, barbiturates, codeine, hydrocodone, oxycodone, and propoxyphene. Treatment requires understanding on the part of the patient, along with complete elimination of the problem medication for at least 2 months. No substitution to another analgesic should occur. Avoidance of tyramine and caffeine in the diet is recommended, whereas use of antidepressants is recommended and helpful. Nonpharmacologic modalities should be employed, more specifically, biofeedback, transcutaneous electrical nerve stimulation, and physical therapy.

Headache from withdrawal of a chronically used substance may also occur. It typically follows a period of abstinence from the agent of less than 12 to 48 hours and is relieved by ingestion of the substance. Persistent elimination of the substance allows resolution of the headache within 14 days. Frequent examples consist of caffeine, ergot derivatives, and narcotics. The headache is diffuse, dull, and mild to moderate in severity. It may be associated with nervousness, restlessness, nausea and vomiting, insomnia, and tremor. Persistent abstinence is the mainstay of treatment but may require hospitalization to prevent the patient from consuming more of the offending medication.

HEADACHE OR FACIAL PAIN ASSOCIATED WITH CRANIOFACIAL OR CERVICAL DISORDERS

Cervicogenic headache is a relatively common condition created by a disorder afflicting the cervical spine often following neck trauma. Women are more frequently affected than men. It is characterized by fluctuating or constant headache that is unilateral, unchanging, dull, and nonpulsatile. It tends to start at the occiput and radiate to the frontal region, where the pain is most intense. Associated symptoms of nausea and photophobia or phonophobia are present in 50% of patients. Neck examination reveals a reduced range of motion of the spine and possibly muscle tenderness, spasm, hypertrophy, or atrophy. Cervical radiographic data reveal abnormalities on flexion and extension films, abnormal posture, or evidence of bone or joint pathology. Treatment consists of physical therapy, stretching exercises, use of NSAIDs, and nerve blockade for refractory cases.

Sinonasal disorders are a frequent source of headaches. Frontal headache and facial pain are two of the three major symptoms suggesting the presence of sinusitis; the other is purulent nasal drainage. The cephalalgia is pressure-like or dull, of moderate intensity, unilateral or bilateral, periorbital, worsened by bending or with Valsalva's maneuver, worse in the morning, and associated with purulent nasal drainage, nasal obstruction, altered sense of smell, exacerbation of asthma, cough, malaise, and dizziness. Pain lasts days or weeks, with fluctuating severity. The location and extent of the sinusitis do not correlate well with the severity or site of pain. On physical examination, tenderness to percussion over involved sinuses may be demonstrated. Other physical findings include inflammatory changes in the nose. Radiographic imaging is helpful to confirm an uncertain diagnosis of sinusitis or to evaluate response to treatment. A screening coronal sinus CT has become the imaging study of choice. Treatment to reverse the inflammatory process includes antibiotics, decongestants, and possibly corticosteroids, with analgesics used in the interim for symptomatic relief until the sinusitis is resolved.

Temporomandibular joint (TMJ) disorders are divided into two major groups: those with demonstrable organic disease (uncommon) and those of myofascial origin from masticatory muscles (very common). Women are far more likely than men to suffer from TMJ pain. The pain is located preauricularly and in the temporal region of the head, is intermittent, lasts hours to days, is mild to moderate in intensity, can be unilateral or bilateral, and is exacerbated by jaw movement. Associated features include otalgia, bruxism, trismus, TMJ crepitus, and jaw locking. Physical findings include audible joint clicking on one side or both and decreased range of motion. Normal vertical opening between central incisors ranges from 42 to 55 mm. If pathology is suspected, a TMJ radiographic series may reveal a joint abnormality. The usual indications for imaging include suspected fractures, degenerative joint disease, ankylosis, or tumors. Management of TMJ disorders includes reassurance, education, NSAIDs, restriction of jaw opening, a soft diet, and physical therapy. Occasionally, biofeedback or corticosteroid injection may be helpful. If pain is chronic, tricyclic antidepressants may be beneficial. Occlusal splints relieving bruxism may help.

CRANIAL NEURALGIAS

Cranial neuralgias are conditions affecting nerves with sensory functions in the head and neck resulting in severe stabbing or throbbing pain in the distribution of the involved nerve. Injury to a nerve can result in chronic neuralgia. Symptoms include hypersensitivity, pain to light touch, and aggravation by cold or emotional duress. The pain is sharp and lancinating. Inflammatory conditions are also well known to cause neuralgia. A prime example is *acute herpes zoster* involvement of a branch of the trigeminal nerve, the seventh cranial nerve, or cervical roots. The ophthalmic branch of cranial nerve V is the most commonly involved. Intense burning or stabbing pain in the distribution of the involved nerve is followed within 1 week by a vesicular eruption of the skin in the distribution of the nerve. Motor divisions of these nerves may be paretic. The pain subsides within 6 months of the onset, but the motor palsies have a poor prognosis for complete recovery. Treatment of the acute phase consists of a 10-day course of prednisone and acyclovir. Nonsteroidal anti-inflammatory drugs or opiates may be necessary to control pain. Acute herpetic neuralgia is common in lymphoma patients, so a new outbreak should raise suspicions about that possible comorbidity. *Chronic postherpetic neuralgia* exists when zoster pain persists greater than 6 months. Nonsteroidal anti-inflammatory drugs and opiates fail to relieve the neuralgia. Instead, anticonvulsants are more effective and may be paired with tricyclic antidepressants or baclofen to enhance their efficacy.

Trigeminal neuralgia is the most common cranial neuralgia and most often affects adults over 50 years old; women are more often affected than men. Typically, recurrent episodes of unilateral, excruciating, stabbing pain occur in the distribution of the maxillary and mandibular branches of the trigeminal nerve. During an episode, ipsilateral twitching may occur—hence the name "painful tic." It occurs without warning, while patients are awake, and recurs several to many times a day, with each episode lasting seconds to minutes. Numbness does not occur. Light touching of the face may precipitate an attack, as can movement of the trigger zone by talking, chewing, or shaving. Physical findings include an intact neurologic examination and the presence of a trigger zone most often located in the nasolabial fold, lips, or gums. Diagnostic evaluation should include an MRI of the head and a lumbar puncture if the MRI is normal, to rule out central causes including vascular anomalies or aneurysm, tumor, cholesteatoma, multiple sclerosis, neurosyphilis, and cryptococcal or tuberculous meningitis. Treatment of idiopathic trigeminal neuralgia includes patient education and reassurance with pharmacologic control. Carbamazepine will provide symptomatic relief acutely in the majority of patients. Tricyclic antidepressants and NSAIDs may also be beneficial. Surgical radiofrequency ablation, specifically trigeminal rhizotomy, is recommended for patients refractory to medical therapy.

UNCLASSIFIABLE FACIAL PAIN (ATYPICAL FACIAL PAIN)

Atypical facial pain fails to fit the profile of any specific craniofacial condition. It does not localize to anatomic regions or have a relation to specific structures as TMJ arthralgia or myofascial pain does. It lasts for years and is exacerbated by stress. Comorbidities include chronic fatigue, depression, personality disorders, irritable bowel syndrome, and other idiopathic pain disorders. Tricyclic antidepressants are the mainstay of therapy; they should be taken at night and titrated up to a desired response.

27

NEOPLASMS OF THE NOSE AND PARANASAL SINUSES

Ara A. Chalian, MD
David Litman, MD

The poor prognosis for patients with nasal and paranasal sinus malignancy has led many investigators to focus their attention on it.

PATHOLOGY

Whereas most sinus neoplasms are malignant, in the nasal cavity, there is a fairly even distribution between benign and malignant disease. The majority of these benign lesions are papillomas that may be subdivided into three categories: fungiform (50%), inverted (45%), and cylindrical cell (5%). Inverted papillomas are characterized by a squamous or transitional cell epithelium surrounding a fibrovascular stroma with endophytic growth. They are most often found on the lateral nasal wall and have been reported to be associated with squamous cell carcinoma in 5 to 15% of patients.

Additional benign tumors of epithelial origin include adenomas, cholesteatomas, and dermoids. Adenomas of the sinonasal tract are histologically identical to those arising in other areas of the body. They occur most commonly in the fourth to seventh decade and usually involve the nasal septum.

Fibrous dysplasia occasionally arises in the maxilla. It occurs in both polyostotic and monostotic forms, with monostotic being more common. Growth is slow, and treatment consists of local excision for lesions that are physically obstructive or cosmetically deforming. The surgery typically is conservative and involves a sculpting excision of the lesion to restore the normal contour.

Malignant epithelial neoplasms constitute the majority of sinonasal tumors, representing 45 to 80% of all sinus neoplasia. Of these, squamous cell carcinoma is the most common. Sixty percent of these neoplasms arise in the maxillary sinus, 20 to 30% in the nasal cavity, 10 to 15% in the ethmoid sinuses, and 1% in the frontal and sphenoid sinuses. As in other areas of the head and neck, the tumor may present with varying degrees of differentiation.

Glandular carcinomas are the next most common tumors, comprising 4 to 15% of all sinus neoplasms. Of these, adenocarcinomas are the most common, representing 5 to 19% of nasal and sinus tumors. In general, these tumors are classified as low grade on the basis of uniform glandular architecture and uniform cytologic characteristics. High-grade adenocarcinomas have a predominantly solid growth pattern and moderate to prominent nuclear pleomorphism.

Adenoid cystic carcinomas are somewhat less common than adenocarcinomas but still comprise a sizable portion of sinonasal tumors in most studies.

Mucoepidermoid carcinoma is an extremely rare form of glandular carcinoma. It is composed of a combination of squamous cells and glandular, mucus-producing, basal cells.

Although rare, two tumors of neuroectodermal origin are occasionally encountered. These are sinonasal melanoma and olfactory neuroblastoma (esthesioneurocytoma, esthesioneuroblastoma).

EPIDEMIOLOGY

Commonly cited data indicate that these neoplasms account for 0.2 to 0.8% of all carcinomas and for 3% of those occurring in the upper aerodigestive tract. Demographically, these tumors occur predominantly in the age range from 50 to 90 years. These tumors occur in all races, and there is no gender predilection.

Squamous cell carcinoma is by far the most frequently encountered malignancy, accounting for up to 80% of all neoplasms according to some studies. This is followed by the salivary gland tumors (4 to 15%) and sarcomas (4 to 6%).

Of the different sites, the maxillary sinus is commonly identified as the primary site, representing 55 to 80%. It is followed by the nasal cavity (27 to 33%), the ethmoid sinuses (9 to 10%), and the frontal and sphenoid sinuses (1 to 2%).

Environmental factors play a large role in the development of paranasal sinus malignancy. Up to 44% of these tumors are attributed to occupational exposures. The most well known is the association between wood dust and adenocarcinoma. Exposure to wood dust increases the relative risk of adenocarcinoma by 540 times.

PATIENT EVALUATION

In contrast to many other areas in the head and neck, paranasal sinus tumors are not characterized by an early presentation. Late symptoms include epistaxis, ocular dysfunction secondary to cranial nerve or extraocular muscle involvement, proptosis, facial pain, facial swelling, facial numbness, loosening of teeth, epiphoria, visual loss, anosmia, trismus, and even facial weakness.

Physical Examination

Proptosis, chemosis, or evidence of extraocular muscle impairment signifies orbital invasion and provides the practitioner with a readily available means of determining tumor extent. Similarly, the oral examination may help to delineate tumor spread. Key findings include mass effect in the palate and gingivobuccal sulcus. Trismus indicates invasion of the pterygoid muscles. A thorough neurologic examination must also be performed. Cranial nerve I dysfunction may be related to either nasal obstruction or nerve involvement. An assessment of visual acuity and oculomotor function should be undertaken.

Imaging

On computed tomography (CT), malignant tumors of the paranasal sinuses and nasal cavity appear as dense, homogeneous, destructive masses. The primary benefit of CT scans is the detailed demonstration of bony structure, but one cannot distinguish between soft tissue and retained mucus with CT.

Magnetic resonance imaging (MRI) is more sensitive in determining the true extent of tumor expansion. On T_1-weighted images, most tumors exhibit a low signal intensity that enhances after the administration of gadolinium. On T_2-weighted images, these tumors show a higher signal intensity than muscle but are not as bright as secretions.

Angiography should be reserved specifically for patients in whom there is suspected internal carotid artery involvement. When carotid artery involvement is suspected, magnetic resonance angiography will often suffice to confirm or refute it. Indications for conventional angiography are (1) preparation for embolization of a vascular lesion preoperatively, (2) to define intracranial arterial anatomy in a patient who is to undergo arterial bypass, and (3) balloon occlusion testing in a patient who will likely have the carotid artery sacrificed.

Computed tomography and MRI provide information on key issues in treatment planning including orbital or skull base invasion, vascular involvement, and transdural extension.

Staging

In the United States, the favored staging system is that proposed by the American Joint Committee on Cancer (AJCC).

It is largely based on Ohngren's line, a theoretical plane drawn from the medial canthus of the eye to the angle of the mandible. Tumors of the maxillary sinus posterior to this plane have a poorer prognosis. As an alternative, many authors now use the staging system proposed by the International Union Against Cancer (UICC). Although the UICC staging system accounts for the most common sites of paranasal sinus malignancy, its variation from the AJCC staging of maxillary cancer makes analysis of studies using the different staging systems difficult.

PROGNOSIS

Because of the previously discussed difficulty in comparing various clinical studies, it is difficult to state the extent that various clinical factors play in prognosis. Clearly, an advanced stage is associated with a worse prognosis. In fact, it has been asserted that the most accurate predictor of poor prognosis is the T category. Lymph node involvement at the time of diagnosis is known to be associated with a uniformly dismal prognosis. Interestingly, many studies have shown that histologic subtype does not play a role in the overall prognosis.

TREATMENT

Surgery

Proposed criteria for unresectable lesions include (1) transdural extension, (2) invasion of the prevertebral fascia, (3) bilateral optic nerve involvement, and (4) gross cavernous sinus invasion.

Operative planning in paranasal sinus surgery includes both the resection and the approach through which the resection takes place. A number of approaches are available, depending on the size and location of the tumor and the excision to be performed. They include the endoscopic approach, midfacial degloving, lateral rhinotomy, lateral facial (Fisch-Mattox) approach, craniotomy, and combined craniofacial approaches.

Endoscopic Sinus Surgery

The endoscopic approach to paranasal sinus neoplasms is an option for treatment for low-grade or benign tumors involving the lateral nasal wall, ethmoid sinuses, or the sphenoid sinus. The primary advantage of this approach is the lack of need for facial incisions. Other advantages include the magnification that modern endoscopy provides. A contraindication to an endoscopic approach is invasion of inaccessible areas, including the lateral part of the maxillary sinus, periorbita, lacrimal sac, supraorbital ethmoid cells, frontal sinus, and skull base.

Midfacial Degloving Appraoch

Midfacial degloving represents one of many open approaches that one may use to approach an intranasal tumor. This approach consists of (1) bilateral intercartilaginous incisions, (2) a septocolumellar complete transfixion incision, (3) bilateral sublabial incisions, and (4) bilateral piriform aperture incisions. This is a versatile approach that can provide access to a wide variety of areas, including the nasal cavity, nasopharynx, maxillary antrum, orbital floor, and zygoma. The primary advantages of the procedure are its lack of extensive facial incisions and good access provided for inferiorly based tumors. Additionally, there is a fairly low complication rate associated with the procedure. Disadvantages include difficulty with access to superiorly based tumors. Other transfacial procedures are preferred for superiorly based tumors unless otherwise contraindicated.

Lateral Rhinotomy

Lateral rhinotomy serves as the basis for the majority of transfacial procedures. It consists of a curvilinear incision beginning at the inferomedial aspect of the brow and extending inferiorly midway between the nasal dorsum and medial canthus to the lateral edge of the alar base. The approach provides fairly wide access to tumors involving the supraorbital ethmoidal area, frontal duct, lacrimal fossa, orbit, or cribriform plate.

The primary advantage of the procedure is the wide access it provides combined with the relative ease in which the incisions may be modified to achieve better access. The disadvantages of the procedure include orbital complications, including blepharitis, epiphora, and intermittent dacryocystitis related to transection of the nasolacrimal duct.

Anterior Lateral Skull Base Approach

Although standard transfacial approaches offer good access to the sinonasal region, tumors that extend to the pterygopalatine fossa, sphenoid sinus, or nasopharynx are best approached through the lateral face/skull base. The most well-described approach is the lateral facial split or the infratemporal fossa type C procedure of Fisch and Mattox. The benefit of this approach is the access it provides to the central part of the skull base. Wide exposure of the internal carotid artery not only allows the opportunity to assess potential involvement with the tumor, it also provides the option of bypass. In extreme cases, this exposure may necessitate division of the facial nerve or result in facial nerve weakness from traction on the nerve. In patients requiring facial nerve division, reconstructive neurorrhaphy is recommended.

Craniotomy/Craniofacial Approach

An alternative approach to paranasal sinus tumors is the transcranial resection. The transfacial approaches described above are difficult to use in tumors adherent to the anterior cranial floor. There is the added risk of cerebrospinal fluid (CSF) leak when attempting extracranial excisions in this area. Transcranial access is the approach of choice in tumors involving the cribriform plate, for tumors in which one suspects dural invasion, or in patients in whom there is known intracranial invasion. In addition to the inherent morbidity of a craniotomy, a significant disadvantage of the approach is the limited access to the inferior and medial parts of the orbit as well as the maxillary sinus. In fact, in most cases, the procedure should be combined with a transfacial approach to allow for exposure and control of the paranasal sinus involvement and definitely when one suspects that the excision will include orbital exenteration. Complications include CSF leak, meningitis, pneumocephalus, and dacryocystitis if the resection includes the ethmoid or maxillary sinuses.

Radiation Therapy

Radiation therapy plays a large role in the treatment of patients with paranasal sinus tumors. Because of the late stage in which most of the patients present, multimodality therapy is nearly universal. Additionally, in rare cases of early-stage cancers, radiation therapy alone has been shown to be as effective as surgical excision. Some neoplasms such as lymphomas, plasmocytomas, and esthesioneuroblastomas appear to be especially radiosensitive.

As with surgery, there are numerous risks to radiation therapy. The majority relate to damage of the orbits and brain. Reported complications include blindness, central nervous system sequelae, otitis media, nasolacrimal duct obstruction, sinusitis, nasal bone destruction, chronic orbital pain, osteoradionecrosis, retinopathy, and medial canthus fistula.

Chemotherapy

Several trials have evaluated the effects of chemotherapy in treating patients with paranasal sinus tumors. Although the results have been promising, there is no definitive evidence that chemotherapy improves survival. However, several studies have shown evidence of tumor regression with the addition of chemotherapy.

CONTROVERSIAL TOPICS IN PARANASAL SINUS TUMORS

Orbital Preservation

In the past, radical excision with orbital exenteration was performed if the tumor approached the orbit. There is a trend toward using preoperative radiotherapy and/or chemotherapy, with the goal of preserving structures such as the orbit. Proponents of orbital preservation argue that the orbit is surrounded by a layer of periosteum that is resistant to tumor invasion.

Surgeons favoring radical excision of the orbit point out that there is no reliable radiographic means to determine the extent of orbital involvement. Additionally, with the use of neoadjuvant radiation treatment, it can be difficult to determine the extent of orbital involvement at the time of surgical excision. The function of the eye must be considered when making the decision to pursue preservation.

Elective Treatment of the Neck

Traditionally, elective treatment of the N0 neck has not been advocated secondary to the low rate of occult lymph nodal disease. Additionally, many argue that the primary lymphatic drainage of the sinonasal region is to the retropharynx. Therefore, the areas most likely to contain cancer reside in this region and not in the neck. This dogma has recently been challenged based on the following reasoning: the rate of lymph nodal recurrence ranges from 12 to 28%. Patients with neck relapse are known to have inferior long-term survival and a higher risk of distant metastasis compared with those who did not have locoregional failure. Le and colleagues demonstrated that elective neck irradiation effectively prevented lymph nodal recurrence in the 25 patients in whom it was used. For this reason, it is now considered reasonable to irradiate the N0 neck in the presence of a primary tumor of advanced stage (T3/T4).

28

RECONSTRUCTION OF THE OUTSTANDING EAR

Daniel G. Becker, MD
Stephen Y. Lai, MD, PhD

Correction of the outstanding ear requires an understanding of the discrete elements that comprise the normal ear. Careful anatomic analysis to determine the precise cause of an abnormality allows appropriate preoperative planning for surgical correction. In selecting appropriate techniques from the many that are described in the literature, the surgeon must place the greatest emphasis on reliably achieving a natural-looking improvement. In general, techniques that reposition rather than resect cartilage may be safer and are therefore preferred.

EMBRYOLOGY

Development of the auricle or pinna is first detectable in the 39-day-old embryo. The auricle is formed from six mesenchymal proliferations (hillocks of His) at the dorsal ends of the first and second pharyngeal arches surrounding the first branchial groove. These elements begin in the lower neck and ascend to the level of the eyes at the side of the head during gestation. Cartilage formation is visible in the seventh week, and hillock fusion occurs in the twelfth week of gestation. The recognizable shape of the auricle is visible by the twentieth week of gestation. Although each of the six hillocks was previously correlated to a specific element of the auricle, current studies suggest that the first branchial arch elements contribute to the tragus and the second branchial arch elements form the remaining structures.

SURFACE ANATOMY

The auricle is 85% of adult size by 3 years of age and is 90 to 95% of full size by 5 to 6 years of age, although it may elongate an additional 1 to 1.5 cm during life. The helical rim along its lateral edge is approximately 1 to 2 cm from the mastoid skin. The angle of protrusion of the auricle or the auriculomastoid angle is usually between 15 and 30 degrees.

Among important surface features is the helix, the prominent rim of the auricle. Parallel and anterior to the helix is another prominence known as the antihelix or antihelical fold. Superiorly, the antihelix divides into a superior and an inferior crus, which surround the fossa triangularis. The depression between the helix and antihelix is known as the scapha or scaphoid fossa. The antihelical fold surrounds the concha, a deep cavity posterior to the external auditory meatus. The crus helicis, which represents the beginning of the helix, divides the concha into a superior portion, the cymba conchae, and an inferior portion, the cavum conchae. The cavity formed by the concha on the anterior (lateral) surface of the ear corresponds to a bulge or convexity on the posterior (medial) surface of the ear that is known as the eminence of the concha.

Anterior to the concha and partially covering the external auditory meatus is the tragus. The antitragus is posteroinferior to the tragus and is separated from it by the intertragic notch. Below the antitragus is the lobule, which is composed of areolar tissue and fat. Anatomic variations such as preauricular tags or Darwin's tubercle, a small projection along the helix, may be present on the ear and should be recognized and documented in the preoperative assessment.

STRUCTURAL FEATURES

Except for the lobule, the auricle is supported by thin, flexible elastic fibrocartilage. This cartilaginous framework is 0.5 to 1.0 mm thick and is covered by a minimum of subcutaneous tissue. The skin is loosely adherent to the posterior surface and helix of the auricular cartilage. The close approximation of the skin to the anterior surface of the cartilage provides the auricle with its unique topographic features.

Malformations of the auricle are not unusual and range from complete absence to macrotia. The incidence of abnormally protruding ears is approximately 5% in Caucasians. As the auricle assumes a recognizable form by the end of the twelfth gestational week, the greatest number of malformations occur. Although they may be a dominant or recessive trait, most ear deformations are inherited as an autosomal dominant trait with incomplete penetrance. Understanding the pathogenesis of these deformities aids the plastic surgeon in developing an operative plan.

The most common cause of outstanding ears is the lack of development of the antihelical fold. This malformation of the antihelix is present in approximately two-thirds of all cases of protruding ears. However, other pathologic features may also contribute to the outstanding ear. A wide, protruding conchal wall is present in approximately one-third of all cases. Additionally, the prominent concha is often accompanied by a thickened antitragus.

The outstanding ear is a single entity within a wide spectrum of auricular malformation. Depending on the degree of severity, the protruding ear may also have structural abnormalities seen in the classically described "lop ear" and/or "cup ear." The term lop ear is used to describe a deformity of the helix characterized by a thin, flat ear that is acutely folded downward at the superior pole. In the cup ear deformity, weak cartilage with resulting limpness of the auricle results in cupping or deepening of the conchal bowl. The cup ear is often smaller than normal and is folded on itself. Poor development of the superior portion of the ear results in a short, thickened helix and a deformed antihelix. The surgical techniques used to correct the outstanding ear may be applied to the lop ear and to the cup ear, but the correction of these malformations extends beyond the scope of this chapter.

PREOPERATIVE EVALUATION

Patients with outstanding ears typically present early in childhood, although some present in adulthood. The optimal age for surgical correction is between 4 and 6 years of age. At this age, the auricle is near or at full adult size, and the child is capable of participating in the postoperative care of the ear. Also, the child is typically about to enter school, and, unfortunately, children with protruding ears are commonly subjected to severe ridicule by their young peers.

Although the classic description of the outstanding ear attributes this deformity to the absence of the antihelical fold, two other attributes must be carefully assessed. Overprojection of the concha and/or the lobule will also contribute to the appearance of the protruding ear. Consideration and correction of these elements will contribute to the ultimate goal of a normal-appearing auricle.

As with any cosmetic procedure, preoperative and postoperative photographs are absolutely critical for careful planning of the surgical procedure and to document changes to the auricle. Uniform lighting and views of the auricle should be used before and after the surgery. The photographs should include a full-face anterior and full-head posterior view, an oblique/lateral view of both sides of the head, and close-up views of the ears. For patients with long hair, a hair clip or headband can be useful to prevent the hair from obstructing accurate photodocumentation.

MATTRESS SUTURE OTOPLASTY

In the mid-1960s, Mustarde described a corrective otoplasty technique that gained quick and ready acceptance and wide popularity as it was seen as a marked improvement over existing techniques. Horizontal mattress sutures placed in the auricular cartilage along the scapha recreate the natural curve of the antihelix, blending gently into the scaphoid fossa. Dimensions of the horizontal mattress sutures have been described, with outer cartilage bites of 1 cm separated by 2 mm. The distance between the outer and inner cartilage bites is 16 mm.

The advantages of this approach included that no through-and-through cartilage incisions are necessary, so the potential sharp edges of other techniques are avoided. Also, transperichondrial sutures may be positioned, test-tied, and then maintained or replaced as necessary to develop a natural antihelix. This was in contrast to the cartilage splitting approach, in which the cartilage incision was irreversible and uncorrectable. Furthermore, the procedure has satisfactory long-term results and requires less dissection of the ear and less surgical trauma than other approaches. Surgeons also found this approach relatively easy to learn and to teach.

Whereas Mustarde's technique addressed the most common deformity of the protruding ear, the absent antihelix, Furnas described a suture fixation method to address the deep conchal bowl. Furnas described the placement of a permanent suture to adjust the apposition of the conchal bowl to the mastoid periosteum, decreasing the angle between the concha and the mastoid. Additionally, a suture from the fossa triangularis to the temporalis fascia may further correct conchal height or contour. Care must be taken when placing the suture to avoid rotation of the auricle anteriorly with resultant external auditory canal narrowing.

COMBINATION TECHNIQUES

Prior to the description of mattress suture techniques, cartilage cutting techniques were the primary method of correction of prominent ears. Subsequent to the description of mattress suture techniques, cartilage cutting approaches have remained useful in combination with suture techniques. Cartilage cutting techniques have been employed by experienced surgeons to create a gently curved appearance to the antihelix and a pleasing appearance to the postoperative ear. The cartilage-cutting techniques may be especially useful when large anatomic deformities must be corrected or when the auricular cartilage is especially inflexible or thick. However, the caveat must be repeated that these are technically difficult procedures that require substantial surgical experience.

MATTRESS SUTURE OTOPLASTY: METHOD OF TARDY

Mattress suture techniques with modifications are widely used today. One approach will be reviewed in detail here. Suture fixation techniques are relatively easy to perform and do not require incisions or excisions of the cartilage that permanently alter cartilage characteristics or leave permanent postoperative stigmata.

Although the horizontal mattress suture is the primary mode of repair in this technique, it is important to emphasize the importance of addressing thick and inflexible cartilage. The mattress suture procedure is frequently augmented by thinning, weakening, and, occasionally, limited incision of the cartilage to achieve natural and symmetric results. Thinning the cartilage by shave excision or with a bur and incisions through the cartilage to facilitate folding will reduce the tension on the horizontal mattress sutures. Thus, every surgeon performing otoplasty must be comfortable addressing the protruding ear with more than one technique. Knowledge of one technique only is inadequate.

In the operating room, the ears are reassessed with regard to the causes of protrusion. Special attention is directed to the depth of the conchal bowl, the position of the lobule, and the strength and flexibility of the auricular cartilage. The periauricular areas are prepared with a sterile cleansing solution (hexachlorophene or povidone-iodine) and draped with sterile towels. The postauricular skin and subcutaneous tissue are infiltrated with local anesthetic (eg, 1% lidocaine with 1/100,000 epinephrine) for analgesia and hemostasis. The head is draped in a manner that permits comparison of both ears intraoperatively.

A fusiform or "elliptical dumbbell"-shaped incision is made posteriorly, exposing the portion of auricular cartilage in the area of the soon to be formed antihelix. Care is taken to avoid removal of skin in the postauricular sulcus, which would cause flattening of the ear against the head. The skin is excised, leaving the posterior deep soft tissue and perichondrium, which facilitates later scar formation, which is the strength of the repair. The remaining skin is undermined to the postauricular sulcus and to the helical rim. Meticulous hemostasis should be maintained at this juncture and throughout the procedure.

A deep conchal bowl, when it exists, may be addressed initially. Undermining along the posterior aspect of the cartilage reveals the posterior eminence of auricular cartilage underlying the conchal bowl. Excess cartilage in the posterior eminence frequently causes this area to impinge on the mastoid process, preventing the ear from resting closer to the head. Using a scalpel, small disks of cartilage can be shaved from this region to allow retropositioning of the auricle. This cartilage sculpturing is often sufficient to retroposition the ear and makes conchal setback sutures unnecessary. Excision of cartilage in this area will weaken the cartilage, reducing overall tension on the mattress sutures that will be placed in the anti-helix region. *Great care is taken to achieve partial-thickness excision of cartilage, and through-and-through excision is avoided.* Nevertheless, on occasion, the auricle with a very deep cavum conchae may require conchal setback sutures or, rarely, the excision of a semilunar segment of cartilage within the cavum conchae to reconstruct the neoantihelix properly.

The new antihelix is created by manipulating the auricular cartilage and blending this fold into the inferior crus. Temporary 4-0 silk marking sutures may be placed from anterior to posterior to mark the location of the horizontal mattress sutures and thereby precisely guide their placement. This method avoids the use of ink or sharp needles to guide placement of the permanent sutures.

Once the new antihelix has been marked, 4-0 braided nylon (Tevdek) horizontal mattress sutures are placed sequentially, from caudal to cephalad along the neoantihelical fold. These horizontal mattress sutures are placed through the posterior perichondrium, auricular cartilage, and anterior perichondrium. Careful palpation with the free hand along the anterior surface of the auricle ensures that the needle does not pass through the anterior skin. Incorporation of the anterior perichondrium in the horizontal mattress suture is necessary to prevent the suture from tearing through the cartilage when it is tied down. Additionally, the sutures are not placed near the incision site to prevent future suture extrusion.

The horizontal mattress sutures are placed from caudal to cephalad and test-tied. Sutures are removed and replaced as necessary to achieve the desired fold on the auricular cartilage and are then held with a hemostat. The sutures are tied securely once the antihelix has been completely formed. Typically, four or more mattress sutures are necessary to distribute the tension evenly and to hold the repair until sufficient scar tissue forms, usually in 2 to 3 months. If the sutures are adequately placed, it is unnecessary to overcorrect the repositioning of the auricle since the sutures will maintain their position without slippage. The postauricular skin is closed with a fast-absorbing 5-0 chromic gut suture in a continuous, intradermal fashion.

Following creation of a neoantihelical fold, the position of the lobule is assessed. Ideally, the helix and antihelix should be in the same plane as the lobule. Commonly, simple skin excision and reattachment are sufficient to position the lobule in the appropriate plane, although more extensive intervention may be required at times.

The procedure is completed on the opposite ear. Frequent comparison between both ears ensures as symmetric a repair as possible. Given the nature of auricular deformities, complete symmetry between both ears is nearly impossible.

At the conclusion of the surgery, a conforming dressing is applied followed by a bulky head dressing. This is removed and replaced with a smaller dressing that the patient wears for an additional 36 to 72 hours.

Outcomes and Complications

Surveys have demonstrated high rates of patient satisfaction (82 to 95%) following otoplasty. Unsatisfactory cosmetic results were reported in 4.8 to 13.6% of cases; the rate was often higher for cartilage cutting techniques. The rates of relapse of auricular protrusion range from 2 to 13%. Interestingly, more than almost half of the patients in this group reported an injury in the postoperative period.

Regardless of the surgical techniques employed, complications are reported to occur at rates ranging from 7.1 to 11.4%. Early complications include hematoma and infection. Infection can be cellulitis or perichondritis/chondritis, which can lead to permanent auricular deformity. Antibiotic treatment must empirically cover *Pseudomonas aeruginosa*. Late complications include paresthesias and hypersensitivity, suture granuloma formation, suture extrusion, hypertrophic scarring, and keloid fomation. Esthetic complications include inadequate correction of the antihelix, overcorrection with a "hidden" helix, telephone ear (in which the middle portion is overcorrected relative to the upper and lower poles) or reverse telephone ear deformity, persistent prominence of the concha, malposition of the lobule, sharp cartilage edges when cartilage cutting approaches are employed, and distortion of the external auditory canal with possible stenosis.

29

NASAL RECONSTRUCTION AND RHINOPLASTY

M. Eugene Tardy Jr, MD

INCISIONS AND EXCISIONS

External nasal incisions should be sited in inconspicuous areas, leading to minimal distortion of nasal features and symmetry. *Junctions of facial landmarks* hide surgical scars well; therefore, incisions along the nasomaxillary groove, the alar-facial junction, and the columellar-labial (or nasolabial) junction heal inconspicuously. Natural folds created by the synergistic interaction of muscle groups at the root of the nose provide ideal sites for incision and excision camouflage. Horizontal, oblique, and vertical wrinkles apparent in this area, blending into the glabellar region, provide wide latitude in scar camouflage in the aging patient. Redundant nasal and glabellar skin allows considerable excisional license without sacrificing normal landmarks.

Epithelial nasal defects commonly result from minor to major excisions of nasal lesions, benign or malignant. Occasionally, epithelial reconstitution is necessary for replacement of irradiated nasal skin of poor quality. Traumatic avulsion defects demand immediate repair if esthetics are to be properly served and unacceptable scarring and contracture avoided. Because it occupies the conspicuous central portion of the face, the nose draws immediate attention to itself, and nasal defects, however minor, accentuate that attention. Therefore, camouflage repair of nasal defects deserves high esthetic and functional priority, with strict attention to achieving reconstructive symmetry by repair that respects topographic subunit principles.

Until recent decades, the split-thickness or full-thickness skin graft served the surgeon well as an effective tissue for immediate epithelial replacement. Skin is readily available around the head and neck, its rate of successful "take" is high, and one-stage repairs conserve the patient's and the surgeon's time and skills.

Gradually, however, the multiple advantages of adjacent or regional pedicle flaps become apparent to head and neck surgeons interested and skilled in a higher degree of esthetic camouflage, effective one-stage (or, on occasion, two-stage) repair and superior defect effacement and color match. Properly designed and executed flaps should replace missing tissue with *like tissue*, a fundamental concept in plastic surgery. Furthermore, flaps possess the following distinct advantages over skin grafts: (1) they provide their own blood supply; (2) they contract less; (3) cosmetically and chromatically, they are superior; (4) they provide bulk and lining; (5) they create superior protection for bone and cartilage; (6) they resist infection; (7) they undergo minimal pigment change; and (8) they may incorporate cartilage, bone, or skin in composite fashion.

In their simplest form, adjacent flaps may be classified as *advancement, rotation, transposition*, and *interposition* flaps, all designed and derived from tissue adjacent to the nasal defect. By far the most versatile adjacent flaps are the transposition flaps, which include bilobed, rhomboid, and Z-plasty flaps. *Regional flaps* are best used when more abundant tissue is required for repair or adjacent skin is inadequate or unsatisfactory. They use unipedicled flaps of similar texture, thickness, and color from adjacent regions (glabella, forehead, scalp, cheek, neck). A second stage of repair is required to transect the bridge of the flap, reconstructing both the defect and donor site to render both inconspicuous. Regional flaps are invariably designed and transposed from areas of relative epithelial excess and redundancy in the head and neck.

Superficial nasal epithelial defects of the lower half of the nose (trauma, burns, surgical excisions) are readily repaired with skin grafts derived from *nasolabial, preauricular*, or *postauricular* skin. The postauricular site has been shown by experience to be a less ideal color match than skin derived from the first two sites. An ideal but neglected donor site in older patients is *redundant skin of the nasolabial fold*. Full-thickness skin donated from this site is abundant and of excellent color match and allows camouflage of the donor defect in the nasolabial crease. Full-thickness defects of the nasal lobule and columella heal beautifully with nasolabial fold full-thickness skin grafts. Similarly, the preauricular and glabellar areas may harbor redundant skin with similar advantages. Seldom does the need arise to graft with skin derived from the more classic distant skin graft sites (inner arm, abdomen, thigh, buttocks).

Split-thickness skin grafts seldom satisfy the need for three-dimensional augmentation or effacement of nasal defects, they may become depressed and thinner with time, they seldom provide appropriate covering for implants of bone and cartilage, and they carry none of their own blood supply. For these reasons and those previously outlined, adjacent flaps remain the tissue of choice for immediate nasal repair in all areas except the nasal tip and infratip lobule. Specifically, grafts are generally inappropriate in areas of dense scarring and/or irradiation with consequently poor recipient site blood supply.

ESTHETIC SEPTORHINOPLASTY

The rhinoplasty surgeon must have wide knowledge of predictable procedures to be implemented in the unlimited variety of nasal configurations encountered. Strict adherence to basic principles does not necessarily always produce the ideal result. It is essential that an understanding of dynamic nasal structure transcends the components of static bone and cartilage; the relationship of shape and form with muscle tension and skin texture, the relationship of bone and cartilage with surrounding structures, the degree of postoperative thickening and/or relaxation of tissues, and the role of interrelated structures in the production of the deformity must be realized and evaluated.

Surgical variations in rhinoplasty are manifold, ranging from minor corrections to complete reconstruction of the nose. Esthetic rhinoplasty aims at the creation of a nose that can be considered ideally proportioned, but proper physiologic function is essential. In post-traumatic deformities and many developmental and congenital deformities, the correction of respiratory derangements is paramount, and esthetic appearance, although significant, is secondary. Some congenital deformities, such as the cleft lip or bifid nose, encompass both functional and cosmetic requirements of a special nature.

Patients seeking rhinoplastic surgery with a gross deformity, an occupational need for improvement, or a wish to appear younger usually have a realistic approach to the operation, whereas those who are excessively anxious about the operation, display obsessive-compulsive traits, or have unrealistic expectations about what the operation will do for their lives have a less ideal or guarded prognosis.

Rhinoplasty remains the most challenging of all esthetic operations because no two procedures are ever identical. Each patient's nasal configuration and structure require individual and unique operative planning and surgical reconstruction. Therefore, no single technique, even though mastered, will prepare the surgeon for the varied anatomic patterns encountered. It is essential to regard rhinoplasty as one operation planned *to reconstitute and shape* the anatomic features of the nose into a new, more pleasing relationship with one another and the surrounding facial features. Rhinoplasty should be approached as an anatomic dissection of the nasal structures requiring alteration, conservatively shaping and repositioning these anatomic elements. Many more problems and complications arise from *overcorrection* of nasal abnormalities than from *conservative* correction. Inappropriate technique applied persistently without regard for existing anatomy creates frequent complications. One truism, "it is not what is removed in rhinoplasty that is important but what is left behind," remains valid. Furthermore, one must comprehend clearly the dynamic aspects of operative rhinoplasty because all surgical steps are interrelated and interdependent, *most maneuvers leading to a temporary deformity to be corrected by the steps that follow.*

Rhinoplasty varies in each patient by the amount of tissue excised and/or the relative repositioning, reorientation, and/or grafting of anatomic structures. Classically, then, rhinoplasty consists of the following interrelated steps: (1) septoplasty; (2) tip remodeling, projection, and cephalic rotation; (3) hump removal (establishing the profile line); (4) narrowing of the nose with osteotomies; and (5) final correction of subtle deformities.

Sculpture of the nasal tip is regarded, and properly so, as the most exacting aspect of nasal plastic surgery. The surgeon is challenged by the essentially bilateral, animate, and mobile nasal anatomic components. Because no single surgical technique may be used successfully in correction of the endless anatomic tip variations encountered, the surgeon must analyze each anatomic situation and make a reasoned judgment about which approaches and tip modification techniques will result in a predictably natural appearance. Factored into this judgment decision must be consideration of, among other things, the strength, thickness, and attitude of the lower lateral cartilages (alar cartilages), the degree of tip projection, the tip skin and subcutaneous thickness, the columellar length, the length of the nose, the width of the tip, and the tip-lip angulation and relationship. The alar cartilages are of variable shape; are composed of medial, lateral, and intermediate crura; frame the nares; and form the alae. The medial crura are attached to each other by fibrous tissue and to the caudal edge of the septal cartilage by skin, making up the columella and membranous septum. The lateral crura may slightly overlap the upper lateral cartilages and are attached to the lower rim of the upper lateral cartilages and the septal cartilage by connective tissue. One fundamental principle of tip surgery is that normal or ideal anatomic features of the tip should be preserved and, if possible, remain undisturbed by surgical dissection, and abnormal features must be analyzed, exposed, reanalyzed, and corrected by reduction, augmentation, or shape modification.

Surgeons have gradually come to understand that radical excision and extensive sacrifice of alar cartilage and other tip support mechanisms all too frequently result in eventual unnatural or "surgical" tips. What appears pleasant and natural in the early postoperative period may heal poorly because of overaggressive attempts to modify the anatomy more extensively than the tissues allow. Cross-cutting or morselization of the lateral crura may provide an excellent early appearance but commonly results in distortion or loss of tip support as the soft tissues "shrink-wrap" the weakened cartilages over time. Rhinoplasty is, after all, a compromise operation, in which tissue sacrifices are made to achieve a more favorable appearance. It therefore becomes judicious to develop a reasoned, planned approach to the nasal tip based entirely on the anatomy encountered coupled with the final result intended. A philosophy of a *systematic incremental anatomic approach* to tip surgery is highly useful to achieve consistently natural results. Conservative reduction of the volume of the cephalic margin of the lateral crus, preserving a substantially complete, undisturbed strip of residual alar cartilage, is a preferred operation in individuals in whom nasal tip changes are intended to be modest. As the tip deformity or asymmetry encountered becomes more profound, more aggressive techniques are required, from weakened and complete strip techniques to significant interruption of the residual complete strip with profound alteration in the alar cartilage size, attitude, and anatomy. Cartilage structural grafts to influence the size, shape, projection, and support of the tip are often invaluable.

Successfully achieving these diverse surgical results requires an understanding of and a healthy respect for the major and minor tip support mechanisms, seasoned by the recognition of the intraoperative surgical tip dynamic principles that interact in every tip operation. It clearly follows that the *appropriate tip incisions and approaches should be planned to preserve as many tip supports as possible.* Alar cartilage sculpturing should similarly respect this principle by conserving the volume and integrity of the lateral crus and avoiding, in all but the most extreme anatomic situation, radical excision and sacrifice of tip cartilage. The surgeon should differentiate clearly among *incisions, approaches, and techniques.*

In anatomic situations in which the nasal tip anatomy is favorable, only conservative refinements are necessary, and *nondelivery* (of the alar cartilages) approaches possess great value. Less dissection and less disturbance of the tip anatomy are necessary and reduce the chance for asymmetry, error, and unfavorable healing. Properly executed (when indicated), nondelivery approaches therefore allow the surgeon to control the healing process more accurately than when more radical approaches and techniques are chosen.

Delivering the alar cartilages as individual bipedicle chondrocutaneous flaps through intercartilaginous and marginal incisions is the preferred approach when the nasal tip anatomy is more abnormal (broad, asymmetric, etc) or when more dramatic tip refinements are necessary. Significant modifications in the alar cartilage shape, attitude, and orientation are more predictably attained when the cartilages are delivered. Interrupted strip techniques (rarely employed) for more radical tip refinement and cephalic rotation are more efficiently accomplished when the cartilages are delivered. The increased surgical exposure provides the surgeon with an improved binocular view of the tip anatomy and affords the added ease of bimanual surgical modifications.

The *external* or *open approach* to the nasal tip is in reality a more aggressive form of the delivery approach and is chosen with discretion in specific nasal tip deformities. When the nasal tip is highly asymmetric, markedly overprojected, severely underprojected, or anatomically confusing in its form (as in certain secondary revision cases), the open approach is considered. The transcolumellar scar is of negligible importance in this decision because it routinely heals inconspicuously when meticulously repaired.

The choice of the *surgical technique* used to modify the alar cartilages and the relationship of the nasal tip with the remaining nasal structures should be *based entirely on the anatomy encountered* and the predicted result desired, as defined from the known dynamics of long-term healing. The astounding diversity of tip anatomic situations encountered demands a broad diversification of surgical planning and execution by the experienced surgeon.

Three broad categories of nasal tip sculpturing procedures may be identified. Although additional subtle technical variations exist, the three primary categories are volume reduction with residual complete strip, volume reduction with suture reorientation of the residual complete strip, and volume reduction with interrupted strip.

Preserving intact the major portion of the *residual complete strip* of the alar cartilage is always preferred when the anatomy of the alar cartilages and their surrounding soft tissue investments allows. Techniques involving a weakened (or suture-reoriented) residual complete strip have all of the foregoing positive virtues and allow the surgeon to effect reorientation of the breadth of the domal angle, projection modification, and narrowing refinement so desirable in the ideal postoperative appearance. The control of favorable healing is enhanced with these techniques, with the risk of complication diminished considerably. Anatomic situations are occasionally encountered in which the shape, breadth, and orientation of the alar cartilages must be changed more radically by *interrupting* the complete strip in a vertical fashion somewhere along its extent to refine severe anatomic deficits. When significant cephalic rotation is indicated, interrupted strip techniques are considered. The risks of asymmetric healing are higher when the alar cartilages are divided, however, and initial loss of tip support occurs immediately. If tip projection is inadequate, several reliable methods may be used singly or in tandem to establish permanent improvement. All involve reorientation of the alar cartilages or addition of autogenous cartilage grafts to strengthen or sculpture the projection and/or attitude of the tip and infratip lobule. Autogenous *cartilage struts* positioned below and/or between medial crura are effective in establishing permanent tip stability and slight additional projection.

In many patients undergoing rhinoplasty, *cephalic rotation* of the nasal tip complex (alar cartilages, columella, and nasal base) assumes major importance in the surgical event, whereas in other individuals, the *prevention* of upward rotation is vital. Certain well-defined and reliable principles may be invoked by the nasal surgeon essentially to calibrate the degree of tip rotation (or prevention thereof). The dynamics of healing play a critical role in tip rotation principles; the control of these postoperative healing changes distinguishes rhinoplasty from less elegant procedures.

Profound facial and nasal disharmony may result from the anatomic facial feature variant termed "*the overprojecting nose.*" Because the entire nose, and especially the normal nasal tip, is composed of distinct, interrelated anatomic components, any one or a combination of several of these components may be responsible for the tip that projects too far forward of the anterior plane of the face. The guidelines for determining appropriate and inappropriate tip projection are now well accepted. When numerous patients with overprojecting tips are analyzed, it becomes apparent that no single anatomic component of the nose is constantly responsible for overprojection; therefore, no single surgical technique is uniformly useful in correcting all of the problems responsible for the various overprojection deformities. Accurate anatomic diagnosis allows preoperative development of a logical individualized strategy for correction and tip retropositioning. In almost every instance, *weakening or reducing of normal tip support mechanisms is required* to achieve normality, supplemented by reduction of the overdeveloped components. The following anatomic variants are commonly responsible individually or collectively for overprojection of the nasal tip.

Overdevelopment of the alar cartilages, commonly associated with thin skin and large nostrils, is frequently encountered in the overprojecting nose. Overprojection and obliteration of a definitive nasolabial angle may be the result of an *overdevelopment of the caudal part of the quadrilateral cartilage*. The nasal spine may, in fact, be of normal size, but if it is even slightly overlarge, it compounds the problem of overprojection. A *high anterior septal angle* caused by an overdeveloped dorsal quadrilateral cartilage component may spuriously elevate the tip to an abnormally forward projecting position, even when associated with otherwise perfectly normal tip anatomy. A less common cause of excess nasal tip projection is an *overlarge nasal bony spine*, which seemingly imparts an upward thrust of the tip components (which may otherwise be of normal dimensions). Compounding this abnormal appearance is often a coexistent blunting of the nasolabial angle, which may appear full, webbed, and excessively obtuse, with no obvious demarcation between the tip and columella. Tip overprojection may occur as a result of an *overly long columella* associated with an excessively long medial crura. In this deformity, the infratip lobule is commonly insufficient, creating the effect of extremely large and disproportionate nostrils. Various *combinations* of the foregoing hypertrophic anatomic problems may contribute to the overprojecting tip problem. In preoperative analysis, each nasal component must be compulsively identified and analyzed; only then can a definitive plan for natural correction be conceived. Generally, a combination of weakening of the major tip support mechanisms associated with reduction of the components responsible for the tip overprojection is carried out incrementally and as conservatively as possible to achieve the desired normal final result in a progressive fashion. *Iatrogenic overprojection* may occur when surgeons intent on profoundly increasing tip projection produce an unnaturally sharp and projected tip configuration (often associated with over-rotation of the tip). These misadventures commonly result from overaggressive tip surgery in which portions of the lateral crus are borrowed and rotated medially to increase medial crural projection.

Appropriate retroprojection of the projecting nose typically requires diminishing the various major and minor tip support mechanisms to reposition the tip closer to the face. A concomitant reduction of the alar component length and lateral flare (occasioned by tip retropositioning) is usually required to improve nasal balance and harmony. *Alar base wedge excisions* of various geometric designs and dimensions are necessary to balance alar length and position. The exact geometry of these excisions is determined by the present and intended shape of the nostril aperture, the degree and attitude of the lateral alar flare, the width and shape of the nostril sill, and the thickness of the alae.

Three anatomic nasal components are responsible for the preoperative profile appearance: *the nasal bones, the cartilaginous septum*, and *the alar cartilages*. Generally, all three must undergo modification to create a pleasing and natural profile alignment. If the nose is overlarge with a convex profile, reduction of the three segments is required. Less commonly (except in revision rhinoplasty), profile *augmentation* with autograft materials must be accomplished.

In planning profile alignment, the two stable reference points are the existing (or planned) *nasofrontal angle* and the *tip-defining point*. Esthetics are generally best served when profile reduction results in a high, straight-line profile in men and the leading edge of the tip just slightly higher in women. The degree and angulation of the "hump removal" depend on various factors, the most important of which are the size of the various involved anatomic components and the surgeon's confidence in the stability of postoperative tip projection. These must be balanced with the personal preference for profile appearance combined with the surgeon's value judgment of facial esthetics.

The plane of tissue elevation over the nasal dorsum is important for several reasons. A relatively avascular potential plane exists intimate (superficial) to the perichondrium of the cartilaginous vault and just below the periosteum of the bony vault. Elevating the soft tissue flap in this important plane preserves the thickest possible ultimate epithelial soft tissue covering to cushion the newly formed bony and cartilaginous profile. Generally, only sufficient skin is elevated to gain access to the bony and cartilaginous profile; therefore, wide undermining is unnecessary in the typical rhinoplasty. In older patients with redundant and less elastic skin, or when access is needed for major autograft augmentation, wider undermining is carried out. Even in the latter instance, the periosteal soft tissue layer over the intended site of the low lateral osteotomies is preserved intact to help stabilize the mobile bony pyramid after in-fracture osteotomy maneuvers. Either of two methods of profile alignment is preferred: *incremental* or *en bloc*. In the first method, the cartilaginous dorsum is reduced by incrementally shaving away the cartilaginous dorsum until an ideal tip–supratip relationship is established, followed by sharp osteotome removal of the residual bony hump. A Rubin osteotome, honed to razor sharpness for each procedure and seated in the opening made by the knife at the osseocartilaginous junction, is advanced cephalically to remove the desired degree of bony hump in continuity with the cartilaginous hump. Any remaining irregularities are corrected under direct vision with a knife and sharp tungsten carbide rasp.

Further profile enhancements may be favorably developed with contouring cartilage grafts positioned along the dorsum, supratip area, infratip lobule, columella, and nasolabial angle. In the last site, so-called "plumping" grafts are commonly used to open an otherwise acute or unsatisfactory nasolabial angle and thereby contribute to improved profile appearance. The illusion of tip rotation and nasal shortening results from this maneuver, reducing the degree of actual shortening required and preserving a longer and often more elegant nose.

Significant advances have been developed over the past two decades in the reduction of osteotomy trauma in rhinoplasty surgery. Osteotomies, the most traumatic of all nasal surgical maneuvers, are best delayed until the final step in the planned surgical sequence, when vasoconstriction exerts its maximal influence and the nasal splint may be promptly positioned.

Profile alignment in the typical reduction rhinoplasty inevitably results in an excessive plateau-like width of the nasal dorsum, requiring narrowing of the bony and cartilaginous pyramid to restore a natural and more narrow frontal appearance to the nose. To facilitate atraumatic low lateral osteotomy execution, medial-oblique osteotomies angled laterally 15 to 20 degrees from the vertical midline are preferred. By creating an osteotomy dehiscence at the intended cephalic apex of the lateral osteotome, the surgeon exerts added control of the exact site of backfracture in the lateral bony sidewall. A 2 or 3 mm sharp micro-osteotome is positioned intranasally at the cephalic extent of the removal of the bony hump (if no hump removal has been necessary, the site of positioning is at the caudal extent of the nasal bones in the midline). The osteotome is advanced cephalo-obliquely to its intended apex at an angle of 10 to 15 degrees, depending on the shape of the nasal bony sidewall. Little trauma results from medial-oblique osteotomies. Trauma may be significantly reduced in lateral osteotomies if 2 or 3 mm micro-osteotomies are used to accomplish a controlled fracture of the bony sidewalls. No need exists for elevation of the periosteum along the pathway of the lateral fractures because the small osteotomies require little space for their cephalic progression. Appropriately, the intact periosteum stabilizes and internally splints the complete fractures, facilitating stable and precise healing. Final subtle nasal refinements are now completed and may include caudal septal reduction, resection of excessive vestibular skin and mucous membrane, trimming of the caudal margins of the upper lateral cartilages (only if overlong or projecting into the vestibule), columellar narrowing, and bilateral alar base reduction. These final maneuvers are carried out with the assistant maintaining constant finger pressure over the lateral osteotomy sites to prevent even minimal oozing and intraoperative swelling. All incisions are closed completely with 5-0 chromic catgut suture. No permanent sutures are used.

No intranasal dressing or packing is necessary in routine rhinoplasty. If septoplasty has been an integral part of the operation, a folded strip of Telfa is placed into each nostril along the floor of the nose to absorb drainage. The previously placed transseptal quilting mattress suture acts as a sole internal nasal splint for the septum, completely obliterating the submucoperichondrial dead spaces and fixing the septal elements in place during healing. The external splint consists of a layer of compressed Gelfoam placed along the dorsum and stabilized in place with flesh-colored micropore tape, extending over and laterally beyond the lateral osteotomy sites. A small aluminum and Velcro splint is applied firmly over the nasal dorsum and removed in 5 to 7 days.

The care of the postrhinoplasty patient is directed toward patient comfort, reduction of swelling and edema, patency of the nasal airway, and compression/stabilization of the nose.

Whether the patient is discharged on the afternoon of or the morning after surgery, all intranasal dressings are removed from the nose before the patient leaves. A detailed list of instructions is supplied for the patient or accompanying family member; the important aspects of these "do's" and "don'ts" are emphasized. Prevention of trauma to the nose is clearly the most important consideration. Oral decongestant therapy is helpful, but the value of corticosteroids and antibiotics in routine rhinoplasty is conjectural.

Nasal Septal Reconstruction

The functions of the nasal septum are (1) support of the external nose, (2) regulation of airflow, and (3) support of nasal mucosa. *Preservative* septal surgery is justified by considering *normal anatomy*. Few "normal" septa are perfectly straight, existing without imperfection. Minor septal irregularities after appropriate reconstruction are inconsequential, provided that they create no obstruction and contribute to no external nasal deformity. Radical septal resections in pursuit of a "straight" septum are therefore generally without virtue.

Septal reconstruction is usually carried out with (and usually as an integral part of) rhinoplasty. Reduction rhinoplasties invariably diminish breathing space. Reconstructive septoplasty can rescue an airway otherwise potentially compromised by a purely esthetic procedure. Invariably, the deformed septum contributes to the anatomic deficit inherent in the twisted nose and is best corrected at the outset of septorhinoplasty. It is frequently remarkable at the operating table how initial septoplasty transforms the crooked nose into near-perfect cartilaginous alignment. As in all surgery for which perfection is the goal, a secondary procedure of lesser magnitude may be occasionally required (less than 5% of all procedures), and all patients deserve to know that fact before undergoing a reconstructive procedure ("the crooked nose has a memory").

Finally, preservative conservation septal surgery should totally negate the most severe sequelae of more radical septal resections: columellar retraction, saddle nose, airway collapse, loss of tip support, and septal perforation. The latter conditions present complex difficult reconstructive exercises and are better avoided than risked.

Certain precepts emerge as cardinal to all septal surgery. These precepts have as their basis an increasingly detailed, atraumatic dissection and mobilization of the septal components, an assessment of the obstructive problem, and, finally, reconstruction and realignment after minimal tissue sacrifice. These major steps involve the following surgical phases, which are not always carried out in this sequence:

1. Whenever possible, elevate a mucoperichondrial flap only on one side.
2. Atraumatically disarticulate the attachment of the quadrilateral cartilage to the perpendicular plate of the ethmoid and to the vomer. If a vertical angulation exists just caudal to this articulation, a common site of deviation, the disarticulation can be positioned at this angulation.
3. Mobilize the quadrilateral cartilage along the floor of the nose at the maxillary crest. A narrow horizontal strip of cartilage may be removed to facilitate this mobilization without compromising septal support.

4. Isolate the *bony* septum between its bilaterally elevated mucoperiosteal flaps and medially reposition or resect the portion creating obstruction (bone grafts are commonly taken at this juncture).

5. Realign the cartilaginous septum with the conservative manipulations to be described subsequently.

6. Stabilize all realigned septal segments with quilting mattress transseptal absorbable sutures during the healing phase.

Certain vital fundamental technical concepts are required to accomplish these goals of septal reconstruction:

1. Perform all septal surgery under direct vision. Intense fiberoptic headlighting, long nasal specula, complete septal mobilization, and effective vasoconstriction make this an easily realized surgical prerequisite.

2. Preserve the contralateral mucoperichondrial flap for support, septal cartilage nutrition, and stability. Exceptions to this principle exist but are infrequent.

3. Preserve the caudal septal relationship with the membranous columella and feet of the medial crura. Severe caudal subluxation may negate this principle.

4. Dissect and mobilize the septal components fully before final deformity diagnosis. Only now should the extent of a conservative resection be planned.

5. Resist the temptation to resect more radically in pursuit of a "perfectly straight" septum.

6. In septorhinoplasty of the twisted nose, generally the septal realignment is best created before tip and profile reconstruction. Septoplasty in combined procedures frequently requires more technical ingenuity than rhinoplasty.

7. Assiduously avoid removal of septal cartilage contributing important strength to the structure of the external nose.

8. Dissect from the "known to the unknown," to best avoid development of tears and flap perforation. If perforations are created, repair with fine suture technique.

9. Unless it contributes to deformity, preserve the upper lateral cartilage attachment to the septum.
10. Control and stabilize final septal alignment with judiciously placed transseptal sutures, thereby preventing cartilage segment overrides, hematoma, and unfavorable fibrosis. The need for long-term septal splints is thereby lessened or negated.
11. Avoid long-term intranasal packing and tamponade, a more traditional than useful exercise.
12. Constantly reassess and diagnose the obstructive problem during the course of septal surgery with inspection *combined with intranasal palpation.* As in rhinoplasty, the anatomic metamorphosis in septoplasty is dynamic and interdependent, each surgical step often dramatically influencing the next. Remain flexible in ideas and approach, ready to incorporate surgical options as required.
13. Understand that airway improvement, particularly in the twisted nose (or as the sequela of old comminuted fractures), may require nasal osteotomies to achieve optimum breathing space.

With progressive use of the foregoing integrated techniques, most deviated septa may be appropriately reconstructed rather than resected and the septal functions preserved without embarrassing septal support. Controlling the healing process totally is not possible, but it can be favorably influenced by the suture techniques to be described.

Following completion of septal reconstruction, a series of transseptal transperichondrial through-and-through sutures are now positioned to coapt the septal flap(s), thereby closing all dead space. Hemostasis is thus promoted, and hematoma is avoided. The presence of one intact undissected mucoperichondrial flap provides a great advantage in stabilizing the septal reconstruction.

30

FACIAL FRACTURES

Paul J. Donald, MD
Jonathan M. Sykes, MD

The emergency management of the patient suffering from a facial fracture includes the establishment of a patent airway, control of hemorrhage, and assessment of neurologic status. Maxillofacial injuries generally have a low priority and are addressed after abdominal, thoracic, and other life-threatening injuries have been ruled out. Especially important in facial injuries is the status of the cervical spine. Injuries to the spine must be ruled out prior to the repair of the fractures of the facial skeleton. Airway compromise may arise from bilateral body fractures of the mandible or those lower jaw fractures that are accompanied by extensive intraoral contusions and lacerations such as those seen in gunshot wounds to the face. Le Fort fractures of the maxilla commonly present with airway obstruction owing to the retrodisplacement of the upper facial skeleton and parapharyngeal edema.

Attention to soft tissue injuries to the face includes the institution of tetanus prophylaxis, adherence to the principles of conservative débridement of marginally viable tissue, and attention to the use of lines of minimum tension and the concept of facial esthetic units during reconstruction.

DENTAL OCCLUSION

A clear understanding of normal dental occlusion and its common variants is essential in making the diagnosis of jaw fractures and the planning of their repair. Class I occlusion is present when the mesiobuccal cusp of the first maxillary molar tooth rides on the buccal surface of the intercuspal groove of the first mandibular molar. Class II occurs when the mesiobuccal cusp is located anterior to the intercuspal groove, and class III occurs when the mesiobuccal cusp is located posterior to the groove.

A class II occlusion usually translates into an overjet of the upper central incisors, pushing them beyond the mandibular central incisors. There is usually an accompanying retrognathism. The lower central incisors will, to a certain extent, often be directed superiorly toward the palate. This is called overbite. When a class III occlusion occurs, the lower incisors are in front of the upper incisors and there is an accompanying prognathism.

The presence of mamelons on the teeth and the presence of wear facets on others also help in establishing the correct premorbid occlusion in patients with fractures of the jaws.

FRACTURES OF THE MANDIBLE

Mandibular fractures are classified according to fracture site, favorability of angulation, severity, complexity, and status of dentition. They are further stratified into those occurring in children with mixed dentition and those occurring in adults. The most common site of mandibular fracture is the subcondylar region. Fractures in the body, parasymphysis, and especially the angle of the jaw are often accompanied by a subcondylar fracture on the opposite side. Favorability and unfavorability are determined by the angle of the fracture as it relates to the pull of the muscles of mastication. Fractures may be greenstick, simple, displaced, compound, or comminuted.

Diagnosis is aided by a detailed account, when possible, of how the trauma occurred and from what direction the blow to the jaw came. Pain localized to the fracture site, malocclusion, visible deformity, and trismus are the usual signs and symptoms. Panorex films supplemented by plain views of the mandible or occasionally computed tomographic (CT) scanning will usually clearly outline the fracture.

Treatment parameters are the restoration of normal occlusion by precise anatomic restoration of the fracture fragments and maintaining the alignment by some form of fixation. A little less precision is required in the edentulous patient. The classic method of fixation is with the Erich arch bar and placement of intermaxillary wires. Intermaxillary fixation can sometimes be successful using eyelet wires, but these are usually reserved for patients with subcondylar fractures who require only short-term fixation. In the edentulous patient, Gunning's splints are used anchored by circummandibular wires, transosseous screws, or Kirschner wires. The patient's own denture makes a good splint and, even if broken, can be repaired with cold-cure acrylic.

In any patient who has some unfavorability of the fracture alignment, a comminuted fracture, or a fracture that is in some way potentially unstable, some form of interosseous fixation is required. Although, in the past, interosseous wires were the common form of treatment, now virtually all open fracture repair is done with titanium plates or lag screws. Currently, the transbuccal systems of intraoral plating allow most mandibular fracture repairs through intraoral incisions, with the screw holes placed through a trocar that has been passed through a stab wound in the cheek skin. Eccentrically placed screw holes in the plate permit some dynamic compression of the fracture fragments to allow primary healing of the bone. An antitension band must be placed near the superior surface of the jaw in the way of an arch bar segment or a small monocortical plate to prevent distraction at the occlusal surface. Champy has designed small low-profile plates to be placed along the lines of osteosynthesis, which are naturally occurring distraction lines that arise because of the pull of the muscles of mastication. These monocortical plates placed at the points of distraction are opposed by the impaction forces that occur opposite to them.

Lag-screw fixation requires a fracture that has an oblique inclination. Screw holes are placed so as to have a gliding hole in the lateral fragment and a smaller hole in the medial fragment that will be captured by the flutes located at the terminal portion of the screw. A countersink is placed in the lateral fragment that will serve as the anchoring purchase as the screw is tightened. As the screw is passed, it glides through the lateral fragment but captures the medial fragment, and as the screw is tightened and locks into the countersink hole, the medial fragment is compressed against the lateral one. Care must be taken to cross the fracture line at a right angle and that enough bone in the medial fragment is engaged. Best fixation is achieved when two or three screws are used.

The Morris biphase appliance is an indispensable tool in the management of large open mandibular fractures such as those resulting from gunshot wounds. Two pins are placed in each fragment, the fracture fragments are aligned by alternatively loosening and tightening the first phase, and, once normal occlusion has been established, the second phase is applied and the first phase is removed. Bone grafting is delayed until all infection is cleared and there is adequate soft tissue coverage.

FRACTURES OF THE ZYGOMA

Fractures of the zygoma may be divided into arch, body, and trimalar fractures. The last two may or may not have a concomitant fracture of the orbital floor. The arch is usually depressed by a direct blow and is characterized by trismus, localized pain, and a depressed area over the upper lateral part of the face. Trimalar fractures are the most common, and in this injury, the zygoma is fractured away from the rest of the facial skeleton. Symptoms of localized facial pain, numbness over the infraorbital nerve distribution, epistaxis, and malar flattening are accompanied by facial swelling and subconjunctival hemorrhage. Step-offs at the zygomaticofrontal suture line and inferior orbital rim are palpable, and irregularity and crepitus are palpable intraorally under the zygomatic arch.

Computed tomographic scanning or plain films will reveal the fracture lines in arch-only fractures. There are usually two fragments, which are depressed medially. In trimalar fractures, the fracture lines are at the lateral and inferior orbital rims, in the arch, along the maxillary face, and sometimes in the orbital floor. Comminuted fractures of the zygomatic body must be identified as they pose a particularly difficult problem in maintaining fixation.

The arch fracture can be simply reduced by the Gillies technique. An incision is made in the temporal area of the scalp; an elevator is inserted under the arch, and the arch is levered into position. The trimalar fracture is approached with a brow incision and an infraorbital incision. The fracture is reduced by levering it into position with the elevator placed under the zygomatic arch in the infratemporal fossa and the pressure exerted laterally and anteriorly. The fracture is fixed in place by a titanium miniplate at the zygomaticofrontal suture line fracture and a microplate at the fracture line in the infraorbital rim. Fractures of the orbital floor are reduced through a Caldwell-Luc antrostomy coupled with manipulation from above and supported with a graft preferably from the nasal septum or maxillary face. For reduction and repair of comminuted fractures of the zygomatic body, an extension of the supraorbital incision into a crease line in a crow's foot line lateral to the eye or an extended gingival-buccal incision over the maxilla or both is needed. The depressed body may have to be manipulated into place by pressure against the malar prominence via the cavity of the maxillary sinus. Miniplates are used to secure the fracture fragments.

FRACTURES OF THE MAXILLA

Maxillary fractures are usually bilateral and are classified according to the Le Fort system. Le Fort I fractures essentially separate the palate from the remainder of the midface skeleton. Le Fort II fractures traverse through the nasal dorsum and sometimes through the infraorbital rim and orbital floor. The Le Fort III fracture is a craniofacial dysjunction separating both maxillae from the cranial skeleton.

These are severe fractures that are often associated with intracranial injury and multiple-other-system trauma. They often present with a compromised airway because of the posterior retraction of the fractured maxillary segment into the upper airway and the edema secondary to the fracture and associated pharyngeal edema. Le Fort II and III fractures have the common finding of a mobile maxilla. An anterior open bite deformity is often seen because of the pull of the pterygoid muscles against the now floating maxilla, drawing it toward the angle of the mandible. Facial swelling, pain, epistaxis, facial numbness, and diplopia are common in Le Fort II and III fractures. Malocclusion and pain usually accompany the Le Fort I injuries.

Computed tomographic scans give the most revealing information regarding the sites and degree of displacement of these fractures. Care is taken to observe for palatal splits and mixed fractures as maxillary fractures are uncommonly symmetric in their pattern. Therefore, it is not uncommon to have, for example, a Le Fort I fracture on one side with a Le Fort III on the other.

In most instances, a tracheostomy should be performed. Repair of these fractures must be directed to restoring the integrity of the stress buttresses of the middle third of the face. First the maxilla is disimpacted, and the normal occlusal relationships of the teeth are established; the teeth are placed in intermaxillary fixation with arch bars. The correct relationship of the maxilla to the cranium is re-established at the zygomaticofrontal suture areas and in the nasofrontal region. Titanium miniplates are appropriately shaped to conform to the maxillary skeleton and fix the key points in these buttresses: under the zygoma as it forms the malar eminence, at the zygomaticofrontal suture area, and at the nasofrontal region. Any fractures at the infraorbital rim are repaired with microplates. If the fixation is stable, it is safe in some instances to remove the arch bars at the end of the operative procedure.

FRONTAL SINUS FRACTURES

Fractures of the frontal sinus may be classified according to which walls are fractured, displacement, and fracture severity. They may involve the anterior wall, posterior wall, nasofrontal duct, or corner or may be through and through. Each fracture may be linear or displaced, and the anterior wall fractures may be compound through the skin. The through-and-through fracture is the most complex and is characterized by involvement of all walls of the sinus in addition to intracranial trauma. The injury tears the skin, and usually there are comminuted depressed anterior and posterior walls of the sinus, torn dura, and contused brain.

Diagnosis is made principally based on the findings on a CT scan of the head, which is usually done in the emergency department at the time of the head injury. Anterior wall fractures, if depressed, will often present with, if not a visual, a palpable depression. However, soon after the initial injury, the depression may be obscured by a blood clot. Moreover, a subgaleal hematoma, even in the presence of an undisplaced fracture, may suggest a depression. A compound fracture will reveal the presence of an anterior wall fracture and intraoperatively provide a portal of entry for an endoscope to check for fractures of the posterior wall or nasofrontal duct region. Posterior wall fractures are obvious on the CT scan, but degrees of displacement are not. Fractures of the nasofrontal duct area are the hardest to pick up on the scan. They are suspected when there is an opacification of the frontal sinus that persists for longer than 2 weeks. A corner fracture is merely the terminal extension of a skull fracture in which the fracture nips the corner of the sinus. The anterior and posterior walls and sinus floor all have a linear fracture that is undisplaced and requires no treatment. A through-and-through fracture victim is usually unconscious and is often in a deep coma. A large laceration in the frontal skin is quite common, and cerebrospinal fluid and even brain often emanate from the wound. The first meeting with the patient is often during the craniotomy, at which time the otolaryngologist is summoned by the neurosurgeon to address the problems posed by the severely damaged frontal sinus.

The treatment of an undisplaced anterior wall fracture is by observation. Displaced fractures are opened through a coronal scalp incision, a butterfly incision in the brows, or any open wound over the sinus, which may be extended along a natural crease line in the forehead. The sinus is inspected for occult posterior wall or nasofrontal duct fractures, the sinus mucosa adjacent to the fracture lines is removed, and the fragments are restored to their correct anatomic position. Fixation can be with wire or titanium miniplates. Posterior wall fractures should all be opened, the sinus cavity divested of mucosa, and then the bony walls lightly drilled, the intersinus septum removed, the nasofrontal duct mucosa inverted on itself, and the cavity obliterated by an abdominal fat graft. Nasofrontal duct fractures should be managed either by removal of the intersinus septum through a trephine hole or by the osteoplastic flap and fat graft obliteration technique.

The through-and-through fracture is managed by cranialization. Anterior wall fragments are removed, cleansed, divested of mucosa, and stored in povidone-iodine. The neurosurgeon stops the intracranial bleeding, débrides any necrotic brain, and repairs the torn dura, usually with a fascia graft. The posterior wall of the sinus is completely removed so that the frontal sinus cavity becomes an extension of the anterior cranial fossa. The mucosa is meticulously dissected from the frontal sinus cavity, and the bony walls are carefully drilled to remove any last vestige of mucosa. Obliteration of the nasofrontal ducts is done with plugs of temporalis muscle. The anterior wall fragments are returned and fixed with miniplates.

NASOFRONTAL-ETHMOIDAL COMPLEX FRACTURES

Fractures of the nasofrontal-ethmoidal complex result from a severe frontal blow. The complex is driven posteriorly and wedged under the nasal processes of the frontal bones. There is often an accompanying tear of the medial canthal tendon. The torn tendon, which inserts on the anterior and posterior lacrimal crests, often takes a small fragment of lacrimal bone with it. Because the major contributing anatomic structures to the tendon are the fibrous extensions of the preseptal and pretarsal parts of the orbicularis oculi, there is a displacement of the medial canthus laterally in such injuries.

The diagnosis is made clinically by the marked flattening of the nasal dorsum, the typical turned-up "pig snout" appearance of the nasal tip, and, when the medial canthal tendon is torn, the telecanthus. In traumatic telecanthus, the medial canthus is dislocated laterally, inferiorly, and anteriorly. There is the absence of the bowstring sign, the natural tightening felt in the medial canthal area when the lateral canthus is retracted laterally. On some occasions, epiphora may occur either because of the ineffective action of the lacrimal pump or injury to the nasolacrimal duct. A CT scan will reveal the depressed nasal skeleton and the compressed, telescoped ethmoid block.

Treatment is aimed at restoring the nasal dorsum to its normal anatomic position, preventing relapse, and placing the medial canthal tendon back into its premorbid location. Reduction of the nose can first be attempted by placing Asch forceps into the nose and applying anterior pressure to disimpact the telescoped nasal bones. The nasal bones are often so severely trapped under the nasal process of the frontal bone that a better purchase in the ethmoid block must be obtained. A pair of bone hooks is placed in the block through bilateral Lynch incisions through which dissection between the periorbita and the fractured lamina has been accomplished. They are engaged so that the hooks face medially, and then a downward and anterior traction is exerted that will reduce the nose. The problem of retaining that reduction is solved by the judicious placement of microplates securing the nasal bones to the frontal bone and any stable part of the maxilla. If the nasal fragments are too small to hold a screw, fixation can be achieved with lead plates and hammock wires. Often the nasal architecture has been so severely disrupted that no semblance of a normal nose can be achieved. In these patients, an on-lay calvarial bone graft cantilevered from the frontal bone is placed over the shattered nasal bones.

Permanent fixation of the medial canthal tendon is difficult to achieve. The constant pull of the orbicularis oculi muscle in a lateral direction coupled with the fragility of the tendon causes many forms of fixation to tear through. Backing up the wire ligature through the tendon with some form of bolster such as a Kazanjian button or a Dacron felt pledget might prevent the wire from cutting through. Care is taken to overcorrect the position of the tendon, especially in the superior and posterior direction. Whereas a unilateral tear can be fixed to the bone of the opposite lamina papyracea, bilateral tendon tears are ligated to one another using the Converse-Hogan open-sky technique.

31

MICROTIA, CANAL ATRESIA, AND MIDDLE EAR ANOMALIES

Simon C. Parisier, MD
Jose N. Fayad, MD
Charles P. Kimmelman, MD

The child born with a malformed ear faces a lifelong hearing and communication impairment along with the social stigma of a facial deformity. Frequently, there are additional anomalies, such as facial and skeletal deformities. There may be dysfunction of associated neural pathways. Associated disturbances of the vestibular system may cause developmental motor delay. Additionally, there are psychological factors to be considered, including parental guilt, peer ridicule, and the shame of "being different." These hearing-impaired children face educational and economic challenges that may limit their achievements and opportunities.

EMBRYOLOGY OF ATRESIA AND MICROTIA

In the 3 to 4 mm embryo (3 to 4 weeks), the first indications of aural ontogenesis are the first and second branchiomeric structures and the otic placode, an ectodermal thickening on the lateral surface of the head opposite the fourth ventricle. The placode invaginates to first form a pit and then a vesicle detached from its surface origin. This otocyst forms the inner ear membranous structures, with the endolymphatic duct developing first at the 6 mm stage, followed by the appearance of the semicircular ducts and the cochlear diverticulum at the 15 mm stage (6 weeks). By the end of the third month, the cochlea is fully coiled. The cranial nerves entering the otocyst exert an inductive influence to produce neuroepithelium. The cochleovestibular ganglia develop from the otic placode epithelium.

As the membranous structures of the inner ear form, they become enveloped in a cartilaginous capsule, which eventually gives rise to the petrous portion of the temporal bone. Concurrently, the first pharyngeal pouch begins to form in the 3 to 4 mm embryo and expands into a tubotympanic recess, which will eventually give rise to the eustachian tube, middle ear space, and mastoid air cell system. The third branchial arch migrates superiorly to the level of the recess, and its artery (the internal carotid) comes to lie dorsal to the eustachian tube. Corresponding grooves develop on the external surface of the nascent cervical region. The first of these branchial clefts deepens until it approaches the tubotympanic recess, being separated only by the thin layer of mesoderm destined to become the middle fibrous layer of the tympanic membrane. Subsequently, in the 30 mm embryo (8 weeks), the primordial external canal becomes occluded by an ectodermal plug. By the twenty-first week, this begins to resorb to form the definitive external auditory canal.

Defects in the canalization process may also be associated with faulty formation of the pinna, which arises in the 8 to 11 mm embryo from six mesodermal thickenings. These hillocks surround the entrance of the first branchial cleft. The first branchial arch cartilage (Meckel's) forms the tragus and superior helical crus; the remainder of the pinna derives from the second arch cartilage (Reichert's). The developing auricular appendage migrates from its initial position in the lower face toward the temporal area. Branchial cleft dysmorphogenesis can impede this migration and leave the pinna in a low, transverse orientation.

As the middle ear forms, the separation between the first pharyngeal pouch and cleft is filled in by mesenchyme. In the

8 mm embryo (6 weeks), part of the connective tissue condenses to form the malleus handle; the subsequent expansion of the tympanic cavity superiorly is delayed until the cartilaginous otic capsule fully forms. The expansion of the first pharyngeal pouch results in the envelopment of the ossicles in an endodermal epithelium. The ossicles predominantly originate from the mesenchymal visceral bars of the first and second arches. The first arch forms the head of the malleus and body of the incus, with the second arch giving rise to the manubrium, long process of the incus, stapes superstructure, and lateral portion of the footplate. The medial lamina of the footplate is derived from the otic capsule. As the derivatives of the first pharyngeal pouch continue to extend into the developing temporal bone, the antrum, mastoid air cells, and petrous pyramid cells begin to form. Most mastoid development is postnatal.

The facial nerve is intimately related to the development of the middle and inner ear structures. The development of the stapes is closely related to that of the facial nerve, and abnormalities in the development of the stapes frequently are coeval with facial nerve anomalies. This relationship of the facial nerve to developing middle ear structures increases the likelihood of an anomalous course of the nerve in the malformed middle ear.

ETIOLOGY OF AURAL ATRESIA

Atresia and microtia can coexist with several known syndromes associated with inherited defects or acquired embryopathies owing to intrauterine infection (rubella, syphilis), ischemic injury (hemifacial microsomia), or toxin exposure (thalidomide, isotretinoin). The genetic basis of external and middle ear anomalies generally remains poorly characterized. Aural atresia occurs in approximately 1 in 20,000 live births. Although the inner and middle ears develop separately, inner ear abnormalities coexist in 12 to 50% of cases. Atresia is bilateral in 30% of cases, occurring more commonly in males and in the right ear. It is not surprising that an embryonic insult severe enough to cause aural atresia would also affect other organ systems. The following may be anomalous in patients with atresia: neurocranium defects (Crouzon's disease or craniofacial dysostosis), central nervous system (mental retardation), oral cavity (first and second branchial arch syndromes), the eye (Goldenhar's syndrome), the neck (branchial fistulae), the CHARGE association (coloboma, heart defect, choanal atresia, retarded growth, genitourinary defects, and ear anomalies), Treacher Collins syndrome (mandibulofacial dysostosis), Duane's syndrome (abducens palsy with retracted bulb), VATER complex (probable disorganization of the primitive streak with early mesodermal migration causing vertebral defects, anal atresia, tracheoesophgeal fistula, renal defects, and genital anomalies), and Pierre Robin syndrome. Chromosomal anomalies affecting the external and middle ears include Turner's syndrome and trisomies 13 to 15, 18, 21, and 22.

Anomalies of the ear in the absence of syndromes are usually not familial. Other congenital anomalies should be assiduously sought. A chromosomal analysis may be indicated. Gene mapping may prove useful in identifying a genetic basis for many of these disorders.

DIAGNOSIS AND EVALUATION

Usually, the diagnosis is evident on inspection of the external ear. Depending on the degree of the abnormality, the microtic ear may be classified in three grades. In grade I, the auricle is developed and, though misshaped, has a readily recognizable, characteristic anatomy. In grade II, the helix is rudimentary, and the lobule is developed. In grade III, an amorphous skin tag is present. In all stages, wide variations of morphology exist. The pinna may be fully formed with a transverse and low-set orientation. There may be accessory appendages of the pinna (pretragal tags with or without cartilage) and preauricular sinus tracts. The external canal may be stenotic or atretic to varying degrees. In cases of stenosis, entrapped squamous epithelium may lead to a retention cholesteatoma with bone destruction. A higher percentage of partially atretic ears have retention cholesteatomas than atretic ears.

Abnormalities of the tympanic cavity alone may occur with a normal tympanic membrane and external ear. In ears with conductive hearing losses and normal otoscopic examinations, isolated ossicular anomalies should be suspected. Ossicular fixation can be produced by a variety of abnormalities and may involve the stapes, incus, or malleus. Ossicular discontinuity may also be present generally involving the incus or the stapes arch. Ossicular malformations caused by abnormalities related to first or second branchial cartilaginous derivatives can frequently be surgically repaired (class I and II). However, ossicular fixation owing to cochlear capsule abnormalities, especially when associated with an aberrant facial nerve, may not be surgically correctable (class III). In class I, the middle ear space is aerated and normal, and the oval window is well developed with a mobile stapes; it is not obstructed by the facial nerve. In class II, the middle ear space is narrow but aerated, and there is an aplasia of the oval window with a fixed stapes. In class III, the middle ear space is hypoplastic and nonaerated, the oval window is obstructed by the facial nerve, and the tegmen is low, obstructing access to the middle ear. Otic capsule abnormalities producing stapedial fixation are frequently associated with abnormal communication between the inner ear and the subarachnoid space. In these instances, manipulation of the stapes results in a gusher of cerebrospinal fluid. Vascular malformations also occur in the middle ear, such as a high jugular bulb, a persistent stapedial artery, and an anomalous course of the carotid artery.

Further delineation of structural abnormalities requires computed tomography (CT). Computed tomographic studies allow determination of the degree of the canal atresia, the thickness of the atresia plate, the extent of pneumatization of the middle ear and mastoid, the intratemporal course of the facial nerve, and the presence or absence of the oval window and the stapes. An unsuspected cholesteatoma may also become apparent. Computed tomography also reveals the normalcy of the osseous inner ear structures.

Brainstem response audiometry should be performed neonatally in all children born with either microtia or atresia. In cases of microtia with fairly normal canals, an ossicular malformation producing a conductive hearing loss may be present. In patients with unilateral atresia, it is not unusual for the seemingly normal contralateral ear to have a hearing loss. Bilateral involvement may cause masking dilemmas; such is the case when one ear has a conductive loss and the other a sensorineural loss. These dilemmas may be minimized by using multichannel analysis of ipsilateral versus contralateral responses to determine the laterality of wave I. As the infant matures, behavioral audiometric evaluations must be obtained to confirm the neurophysiologic tests of hearing. In children older than 1 year, conditioned free-field play audiometry should help to quantify the overall hearing levels. Eventually, pure-tone and speech testing with masking should be obtained in children with fairly normal canals. Impedance and stapedial reflex measures in a seemingly normal ear can provide valuable information as well.

The otologist should consider evaluation of the function of other organ systems to detect any coexisting developmental defects.

MANAGEMENT OF AURAL ATRESIA AND MICROTIA

Nonsurgical

Early amplification, auditory training, and speech therapy can improve speech and language skills. In children with bilateral atresia, amplification with bone-conduction aids should be provided as soon as possible, preferably within the first few months of life. In infants with unilateral atresia and conductive hearing loss in the seemingly normal ear, an air-conduction aid should be fitted to the ear with a canal.

Surgical

In the unilateral case with normal contralateral hearing, repair of either the microtia or the atresia is considered elective, and there is less urgency to intervene during childhood. When the atresia is bilateral, with acceptable-appearing auricles, reconstructive surgery can be performed at a fairly young age. However, in cases of microtia that require reconstruction, atresia repair should be deferred until the initial stages of the auricular repair are completed. Generally, microtia surgery requires a scaffold that can either be sculpted from a cartilage graft that is obtained from the costochondral region or by using a synthetic allograft. An adequate cartilage graft requires sufficient growth and fusion at the donor site, which has usually occurred by 5 to 6 years of age. Additionally, in bilateral cases, many authorities recommend postponing surgery for the restoration of hearing until at least age 5 years so that pneumatization can develop.

Surgical Procedures for Congenital Conductive Hearing Loss

The success of the surgical correction of congenital conductive hearing losses is related to the abnormality since a wide range of malformations is possible. In class I ears, the potential for achieving an excellent hearing result is great. Conversely, in class III ears, the chances of achieving good hearing are slim. Before assuming the responsibility of correcting congenital conductive hearing losses and embarking on a procedure with significant potential complications, especially in children, the otologic surgeon must have sufficient experience to maximize the likelihood of a successful outcome.

Once the middle ear is entered, the surgeon must decide if the chain is fixed, and if it is, where is the fixation? Is it in the epitympanum? Is the stapes fixed? Or is it a fixation of the stapedial tendon?

A gap interrupting the ossicular chain's continuity occurs most commonly at the incudostapedial joint. The presence of a mobile stapes facilitates the surgery and greatly improves the surgical result. If there is a small distance between the stapes capitulum and the long process of the incus, a bone or cartilage graft can successfully negotiate the gap. Deficiencies of the long process of the incus can be corrected by either interposing the reshaped incus between the mobile stapes and the malleus handle or using an alloplastic prosthesis designed for this purpose (type III tympanoplasty). When the stapes arch is absent, similar procedures can be performed to bridge the gap from either the under surface of the drumhead to the mobile footplate (type IV tympanoplasty). A coexisting fixation of the stapes or obstruction of the oval window by the facial nerve increases the technical difficulty, yields poorer hearing results, and increases the chances of complications, such as sensorineural hearing loss or facial nerve injury.

Surgery for Microtia and Canal Stenosis or Atresia

Reconstruction of the external ear is usually performed by a plastic surgeon while the otologist corrects the external auditory canal and middle ear defects. Both work as a team to achieve optimal results. Microtia surgery is technically difficult, and overly optimistic expectations should be eschewed.

Correction of a severe grade III microtia requires several staged procedures. During the first stage, either an alloplastic scaffold or a segment of cartilage obtained from the lower costochondral skeleton is carved to mimic the auricle's shape and implanted into a subcutaneous pocket at the appropriate position. A portion of the microtic skin tag is maintained to construct the lobule. During the second stage, the auricle is freed from the scalp, and a split-thickness skin graft is used to create a postauricular sulcus. At a third stage, the tragus is created. An alternative technique for the treatment of severe grade III microtia is to use a lifelike prosthetic ear, which is attached to surgically implanted titanium posts that securely hold the auricle in a normal anatomic position.

Reconstruction of the atresia is deferred until the auricular cartilaginous scaffolding is completed. It is performed as part of the second or third stage of the auricular reconstruction. A postauricular approach is used, with great care being taken not to expose the scaffold. Temporalis fascia is harvested for reconstruction of the tympanic membrane. After elevation of the periosteum, a bony circular canal is created by drilling between the glenoid fossa anteriorly and the tegmen plate superiorly while trying to avoid entering mastoid air cells posteriorly. The surgeon should anticipate that the facial nerve will be located more anteriorly and more laterally than in the normal temporal bone. The purposeful identification of the facial nerve lessens the chance of inadvertent injury. Facial nerve monitoring may facilitate identification of the nerve in these atretic ears. Drilling away the atretic plate permits opening to the middle ear space. Precautions must be taken to avoid drilling on the mobilized atresia remnant since this may transmit traumatic vibratory energy through the ossicular chain to the inner ear and result in permanent sensorineural hearing loss.

The status of the ossicular chain is assessed. If the stapes is mobile, an appropriate reconstruction is performed. If it is fixed or the oval window is obscured by the facial nerve, the ossicular reconstruction should be deferred. Temporalis fascia is used to fabricate a new tympanic membrane. A meatal opening is made in the imperforate concha, incising the skin to create a rectangularly shaped, anteriorly based conchal skin flap. The underlying cartilage and soft tissue are removed to debulk the flap and create an opening that communicates with the drilled out external canal. The conchal flap is rotated to resurface the anterior third of the external canal and is stabilized by suturing to adjacent soft tissues. A thin split-thickness skin graft is harvested from the lower abdomen and used to resurface the remaining ear canal. The canal is packed snugly with Gelfoam to compress the skin grafts against the underlying bone and soft tissue. The postauricular incision is approximated using absorbable sutures.

Results of Atresia Surgery: Risks and Benefits

Atresia surgery is technically demanding. The results achieved are directly related to the experience and skill of the operating surgeon. Generally, hearing improvement to a serviceable level can be achieved in approximately two-thirds of selected patients. The complications of surgery include a small risk of facial paralysis, severe to profound sensorineural hearing loss, stenosis requiring additional surgery, persistent otorrhea, and tympanic membrane graft failure with perforation.

In children with unilateral atresia and a normal contralateral ear, surgery is not routinely indicated. The potential benefit of this difficult surgery may not justify the risk of complications. In binaural cases, the successful creation of an external canal, even when hearing cannot be improved, will allow the use of an ear-level air-conduction hearing aid to restore hearing without using a cumbersome bone-conduction aid. In selected cases, a bone-anchored hearing aid may also be indicated. Thus, in bilateral cases in which the facial nerve obstructs the oval window or when hearing improvement cannot be achieved, providing the patient with a stable, skin-lined canal is a worthy goal in its own right.

32

DISEASES OF THE ORAL CAVITY, OROPHARYNX, AND NASOPHARYNX

Lawrence W. C. Tom, MD
Ian N. Jacobs, MD

ORAL MANIFESTATIONS OF SYSTEMIC DISEASES

Lesions of the oral cavity and oropharynx may be signs of an undetected systemic condition.

Infections

Koplik's spots are found in rubeola (measles). They are red lesions with a pale blue center on the buccal mucosa usually opposite the lower molars. In varicella (chickenpox), vesicles of the oral cavity and pharynx, which progress to shallow ulcers, appear before the pruritic vesicular skin eruption.

Inflammatory Diseases

Behçet's syndrome is rare in children and is characterized by recurrent oral and genital ulcers and ocular inflammation such as uveitis and iridocyclitis.

Reiter's syndrome occurs primarily in young men and presents with urethritis, uveitis, conjunctivitis, and arthritis. Oral lesions are characterized by superficial, erythematous ulcers, which are surrounded by white annular lines.

In Wegener's granulomatosis, gingival hyperplasia is the most common early oral lesion. Lingual, palatal, and buccal ulcers are also common.

Erythema multiforme is a disorder involving the skin and mucous membranes. Erythema multiforme minor causes minimal skin and mucosal damage and is self-limited, lasting 2 to 3 weeks. Erythema multiforme major (Stevens-Johnson syndrome) is associated with systemic manifestations, purulent conjunctivitis, and hemorrhagic necrotic skin and mucosal lesions. Oral lesions occur in 50% of cases, and the lips, tongue, and floor of the mouth are most often affected. The lesions begin as vesicles and bullae that rupture, forming superficial ulcers and hemorrhagic crusts, especially about the lips. Treatment of Stevens-Johnson syndrome requires systemic corticosteroids and elimination of the causative agent.

Kawasaki's disease is a multisystem vasculitis of unknown origin occurring primarily in children under 5 years of age. It is characterized by high fever, bilateral conjunctivitis, polymorphous erythematous rash, erythema and edema of the extremities, cervical lymphadenopathy, pharyngeal injection, and necrotic pharyngitis. It is the most common cause of acquired cardiac disease in children under 5 years of age. Patients are treated with intravenous gamma globulin and aspirin.

Miscellaneous Disorders

Iron deficiency anemia is common in children. Its oral manifestations include burning of the tongue, pallor of the mucous membranes and gingiva, atrophic smooth erythematous tongue, angular cheilitis, and, occasionally, hyperkeratotic lesions on the oral mucosa. Niacin; folic acid; vitamin B_2, B_{12}, and C deficiencies; and mineral disorders also have oral manifestations.

Petechiae, ecchymoses, and hemorrhages appear with thrombocytopenia, whereas pallor of the mucous membranes may occur with anemia. In addition to anemia and thrombocytopenia, patients with leukemia often have neutropenia, and secondary infections of the oral cavity and oropharynx with ulceration are common. Leukemic cells may infiltrate the soft tissues of the oral cavity, especially the gingiva.

INFECTIONS

Viral

Most viral infections are self-limited, and most can be treated symptomatically. Herpangina is usually caused by coxsackie A virus. Symptoms include severe sore throat, pyrexia, and malaise. Examination reveals erythema of the oral cavity and multiple small vesicles and superficial ulcers on the mucosa. Hand-foot-and-mouth disease is similar to herpangina, but accompanying vesiculopapular lesions are found on the palms and soles.

Primary herpetic gingivostomatitis is common in preschool children. Oral vesicles form and rupture and heal as ulcers. The ulcers form a gray pseudomembrane, may coalesce, and cover most of the oral cavity. Recurrent herpes occurs with activation of the herpes simplex virus. Multiple vesicles form and rupture over a course of 10 to 14 days. These vesicles appear on the oral mucosa and near the vermilion borders, forming typical "cold sores."

Herpes zoster results from reactivation of the varicella virus in the sensory ganglia. Oral and skin lesions develop along the course of the second or third branches of the trigeminal nerve.

In the oral cavity, cytomegalovirus infections are manifest by large ulcers of the oral mucosa and exudative pharyngotonsillitis.

Patients with infectious mononucleosis frequently present with a sore throat, enlarged tonsils with a gray membranous exudate, and edema and petechiae of the soft palate. When the tonsillar hypertrophy and pharyngeal edema cause respiratory distress, corticosteroids are used.

Oral manifestations of human immunodeficiency virus infections include candidiasis, recurrent herpetic and aphthous ulcers, angular cheilitis, hairy leukoplakia, peridontitis, bleeding ulcerative gingivitis, papillomas, Kaposi's sarcoma, and diffuse parotitis.

The human papillomavirus causes exophytic, cauliflower-like lesions, which are found most commonly on the soft palate and tongue.

Bacterial

Group A beta-hemolytic strepococcus (GABHS) may cause pharyngitis. The oropharynx and the oral cavity are swollen and red, and the tonsils are covered with exudates. Scarlet fever, rheumatic fever, and glomerulonephritis are potential complications. Penicillin and amoxicillin are initial antibiotics of choice.

Diphtheria presents as a necrotizing pharyngitis associated with erythema and a thick pseudomembrane and may involve the larynx and trachea, leading to airway obstruction. Treatment consists of airway support, antitoxin, and antibiotics.

Fungal

Candidiasis is the most common fungal infection of the oral cavity. Pseudomembranous candidiasis (thrush), the most common form, is characterized by fine white lacey plaques covering the mucosa, usually the tongue, hard palate, and buccal mucosa. When the plaque is disrupted, a raw surface remains. Acute atrophic candidiasis and angular cheilitis are other forms.

Miscellaneous Conditions of the Oral Cavity

Leukoplakia is characterized by white plaques on the oral mucosa. It is a precancerous lesion, with malignant transformation occurring in 2 to 6% of patients. It has been noted in children with candidiasis and some viral infections.

Hairy leukoplakia is characterized by elevated, corrugated white plaques usually on the lateral borders of the tongue and suggests acquired immune deficiency syndrome.

There are three forms of recurrent aphthous stomatitis. Minor aphthous ulcers are painful, shallow, ovoid ulcers less than 0.6 cm in size. Major aphthous ulcers are larger than 0.6 cm and more painful than minor ulcers. Herpetiform ulcers are characterized by crops of painful, multiple, pinpoint ulcers. Treatment for all forms of aphthous stomatitis is symptomatic.

There are two forms of oral lichen planus. The reticular form, the most common type, is characterized by small white papules, which may be isolated or may coalesce to form interlacing white lines (Wickham's striae). It causes no symptoms. The erosive form is manifest by painful ulcers with papules or lines at the periphery.

Median rhomboid glossitis is caused by the persistence of the tuberculum impar. As a result, a rhomboid area free of papillae appears on the dorsal surface of the tongue.

Geographic tongue results from a loss of filiform papillae and is characterized by a white margin of desquamating epithelium of various sizes and shapes on the dorsum of the tongue surrounding a central, red, atrophic area. No treatment is required.

The fissured tongue is characterized by multiple fissures on the lingual dorsum. It has been associated with the genetic disorders Melkersson-Rosenthal syndrome and Down syndrome.

Hairy tongue is characterized by the hypertrophy and growth of the filiform papillae on the dorsal surface of the tongue, giving the tongue a hairy appearance.

The tongue may appear enlarged in many conditions. Relative macroglossia occurs when the tongue is normal in size, but anomalies of the surrounding structures make it appear large. Primary macroglossia is hypertrophy of the tongue musculature, whereas secondary macroglossia is owing to infiltration of tongue tissue. The causes of primary macroglossia include hypothyroidism, acromegaly, Beckwith-Wiedemann syndrome. The causes of secondary macroglossia are numerous.

The simple ranula is a blue, superficial, nontender fluctuant mass and is usually found in one side of the floor of the mouth. Small ranulas are asymptomatic, whereas larger ones may cause speech and swallowing problems. The plunging ranula is less common and appears as a soft, painless, ballottable submandibular mass. It may present with or without intraoral involvement.

DENTAL INFECTIONS AND CYSTS

Dental infections arise from dental caries, trauma to the teeth, and periodontal disease. The pulp of the tooth becomes inflamed and then necroses, leading to low-grade chronic inflammation or abscess formation. Dental infections may remain localized, spread along fascial planes, or become disseminated. Treatment of dental infections consists of antibiotics and root canal therapy or tooth extraction.

Inflammation of the tooth pulp, gingiva, and periodontal structures leads to the development of certain odontogenic cysts, including the periapical cyst. The dentigerous cyst develops from expansion of an impacted tooth follicle.

BENIGN LESIONS OF THE GINGIVA, MANDIBLE, AND MAXILLA

Many benign soft tissue lesions arise from the gingiva, including the pyogenic granuloma, peripheral giant cell reparative granuloma, Epstein's pearls, and congenital epulis.

Odontogenic tumors arise from the precursors of tooth formation and include odontomas, ameloblastomas, and myxomas. Nonodontogenic tumors arise from tissues other than dental precursors and include the torus of the palate, torus of the mandible, and fibrous dysplasia.

TONSILS AND ADENOID

Infections

The symptoms of acute tonsillitis include sore throat, fever, and odynophagia. Signs include tonsillar hypertrophy, erythema, and tonsillar exudates. It is self-limited, usually lasting from 7 to 14 days. An episode of acute tonsillitis may progress to recurrent acute tonsillitis. Many pathogens may cause acute tonsillitis. Of greatest concern is GABHS because it may cause rheumatic fever and glomerulonephritis. In most cases, penicillin and amoxicillin are the initial drugs of choice. If there is a history of treated recurrent acute tonsillitis, a β-lactamase-stable antibiotic should be used. Children who experience three or more episodes of acute tonsillitis despite adequate antibiotic therapy should be considered for tonsillectomy and adenoidectomy

Some patients may be carriers of GABHS. Carriers who experience frequent episodes of acute tonsillitis, infect other patients, or develop complications should be treated. If antibiotics fail, adenotonsillectomy is recommended.

Patients with chronic tonsillitis have a persistent tonsil infection. They complain of constant throat pain, halitosis, and fatigue. Examination reveals hypertrophy and erythema of the tonsils and enlarged crypts filled with debris. Symptomatic patients are treated with tonsillectomy.

Peritonsillar infection occurs when infection of the tonsil extends into the peritonsillar space The infection begins as a cellulitis and may progress to an abscess. Patients complain of fever, unilateral sore throat, odynophagia, and trismus. The classic signs include a muffled voice, drooling, unilateral swelling and erythema of the superior tonsillar pole, deviation of the uvula to the opposite side, and bulging of the posterolateral part of the soft palate. Patients with peritonsillar infections should be hydrated, placed on intravenous antibiotics, and given pain medications. If there is no improvement after 48 hours, airway compromise, or definite abscess, drainage should be considered. Options include needle aspiration, incision and drainage, and tonsillectomy.

The adenoid may become infected during an upper respiratory tract infection, causing fever, nasal obstruction, purulent rhinorrhea, postnasal discharge, and cough. These signs and symptoms are nonspecific and can occur with respiratory tract infections and sinusitis. Adenoiditis may be misdiagnosed as sinusitis, and adenoiditis may be a causal factor in pediatric sinusitis. Treatment is with antibiotics. If the condition persists, adenoidectomy is performed.

Obstruction

Upper airway obstruction may present in an acute or chronic fashion. With acute obstruction, there is a history of a sore throat, dysphagia, and increasing obstruction. Examination reveals an acute infection with signs of airway obstruction. Some children may be managed as outpatients with antibiotics and corticosteroids. Others may require hospitalization, especially to monitor and secure the airway. If symptoms persist, a tonsillectomy and adenoidectomy may be required. Sudden relief of acute upper airway obstruction may cause postobstructive pulmonary edema.

Chronic upper airway obstruction most often occurs from enlarged tonsils and adenoid but may occur when only one structure is enlarged. Collapse of the pharyngeal musculature and lymphoid structures into the airway during sleep increases the obstruction. Tonsillectomy and/or adenoidectomy should be considered.

Children with obstructing tonsils and adenoid may have obstructive sleep apnea (OSA). Sleep apnea is the intermittent cessation of airflow at the mouth and nose during sleep. Obstructive sleep apnea is caused by an obstruction in the upper airway and must be distinguished from the less common central sleep apnea (CSA), in which the cause is in the brainstem. With CSA, the neural drive to the respiratory muscles is temporarily abolished, and there is little effort to breathe.

If the diagnosis is equivocal, lateral neck radiography can be performed to assess the size of the tonsils, adenoid, and nasopharyngeal airway. Either polysomnography or sleep sonography will provide objective data regarding the presence and degree of obstruction.

Miscellaneous Conditions

Tonsilloliths are concretions of epithelial debris. They appear as gritty, caseous white, or yellow calculi up to 1 cm in size and have a foul odor.

The finding of a unilaterally enlarged tonsil often raises the concern of a neoplasm. In most cases, the larger-appearing tonsil is situated more medially within the tonsillar fossa, giving the impression of enlargement. Only rarely is the enlargement caused by a malignancy. In these cases, the tonsil is not only enlarged, but the surface appears abnormal.

Adenoid tissue may affect eustachian tube function. Removal of the adenoid reduces the extrinsic mechanical obstruction of the eustachian tube, improving ventilation. Adenoidectomy decreases the recurrence rates of otitis media. Adenoidectomy should be considered in any child with nasal obstruction or adenoiditis who is undergoing tympanostomy tube placement or in whom tympanostomy tubes are being replaced.

Tonsillectomy and Adenoidectomy

There are a variety of techniques for tonsillectomy and adenoidectomy. For a tonsillectomy, dissection can be performed with a knife, protected electrocautery blade, harmonic scalpel, or laser. Hemostasis can be obtained with electrocautery, ties, suture ligation, and thrombin. Adenoid tissue can be removed with a curette, adenotome, or powered instrument.

Bleeding, the most serious complication of tonsillectomy, occurs in up to 3% of patients. Dehydration, temporary hypernasal speech, and torticollis are common, whereas velopharyngeal insufficiency is uncommon. Nasopharyngeal and oropharyngeal stenosis are rare complications.

HEAD AND NECK SPACE INFECTIONS

Fascia envelops the muscles, vessels, and viscera of the neck. Fascial planes form where adjacent fascia condenses. Fascial spaces are potential spaces between these planes.

The cervical fascia consists of two layers, the superficial or investing layer and deep fascia. The superficial layer lies just below the skin and completely encircles the neck. The deep fascia comprises three layers: the anterior layer, middle or visceral layer, and prevertebral layer.

Fascial spaces are potential avenues for the spread of infection. Clinically, the most important spaces are the prevertebral, retropharyngeal, lateral pharyngeal, and submandibular.

The prevertebral space lies between prevertebral fascia and the vertebral bodies and extends from the base of the skull to the coccyx. The retropharyngeal space lies between the prevertebral fascia and the fascia covering the posterior pharyngeal wall and esophagus. It extends from the skull base to the tracheal bifurcation. The lateral pharyngeal (parapharyngeal) space is cone shaped, with its base at the petrous portion of the temporal bone and its apex at the hyoid bone. The carotid sheath pierces this space. The lateral pharyngeal space communicates with the submandibular, retropharyngeal, and parotid spaces and is close to the masticator and peritonsillar spaces. It is the most often involved with serious infections and most frequent route of spread of infection from one region to another. The submandibular space is bound by the floor of the mouth, tongue, mandible, anterior layer of deep cervical fascia, and hyoid bone.

Gram-positive aerobes are the predominant pathogens of these infections. Gram-negative aerobes, anaerobes, and β-lactamase-producing bacteria are also common. Antibiotic combinations should have activity against all of these microbes.

The diagnosis of a head and neck space infection can often be made after a history and physical examination. Specific radiologic studies are determined in the individual case. Lateral and anteroposterior neck films may demonstrate airway compromise, tracheal deviation, and widening of the retropharyngeal space. Chest radiographs are required to evaluate the airway and the mediastinum.

Contrast-enhanced computed tomography (CT) is the most valuable radiologic study. It evaluates all spaces, reveals findings of infection, differentiates cellulitis from abscess, and demonstrates the size and location of an abscess and its position relative to the carotid artery and internal jugular vein.

Several important principles apply to most of these infections. In children, upper aerodigestive tract infections are the most common cause of head and neck space infections, whereas dental infections are the most common cause in adults. It is not uncommon to fail to identify a primary source of infection. Oropharyngeal pain, fever, and limitation of jaw and/or neck movement are present in most infections. Initial treatment requires hydration, analgesia, and antibiotics.

Peritonsillar abscess is the most frequent head and neck space infection in children. Ludwig's angina is a rapidly spreading cellulitis of the submandibular space. Airway obstruction is a concern with Ludwig's angina, and when in doubt, the airway must be secured.

Retropharyngeal infections occur primarily in young children, usually as a sequela to upper respiratory tract infections. Infections may spread easily to and from the lateral pharyngeal space. Computed tomography with contrast should be performed in any patient with a suspected infection of the lateral pharyngeal space. The position, size, and extent of the abscess and its relationship to the great vessels can be established. If the abscess is medial to the great vessels, drainage of the abscess can be performed through a transoral approach. The external, cervical approach is the choice for abscesses that dissect along or are lateral to the great vessels.

DIFFERENTIAL DIAGNOSIS OF A NECK MASS

The differential diagnosis of a neck mass in adults and children is quite different. In adults, the incidence of malignancy may be as high as 50%, but in children, the incidence is low.

The age of the patient often suggests the type of lesion. In children, the most common causes of neck masses are inflammatory and congenital lesions. In adolescents and adults up to 40 years of age, congenital and developmental lesions and sialadenopathies are common. In adults over 40 years of age, the first consideration must be a metastatic neoplasm.

A history and head and neck examination may help to narrow the diagnostic possibilities. All neck masses should be examined for size, multiplicity, laterality, tenderness, color, mobility, consistency, surrounding tissue changes, and the presence of bruits and thrills. The location is important. Congenital lesions are usually found in the midline or anterior cervical triangle. Metastatic malignancies are distributed along the cervical lymphatic channels. In children, a supraclavicular mass is suggestive of a lymphoma.

Diagnostic studies include blood and urine studies, skin tests, plain radiography, ultrasonography, CT, magnetic resonance imaging (MRI), biopsy, and endoscopy. In a child with a suspected malignancy, a chest radiograph should always be performed because many children with cervical lymphoma have abnormal chest radiographs. Magnetic resonance imaging is preferred over CT. Magnetic resonance imaging provides superior resolution, demonstrates better anatomic detail, has multiplanar capability, and does not involve radiation.

If no diagnosis can be established or a malignancy is suspected in a child, an excisional biopsy is preferred. A needle biopsy is preferred in adults. If the diagnosis is a metastatic malignancy, endoscopy of the entire upper aerodigestive tract and biopsies of any suspicious mucosal areas and any likely primary sites should be performed.

NASOPHARYNX

The nasopharynx extends from the skull base to the soft palate. The adenoid tissue is on the posterosuperior wall. The eustachian tube orifice is located along the lateral wall. The torus tubarius marks the posterior boundary of the orifice. The fossa of Rosenmüller is the recess just posterior to the torus tubarius. The isthmus, the narrowest portion of the nasopharynx, opens into the oropharynx.

The nasopharynx functions as a conduit for respired air and secretions from the eustachian tube and nose to pass to the oropharynx. During swallowing and most phonation, the velopharyngeal valve separates the nasopharynx from the oropharynx. Velopharyngeal insufficiency results in regurgitation of food and fluids into the nose and hypernasal speech. Along with the nose, the nasopharynx is a resonating chamber that contributes to the quality of voice. The eustachian tube protects, ventilates, and clears fluid from the middle ear.

Benign Lesions of the Nasopharynx

Rathke's pouch develops when remnants of the buccal mucosal invagination that forms the anterior lobe of the pituitary gland persist. A craniopharyngioma is a tumor that arises from these remnants. Thornwaldt's cysts develop when the endodermal attachment to the pharyngeal end of the notochord persists. These conditions are discussed in Chapter 34.

Choanal Atresia

Choanal atresia results from failure of the buccopharyngeal membrane to regress so that the posterior part of the nasal cavity does not open into the nasopharynx. This developmental anomaly is discussed in Chapter 34.

Juvenile Angiofibroma

Juvenile angiofibroma of the nasopharynx is rare but is the most common benign neoplasm of the nasopharynx. It is discussed in Chapter 41.

Nasopharyngeal Stenosis

Nasopharyngeal stenosis occurs when scar tissue obstructs the nasopharynx. The posterior tonsillar pillars and soft palate adhere to the posterior pharyngeal wall. Most cases result from tonsillectomy and adenoidectomy. Treatment includes corticosteroid injection, lysis of adhesions, and rotation and advancement flaps.

SLEEP APNEA

Sleep apnea is an increasingly recognized and important condition in adults. In OSA, the obstruction is caused by pharyngeal collapse. The etiology of OSA is multifactorial. Reduced neuromuscular control of the pharyngeal dilator muscles accentuates the normal physiologic pharyngeal narrowing that occurs during sleep. Anatomic abnormalities cause obstruction, and with obstruction, greater inspiratory pressure is needed to generate airflow. This increased negative pressure contributes to pharyngeal collapse. Alcohol ingestion, neuromuscular diseases, and structural abnormalities are causes of OSA. Cardiac disease, chronic obstructive pulmonary disease, obesity, caffeine, and tobacco are predisposing or exacerbating factors.

The most common symptoms of OSA are snoring and excessive daytime somnolence. Other symptoms include frequent nocturnal arousal periods, restless sleep, memory loss, fatigue, irritability, morning headache, sexual dysfunction, and nocturia. Assessment of the patient's general medical condition, height, weight, blood pressure, neck size, and cardiopulmonary status is mandatory. The upper airway is thoroughly examined, and flexible fiberoptic endoscopy is essential. Polysomnography is the definitive diagnostic study.

Any predisposing or associated factors must be treated. Nonsurgical treatment includes positioning, artificial airways, appliances, continuous positive airway pressure (CPAP), and biphasic positive airway pressure (BiPAP). The goal of surgery for OSA is relief of airway obstruction by increasing pharyngeal size, decreasing pharyngeal compliance, or both to maintain adequate airflow. The specific procedure depends on the site of obstruction, and consideration includes nasal surgery, tonsillectomy, adenoidectomy, palatal surgery, uvulopalatoplasty and uvulopharyngopalatoplasty, tongue-base reduction, genioglossal advancement with hyoid myotomy, and maxillomandibular osteotomy with advancement. In severe, acute cases, tracheostomy may be considered.

Central sleep apnea is much less common than OSA and must be distinguished from it. It occurs when there is an absence of respiratory effort. During sleep, respiration is controlled by an automatic feedback system. Any condition affecting this system may cause CSA. Congenital central alveolar hypoventilation, chronic neuropathies, bilateral brainstem lesions, neuromuscular diseases, chronic obstructive pulmonary disease, and congestive heart failure are causes of CSA.

Polysomnography is the definitive study for diagnosis of CSA. Measurement of esophageal pressure may help to make the diagnosis of CSA.

The primary treatment for CSA is nasal mask ventilation using CPAP, BiPAP, or intermittent positive pressure ventilation. Medications have had limited success. In the most severe cases, tracheostomy with ventilation may be required.

33

CONGENITAL ANOMALIES OF THE LARYNX

Rodney P. Lusk, MD

Respiratory distress may range from minor types of stridor to complete obstruction with no air movement. Dysphonia may be caused by laryngeal lesions that interfere with vocalization, with voice quality ranging from hoarseness to complete aphonia. Failure of the larynx to close the airway during swallowing may cause feeding difficulties, with aspiration, cyanosis, or respiratory compromise. When evaluating patients with these signs, a history and examination of the entire airway should be performed.

LARYNGOMALACIA

Laryngomalacia is a condition in which the laryngeal inlet collapses on inspiration, causing stridor. It is the most common cause of stridor in the newborn. The most common symptoms produced by laryngomalacia are inspiratory stridor, feeding problems, and gastric reflux. The inspiratory stridor worsens with increased respiratory effort, such as crying or feeding, and in the supine position. Feeding problems are frequent with laryngomalacia. Radiographic evidence of gastric reflux occurs in 80% and regurgitation in 40% past 3 months of age.

The diagnosis is most frequently based on the symptoms and signs, flexible laryngoscopy, rigid laryngoscopy, and radiography of the neck and chest to identify possible subglottic lesions. The disadvantage of using a flexible laryngoscope is that one cannot accurately assess the subglottis. The necessity for rigid bronchoscopy is controversial. If symptoms are not compatible with laryngomalacia or if the patient fails to thrive, direct laryngoscopy and bronchoscopy should be performed to rule out secondary lesions. The flexible laryngoscope should not take the place of rigid endoscopy especially if a subglottic lesion is suspected.

The primary treatment is expectant observation in most cases. The small percentage of patients (10 to 15%) with failure to thrive or more than one lesion will require surgical intervention. The term supraglottoplasty is used to describe the surgical procedure for removing the flaccid supraglottic tissues. Care must be taken not to excise or traumatize the strip of mucosa between the arytenoid cartilages in the posterior part of the glottis.

SUPRAGLOTTIC LESIONS

Congenital supraglottic lesions, such as bifid epiglottis, are rare and can be associated with stridor and aspiration. There is a high incidence of other multiple congenital anomalies. A 44% incidence of polydactyly has been reported. The only means of diagnosing a bifid epiglottis is with flexible or direct laryngoscopy. If the airway distress is significant, a tracheostomy is warranted.

LARYNGEAL ATRESIA

Atresia occurs when the laryngeal opening fails to develop and an obstruction is created at or near the glottis. Congenital laryngeal atresia is a rare lesion. The lesion is thought to arise from the premature arrest of normal vigorous epithelial ingrowth into the larynx.

At delivery, the child makes strong respiratory efforts but does not move air, cry, or manifest any stridor. The child becomes markedly cyanotic when the umbilical cord is clamped. The diagnosis is most frequently made at autopsy. With the increased use of ultrasonography, the diagnosis of laryngeal atresia can be made before birth by noting enlarged edematous lungs, compressed fetal heart, severe ascites, and fetal hydrops.

These patients will not survive unless an emergency tracheostomy is performed or the patient is ventilated through a patent tracheoesophageal fistula. Tracheoesophageal fistulae are frequently associated with this condition and usually arise at the tracheal bifurcation.

LARYNGEAL WEBS

Laryngeal webs occur in the glottis. Most webs are located anteriorly and extend a varying length toward the arytenoids. The webs vary in thickness from a thin structure to one that is thicker and more difficult to eradicate. Congenital laryngeal webs are uncommon, constituting 5% of all congenital laryngeal lesions. Acquired webs are more common than congenital lesions.

Symptoms of laryngeal webs are present at birth in 75% of patients and within 1 year in all patients. The types of symptoms depend on the severity of the web. Vocal dysfunction is the most frequent symptom, and the severity of the dysphonia is not necessarily indicative of the severity of the web. The second most common symptom is airway obstruction, and the severity is directly proportional to the degree of obstruction. If stridor is present, it will occur in both inspiratory and expiratory phases, and if stridor is severe, the airway must be secured with intubation or a tracheostomy. Reflux of gastric contents is also frequent in infants with laryngeal webs.

The only way to make the correct diagnosis is by direct laryngoscopy under general anesthesia. The flexible laryngoscope may also have a role, but experience in using it in patients with laryngeal webs is limited.

Approximately 60% of patients require surgical intervention. Of all patients with laryngeal webs, 30 to 40% require a tracheostomy. In general, the thinner webs are easier to treat; the more severe webs are resistant to surgical management. It is difficult to obtain a crisp anterior commissure, and even if one is obtained, this does not ensure a good voice.

SACCULAR CYSTS AND LARYNGOCELES

Laryngoceles and laryngeal saccular cysts are thought to arise from the laryngeal or saccular appendage or from retention cysts resulting from obstruction of mucous gland ducts. The appendage arises from the anterior part of the ventricle, extends superiorly, and curves slightly posteriorly deep to the false vocal cords and aryepiglottic folds. The type of lesion that develops is based on the size of the saccule, whether there is free communication with the laryngeal lumen, and whether there is inflammation within the sac.

Saccular Cysts

Laryngeal saccular cysts are most likely to become manifest in infancy. Forty percent of congenital laryngeal cysts are discovered within a few hours of birth, and 95% of the children have symptoms before 6 months of age. The most frequent symptom is stridor (90%), which is primarily inspiratory, although it may be biphasic. The cry has been reported as feeble, muffled, shrill, hoarse, or normal. Dyspnea, apnea, and cyanosis have been noted in 55% of patients.

Chest and lateral neck radiographs, barium swallow, and computed tomographic scan are useful preoperative evaluations of the stridor, but they are not diagnostic. The only way to make the diagnosis definitively is with direct laryngoscopy. The cysts are typically divided into lateral wall saccular cysts and anterior saccular cysts. Lateral saccular cysts are most frequently located in the aryepiglottic fold, epiglottis, or lateral wall of the larynx. Anterior saccular cysts extend medially and posteriorly between the true and false vocal cords and directly into the laryngeal lumen.

Treatment of laryngeal cysts may require emergency tracheostomy. In the infant, the cysts should be treated primarily with endoscopic deroofing. Aspiration has also been recommended, but the incidence of recurrence is high.

Laryngoceles

Laryngoceles may occur in infants and children, and they cause airway obstruction. Laryngoceles are much more common in adults and appear most commonly in the fifth decade. Laryngoceles are symptomatic only when they are filled with air or fluid, so the symptoms may be intermittent. Because the laryngocele may rapidly inflate and deflate, several radiographs may be necessary to document the lesion. If it becomes infected, it fills with mucopus and is called a laryngopyocele.

The definitive diagnosis is made with direct laryngoscopy. Laryngoceles originate from the ventricle and bulge out between the true and false vocal cords or dissect posteriorly into the arytenoid and aryepiglottic fold. Laryngoceles should be diagnosed with direct laryngoscopy, when they are symptomatic, in addition to radiographic findings.

Only symptomatic lesions require treatment. Holinger and associates emphasized that true laryngoceles are rare in children and should be treated endoscopically by deroofing with cup forceps or a laser.

LARYNGEAL CLEFTS

Congenital laryngotracheoesophageal cleft is characterized by a deficiency in the separation between the esophagus and the trachea or larynx. Clefts of the larynx alone are less common.

Most clefts occur through the posterior part of the glottis; however, rare ventral or anterior clefts have been reported. Type I is called the laryngeal cleft and is found only in the posterior part of the glottis. Types II and III involve the trachea in addition to the larynx. Type II extends down to but not beyond the sixth tracheal ring, and type III can extend to the carina. Posterior glottic clefts have been associated with tracheal agenesis, as well as many other congenital anomalies.

The following manifestations, in order of frequency, are associated with laryngotracheoesophageal clefts: aspiration and cyanosis (53%), postpartum asphyxia (33%), increased mucus production (23%), recurrent pneumonia (16%), voiceless crying (16%), stridor (10%), and impaired swallowing (5%). The inspiratory stridor is produced by the collapse of redundant mucosa around the cleft and from the intrusion of the arytenoid into the airway. Cohen reported that the stridor may be expiratory because of aspirated secretions. One sees a frequent combination of posterior laryngeal clefts and tracheoesophageal fistulae.

A laryngeal cleft is frequently demonstrated by an esophagram with water-soluble contrast medium or is suggested by aspiration pneumonia on a chest radiograph. The most important diagnostic test, however, is direct laryngoscopy. If one does not specifically look for the entity, it frequently escapes detection. When the larynx is examined, redundant mucosa in the posterior cleft is usually the first clue to the defect. The cleft can best be demonstrated by placing a laryngoscope, such as a Dedo or Jako, into the supraglottis and examining the posterior part of the glottis. The posterior part of the glottis can also be palpated with a spatula or a similar thin instrument to demonstrate the defect.

Three surgical approaches to the posterior aspect of the larynx have been described: (1) minor (type I) clefts can be repaired endoscopically; (2) lateral pharyngotomy has been used frequently, especially for the smaller laryngeal clefts; and (3) anterior laryngofissure does not risk injury to the recurrent laryngeal nerve and has been used in neonates. Cotton and Schreiber have noted that, after repair of a posterior cleft, the patient may have continued esophageal reflux and aspiration of gastric contents.

VOCAL CORD PARALYSIS

Vocal cord paralysis can be categorized into congenital and acquired lesions. Congenital lesions are frequently associated with central nervous system lesions, including hydrocephalus, meningomyelocele, Arnold-Chiari malformation, meningocele, encephalocele, cerebral agenesis, nucleus ambiguus dysgenesis, neuromuscular disorders, and myasthenia gravis.

Estimates of the frequency of vocal cord paralysis among congenital laryngeal anomalies range from 1.5 to 23%; according to some authorities, it ranks second in frequency among congenital laryngeal lesions. Holinger and associates found that congenital lesions were more frequent than acquired. The acquired group can be further categorized into traumatic, infectious, or neoplastic. Traumatic lesions are most frequent secondary to stretching of the recurrent laryngeal nerve during vaginal delivery or surgical trauma in management of bronchogenic cysts, tracheoesophageal fistulae, or patent ductus arteriosus.

The pathophysiology of bilateral vocal cord paralysis may result from (1) compression of the vagus nerves in their course through the foramen magnum, (2) traction of the cervical rootlets of the vagus nerves by the caudal displacement of the brainstem, or (3) brainstem dysgenesis. Most authors favor the compression theory because, with timely decompression of hydrocephalus or the Arnold-Chiari malformation, the vocal cords regain function.

Any of the three laryngeal functions of respiration, voice production, and deglutition can be affected by vocal cord paralysis. With unilateral vocal cord paralysis, the voice is breathy and weak, but the patient has an adequate airway unless stressed. Stridor, weak cry, and some degree of respiratory distress can be seen in all patients with bilateral vocal cord paralysis. If the recurrent and superior laryngeal nerves are paralyzed, the vocal cords will be in the intermediate position, and the airway then will frequently be sufficient to allow adequate ventilation. If only the recurrent nerves are paralyzed, the vocal cords will be in the paramedian position, resulting in an inadequate airway.

Stridor is the most frequent presenting symptom of bilateral vocal cord paralysis. The airway becomes narrower, and there will be an increase in stridor and the development of nasal flaring, restlessness, and the use of accessory respiratory muscles, with an indrawing of the sternum and epigastrium. The stridor may progress to cyanosis, apnea, and respiratory and cardiac arrest if not recognized and treated. Aspiration and dysphagia are frequently noted in patients with bilateral vocal cord paralysis.

The diagnosis is made by flexible laryngoscopy or direct laryngoscopy. Once the diagnosis of vocal cord paralysis is made, the airway should be secured if the patient has significant airway distress. The airway is best established with intubation, followed by a full workup to ascertain the cause of the vocal cord paralysis. One must look specifically for associated findings of meningomyelocele, Arnold-Chiari malformation, and hydrocephalus. If the compression of the nerve is relieved within 24 hours, the vocal cords will regain function within 2 weeks; otherwise, vocal cord function may not return for 1.5 years, if at all. If the patient shows no evidence of function within 1 to 2 weeks, a tracheostomy should be performed to relieve the airway distress. Approximately 50% of children with bilateral vocal cord paralysis require tracheostomy.

SUBGLOTTIC LESIONS

Cricoid cartilage deformities are usually congenital and consist of abnormal shapes and sizes. They may be elliptical, flattened, or otherwise distorted. A subglottic stenosis is considered to be congenital when the patient has no history of endotracheal intubation or trauma. It is the third most common congenital abnormality. If the stenosis is congenital, the only manifestation may be prolonged or recurrent croup.

The primary causes of acquired or membranous subglottic stenosis in children are external injury from blunt trauma or a high tracheostomy and internal injury from prolonged intubation and chemical or thermal burns. Internal trauma, secondary to prolonged intubation, is thought to account for approximately 90% of acquired subglottic stenosis. The incidence of stenoses after intubation ranges from 0.9 to 8.3%.

The pathophysiology of acquired subglottic stenoses is well described. The endotracheal tube causes pressure necrosis of the respiratory epithelium. Edema and superficial ulceration begin, and the normal ciliary flow is interrupted. As the ulcer deepens, secondary infection of the areolar tissue and perichondrium begins. An oversized endotracheal tube or a tube of appropriate size in a patient with a small cricoid cartilage can increase the mucosal pressure and result in a deep ulceration. In children, an endotracheal tube that allows a leak at pressure less than 20 cm H_2O should be chosen. Gastroesophageal reflux can increase the inflammation and tissue trauma. Systemic factors such as immunodeficiency, anemia, neutropenia, toxicity, hypoxia, dehydration, and poor perfusion increase the risk of developing mucosal ulceration and subsequent scar formation.

Neonates tolerate prolonged intubation better than adults. The reason for this is unclear, but more pliable cartilage and the higher position of the larynx in the neck have been suggested as considerations. In the intubated neonate, evidence of subglottic stenosis may not manifest until the patient is ready for extubation. If a subglottic ulcer is present, the airway may be compromised immediately, or edema may accumulate over a few hours. If the patient has mild to moderate congenital subglottic stenosis, symptoms may not appear until an infection of the upper respiratory tract causes additional narrowing and respiratory distress.

The main symptoms and signs relate to airway, voice, and feeding. Stridor is the primary sign and is biphasic, with the inspiratory phase always louder. With progressive narrowing of the airway, respiratory distress ensues. If the vocal cords are affected, hoarseness, abnormal cry, and aphonia will indicate that an anterior web is present. Dysphagia and aspiration pneumonia can occur.

Soft tissue radiographs of the lateral neck may demonstrate subglottic narrowing. Computed tomographic scans do not give adequate additional information. Direct laryngoscopy is the most important diagnostic step in assessing the thickness and length of the stenosis and involvement of the larynx. Flexible fiberoptic laryngoscopy is most useful in assessing vocal cord function. Because the flexible scope provides only a limited view of the posterior part of the glottis and subglottis, rigid endoscopy is necessary to assess the size and patency of the lumen. The airway may be sized with the bronchoscope or endotracheal tubes.

Congenital subglottic stenosis that is mild and causing mild symptoms and signs can be treated expectantly. Tracheostomy is required in fewer than half of patients with congenital subglottic stenosis.

The anterior cricoid split operation was initially devised to treat acquired subglottic stenosis. This procedure breaks the cartilaginous cricoid ring anteriorly to allow expansion of the subglottis. The procedure involves making a vertical incision through the lower third of the thyroid cartilage, the cricoid cartilage, and the first two tracheal rings. Some surgeons have recommended placement of auricular or rib grafts at the time of the decompression. The patient is left intubated with an endotracheal tube one size larger for 5 to 7 days, treated with corticosteroids, and re-examined prior to extubation. Dilatation is useful if the ulceration is still present and granulation tissue is forming.

A variety of methods for endoscopic correction of subglottic stenosis have been suggested. The carbon-dioxide laser appears to be the current modality of choice. The laser can only be used to resect membranous stenosis, and the procedure has to be performed in stages. Prophylactic systemic antibiotic therapy is recommended for endoscopic procedures. Thin webs are most appropriately treated with the laser.

The open procedures have been traditionally used for the more severe lesions. Surgeons are increasingly using single-stage reconstruction. The costal cartilage reconstruction has been the standard method for subglottic reconstruction for the past several years. The fifth or sixth cartilaginous rib or costal margin cartilage is harvested.

The larynx and trachea are exposed, and a midline incision is made through the length of the stenosis. When only an anterior graft is used, the incision usually extends from the tracheal rings through the lower third of the larynx. If a posterior graft and stent are required, a full laryngofissure will be necessary.

In patients with more severe subglottic stenosis, a posterior graft is needed, and the posterior cricoid lamina is divided in the midline to, but not through, the hypopharyngeal mucosa. In complete stenosis, a four-quadrant split or segmented resection with stenting has been recommended.

Recently, auricular cartilage has been used as a graft material. It is useful because it is malleable; its curved shape allows for greater dimensions than available with the rib graft.

The results of successful decannulation depend, in part, on the severity of the stenosis. The ultimate outcome of grade 1 is

92% successful, that of grade 2 is 85% successful, that of grade 3 is 70% successful and that of grade 4 is 36% successful.

SUBGLOTTIC HEMANGIOMA

Congenital subglottic hemangiomas are relatively rare lesions and develop primarily in the submucosa. Fifty percent are associated with cutaneous hemangiomas. Almost all of these lesions will become manifest before 6 months of age. The stridor is more prominent on inspiration but is also present during expiration. Altered cry, hoarseness, barking cough, and failure to thrive are the other frequently noted manifestations. Recurrent croup is the most frequent erroneous diagnosis.

The diagnosis can only be made endoscopically. The appearance of these lesions is characteristic and can be made by the experienced endoscopist without a biopsy. The lesion is sessile, fairly firm, but compressible; pink, red, or bluish; and poorly defined. If the airway distress is significant at the time of diagnosis, immediate airway control will be necessary through intubation or a tracheostomy.

The judicious use of a laser to excise the lesion in stages, with the patient's airway protected by a tracheostomy when necessary, appears to be the treatment favored by most surgeons. External beam irradiation has been reported to have a cue rate of 93%, but the threat of radiation-induced malignant tumors of the thyroid gland strictly limits its use. Excision through an external incision is also recommended in some patients.

34

CONGENITAL ANOMALIES OF THE HEAD AND NECK

Lee D. Rowe, MD

Congenital head and neck anomalies represent a diverse group of clinical disorders. They present as upper aerodigestive tract neoplasms and neck masses with thyroglossal duct abnormalities most common, followed by branchial arch defects, lymphangiomas, and subcutaneous vascular anomalies. Less common are teratomas, heterotopic neural tissue, and nasopharyngeal neoplasms. Additional disorders include congenital anomalies of the oral cavity including cleft lip and palate, Pierre Robin sequence (PRS), and other aberrations such as primary ciliary dyskinesia, Kartagener's syndrome, and craniofacial anomalies.

BRANCHIAL CLEFT ANOMALIES

Lateral cervical lesions, termed branchial cleft cysts, are congenital developmental defects that arise from the primitive branchial apparatus. The branchial arches consist of five parallel mesodermal bars, each with its nerve supply and blood vessel. The branchial arches are separated externally by branchial clefts consisting of ectoderm and internally by endodermally lined branchial pouches. A branchial plate is located between each arch, separating the pouch and cleft. The most widely accepted theory of the development of branchial cleft anomalies is that fistulae, sinuses, and cysts result from incomplete closure of the connection between the cleft and the pouch with rupture of the branchial plate.

Typically, branchial clefts present as smooth, round, fluctuant, and nontender masses along the anterior border of the sternocleidomastoid muscle. During upper respiratory tract infections, a painful increase in size may occur and may be associated with external drainage through an unrecognized fistula.

Second branchial cleft anomalies are the most common and are located in the anterior triangle of the neck. *Third branchial cleft anomalies* are unusual and constitute less than 1% of all branchial cleft anomalies. *Fourth branchial cleft anomalies* are extremely rare. Preoperative assessment with computed tomography (CT) or magnetic resonance imaging (MRI) is essential. Complete surgical excision is the treatment of choice and is indicated for recurrent infection, cosmetic deformity, and because of the potential for malignant degeneration.

The hypothesis that squamous cell carcinoma arises in a branchial cleft cyst (branchiogenic carcinoma) is controversial. Cystic squamous cell carcinoma presenting in the neck without an apparent primary is almost universally secondary to metastasis from a neoplasm arising in the palatine or lingual tonsils or nasopharyngeal tissue.

LYMPHANGIOMAS

Congenital lymphangiomatous malformations of the head and neck represent a wide clinical spectrum. Lymphangiomas result from abnormal development of the lymphatic system at sites of lymphatic-venous connection with obstruction of lymph drainage from the affected area causing multicystic, endothelium-lined spaces. The neck is the most common site (25%) of all cases. Over half of these lesions present at birth, with 90% becoming apparent by 2 years of age.

Cystic hygromas are large lymphangiomas most commonly found in the posterior triangle of the neck and axilla in children. They are soft, painless, and compressible masses that may increase when the patient cries. Two-thirds are asymptomatic. After an upper respiratory tract infection, however, sudden enlargement with inflammation, infection, dysphagia, and stridor may develop. Other congenital vascular lesions of the head and neck include hemangiomas and arteriovenous malformations or lymphovenous lesions. Diagnostic imaging of these anomalies is based on the need for surgical treatment. Only those lesions that cause functional impairment or developmental disturbance are surgically addressed.

ABERRANT THYROID TISSUE

Ectopic thyroid tissue can occur anywhere from the foramen cecum to the lower neck. Most frequently, it occurs as a thyroglossal duct cyst associated with a normal thyroid gland. The primitive thyroid gland begins as a ventral diverticulum of endodermal origin arising in the floor of the pharynx. The thyroid descends caudally through or adjacent to the primitive hyoid bone. Thyroglossal duct anomalies result from failure of complete obliteration of the thyroglossal duct and are located anywhere along the descent of the gland.

Lingual thyroid presents in the midline as a sessile nontender reddish mass in the base of the tongue anterior to the valleculae. It is the most frequent benign mass encountered in the oropharynx, and symptoms may include dysphagia, cough, dysphonia, dyspnea, and hemorrhage. Indications for surgical removal include uncontrolled hyperthyroidism, hemorrhage, symptomatic enlargement, or a question of malignancy. Excision is performed by the transhyoid route. *Thyroglossal duct cysts* may be recurrently infected during upper respiratory tract infections, which can cause cyst enlargement, abscess development, and rupture with external sinus formation. As with the lingual thyroid, a preoperative thyroid scan is mandatory. Malignant degeneration, recurrent infections, undesirable cosmetic appearance, and, rarely, intermittent upper airway obstruction are indications for surgical excision of the thyroglossal duct cyst and fistula. The Sistrunk procedure is recommended to prevent recurrence. This involves a transverse incision over the cyst or fusiform incision around an external fistula with resection of the cyst, fistula, body of the hyoid, and fibrous cord extending to the foramen cecum. Fortunately, malignant degeneration of the thyroglossal duct cyst is rare.

THYMIC CYSTS

Cervical thymic cysts are extremely rare. Cysts can arise from a mass of thymic tissue anywhere along the descent of the thymic primordia from the angle of the mandible to the mediastinum and are primarily located anterior and deep to the middle third of the sternocleidomastoid muscle. Surgery is the definitive treatment.

NEUROGENIC NEOPLASMS

Congenital neurogenic lesions involving the head and neck include all neoplasms or anomalies originating in the neural tissue or its covering. Two groups have been recognized: heterotopic brain lesions with developmental defects and neoplasms of neurogenic origin including neurinomas, neurofibromas, ganglioneuromas, and menigiomas. Neurinomas originating from the connective tissue sheath of the nerve are termed schwannomas and may appear as multiple neurofibromas arising from cutaneous, visceral, and cranial nerves in neurofibromatosis (NF) 1 or 2. In NF1 (classic von Recklinghausen's disease), functional deficits include speech and voice abnormalities, airway obstruction, dysphagia, facial paresis, lip incompetence, and impaired mastication. Patients with NF2 (bilateral acoustic schwannomas) present with hearing loss. In all cases, symptoms depend on the size and location of the tumor. Treatment is surgical excision and must be complete because recurrence is common.

CONGENITAL DISORDERS OF THE NOSE AND PARANASAL SINUSES

Heterotopic Neural Tissue

Heterotopic neural tissue or gliomas may manifest as isolated ectopic brain tissue with only a fibrous band connecting it to the endocranium. Gliomas may be of the external or endonasal type. The external nasal glioma is typically found in the nasion as a red, relatively firm, mobile mass located subcutaneously. It does not increase in size when the patient cries. The endonasal glioma is less common and arises from the middle turbinate or the lateral nasal wall. A meningocele is a hernial protrusion of the meninges and if it contains brain tissue is called an encephalocele. Two types have been identified: sincipital and basal. The sincipital type is uncommon and is associated with termination of the meninges near the base of the nose. The basal type, in which the hernia extends into the nasal, orbital, or pharyngeal region, is rarer than the sincipital. In all cases, unlike with gliomas, the pulsations and increase in size of the mass can be observed when the patient coughs or strains. Computed tomography and MRI are necessary to determine the appropriate combined transfacial and intracranial approach for surgical resection.

Dermoid Cysts

Dermoid cysts occasionally occur in the neck and usually in the midline. Overall, fewer than 10% of all dermoids occur in the head and neck. One-fourth are found in the floor of the mouth, with the remainder in the periorbital region. Because of the variability in clinical presentation and contiguous structure involvement, the segregation of periorbital dermoids into three distinct subgroups is helpful. These include brow, orbital, and nasoglabellar region dermoids. The treatment of choice is surgical excision after CT and MRI to evaluate for possible intracranial extension.

Choanal Atresia

Bilateral choanal atresia is the most frequently encountered congenital nasal anomaly (1 in 7,000 to 8,000 live births) and is a common cause of neonatal respiratory distress. Fifty to 60% of cases are unilateral. A female predisposition is seen in choanal atresia, and recent evidence points to an autosomal recessive mode of inheritance. Failure of breakdown of the buccopharyngeal membrane on gestational day 45 is considered to be the cause of choanal atresia. Severe craniofacial abnormalities, including skull base defects and systemic malformations, have been described in association with choanal atresia. This includes the CHARGE association (coloboma of the eye, heart anomaly, choanal atresia, retardation, and genital and ear anomalies), which is a nonrandom pattern of congenital anomalies that has an estimated prevalence of 1 in 10,000 births. Respiratory distress at birth is the sine qua non of bilateral choanal atresia. Effective air exchange does not occur until the neonate begins to cry, bypassing the nasal obstruction. Because neonates are obligatory nasal breathers, placement of an oral airway or a McGovern nipple is lifesaving. The diagnosis is confirmed with nasofiberoptic endoscopy and CT scanning. Multiple methods are available to repair choanal atresia. The appropriate method is determined by the age of the patient and whether the atresia is bilateral or unilateral. Surgical treatment must provide adequate mucosal lining to the new choana and prevent granulation tissue formation and subsequent stenosis. Treatment requires perforation of the atresia plate followed by stenting for 6 weeks.

The most direct and simplest route for choanal atresia repair is a transnasal approach with curettage. Unfortunately, transnasal curettage has a higher incidence of restenosis and requires additional revisions or dilatations. An endoscopic approach with a 2.5 or 4 mm telescope and powered instrumentation using attachable burs and blades with continuous suction is preferred. After removal of the atresia plate, effective stenting, and the use of topical corticosteroids, stenosis may still occur, and dilatation may be necessary. If this fails, a transpalatal approach will be required. This approach provides superior visualization of the membranous or bony atresia and may be useful for both bilateral and unilateral atresia.

CONGENITAL DISORDERS OF THE NASOPHARYNX AND OROPHARYNX

Thornwaldt's Cysts and Rathke's Cysts

If the pharyngeal segments of the primitive notochord remain connected to the endoderm in the nasopharynx, a bursa or embryonic pouch occurs. In approximately 3% of individuals, this invaginated connection persists, and the resulting sac and canal extend posteriorly and cephalically toward the occipital bone. If the bursa is occluded by inflammation, a Thornwaldt's cyst will develop. Anterior to the invagination above the bursa is a small pharyngeal hypophysis developed from Rathke's pouch, which sometimes persists as the craniopharyngeal canal running from the sella turcica through the body of the sphenoid. Most Thornwaldt's cysts appear clinically in the second and third decades of life. Symptoms include intermittent or persistent postnasal discharge of tenacious or purulent material associated with odynophagia, halitosis, and, occasionally, a dull occipital headache. Nasopharyngoscopy reveals a smooth submucosal 1 to 2 cm midline cystic mass superior to the adenoidal pad. Treatment requires either excision to the periosteum or wide marsupialization of the Thornwaldt's cyst. Rathke's cysts become clinically apparent when they become infected and rupture intracranially. They are most commonly associated with headache followed by galactorrhea, visual field loss, and hypopituitarism. Treatment is transsphenoidal drainage of the cyst with biopsy of the wall.

Chordomas

Chordomas are rare malignant neoplasms arising from primitive notochordal remnants primarily in the fifth or sixth decade of life. Fifty percent occur in the spheno-occipital area. Presenting signs and symptoms include an expanding nasopharyngeal mass, frontal headaches, cranial nerve palsies, and pituitary abnormalities. Children under 5 years of age have a wider range of presenting symptoms, a greater prevalence of atypical histologic findings with aggressive behavior, and a higher incidence of metastasis to the lung and lymph nodes. Treatment is surgical excision via a skull base approach combined with postoperative radiation therapy.

Craniopharyngiomas

Craniopharyngiomas arise from Rathke's pouch and are located in the sellar, parasellar, and third ventricle regions. They are composed of well-differentiated epitheliomas, including bones, cysts, and ameloblasts. This tumor accounts for 10 to 15% of all childhood and adolescent intracranial neoplasms. Clinical manifestations include visual field defects, sudden blindness, extraocular motor paralysis, and hypopituitarism. Currently, surgical resection followed by radiation therapy achieves long-term control, with low morbidity for tumors smaller than 5 cm.

Teratomas

Teratomas are true neoplasms that contain tissues foreign to the site in which they arise. They grow aggressively and, in the head and neck, most commonly occur in the cervical area followed by the nasopharynx. Nasopharyngeal teratomas occur with a female to male ratio of 6 to 1, and overall, teratomas of the head and neck comprise approximately 2 to 9% of all teratomas. Teratomas of the nasopharynx typically arise on the lateral or superior wall. Four basic types are recognized: (1) dermoid cyst, which is the most common form with ectodermal and mesodermal elements; (2) teratoid cyst derived from all three germ layers but poorly differentiated; (3) true teratoma composed of ectoderm, mesoderm, and endoderm with specific tissue and organ differentiation; and (4) epignathus, in which well-developed fetal parts are recognizable. Computed tomography and MRI are critical to define the extent of these neoplasms and to exclude either a nasoencephalomeningocele or intracranial extension of a sphenoid-based teratoma through the craniopharyngeal canal. Fortunately, most cervical teratomas occurring in the neonate are benign. The tumor can surround or encroach on the airway, causing progressive dysphagia and airway obstruction. Surgical removal is planned to ensure a controlled airway throughout the intraoperative and postoperative periods.

CONGENITAL DISORDERS OF THE ORAL CAVITY AND LIP

Cleft Lip and Palate

Cleft lip and palate are the most common congenital malformations of the head neck, occurring once in every 700 births. Both cleft lip with or without cleft palate and isolated cleft palate can be further segregated into those classes associated with (syndromic) or without (nonsyndromic) another recognized malformation. The cause of syndromic clefting may be single-gene transmission, chromosome aberrations, teratogenicity, or environmental factors. Nonsyndromic clefting is associated with no obvious first or second arch anomalies or systemic organ malformation. Multifactoral inheritance is the cause of these clefts.

Clefts of the lip, alveolar process, or palate are mid-facial soft tissue and skeletal fusion abnormalities. Failure of ingrowth of mesodermal tissue between fetal weeks 8 and 10 results in a lack of cohesion of the palatal segments, causing a cleft palate, which may be seen in conjunction with clefts of the lip and/or alveolar processes or alone. Interruption in the migration of mesodermal tissue during the first 2 months of embryonic life results in cleft lip deformities. Ultimately, a lack of fusion of the median nasal processes with the maxillary processes causes a cleft of the upper lip, premaxilla, and alveolar process. The incidence of cleft palate increases in the presence of cleft lip, which occurs at an earlier stage than cleft palate.

The initial priority for infants with clefts is to establish adequate feeding and nutrition. Infants with a unilateral or bilateral cleft lip and alveolar ridge feed generally well by either breast or bottle. Infants with bilateral cleft lip, alveolar ridge, and palate have significant feeding problems and require modified nipples with feeding in the upright position to minimize nasal regurgitation. Most experts perform cleft lip repair at 3 months and cleft palate repair at 12 months of life. Two schools of thought have evolved: one advocating early closure of the lip and palate, a procedure imparting a high priority to early speech development, and the other recommending delayed closure of the hard palate, thus according a high priority to maxillary growth. In the basic complete unilateral cleft lip defect, the floor of the nose communicates with the oral cavity, and the alveolar defect passes through the developing dentition. The goals of surgical repair are restoration of orbicularis muscle function, alar base, and columellar height and creation of symmetry of the philtral columns, tip height, cupid's bow, and vermilion. In the bilateral cleft lip deformity, the floor of the nose is absent bilaterally, and the nasal and oral cavities communicate freely. Bilateral lip adhesion, if indicated, is performed when the patient is 2 to 4 weeks old, with definitive lip repair following at 4 to 6 months of age.

In cleft palate, the basic defect, absence of the nasal floor, may be complete or incomplete, with or without associated cleft lip. The goals of cleft palate repair are to close the defect when the patient is 10 to 18 months of age. This may require preoperative orthopedic devices to move the premaxilla posteriorly and expand the lateral maxillary segments, facilitating surgical closure of the lip.

Pierre Robin Sequence

The PRS of glossoptosis, micrognathia, and cleft palate (all three findings present in 50% of cases) may occur as an isolated nonsyndromic congenital disorder or as part of a larger anomaly that may include facial dysmorphism, cardiac defects, mental retardation, and/or musculoskeletal anomalies. Syndromic PRS is often associated with ocular or aural anomalies. Heredity appears to be a factor in isolated nonsyndromic PRS, and usually, a completely U-shaped cleft palate is the primary determinator of the associated triad. Infants with PRS are at increased risk of airway obstruction and resulting hypoxemia, cor pulmonale, failure to thrive, and cerebral anoxia. They are initially given a trial of prone positional management with high-calorie gavage feedings. If continued respiratory distress and failure to thrive develop, a modified glossopexy is performed. Tracheostomy is reserved for those patients following tongue lip adhesion who have continued failure to thrive and respiratory embarrassment. Patients with syndromic PRS have a higher rate of tracheostomy and gastrostomy tube placement.

Congenital Disorders of the Salivary Glands

Congenital anomalies of the salivary gland are uncommon. Rarely, the parotid gland may be absent in the first and second branchial arch syndromes. The *first branchial cleft anomalies* have been classified into two groups, type 1 and type 2. Type 1 are first cleft ectodermal defects or duplication anomalies of the membranous external auditory canal. In type 1, the cysts are anterior and inferior to the pinnae, and the fistulous tracts terminate in the external auditory canal. Type 2 branchial cysts are primarily first cleft and arch defects with duplication of the external auditory canal and pinna. In type 2, the cysts are found below the angle of the mandible along the sternocleidomastoid muscle, and the fistulous tracts open into the external auditory canal. Clinically, first branchial cleft cysts are associated with repeated infection and may require incision and drainage of the apparent neck abscess. Because of the intimate relationship between the 7th nerve and sinus tract, it is critical in these cases to expose the 7th nerve to preserve it, as in a parotidectomy.

Primary Ciliary Dyskinesia (Kartagener's Syndrome)

Primary ciliary dyskinesia is an inherited disorder characterized by recurrent upper and lower respiratory tract infections secondary to abnormal ciliary structure and function. Also termed immotile cilia syndrome, its most recognized form is in Kartagener's syndrome (bronchiectasis, chronic sinusitis, sinus inversus, and sterility). This disorder is characterized by defects in axonemal dynein complexes probably secondary to mutations in the genes encoding cytoplasmic heavy chains of the outer arms of the axonemes.

35

DISORDERS OF VOICE, SPEECH, AND LANGUAGE

Fred D. Minifie, PhD

Disorders of voice, speech, and language comprise an important category of problems faced by the physician because treatment of these disorders can have a large influence on vocational, social, and emotional adjustments of the patient.

VOICE DISORDERS

A normal voice falls within the accepted ranges of pitch, loudness, and quality found in a majority of individuals of the same age and sex. Abnormal vocal fold vibrations take many forms, each of which creates acoustic patterns that cause the voice to be perceived as disordered.

Pitch Disorders

Pitch disorders are present when the voice is consistently higher or lower than would be expected for an individual of a given gender and age or when the sound is tremulous, monotonous, or bizarre. Vocal pitch disorders may be functional or organic.

High Pitch Disorders

High-pitched male voices frequently have functional origins. For some patients, psychological conflict is implied as a basis for the disorder. In other patients, the disorder may simply reflect a learned pattern. Most of these patients respond readily to voice therapy and adopt the new voice after a brief period of self-consciousness. High pitch disorders with organic causes are not uncommon and usually fall into four categories: underdeveloped larynx, laryngeal web, structural asymmetry, and swelling in the anterior commissure.

Low Pitch Disorders

Excessively low pitch in both men and women is usually associated with organic change; however, functional disorders are observed in persons who attempt to speak at a pitch below that which is optimum for the structures involved. The most common organic origins of low-pitched voices are Reinke's edema, virilization, glottalization or "vocal fry," and tremulousness.

Loudness Disorders

Atypical loudness is often an indicator of personality aberrations (eg, overly aggressive, shy, or socially insecure persons). Alternatively, some persons are required to speak loudly in their occupations. This vocal requirement often creates laryngeal trauma, subsequent changes in the vocal organs, and consequent voice disorders. Organically based loudness disorders are suspected when a slowness, weakness, or absence of complete glottal closure occurs or when the voice is weak and breathy. Peripheral paralyses and pareses usually affect only one vocal fold. Bowed vocal folds stem from long-term heavy use of the voice, particularly in elderly patients. Other organic causes include sulcus vocalis or a hearing loss.

Voice Quality Disorders

Voice quality disorders encompass both resonance and phonatory components.

Aphonia

The absence of phonated sound is revealed as a whispered voice, which indicates that the vocal folds are not vibrating.

Aphonia can result from organic disease ranging from paralyses and other neural impairments to various tumors, inflammatory disease, scarring, and other localized laryngeal lesions. Aphonia also may be indicative of a functional disorder of psychogenic origin.

Breathiness

Chronic breathiness can be recognized by excessively audible breath-flow noise that is accompanied by a relatively low vocal loudness level. Several organic conditions modify the glottal configuration sufficiently to create incomplete glottal closure associated with a breathy voice.

Harshness

When the vocal folds remain in contact for a disproportionately long time in the vibratory cycle, a voice quality known as harshness results. Organic causes of harshness include edematous vocal folds, neoplasms, and any other structural alteration that may prolong the closed phase of the vibratory cycle.

Hoarseness

Hoarseness and harshness are often confused with each other. The differentiating, audible feature of hoarseness is a roughness that results from random variations in the periodicity of the glottal waveform and/or random variations in the intensity of sound.

Spasmodic Dysphonia

Spasmodic dysphonia designates a sudden, momentary interruption of the voice caused by brief, spasmodic glottal closure. As patients attempt to "speak through" the spasmodic closure, the voice may be described as "squeezed," "effortful," or "struggle strained." Inconsistency of symptoms undoubtedly contributes to the traditional assumption that spasmodic dysphonia is psychogenic. Indeed, it may be, but research evidence indicates the possibility of a neural etiologic component.

Resonance and Resonance Disorders

The two most common resonance defects are too much nasal resonance (hypernasality) and insufficient nasal resonance (hyponasality). The first is caused by incomplete closure of the velopharyngeal valve or by a fistula in the structures separating the oral and nasal spaces, and the second is caused by blockage of the nasal passageway.

Therapy for Voice Disorders

Medical and surgical treatment may eliminate some types of voice disorders, but such treatment cannot always restore normal function. Nonmedical rehabilitative measures may be necessary to help compensate for altered anatomic and physiologic conditions, and re-educative procedures are usually indicated in the treatment of habitual or functional disorders.

Environmental Factors

A program of voice therapy that does not recognize the demands of the environment on the communication needs of the patient is incomplete and may be doomed to failure. The person who must talk more or less continuously in a noisy environment may develop detrimental vocal habits and may also abuse the larynx and create tissue changes.

Psychological Factors

An individual's attitude toward self and the environment often is reflected in such vocal elements as the rate of speaking, choice of words, vocal pitch, loudness of the voice, and vocal quality. These factors often indicate the patient's degree of poise, anxieties, emotional states, feelings of friendship or hostility, and belief about acceptance or rejection. When these concepts cause the individual to use an unpleasant, inadequate, or defective voice, any successful modification of the problem must include a consideration of the person's concepts about self, the environment, and his or her speech.

Analysis of the Voice Problem

The individual who provides voice therapy must know the capacities and limitations of the patient's voice because this information not only provides diagnostic data, it also determines the pattern of rehabilitation. Speech-language pathologists are well prepared to conduct such an analysis.

Patient's Evaluation of the Voice Problem

Two basic premises support the concept that one must evaluate one's own voice problem if one wishes to modify it. First, an individual does not hear his or her own voice as others hear it; second, the clearer and more specific a goal or task can be made, the faster it will be accomplished.

Voice Therapy

Direct voice therapy is used to address "recovery" and "training." Recovery procedures presume a need for healing—a return of the structures to normal. In addition, voice therapy must include a period of training that modifies previous habit patterns and replaces them with more efficient phonatory behavior. With voice disorders in which vocal abuse is present, the patient usually has excessive tension in the muscles of the larynx. Unless this tension can be controlled, vocal therapy cannot progress. Many persons, particularly men, attempt to use a vocal pitch that is lower than that which is normal for their laryngeal structures. Direct instruction can be given to establish a habitual pitch that averages four or five musical notes above the lowest tone that the patient can produce. If the physician finds it necessary or desirable to direct the vocal practice of a patient, the focus should be on the use of a quiet voice.

Laryngeal Cancer and Vocal Rehabilitation

Hoarseness, laryngeal cancer, and speech rehabilitation are intimately related. The sound of the voice is often the first evidence of disease and, consequently, is important in diagnosis. The choice of medical treatment for the disease, whether it be irradiation, chemotherapy, partial laryngectomy, total laryngectomy, or combinations of these procedures, influences the type and amount of speech therapy to be used after control of the disease. There appears to be little change in the proportion of cases of cancer of the larynx in the general population over a 25-year period, but the female-to-male ratio has increased progressively from 0.144 in 1974 to 0.246 in 2000. Training in communication skills is almost always desirable for patients who have had a total laryngectomy.

Presurgical Considerations

Presurgical management of the person who must have the larynx removed is extremely important in the total therapy and should be handled with great care. The most satisfactory way to plan for postsurgical speech rehabilitation and to handle the many questions about work, family, and social relationships is to introduce a mature speech-language pathologist who has had extensive experience with laryngectomized persons. The speech-language pathologist's function is to encourage and motivate the patient to make plans for the postsurgical period.

Early Postsurgical Period

Early restoration of the ability to communicate is a major consideration in successful rehabilitation. Every possible effort should be made while the patient is still in the hospital to establish communication by computer, writing, picture boards, signing, or the use of an artificial larynx. Plans should be made for direct work with the patient, the spouse, and other family members.

Subsequent hospital care of laryngectomees deserves special attention from all service levels. The inability of the patient to communicate creates serious problems, especially when specialized nursing care is not available (aides splashing water into the stoma during bathing, application of oxygen to the nose, failure to open a plugged stoma, etc). A special "warning" sign might be placed at the bed and on the patient's chart to identify every hospitalized laryngectomee, and care providers should be given specific instructions.

Restoring Speech Communication
Following Laryngectomy

Any form of substitute voice is inferior to that produced normally. Similarly, any usable speech is superior to mutism, whispering, writing, or signing. Clinicians must search for the best substitute voice sources in relation to the needs and capacities of the individual patient.

Engineering Approach. The engineering approach involves the development of artificial sound generators. These handheld devices are separated into two types according to the driving force used in the production of sound: one is powered by the breath stream; the other by electricity from batteries (artificial larynx).

Surgical Approach. Surgical efforts to produce substitute vocal sound have extended over many years and can be classified into three forms: tracheoesophageal shunts, construction of a pseudoglottis, or combined surgical and artificial devices.

Esophageal Speech Approach. This procedure allows the patient to control and refine the natural eructation sound as the basis for speech. Its advantages are that (1) natural physiologic structures and functions are used, thereby obviating the need for an artificial device; (2) both hands are free for normal activities during speech; and (3) the good esophageal speaker presents a relatively normal appearance and speaking manner. The disadvantages of esophageal speech are that (1) it is often difficult to learn; (2) phrasing is usually changed, so fewer words than normal are uttered in a sequence without pause for phonatory air; and (3) the voice lacks sufficient loudness to be heard easily over common environmental noise. Air must be either "inhaled" or "injected" into the esophagus.

SPEECH DISORDERS

Speech-language pathologists recognize that substantial segments of the adult population as well as the younger groups have serious speech and language disorders that involve otolaryngologists most directly. Speech and language disorders can be divided into three major categories: articulation disorders, fluency disorders, and language impairments.

Normal Speech Development in Children

The normal acquisition of speech may be expected to follow much the same pattern as the motor, adaptive, and personal-social behavior of the child. A "speech readiness period" extends from birth to the fifth year of life, when the child acquires the ability to develop speech as a method of communication. The development of speech can be classified into a sequence of five stages: the cry, babbling, reduplicated babbling, echolalia, and intentional speech, which blend cumulatively.

Articulation Disorders

Disorders of speech articulation may be described as faulty or atypical production of sounds in the spoken language. These problems encompass many kinds of articulatory defects, both functional and organic, and constitute the most frequent type of speech disorder observed within the population.

Functional Articulation Disorders

A child with a delay profile demonstrates performance similar to that of a normal but younger speaker. In contrast, deviant speech refers to an articulation profile unlike that of a normally developing child, even a younger one. Functional articulation disorders usually display four speech sound error types: substitutions, omissions, distortions, and additions.

Organic Articulation Disorders in Children

Structural deviations can affect articulation by interfering with articulatory contact points, breath stream flow (force and direction), oral breath pressure, and oral-nasal cavity coupling. Disorders such as cleft lip and palate can involve all of these aspects, whereas the normal loss of front teeth in a growing child might create involvement of only the first two factors.

Structural and Syndrome-Related Speech Disorders. Many structural deviations (eg, clefts of the lip and/or palate) are associated with speech, hearing, and language disorders. The physician should be sensitive to the possibility that structural anomalies concomitant to speech disorders can result from dysmorphisms of genetic origin. When multiple dysmorphisms appear in the same patient, consultation with a medical geneticist is prudent to determine whether evaluation and treatment of the family as well as the patient are necessary.

Tongue-Tie. The term "tongue-tied" (ankyloglossia) is used when the lingual frenum appears to be abnormally short or taut, restricting the movement of the tongue so that it cannot move upward to the alveolar ridge. Although this condition is known to exist, its interference with articulation is considered comparatively rare.

Dental Abnormalities and Tongue Thrust. Professional debate related to the developmental nature of swallowing (normal and abnormal), the impact of tongue thrust on dentition and articulation, and the efficacy of speech and/or myofunctional therapy has created an ongoing controversy that is still unresolved.

Treatment Of Articulation Disorders In Children

The goal in treating articulation disorders is to identify and correct defective sounds. Most treatment is directed at improving performance accuracy and consistency. The four general steps of remediation are (1) training the speaker's perceptual skills (phonologic process or sound identification and discrimination), (2) establishing the new response (correct sound production), (3) strengthening and generalizing the correct sound production or phonologic process to connected speech levels, and (4) carrying over the new response to conversational speech both within and outside the clinical setting.

Disorders of Speech Motor Control

Neuromotor speech disorders result in the talker being imperfectly understood or creating the impression that something is unusual or bizarre about his or her speech pattern. The two major types of neuromotor speech disorders are dysarthria and apraxia. With both conditions, articulation proficiency of the speaker is adversely affected. The causes of these disorders include, for example, myasthenia gravis, Parkinson's disease, amyotrophic lateral sclerosis, cortical lesions, cerebellar ataxias, etc.

Dysarthria

Dysarthria may be defined as a defect of articulation resulting from a lesion in the central or peripheral nervous system, which directly regulates the muscles used for speaking. It involves an impairment in the control and execution of speech movements because of muscle weakness, slowness, incoordination, or altered muscle tone.

Apraxia

In contrast, apraxia of speech represents an impairment in the programming of speech movements in the absence of muscle impairments associated with dysarthria.

Treatment of the Motor Speech Disorders

Any treatment program for motor speech disorders should incorporate five fundamental principles: (1) the patient must be assisted to develop functional compensation from the healthy body systems; (2) the patient must develop the perspective that speech production must now become a highly conscious, deliberate effort; (3) the patient must develop the ability to monitor speech performance continuously; (4) remediation must begin as soon as possible because waiting is not beneficial; and (5) the patient must receive continued support and reassurance.

Disorders of Fluency (Stuttering)

Stuttering is one of the most enigmatic speech defects encountered by the speech-language pathologist. Wingate's commonly used definition of fluency disorders follows:

> Disruption in the fluency of verbal expression is characterized by involuntary, audible or silent, repetitions or prolongations in the utterance of short speech elements, namely: sounds, syllables, and words of one syllable. These disruptions usually occur frequently or are marked in character and are not readily controllable. Sometimes the disruptions are accompanied by accessory activities involving the speech apparatus, related or unrelated body structures, or stereotyped speech utterances. These activities give the appearance of being speech-related struggles. Also, there are not infrequently indications or report of the presence of an emotional state, ranging from a general condition of "excitement" or "tension" to more specific emotions of a negative nature such as fear, embarrassment, irritation, or the like. The immediate source of stuttering is some incoordination expressed in the peripheral speech mechanism; the ultimate cause is presently unknown and may be complex or compound.

Stuttering is more common among boys than girls in a ratio of approximately 3 to 1. The typical onset occurs during the preschool years, usually 1 or 2 years after the child first learns to speak (onset is rare in adulthood). The onset is usually gradual and is most often characterized by an excessive amount of repetitive speech (sounds or syllables), usually without tension or effort. Although the exact nature of development varies among stutterers, virtually all demonstrate a change of behavior as long as the disorder persists. Reactions by listeners, important "others," and the stutterer tend to create fear, anxiety, and self-doubt.

Most children experience periods of "normal nonfluency" during their early years that look and sound similar to the behavior described as the onset characteristic of stuttering. The number and duration of such episodes vary among children, but their occurrence does not automatically confirm the existence of stuttering.

Parents of a young child who demonstrates minor hesitations and repetitions during speech should remain unemotional about these speech patterns to prevent the development of undue awareness and concern on the part of the child. Being an attentive, thoughtful listener is the best response. The young child with incipient stuttering should not be subjected to direct speech therapy or any type of therapy related to speech production. In advanced stages of stuttering, the patient experiences considerable struggle to speak. Clinical management of stuttering involves changing the stutterer's attitude, method of talking, and/or environment. The advanced or secondary stutterer must perceive the need for therapy. Frequently, the family of the secondary stutterer is also in need of appropriate treatment.

DISORDERS OF SYMBOLIZATION (LANGUAGE)

Language may be defined as an organized symbolic representation of thought and action used as a means of communication on an abstract level by human beings. When this process is disturbed, the result may be classified as a communication disorder that is manifested in the inability, or limited ability, to use linguistic symbols as a means of oral communication.

Children with Specific Language Impairment

Children with specific language impairment generally have a disorder profile limited to the area of language. The particular difficulty may be in some or all of the following components of language: (1) lexicon (the concepts and labels of our vocabulary), (2) syntax (word order), (3) morphology (word forms), (4) semantics (word meaning), and (5) pragmatics (use of language in social contexts).

Children with Acquired Aphasia

Myklebust's definition of this disorder is as follows:

> Childhood aphasia refers to one or more significant deficits in essential processes as they relate to facility in use of auditory language. Children having this disability demonstrate a discrepancy between expected and actual achievement in one or more of the following functions: auditory perception, auditory memory, integration, comprehension, and expression. The deficits referred to are not the result of sensory, motor, intellectual, or emotional impairment, or of the lack of opportunity to learn. They are assumed to derive from dysfunctions in the brain, though the evidence for such dysfunctioning may be mainly behavioral, rather than neurological, in nature.

Following an initial period of normal language development, children with acquired aphasia lose that ability usually because of some known brain damage caused by either illness or trauma. Many recover quickly. When deficits persist, intensive interdisciplinary remediation is required.

Aphasia (Dysphasia) in Adults

Aphasia is associated with cortical disturbances or lesions resulting from vascular impairment (thrombosis, embolism, and hemorrhage), tumors, degenerating and infectious disease, and trauma. Aphasia is a general term applied to different but related syndromes that impair the ability to formulate, retrieve, and/or decode the symbols of language. The linguistic disturbances may be classified as follows:

1. Broca's or motor aphasia—marked reduction in speech output, common oral-verbal apraxia, relatively good speech comprehension, word retrieval problem, writing performance matches speech output
2. Transcortical motor aphasia—a fairly rare type with significant struggle in producing an utterance, telegraphic speech is common, relatively good speech comprehension, impaired writing skills
3. Anomic aphasia—word retrieval problems predominate for both speech and writing, nearly normal comprehension for speech and reading
4. Wernicke's or jargon aphasia—significant comprehension deficit for speech and reading; fluent but jargon-like verbal output, writing parallels speech patterns
5. Conduction aphasia—nearly normal comprehension for speech and reading, marked deficit in speech repetition, fluent speech output with numerous sound and word errors
6. Global aphasia—the most severe and most common type; profound problems with both verbal output and comprehension, and both reading and writing functions are poor

The emotional language of the adult aphasic is usually better than propositional language. The patient may find it easier to swear, count, or use other forms of automatic speech or nonpropositional forms of speech but is at a loss when requested to develop this emotional language into abstract or propositional language situations. The patient experiences difficulty in combining simple linguistic symbols into more complex linguistic units. The patient is not without words but rather cannot quickly command the response that is appropriate to the situation. Ideally, the adult aphasic should be started on a program of rehabilitation as soon after the traumatic episode as possible.

36

AIRWAY CONTROL AND LARYNGOTRACHEAL STENOSIS IN ADULTS

Joseph C. Sniezek, MD
Brian B. Burkey, MD

The successful management of the airway is of paramount importance. Airway control requires a logical and systematic approach guided by the principles of basic and advanced life support techniques and a working knowledge of relevant pharmacology. Most importantly, the health professional must possess a mastery of the anatomy and physiology of the upper aerodigestive tract. The airway surgeon is also uniquely responsible for the diagnosis and treatment of airway lesions such as laryngotracheal stenosis and arytenoid fixation.

AIRWAY CONTROL

Clinical Evaluation of the Airway

The clinical evaluation of the airway must begin with a rapid assessment of the patient's ventilatory and respiratory status. The symptoms and signs that indicate upper respiratory obstruction include hoarseness; dyspnea; stridor; intercostal, suprasternal, and supraclavicular retractions; restlessness; cyanosis; and drooling. The signs of trauma to the airway include bloody sputum, subcutaneous emphysema, and palpable laryngotracheal fractures.

Airway Management

If the patient is in impending airway distress, prophylactic measures to prevent deterioration of the airway must be employed. If the patient does not appear to be ventilating adequately, the airway must be secured through medical or surgical techniques. If medical control of the airway fails and intubation is impossible owing to an airway injury or upper airway obstruction, an urgent tracheostomy or cricothyroidotomy must be performed.

Although the management of the airway in the controlled environment of the operating room is straightforward, patients presenting in the emergency department pose unique problems such as cervical spine injuries, closed head injuries with the possibility of increased intracranial pressure, laryngotracheal disruption, airway hemorrhage, and facial deformities. The intensive care unit setting also offers challenges such as confounding medical issues. These complicating factors can be handled only through an individualized approach that is guided by a stepwise progression of techniques aimed at controlling the increasingly difficult airway.

Supplemental oxygen is the most simple measure of airway support and should be given almost universally to patients with airway distress. After this intervention, the clinician should evaluate for airway obstruction from foreign bodies such as displaced teeth or tongue and soft tissue collapse into the pharynx. Because of its efficacy and lack of cervical movement, the jaw thrust is the most appropriate positioning maneuver. Lifting the chin and extending the neck may be successful in improving the airway but risks cervical spinal cord injury in a trauma patient. An oropharyngeal airway may relieve soft tissue obstruction of the airway. It serves to displace the tongue anteriorly, providing an unobstructed airway. A nasopharyngeal airway (trumpet) may be placed transnasally into the posterior part of the hypopharynx, thus relieving soft tissue obstruction of the oropharynx.

Nasopharyngeal airways tend to be less stimulating than oral airways in awake patients but risk epistaxis. Nasopharyngeal trumpets should not be used in patients with known or suspected basilar skull fractures owing to the risk of inadvertent intracranial placement.

A laryngeal mask airway is a nondefinitive technique sometimes employed by emergency medical technicians or anesthesiologists to obtain a temporary airway for positive pressure ventilation. This device forms a "seal" over the larynx and provides a route for oxygen flow into the trachea. If a definitive airway is required, endotracheal intubation is the quickest and most successful option whenever possible. It allows ventilatory control with the ability to deliver high levels of oxygen and temporarily protects against aspiration. Endotracheal intubation may be achieved through either an oral or a transnasal route. In the case of head and neck trauma, transoral intubation may be achieved while holding in-line cervical traction and maintaining cervical stabilization. Manual in-line immobilization is the optimal method of stabilization and results in significantly less cervical spine movement than stabilization in a Philadelphia collar.

The most common technique employed for oral intubation in the emergent situation is the rapid sequence induction, which uses preoxygenation and denitrogenation followed by a short-acting hypnotic agent such as thiopental or midazolam followed by a neuromuscular blocking agent. An assistant may hold cricoid pressure to prevent aspiration if the patient is unconscious. If a cervical spine injury is suspected, a second assistant maintains in-line stabilization during the intubation. A fiberoptic endoscope may also be placed inside an endotracheal tube to facilitate the localization of the airway. The tube can then be passed over the endoscope after the airway has been identified and entered. One disadvantage of this endoscopic technique is that the presence of blood and secretions may obscure visualization through the endoscope.

Cricothyroidotomy

If the airway cannot be controlled through endotracheal intubation or other medical maneuvers, a surgical airway must be obtained. Cricothyroidotomy involves the creation of an opening into the cricothyroid membrane followed by the placement of a stenting tube. A horizontal incision is made over the middle third of the cricothyroid membrane and is carried directly into the airway. Although cricothyroidotomy has been used for long-term airway management, it is most useful in the emergency setting, where a surgical airway must be rapidly gained. Cricothyroidotomy is faster and usually easier to perform than a tracheostomy, especially in the hands of a nonsurgeon, requiring little surgical skill other than a knowledge of anatomy. Reported complications of cricothyroidotomy include bleeding, tube displacement, infection, true vocal cord damage, subcutaneous emphysema, and the development of subglottic or tracheal stenosis.

Tracheostomy

Tracheostomies have been performed for over 2,000 years. Until the early 1900s, however, the procedure was reserved for essentially moribund patients owing to high rates of morbidity and mortality. Attitudes toward tracheostomy changed in 1909, when Chevalier Jackson described the modern tracheostomy. The unacceptably high rates of laryngeal and tracheal stenosis associated with tracheostomies preceding his description were attributable to damage to the thyroid and cricoid cartilages incurred during the performance of "high" tracheostomies. Jackson implored that tracheostomies be performed below the second tracheal ring, thereby avoiding these dreaded complications. This dictum has been followed to the present day.

Although horizontal and vertical incisions into the tracheal wall have been proposed, an inferiorly based Björk flap consisting of several tracheal rings is a superior option for adults. Following Jackson's principles, a horizontal incision is made between the second or third tracheal rings and carried inferiorly with Mayo scissors to fashion an inferiorly based flap. The space between the rings may be calcified in older patients. The Bjork flap may be sewn to the subcutaneous tissue of the inferior skin margin with an absorbable suture. This tracheal flap makes reintubation safer in the event of accidental extubation but does lead to a slightly increased risk of tracheocutaneous fistula. For this reason, a horizontal H incision based on the third tracheal ring or the removal of an anterior section of a single tracheal ring may be preferable in patients who are expected to require only a tracheostomy for a short period of time.

When a tracheostomy is permanent or of long duration, the surrounding skin may be surgically defatted and sutured to the tracheostoma circumferentially. This is particularly useful in obese patients, in whom a semipermanent tracheostoma can be fashioned, which is less prone to maceration or the formation of granulation tissue and stenosis because the skin directly abuts the respiratory mucosa of the trachea. The creation of a semipermanent tracheostoma in this fashion also serves to decrease the length of the tract of the tracheostomy, thereby facilitating removal and reinsertion of the tracheostomy tube.

The tracheostomy incision should never be closed tightly and must allow the passive egress of air from the wound to prevent subcutaneous emphysema, which could lead to pneumomediastinum, pneumothorax, or infection.

Tracheostomy decreases the protective glottic closure reflexes and predisposes the patient to aspiration. A soft, solid diet, as opposed to liquids, and maintaining an upright position tend to prevent aspiration. Although inflating the tracheostomy tube cuff can afford temporary airway protection, hyperinflation of the cuff actually exacerbates aspiration owing to compression of the esophagus.

A particularly dangerous late complication of tracheostomy is rupture of the innominate artery that results from erosion of the tracheal wall by the tip or the cuff of the tracheostomy tube. The tracheostomy tube should be immediately removed and replaced with a longer cuffed endotracheal tube to allow ventilation of the patient, and the innominate artery should be digitally compressed against the manubrium. The patient should be taken to the operating room for median sternotomy and ligation of the artery.

LARYNGEAL AND TRACHEAL STENOSIS IN THE ADULT

The management of laryngeal and tracheal stenosis in adults is both challenging and intriguing. The diagnosis and evaluation of these lesions require a complete mastery of the anatomy and physiology of the upper aerodigestive tract. The incredible variability of stenotic areas in the adult larynx and trachea requires the head and neck surgeon carefully to individualize treatment and provide unique strategies for the management of these diverse lesions.

Etiology

There are many factors that can lead to laryngotracheal stenosis (LTS). Most cases of adult LTS result from external trauma or prolonged endotracheal intubation. External trauma causes cartilage damage and mucosal disruption with hematoma formation. These hematomas eventually organize and result in collagen deposition and scar tissue formation. Endotracheal intubation can cause direct injury, and mucosal damage through pressure necrosis can result from the pressure of the endotracheal tube or cuff. Mucosal ulceration also leads to healing through collagen deposition, fibrosis, and scar tissue formation. Lesions from endotracheal intubation are usually located in the posterior part of the glottis, where the tube most often contacts mucosa, or in the trachea, where the cuff or tube tip causes mucosal damage. Low-pressure endotracheal tube cuffs have somewhat reduced the rate of cuff-induced damage. The length of intubation, tube movement, tube size, and gastroesophageal reflux can also contribute to the development of LTS.

Classification

Since areas of LTS are so variable in their size, consistency, and location, a rigid classification scheme is essentially impossible, and the surgeon must describe and document the lesion in a way that is widely understandable and reproducible. The classification of LTS in adults begins with the anatomic location of the lesion as glottis, subglottis, trachea, or a combination of these. These stenotic segments may be further described as anterior, posterior, or circumferential. The diameter and length of the stenotic area are critical in classifying the lesion.

Diagnostic Assessment

The evaluation of LTS must begin with a meticulous history and physical examination. Since most cases of LTS result from laryngotracheal trauma or endotracheal intubation, the timing of the predisposing incident should be recorded. Any previous airway evaluations or attempts at repair should also be noted. The patient should be questioned regarding the onset, duration, and severity of symptoms such as exercise intolerance, disruption of lifestyle, and tracheostomy dependence. Patients who do require a tracheostomy should be questioned as to how often the tube may be plugged. Symptoms of aspiration, voice change, or dysphagia may indicate the degree of glottic involvement.

The entire upper aerodigestive tract must be carefully examined in a patient with suspected LTS. Indirect laryngoscopy and flexible fiberoptic laryngoscopy offer critical information regarding the supraglottic airway and mobility of the true vocal folds. In extreme abduction, areas of subglottic stenosis may be visible using these techniques. Video documentation of these procedures offers a valuable method of treatment planning and patient education.

Although imaging studies such as airway radiographs, computed tomography, and magnetic resonance imaging occasionally provide useful information, the most valuable diagnostic assessment stems from the examination of the patient with endoscopy. After the patient has been examined by indirect laryngoscopy and flexible fiberoptic techniques, rigid endoscopic evaluation under general anesthesia should be performed in all patients with symptomatic airway abnormalities. Direct measurement and documentation of the diameter and length of stenotic areas are critical steps in the management of these lesions. Measurement of the diameter of stenotic segments is best evaluated by passing an endoscope, with a known diameter, that just fits through the stenotic area. Measurement of stenosis length may be performed by placing the endoscope at the distal end of the stenotic segment and marking the instrument at the incisors. The endoscope is withdrawn to the proximal aspect of the stenosis and remarked. The length of stenosis may be measured on the endoscope.

Treatment of Laryngotracheal Stenosis

Endoscopic Treatment

Some areas of LTS are amenable to endoscopic treatment techniques such as laser vaporization and dilation, excision using a microtrapdoor technique, or serial dilation with radial incisions of the stenotic segment. Intralesional corticosteroids may also be injected under endoscopic guidance. Lasers allow the precise treatment of tissue throughout the airway while avoiding external incisions and providing an excellent method of cutting, coagulating, or vaporizing tissue. Hemostasis may be achieved, and perioperative edema is often decreased with the use of lasers owing to smaller amounts of tissue sustaining thermal damage when compared to electrocautery.

Owing to its precision (small spot size) and availability, the carbon-dioxide laser, which produces light in the mid-infrared region, remains the instrument of choice in the endoscopic management of LTS. It can be used to coagulate vessels up to 0.5 mm in diameter. If the stenotic area is vascular, a laser with better hemoglobin absorption, such as the potassium titanyl phosphate/532 (KTP/532) or neodymium:yttrium-aluminum-garnet (Nd:YAG), is recommended. One further disadvantage of the carbon-dioxide laser is that it lacks a good fiberoptic delivery system and must generally be controlled with a micro-manipulator system mounted on a microscope.

Laser ablation of stenosis is a useful technique that may be combined with dilation of the stenotic segment or place-ment of an intraluminal stent. This procedure is most suc-cessful in the management of early lesions composed mostly of granulation tissue that have not yet evolved into a mature scar. Stenotic segments less than 1 cm in length may also be addressed with this method.

Areas of circumferential stenosis may be addressed endo-scopically by making radial incisions in the scar tissue with a laser and dilating the treated area with a bronchoscope or dilating instrument. The laser is used to create radial inci-sions in the scar tissue in four to six areas. The laser may be coupled to a ventilating bronchoscope if the patient is not tra-cheostomy dependent. The incisions break up the circumfer-ential scar band and leave islands of intact mucosa. The leaving of areas of intact mucosa is critical to prevent cir-cumferential areas denuded of mucosa that would ultimately reform scar tissue similar to the original lesion or possibly even make the scarring worse. The stenotic segment may be sequentially dilated. The procedure generally needs to be repeated at several 3- to 4-week intervals before an adequate airway is achieved.

Open Surgical Techniques

Severe areas of LTS that do not respond to endoscopic techniques require an open surgical procedure. Open techniques attempt to either excise the stenotic segment and reanastomose the airway or augment the circumference of the stenotic segment with transplanted tissue. Stenoses that are longer than 1 cm, have glottic or extensive tracheal involvement, and have failed endoscopic treatment and near-complete stenoses are candidates for an open technique. In patients with diabetes or severe systemic illnesses, open approaches must be considered with great care. Such patients suffer from poor wound healing, have a high risk of perioperative complications, and have a lower rate of successful outcome after open procedures. In these high-risk patients, a tracheostomy may be the most prudent choice of management.

Tracheal Resection and Reanastomosis

Areas of cervical tracheal stenosis up to about 5 cm can generally be excised, and the proximal and distal tracheal segments reanastomosed primarily. A suprahyoid laryngeal release may be required to allow for closure under minimal tension. When performing this procedure, the surgeon must keep in mind the age and body habitus of the patient. Older patients tend to have calcifications between the tracheal rings, resulting in decreased tracheal elasticity. Patients with large, thick necks and older patients with cervical kyphosis also tend to lack tracheal mobility.

Cricoarytenoid Joint Fixation

The cricoarytenoid joint is a synovial joint formed by the articulation of the arytenoid cartilage with the posterosuperior aspect of the cricoid cartilage. The vocal process of the arytenoid cartilage is usually free to rotate in three dimensions to allow proper apposition of the true vocal folds. This normal mobility of the arytenoid cartilages can be impaired by several factors. Dislocation of the arytenoid cartilage may occur owing to external trauma or intubation. The arytenoid cartilage may be dislocated anteriorly or posteriorly, with anterior dislocation being slightly more common owing to the force vector exerted through the blade of a laryngoscope. Several inflammatory disorders such as rheumatoid arthritis and gout may also involve the cricoarytenoid joint and result in an abnormal "fixation" of the joint. Inflammatory disorders can result in unilateral or bilateral cricoarytenoid joint dysfunction. With cricoarytenoid arthritis, the patient generally presents with symptoms of stridor and dyspnea with a variable degree of dysphonia. The dysfunction results from fixing the vocal cords in the paramedian position and the inability to achieve normal apposition of the true vocal folds on phonation or normal abduction with inspiration. Also, denervation of the larynx may limit the normal mobility of the arytenoid cartilages.

In the patient with suspected cricoarytenoid joint dysfunction, the differential diagnosis is three-fold. First, the posterior cricoarytenoid muscle may be denervated. Second, the arytenoid cartilage may be dislocated. A history of trauma should be carefully elicited in this group of patients. Finally, the joint may be fixed owing to an inflammatory condition. The proper location of the arytenoid cartilage and mobility of the cricoarytenoid joint are best assessed under general anesthesia by gently rocking the arytenoid cartilage back and forth. A "fixed" cricoarytenoid joint can be diagnosed with this method. An electromyogram of the intrinsic laryngeal musculature can determine if the immobility is caused by denervation or is secondary to fixation of the cricoarytenoid joint. A careful history aids in the diagnosis of a systemic inflammatory condition.

The treatment of cricoarytenoid joint dysfunction must be carefully individualized to the patient and the disease process. A patient with an inflammatory disease should be treated medically with the aid of a rheumatologist. Stable patients who are able to phonate, breathe, and swallow well without aspiration may be safely observed. Unstable patients or patients who do not improve on medical and rehabilitative strategies must be treated surgically. Patients with inadequate ventilation may undergo a tracheostomy, which would likely result in maintenance of an excellent voice owing to the medial position of the vocal cords. Patients who wish to be decannulated can be offered a cordectomy or arytenoidectomy, but they must be carefully counseled that a more patent airway will result in an inferior voice. A successful treatment strategy requires excellent communication between the surgeon and the patient and intensive patient education and counseling.

37

TRAUMA TO THE LARYNX

Peak Woo, MD
Philip Passalaqua, MD

ETIOLOGY

The position of the larynx in the neck, protected by the mandible superiorly and the clavicles and sternum below, shields it from falls and blows. Although the cartilaginous framework provides protection to the larynx, once this framework has been violated by trauma, the tight space defined by the laryngeal skeleton makes rapid airway compromise possible.

External laryngeal trauma is a relatively uncommon injury. The incidence of blunt trauma to the larynx has been reported as 1 in 137,000 in an analysis of 54 million inpatients over a 5-year period in 11 US states. In addition to the obvious possibility of acute airway obstruction, the complications of late diagnosed or undiagnosed laryngeal injuries can be severe, including glottic insufficiency, aspiration, and laryngeal stenosis. Furthermore, studies have demonstrated that early diagnosis and surgical management result in improved functional outcomes.

BIOMECHANICS OF LARYNGEAL TRAUMA

The larynx may be injured by blunt and penetrating trauma. In motor vehicle trauma, the head is often in extension. During deceleration, the larynx and neck are pulled forward, while the thorax is held in restraint. The larynx is decelerated against blunt objects, such as the steering wheel and dashboard, and is crushed against the vertebral column. The other major causes of blunt trauma to the larynx are of the "clothesline" type. Injuries of this type occur when the anterior part of the neck strikes a clothesline, chain, or tree branch during bicycling, snowmobiling, or riding in all-terrain vehicles. In clothesline injuries, the possibility of cricotracheal separation is a special concern.

TYPES OF LARYNGEAL TRAUMA

Soft tissue injuries to the larynx from blunt trauma include laryngeal edema, hematoma, and mucosal tears. Often edema or hematoma involves the aryepiglottic folds and false vocal cords owing to the supraglottic submucosal distensibility. In the course of a laryngeal trauma, the thyroid cartilage may be compressed against the vertebral column. This pressure against the thyroid cartilage will splay the angle of the thyroid cartilage to a more obtuse angle. Therefore, most fractures of the thyroid cartilage occur in the midline, with loss of the normal acute angulation of the thyroid alae. A similar force applied to the cricoid cartilage against the vertebral column will result in a comminuted fracture of the signet ring–shaped cartilage. Because of the prominence of the thyroid cartilage and its thyroid notch, it is the cartilage most usually fractured.

Gunshot and knife wounds account for the majority of penetrating injuries. Gunshot wounds produce a greater degree of soft tissue injury depending on the velocity and mass of the bullet. The higher-velocity bullets will result in greater injury to the surrounding soft tissues. Knife injuries usually result in less soft tissue damage but can be associated with injuries of vessels and nerves at some distance from the wound of entrance.

Laryngeal trauma in children tends to be less severe because of the higher position of the larynx in the neck in the pediatric population. Furthermore, owing to the pliable cartilage of a child's larynx, there is a lower incidence of laryngeal fractures. In addition, there is a lower incidence of laryngotracheal separation in the pediatric population because of the narrow cricothyroid membrane.

DIAGNOSIS

All patients with injury to the anterior part of the neck should be carefully evaluated for the existence of laryngeal trauma. The symptoms suggestive of laryngeal injury include cough and expectoration. Pain is present in nearly every patient with laryngeal injury and is accentuated by phonation or deglutition. Tenderness and swelling may be quite marked. Swelling of the neck may be accompanied by loss of laryngeal landmarks in the anterior part of the neck. Dyspnea is often present in varying degrees owing to edema of the soft tissue or blood in the trachea. Hemoptysis may be present but is usually not severe. Stridor and voice change are other signs that suggest laryngeal trauma. Although dysphagia may be present with endolaryngeal trauma, it may also be suggestive of esophageal or hypopharyngeal injury. Emphysema of the neck suggests a perforation of a viscus, such as the larynx or hypopharynx. Crepitation of the neck secondary to subcutaneous air may be elicited. Soft tissue injuries may be accompanied by ecchymosis of the skin. In more severe injuries of the larynx in which the airway compromise is marked, asphyxiation and massive hemoptysis may occur.

WORKUP FOR LARYNGEAL TRAUMA

The field management of the patient with suspected laryngeal injury consists of stabilization of the cervical spine and establishment of an airway. In the event of life-threatening airway compromise, intubation or tracheostomy in the field may be necessary.

After the patient has been stabilized and other potential life-threatening injuries are under control, the physical examination and assessment of the neck may commence for evaluation for laryngeal trauma. The workup for laryngeal trauma consists of physical examination of the neck, fiberoptic laryngoscopic examination, radiologic examination, and operative laryngoscopy.

Stridor is the most common sign in patients with upper airway compromise. The type of stridor may be indicative of the location of the injury. Combined inspiratory and expiratory stridor suggests some degree of obstruction at the level of the glottis. Expiratory stridor is more consistent with a lower airway injury. On the other hand, inspiratory stridor is indicative of supraglottic airway obstruction. The presence of both stridor and hemoptysis has been associated with severe laryngeal trauma, including displaced fractures of laryngeal cartilage, significant endolaryngeal or laryngopharyngeal edema or hematoma, or large mucosal tears exposing cartilage.

A thorough physical examination must be performed with special attention to the presence of neck tenderness, crepitus owing to subcutaneous emphysema, soft tissue swelling, and loss of thyroid cartilage prominence. Fiberoptic laryngoscopy in the stable patient is an essential element of the physical examination and should focus on vocal cord mobility, tears, mucosal edema, hematoma, and dislocated or exposed cartilage. If limited range of motion of the vocal cords is noted, a structural deformity or arytenoid cartilage dislocation is likely. On the other hand, immobility of the vocal cords suggests recurrent nerve injury. The patient presenting with soft tissue injury alone will often display edema, submucosal hemorrhage, and ecchymosis. Laceration of the mucosa, exposed cartilage, arytenoid cartilage dislocation, and disruption of the laryngeal architecture are highly suspicious of laryngeal framework injury.

RADIOLOGIC EVALUATION

If cervical spine injury is suspected, it must be evaluated with cervical films prior to movement of the head. Chest radiography should be done to rule out a pneumothorax. The laryngeal computed tomography (CT) scan is the most useful radiologic examination for evaluating laryngeal injury. There is some debate regarding the utility of CT scans in cases at the ends of the disease spectrum. Some authors do not recommend CT scan in those individuals with minimal cervical trauma and a normal physical examination as the scan will not change the management. They also do not recommend CT scans in individuals who have penetrating injuries, obvious fractures, and large lacerations and those who will require open exploration. They do note that there are exceptions in which the CT scan can serve as a road map for structural repair. Others routinely used CT scans to evaluate severe injuries that required operative management. They found that CT scans assisted in anticipating specific injuries and aided with the planning of the operative procedure. In the vast majority of laryngeal trauma cases, CT scans offer better visualization of the subglottic and anterior commissure areas, can help identify clinically unapparent cartilage fractures, and can verify laryngoscopic findings. Provided that the radiographic facilities are present and the patient is stable, a 2 mm CT scan or a spiral CT scan through the larynx offers the maximal detail as to the extent of laryngeal framework injury.

Carotid arteriography may be indicated in penetrating injuries to help reveal vascular injuries. If esophageal or pharyngeal tears are suspected, a Gastrografin swallow may be indicated.

EMERGENCY MANAGEMENT

In the initial management of laryngeal trauma, securing and stabilizing the airway are of paramount importance. However, there is controversy regarding the optimal method of establishing a patent airway. Oral intubation in the setting of laryngeal trauma can be precarious owing to the possibility of further damaging the larynx, the creation of false passages, and precipitating loss of a tenuous airway. For these reasons, it is recommended that if intubation is necessary, it is to be done after cervical spine injuries have been ruled out and the laryngeal anatomy has been defined by prior fiberoptic laryngoscopy and that it be done in a setting with access to direct visualization with operative bronchoscopes and with equipment and personnel required for a tracheostomy. An experienced clinician in airway management should carry out the procedure of intubation.

Owing to the inherent risks of intubation in the setting of laryngeal trauma, many authors recommend a tracheostomy under local anesthesia. Optimally, tracheostomies for laryngeal trauma should be performed at the fourth to fifth ring of the trachea. A vertical incision also affords better exposure so that, in the case of laryngotracheal separation, the trachea may be better accessed if it has retracted inferiorly. Cricothyrotomy should be used only as an emergency method of airway establishment and should be converted to a standard tracheostomy as soon as possible

CONSERVATIVE MANAGEMENT

After the initial evaluation and management of emergent airway issues, further treatment is divided into nonoperative and operative management. A conservative approach can be taken in patients with minimal soft tissue swelling or small hematomas and nondisplaced laryngeal fractures who are stable and without evidence of respiratory compromise. Hematoma and edema of the larynx often resolve spontaneously if there is no evidence of other injury.

Conservative management consists of observation, bed rest, voice rest, humidification of inspired air, antacids, and antibiotics. If a tracheostomy is not necessary, the patient is observed for 24 hours in an inpatient setting. During the 24 hours of observation, the patient should be followed for evidence of airway compromise from progressive swelling. Corticosteroids have been used for their anti-inflammatory properties and anecdotally prevent the progression of edema. Humidification of inspired air is thought to prevent crust formation if mucosal damage is present. Some authorities have suggested that antacid use may be beneficial by decreasing the incidence of mucosal irritation and possible laryngeal stenosis from gastroesophageal reflux. Antibiotics are indicated, especially in patients with multiple fractures in whom there is an increased risk of infection and perichondritis. Furthermore, a clear liquid diet may be beneficial initially. A nasogastric tube should be avoided if possible owing to the risk of further injury during placement. In addition, with extended placement of a nasogastric tube, there is a risk of mucosal ulceration in the postcricoid region.

SURGICAL MANAGEMENT

Injuries requiring surgical intervention include those with (1) exposed cartilage, (2) large mucosal lacerations, (3) lacerations involving the free edge of the vocal cord, (4) vocal cord immobility, (5) dislocated arytenoid cartilages, (6) displaced cartilage fractures, and (7) any neck injury with airway obstruction. The timing of surgical repair has been debated in the past, with some authors arguing that delaying surgery 3 to 5 days allowed resolution of edema and, therefore, better recognition of the anatomy. However, the current consensus is that outcomes are improved with early intervention. A delay of greater than 24 hours to surgical repair has also been found to be associated with an increased incidence of wound infections, especially with supraglottic injuries.

The early goals of surgical intervention should be to establish a safe airway, document the injury, repair cartilage injuries and restore the laryngeal framework, repair soft tissue lacerations, and promote early healing of the injury by prevention of infection and tissue necrosis. In the repair of laryngeal trauma, the long-term goals should be optimum functional restoration of the voice, airway, and swallowing.

After exposure of the endolarynx, any mucosal lacerations are approximated with fine absorbable sutures. The importance of restoring the lining of the larynx is attributable to the inherent tendency of exposed cartilage to facilitate the formation of granulation tissue, subsequently leading to fibrosis and laryngeal stenosis.

Another basic principle of laryngeal trauma surgery is to preserve as much cartilage as possible. Even free fragments of cartilage can be used to provide a scaffolding and stability, provided that they are covered with viable mucosa. If free cartilage fragments are used, they should be fixated with suture or miniplates.

Displaced fractures of laryngeal cartilage are reduced and immobilized. Fractures can be fixated with wire, nonabsorbable suture, or miniplates. Titanium miniplates offer the advantage of superior alignment of displaced fractures because of the three-dimensional nature of miniplates.

In situations in which rigid internal fixation or immobilization cannot be achieved, laryngeal stenting will be necessary. Stents are also indicated when there is injury to the anterior commissure or when extensive soft tissue injury is present. If mucosal grafting is required, the internal stent serves to hold the graft in approximation to the raw surface to be grafted. The goal of stenting is to provide stability and prevent mucosal adhesions and subsequent laryngeal scarring.

There has been controversy regarding the optimal time period that stents should remain in place. The beneficial effects of laryngeal stabilization and prevention of scar formation should be weighed against the risk of infection and irritation leading to granulation tissue and scar formation with subsequent laryngeal stenosis. Previously longer periods of time, up to 6 weeks, were favored for stent placement. Currently, most authors recommend that stents be removed after about 2 to 3 weeks, providing that fractures have been stabilized and lacerations closed effectively.

COMPLICATIONS

Even with the prompt recognition of laryngeal injuries and appropriate management, complications including granulation tissue, laryngeal stenosis, vocal cord paralysis, and aspiration are possible. Untreated displaced fractures may heal with dystrophic chondrification. Chondronecrosis with prolonged granulation tissue and progressive cicatrix formation is a feared complication of laryngeal fracture. Factors that increase the formation of granulation tissue include the presence of cartilage without mucosal covering and the presence of a stent.

Laryngeal stenosis may develop despite meticulous care after injury. In the case of supraglottic stenosis, the scar tissue may be excised with the carbon-dioxide laser. If needed for wound coverage, local mucosal flaps or buccal mucosal grafts can be used. In these severe cases, a stent with a tissue graft is often placed to facilitate re-epithelialization. In late or repeat reconstructions of the larynx in which laryngeal stenosis is an ongoing issue, the use of a conforming laryngeal prosthesis is invaluable.

Laryngeal stenosis in the subglottic area is more difficult to treat effectively. With limited subglottic stenosis, excision of fibrotic tissue with a carbon-dioxide laser and repeated dilations of the stenotic area may be adequate. In cases of more severe subglottic stenosis, cricoid splits with cartilage grafting are required. To stabilize the restructuring postoperatively, a stent is often needed. Tracheal stenosis of up to 4 cm can be resected with subsequent end-to-end tracheal anastomosis. Late reconstructions of the larynx using pedicled and autogenous grafts have been used with good results in adults suffering from laryngeal stenosis after laryngeal trauma.

In addition to laryngeal stenosis, another possible complication is paralysis of the vocal cords. The cause of an immobile vocal cord must be determined to make appropriate management decisions. To evaluate whether an injured recurrent laryngeal nerve or a cricoarytenoid joint fixation is responsible for vocal fold dysfunction, direct laryngoscopy is performed. During the laryngoscopy, the arytenoid cartilage is palpated to evaluate mobility. If the arytenoid cartilage is mobile, injury of the recurrent laryngeal nerve is the probable cause. If any question still exists, laryngeal electromyography (EMG) can also be performed. Electromyography is a valuable way to evaluate if the laryngeal muscles are denervated or the recurrent laryngeal nerve is intact. If the recurrent laryngeal nerve is severed, the EMG will show total denervation of the muscles. If the nerve is injured but recovering, the EMG will show signs of electrical recovery. If the EMG shows that the muscle activity is intact, the vocal cord immobility is likely secondary to cricoarytenoid joint fixation.

Bilateral vocal fold fixation or bilateral laryngeal nerve paralysis is especially challenging in the management of late effects of laryngeal trauma. Patients with bilateral cricoarytenoid joint ankylosis owing to intubation or laryngeal fracture are tracheostomy dependent unless additional surgery can be done. The surgery for bilateral cricoarytenoid ankylosis varies from open surgical arytenoidectomy to arytenoidpexy to endoscopic arytenoidectomy or transverse cordectomy. All have their advantages and disadvantages.

Beside laryngeal stenosis, laryngeal incompetence may result in disabling aspiration or dysphonia. The cause of late glottic incompetence may be attributable to loss of soft tissue, vocal fold paralysis, and laryngeal ankylosis, as well as inadequate repair and reconstruction of the normal endolaryngeal volume or inadequate approximation of the laryngeal fragments. These problems may result in inadequate soft tissue needed for glottic closure during deglutition or phonation. Since spontaneous recovery of vocal cord function with injury of the recurrent laryngeal nerve is likely unless the nerve is severed, observation for up to 8 months is indicated. However, if dysphonia or aspiration is caused by laryngeal ankylosis or anatomic deficits, repair of laryngeal incompetence by laryngoplasty is indicated. Using modern phono-surgery techniques, the vocal folds can be medialized as a temporizing measure with Gelfoam or fat injection. In situations in which the paralysis does not resolve, vocal cord medialization by laryngoplasty with or without arytenoid cartilage adduction may be performed.

RADIATION INJURY

External beam radiation has been used successfully for the treatment of laryngeal carcinoma for many decades. Radiation therapy can cause permanent morbidity of the larynx. The spectrum of injury ranges from edema to perichondritis and cartilage necrosis.

Pathology

The first effects of radiation therapy are in the epithelium. There is loss of glandular secretions, and ciliary function is damaged. This leads to dry, irritated mucosa that is prone to infection. Radiation induces fibrosis of the submucosal layer, thereby reducing venous outflow that, in turn, causes acute edema. With higher doses, the perichondrium degenerates, and a lymphocytic infiltration occurs. When the dose exceeds 1,000 to 1,200 cGy, irreversible vascular and lymphatic injury occurs. Subintimal fibrosis and proliferation of the endothelium cause obstruction of small arterioles. These changes in the endothelium are permanent and are the main cause of subsequent perichondritis and chondronecrosis.

Clinical Presentation and Management

Clinical symptoms and signs of radiation injury to the larynx include dysphonia, dysphagia, cough, pain, odynophagia, weight loss, aspiration, upper airway obstruction, malodorous breath, and sepsis. Chandler described a clinical grading system for radiation-induced changes in the larynx. Grades I and II include moderate hoarseness, moderate dryness, moderate edema and erythema, and mild impairment of vocal cord mobility. These symptoms and signs are expected in all patients receiving radiation therapy. These patients can often be successfully treated with humidification, antireflux medication, and sialagogues.

Grade III consists of severe hoarseness, dyspnea, moderate dysphagia, and odynophagia. On examination, there is fixation of the vocal folds with marked edema and erythema. Treatment consists of humidification, antireflux medication, antibiotics, and corticosteroids. A 2- to 3-week course of this treatment often results in marked improvement in symptoms.

If there is no response or recurrent episodes, the patient is likely progressing to frank chondronecrosis. Grade IV involves respiratory distress, severe pain, dehydration, and fever. There is evidence of airway obstruction and fetid odor, with possible skin necrosis. Treatment is the same as for grade III reactions, except that tracheostomy is often needed for airway control and gastrostomy is often needed for adequate nutritional support.

Often patients with radiation-induced changes in the larynx become a diagnostic dilemma for the clinician. It is often impossible to distinguish between recurrent carcinoma and radiation reaction, particularly in the face of increasing edema and impairment of vocal fold mobility. If a patient fails to respond to conservative management (corticosteroids, antibiotics, antireflux medication, and humidification), direct laryngoscopy and biopsy are necessary. If tumor is present at biopsy, total laryngectomy is performed. If no tumor is demonstrated, conservative measures can be continued for several weeks with frequent follow-up to detect recurrent carcinoma. In addition, hyperbaric oxygen has been used successfully in preventing the need for laryngectomy and tracheostomy in patients with grade IV laryngeal radionecrosis. If, after a few months, the larynx remains nonfunctional (tracheostomy dependent, severe pain, aphonia, and aspiration), total laryngectomy should be considered even if no tumor is present at biopsy.

Many clinicians are reluctant to biopsy a radiated larynx unless their index of suspicion for recurrent tumor is very high. The already compromised laryngeal cartilage will suffer further ischemia and potential salivary contamination at biopsy, thus increasing the risk of irreversible necrosis. The problem arises in distinguishing who is at high risk for recurrent carcinoma. Computed tomographic scanning and magnetic resonance imaging have not consistently been useful in distinguishing between radiation changes and tumor. Positron emission tomographic scanning has shown some promise in this area by appropriately distinguishing tumor from radiation changes.

LARYNGEAL BURNS

The most common type of thermal injury to the larynx occurs with inhalation of hot gases or smoke in burning buildings. Rarely are thermal injuries secondary to ingestion of hot liquids or foods. Isolated burns to the supraglottis can mimic acute infectious epiglottitis. If this occurs, the airway should be controlled by either tracheostomy or intubation in the operating room. The edema secondary to hot liquid or solid burns usually resolves rapidly, and decannulation or extubation can be accomplished in a short time. Rarely do hot liquids or solids cause long-term sequelae in the larynx.

In contrast, inhalation injuries frequently cause severe and potentially life-threatening acute and long-term complications. Both heat and irritant inhalation produce severe tracheobronchitis with sloughing of mucosa. If the basal cell layer is lost owing to the original insult or subsequent local trauma, delayed repair will result in granulation tissue formation and potential airway stenosis. Thermal injury induces rapid edema that can cause airway obstruction.

Patients with inhalation injury have a wide variability of presenting symptoms and signs. These range from cough to stridor to respiratory arrest. Some authors have advocated elective intubation of all patients with suspected inhalation injury. Others argue that this leads to many unnecessary intubations, and expectant management of the airway can be safely performed for stable patients. Most authors agree that if a patient presents with stridor, loss of consciousness, or massive burns, immediate intubation should be carried out.

If the patient is stable, the decision regarding intubation can be deferred until fiberoptic laryngoscopy and bronchoscopy have been performed to assess the airway. Some centers use flow-volume loops and ventilation-perfusion nuclear medicine scans to assess the damage to the lower airway and predict who requires intubation. If, on fiberoptic laryngoscopy and bronchoscopy, soot or mucosal injury is found, intubation should be performed. Patients who require intubation are at risk for late laryngeal and tracheal complications because their mucosas have already been damaged by the burns. No definitive improvement in outcome has been demonstrated with empiric treatment with antibiotics and corticosteroids in inhalation burns.

38

INFECTIOUS AND INFLAMMATORY DISEASES OF THE LARYNX

James A. Koufman, MD
Peter C. Belafsky, MD, PhD

The majority of patients with disorders of the larynx and voice suffer from infectious and noninfectious inflammatory conditions. It is important to remember that the term *inflammation* implies a local response to tissue injury, characterized by capillary dilation and leukocyte infiltration. The typical signs and symptoms of inflammation are swelling, redness, and, sometimes, discomfort or pain. The term *laryngitis* is synonymous with laryngeal inflammation, although not with hoarseness. Laryngitis (laryngeal inflammation) may result from infection by an invading microorganism or from irritative, traumatic, metabolic, allergic, autoimmune, or idiopathic causes.

Acute and chronic laryngitis are very common in otolaryngologic practice, and the causes (differential diagnoses) in pediatric and in adult patients are different. In infants and children, for example, the most common cause of laryngitis is acute infection, whereas, in adults, laryngitis generally tends to have a chronic, noninfectious cause.

Within the last 20 years, laryngopharyngeal (gastroesophageal) reflux has been discovered to be a far more important cause of laryngeal inflammation than was previously recognized. In addition, primarily because of acquired immune deficiency syndrome (AIDS), infecting microorganisms that were rarely encountered in the practice of oto-laryngology just a few years ago are re-emerging. Thus, the otolaryngologist today must again become familiar with the clinical manifestations of infection by a wide spectrum of microorganisms.

Laryngeal inflammatory disorders are unusual in that often more than one causative factor or condition can be identified. For example, patients with Reinke's edema are frequently smokers who also misuse their voices and have reflux. Such patients may also develop laryngeal carcinoma.

Each of the underlying causes must be identified and corrected if treatment is to be successful. As more has been learned about the larynx, environmental influences, and the effects of systemic disorders on the larynx, imprecise diagnostic terms, such as "nonspecific laryngitis," have appropriately begun to disappear from the otolaryngologic literature.

LARYNGOPHARYNGEAL (GASTROESOPHAGEAL) REFLUX DISEASE

It has been estimated that 10% of Americans have heartburn on a daily basis and an additional 30 to 50% have it less frequently. Of all of the causes of laryngeal inflammation, gastroesophageal reflux disease (GER, GERD) is the most common cause, and as many as 10 to 50% of patients with laryngeal complaints have a GER-related underlying cause.

The term *reflux* literally means "back flow." Reflux of stomach contents into the esophagus is common, and many patients with GERD have symptoms such as heartburn and regurgitation related to inflammation of the esophagus by acid and digestive enzymes. When refluxed material escapes the esophagus and enters the laryngopharynx above, the event is termed *laryngopharyngeal reflux* (LPR). Although the terms *gastroesophageal reflux* and *laryngopharyngeal reflux* are often used interchangeably, the latter is more specific.

Laryngopharyngeal reflux is the preferred term for use in otolaryngology because the patterns, mechanisms, and manifestations of LPR differ from classic GERD.

Laryngopharyngeal reflux affects both children and adults and may be associated with an acute, chronic, or intermittent pattern of laryngitis, with or without granuloma formation. Indeed, LPR has also been implicated in the development of laryngeal carcinoma and stenosis, recurrent laryngospasm, and cricoarytenoid joint fixation, as well as with many other otolaryngology-related conditions, including globus pharyngeus, cervical dysphagia, and subglottic stenosis.

The symptoms of LPR are quite different from those of classic GERD, as seen in the gastroenterology patient, who characteristically has heartburn, regurgitation, and esophagitis. Patients with "reflux laryngitis" (LPR) present with hoarseness, but almost two-thirds deny ever having heartburn. Other throat symptoms, such as globus pharyngeus (a sensation of a lump in the throat), dysphagia, chronic throat clearing, and cough, are often associated with LPR. The pattern of reflux is predominantly during the day in the upright position in LPR, whereas it is more likely nocturnal in the supine position with GERD. Gastroenterologists call reflux patients who deny gastrointestinal symptoms "atypical refluxers," but these patients are quite typical of those encountered in otolaryngologic practice. The physical findings of LPR can range from mild, isolated erythema of the area of the arytenoid cartilages to diffuse laryngeal edema and hyperemia with granuloma formation and airway obstruction. The particular laryngeal findings include pseudosulcus vocalis (subglottic edema that extends from the anterior commissure to the posterior part of the larynx; it appears like a groove or sulcus). It can easily be differentiated from a true sulcus (sulcus vergeture) that is the adherence of the vocal fold epithelium to the vocal ligament secondary to the absence of the superficial layer of lamina propria. It is scarring in the phonatory striking zone. Although the particular laryngeal findings are highly suggestive of LPR, ambulatory 24-hour double-probe (simultaneous esophageal and pharyngeal) pH monitoring (pH-metry) is the current gold standard for the diagnosis of reflux in otolaryngology patients. The distal probe is placed 5 cm above the lower esophageal sphincter, and the proximal probe is placed in the hypopharynx 1 cm above the upper esophageal sphincter, just behind the laryngeal inlet.

There are three levels of antireflux treatment: *level I*, dietary and lifestyle modification plus antacids; *level II*, level I plus use of a histamine H_2-receptor antagonist (such as cimetidine, ranitidine, or famotidine); and *level III*, antireflux surgery (eg, fundoplication) or proton pump inhibitor (PPI) therapy (eg, omeprazole, esomeprazole, lansoprazole, pantoprazole, or rabeprazole). In contrast to GERD, which often responds to level I or II therapy, high-dose, prolonged treatment with PPIs is often required to reverse the tissue injury in patients with LPR.

Potentially life-threatening manifestations of LPR include paroxysmal laryngospasm, laryngeal stenosis, and laryngeal carcinoma. Laryngospasm is an uncommon complaint, but patients who experience this frightening symptom usually are able to describe the event in vivid detail. Laryngospasm is often paroxysmal and usually occurs without warning. The attacks may have a predictable pattern (eg, occurring postcibal or during exercise), and some patients are aware of a relationship between reflux and the attacks (others are not). Loughlin and Koufman studied 12 patients with recurrent paroxysmal laryngospasm, 11 of whom had documented LPR by pH-metry, and all of whom responded to treatment with PPIs by a cessation of laryngospastic episodes. Excluding trauma, LPR is the primary cause of laryngeal stenosis, including subglottic stenosis and posterior laryngeal stenosis; pH-metry-documented LPR has been found in 92% of patients. Treatment with PPIs or fundoplication will result in subsequent decannulation of the vast majority of patients with such stenosis, in some cases without surgery. The risk factors for the development of laryngeal carcinoma include LPR. Koufman reported a series of 31 consecutive patients with laryngeal carcinoma in whom abnormal reflux was documented in 84%, but only 58% were active smokers. The relationship between LPR and malignant degeneration remains unproven, but the available pH-metry data suggest that most patients who develop laryngeal malignancy both smoke and have LPR. In addition, apparently premalignant lesions may resolve with appropriate antireflux therapy.

PEDIATRIC LARYNGITIS

Pediatric patients with laryngeal inflammation and edema present with one or more of the following symptoms: dysphonia, odynophonia, cough, dysphagia, odynophagia, stridor, and dyspnea. Airway obstruction from inflammatory laryngeal edema is more common in children than in adults owing to the small size of the pediatric larynx. Equivalent amounts of mucosal swelling may result in critical narrowing and obstruction in a child, while causing only minimal symptoms in an adult.

Viral laryngotracheitis is the most common laryngeal inflammatory disorder of childhood. It is responsible for 15% of respiratory disease seen in pediatric practice. Usually, this condition is self-limited, occurs in children under the age of 3 years, and has a seasonal peak, with most cases occurring during the winter. The need for inpatient hospitalization depends on the degree of airway obstruction. Treatment is aimed at decreasing laryngeal edema and preventing stasis and crusting of secretions within the airway. Therapy usually includes hydration, humidification of inspired air, and treatments with nebulized racemic epinephrine. Antipyretics, decongestants, and parenteral corticosteroids are often administered. Artificial airway support (eg, intubation) is necessary in only a small proportion of patients.

Acute supraglottitis is a life-threatening infection of the supraglottic larynx traditionally caused by *Haemophilus influenzae* type B. Since childhood immunization against type B *H. influenzae* has become commonplace, however, the disease is significantly less prevalent, and epidemiologic data suggest that non–type B *H. influenzae* is more frequent among those vaccinated children who are affected. The illness begins rapidly over 2 to 6 hours with the onset of fever, sore throat, and inspiratory stridor. The voice tends to be muffled, and there is no "barky" cough, as in croup. As the supraglottic structures become more edematous, airway obstruction develops. The child is generally ill-appearing, stridulous, sitting upright, and drooling because swallowing is painful. The diagnosis is usually based purely on the history and clinical findings. Examination of the epiglottis (in the emergency room) may precipitate airway obstruction and thus is not recommended. Lateral soft tissue radiographs may reveal the classic "thumb" sign of the edematous epiglottis with a dilated hypopharynx. In severe cases, treatment should not be delayed to obtain radiographs. If radiographs are deemed necessary, the study should be carried out in the presence of personnel capable of immediately intubating the patient should airway obstruction occur. The child with suspected epiglottitis should be taken to the operating room immediately to establish the diagnosis and secure an airway. Treatment is directed at airway maintenance and then toward providing appropriate antimicrobial and supportive care.

Diphtheria, spasmodic croup, and vocal misuse and abuse are other less frequent causes of pediatric laryngitis. Laryngeal diphtheria is caused by *Corynebacterium diphtheriae* and generally affects children over the age of 5 years. A febrile illness of slow onset associated with sore throat and hoarseness is then followed by progressive airway obstruction. Treatment consists of establishing a safe airway via a tracheostomy (intubation is contraindicated because it may dislodge a portion of the plaque and cause airway obstruction) and administering diphtheria antitoxin and penicillin or erythromycin to eradicate the microorganisms. Spasmodic croup, or "false croup," is a noninfectious form of laryngeal inflammation, associated with a mild, chronic-intermittent, croup-like pattern. Although the etiology of spasmodic croup remains uncertain, recent evidence suggests that extra-esophageal reflux may frequently be the cause. When spasmodic croup is suspected, 24-hour pH monitoring may be diagnostic. If, after a positive pH study, the patient's condition is alleviated by antireflux therapy, it may be concluded appropriately that reflux was the cause.

Traumatic laryngitis is most commonly caused by vocal abuse, such as excessive shouting or yelling, but it also can result from persistent coughing, inhalation of toxic fumes, or direct endolaryngeal injury. Such patients present with varying degrees of hoarseness and odynophonia. The mucosa of the true vocal folds is hyperemic from dilated vessels present on the superior and free surfaces. Edema within Reinke's space develops, and submucosal hemorrhage may occur. This form of laryngitis is self-limited and subsides within a few days when treated with voice conservation and humidification. Vocal nodules may become chronic in children who continually abuse their voices. Surgical treatment is only rarely indicated.

ACUTE LARYNGEAL INFECTIONS OF ADULTS

Acute viral laryngitis in adults is common, and it is generally less serious than in children because of the larger adult airway, which is able to accommodate more swelling without compromise of the airway. The typical type of acute laryngitis seen in adults is almost always viral. Influenza and parainfluenza viruses, rhinoviruses, and adenoviruses are the most common causative agents, although many other viruses have been implicated. The disease is self-limited and is best treated symptomatically with humidification, voice rest, hydration, cough suppressants, and expectorants. Antibiotic treatment is not usually necessary. In the professional vocalist, corticosteroids are sometimes used to reduce the vocal fold edema, particularly during the recovery phase.

Bacterial laryngitis may develop secondary to purulent rhinosinusitis or tracheobronchitis and generally is less commonly diagnosed in adults than in children. Supraglottic involvement (epiglottitis), as in pediatric patients, is the most common form of bacterial laryngitis. Supraglottitis in adults has a slightly different clinical picture. In adults, the infectious agent is less likely *Haemophilus* and more likely group A streptococcus. The clinical course appears less severe, with less seasonal variation and airway compromise. Although one must never be complacent with management of the airway, conservative airway management in an intensive care setting is often successful, and tracheostomy is rarely required. In adults, two useful clinical predictors of the need for endotracheal intubation are presentation to the emergency department less than 8 hours after the onset of a sore throat and drooling (in preference to swallowing because of severe odynophagia) at presentation. Conservative measures include oxygenation, humidification, hydration, corticosteroids, and intravenous antibiotics. A high index of suspicion should be maintained for progression to laryngeal/epiglottic abscess that is more common in adults.

CHRONIC INFECTIONS (GRANULOMATOUS DISEASES)

Granulomatous infections (eg, tuberculosis and syphilis) were recognized long ago and continued to be common afflictions throughout the world in the preantibiotic era. During the twentieth century, these conditions appeared to be on the decline, and some of them had all but disappeared, until relatively recently. With the advent of effective anticancer chemotherapy, organ transplantation, and human immunodeficiency virus (HIV) infection, it was discovered that the microorganisms causing many of the granulomatous diseases thrive in the immunocompromised host.

Granulomas are nodular histopathologic lesions, characterized by a central mass of epithelioid and giant cells surrounded by lymphocytes and other inflammatory cells. Central necrosis (caseation) is seen in many granulomatous conditions and is conspicuously absent in others.

Unlike children, adults have many chronic forms of granulomatous laryngitis, and these may go unrecognized for many years. Chronic granulomatous conditions involving the larynx may be attributable to numerous different types of microorganisms (bacteria, fungi, viruses), to an autoimmune process, or to an idiopathic cause. Some parasitic infections may also cause laryngeal granulomas.

Granulomatous lesions of the larynx may appear as smooth, diffuse swellings of the affected tissues; diffuse cobblestone mucosa; well-defined, discrete nodules; or an ulcerated inflammatory mass. Sometimes granulomatous diseases mimic laryngeal carcinoma. The necessity for biopsy cannot be understated. Granulomatous diseases caused by bacteria include tuberculosis, leprosy, syphilis, and scleroma, among others. In the past, tuberculous laryngitis usually was accompanied by advanced pulmonary tuberculosis. More recently, slightly more than one-third of patients with tuberculous laryngitis have active cavitary lung disease. Tuberculous laryngitis remains one of the most common granulomatous diseases of the larynx. Approximately one-quarter of the patients present with airway obstruction. In the past, tuberculosis tended to involve the posterior part of the larynx, but, more recently, the true vocal folds appear to be the most commonly involved site. Mycotic granulomatous diseases of the larynx include candidiasis, blastomycosis, and histoplasmosis. A relatively benign but common isolated form of laryngeal candidiasis (without the involvement of other contiguous anatomic structures) occurs in some patients who use corticosteroid inhalers for asthma. Treatment is targeted at the specific etiologic agent. Idiopathic granulomatous diseases include sarcoidosis and Wegener's granulomatosis. Recommended treatment includes corticosteroids and possibly other immunosuppressive agents.

ALLERGIC, IMMUNE, AND IDIOPATHIC DISORDERS

Anaphylaxis, an acute and profoundly life-threatening immune-mediated allergic response, is made up of a triad of clinical manifestations: (1) flushing, pruritus, and/or urticaria; (2) airway obstruction (angioedema, laryngospasm, and/or bronchospasm); and (3) circulatory collapse (shock). Angioedema, which may occur with or without anaphylaxis, is an acute, allergic, histamine-mediated, inflammatory reaction characterized by acute vascular dilation and capillary permeability.

Angioedema can be precipitated by medications (eg, penicillin, aspirin, other nonsteroidal anti-inflammatory drugs, and angiotensin converting enzyme inhibitors), food additives and preservatives, blood transfusions, infections, or insect bites. *Hereditary angioedema* is an autosomally dominant inherited deficiency of C1 esterase inhibitor that leads to recurrent attacks of mucocutaneous edema.

Treatment of both types of angioedema includes epinephrine, corticosteroids, antihistamines, and aminophylline. Intubation or tracheostomy may be required. "Pretreatment" of hereditary angioedema with danazol appears to elevate levels of functional C1 esterase inhibitor and to help prevent recurrent episodes.

Immunocompromised patients, whether immunocompromised from diabetes, long-term corticosteroid therapy, chemotherapy, or AIDS, are at risk of developing opportunistic infections of the aerodigestive tract. The most commonly reported opportunistic infections that affect the larynx are candidiasis, tuberculosis, and herpes infections.

Systemic autoimmune disorders that affect the larynx include rheumatoid arthritis, systemic lupus erythematosus, cicatricial pemphigoid, relapsing polychondritis, and Sjögren's syndrome. Presenting symptoms and findings include dysphonia, ulceration, granulation tissue, glottic and subglottic stenosis, and vocal fold immobility secondary to cricoarytenoid arthritis. Treatment includes airway maintenance, systemic corticosteroids, and other immunosuppressive agents.

MISCELLANEOUS INFLAMMATORY CONDITIONS

Parasitic infections that affect the larynx include trichinosis, leishmaniasis, schistosomiasis, and syngamosis. Trichinosis is suspected from the history and eosinophilia, and the diagnosis is made with serologic testing and muscle biopsy. The diagnosis of leishmaniasis is based on demonstrating the parasite in a biopsy of the granuloma. Diagnosis of schistosomiasis may be suspected by the histologic examination. Confirmation of the diagnosis may be made by identification of parasitic ova in the urine or feces. Treatment of schistosomiasis is with the appropriate antihelminthic medication (praziquantel or oxamniquine).

The size and anatomic configuration of the larynx (having the narrowest and most convoluted lumen of the upper airway) make it particularly susceptible to inhalation laryngitis. Acute thermal and toxic injuries are often seen in patients with facial burns. In this regard, thermal injury usually plays a greater role than chemical injury in the larynx. Intense heat produces excessive vasodilation, capillary permeability, massive edema, and thus airway obstruction. The edema usually peaks at 8 to 24 hours following injury and resolves within 4 to 5 days. The severity of permanent damage depends on the severity of the burn. Complete laryngeal stenosis can occur. Treatment consists of providing humidified oxygen and maintaining the airway. In most cases, corticosteroids and antibiotics should be avoided. Weeks after the acute injury has resolved, laryngeal dilation and surgical procedures to re-establish the airway, if necessary, may be performed.

The common clinical manifestations of allergy to inhalants are well known to otolaryngologists: sneezing, watery rhinorrhea, nasal congestion, and obstruction. The most common offending allergens are dusts, pollens, molds, and chemicals. Allergic reactions of the larynx, similar to those seen in the nose, are uncommon but do occur. The diagnosis is made by the history, clinical findings, and intradermal skin testing. Treatment should be removal of the offending allergen(s), if possible, and desensitization. Corticosteroid inhalers are ineffective in laryngeal allergy and should be avoided.

Tobacco and several other carcinogens cause chronic inflammation of the larynx. These substances can cause mucosal thickening, submucosal edema, hyperkeratosis, dysplasia, and, eventually, carcinoma. In the larynx, leukoplakia, pachydermia, and Reinke's edema (polypoid degeneration) should be viewed as precursors to the development of carcinoma.

Radiation therapy for laryngeal carcinoma, as well as for tumors in other head and neck sites, may deliver significant radiation doses to normal laryngeal tissue. The initial effects produce an intense inflammatory response, characterized by increased capillary permeability, edema, neutrophilic infiltration, vascular thrombosis, and obliteration of lymphatic channels.

Patients undergoing radiation treatment complain of a globus sensation, dysphagia, odynophagia, dysphonia, and odynophonia. On laryngeal examination, the larynx appears red and swollen, and a fibrinous exudate may be present. The symptoms tend to worsen as the treatment progresses; they are worst at the completion of treatment and gradually abate thereafter. Late tissue sequelae consist of degenerative changes and fibrosis in adipose, connective, and glandular tissues and a pronounced obliterative endarteritis of small blood vessels. These changes may take place over a period of years, and the symptoms of many patients worsen with time. Treatment is symptomatic, consisting of hydration, administration of expectorants, and environmental humidification. Radionecrosis is a late complication of laryngeal irradiation, being the result of ischemia of the cartilaginous framework. When a patient presents after radiation therapy with increasing symptoms and laryngeal edema, the clinician must determine the cause or causes. The differential diagnosis of laryngeal radionecrosis also includes tumor recurrence and reflux. Which of these, known as "the three r's" (radionecrosis, recurrence, reflux), has caused the patient's increasing symptoms will determine the treatment. Each patient must be evaluated for each of the three possibilities. Treatment for radionecrosis should be individualized. In some cases, necrotic cartilage and soft tissue can be removed through an endoscopic approach. Often, however, an open surgical procedure is needed.

Screaming and other forms of vocal abuse can lead to acute submucosal hemorrhage of the vocal folds. By history, such hemorrhage occurs abruptly and produces severe dysphonia. On examination, the appearance of hematoma is unmistakable. Voice rest is the usual treatment, although some laryngologists recommend surgical drainage in selected cases.

Muscle tension dysphonia is a generic term for any "functional" voice disorder caused by chronic vocal abuse or misuse. Patients with vocal nodules, contact ulcers, and granulomas or the Bogart-Bacall syndrome fit into this category, as do patients with psychogenic voice disorders. Muscle tension dysphonia can be classified as primary or secondary. Primary muscle tension dysphonia is attributable to nonorganic vocal fold pathology. The behavior may be learned or entirely psychogenic. Secondary, or compensatory, muscle tension dysphonia is a result of an underlying glottal insufficiency. The glottal incompetence may be caused by presbylaryngis, vocal fold paralysis, or vocal fold paresis. The findings are supraglottic hyperfunction that may be a physiologic attempt to compensate for underlying glottal closure problems. Muscle tension dysphonias are common in professional voice users and are frequently initiated or complicated by reflux laryngitis. Treatment with voice therapy, surgery, and, when appropriate, antireflux therapy often successfully resolves the problem.

Anatomically, only a thin layer of mucosa and perichondrium overlies the cartilaginous vocal processes, so ulceration over a vocal process can occur from a variety of insults, including vocal abuse, coughing, viral infection, GER, and endotracheal intubation.

Granulomas over the vocal process are five times more common than ulcers. Chronic ulcers over the vocal processes are uncommon because most either heal or go on to form granulomas. Regardless of the inciting cause, patients with these lesions should initially be treated with "voice modification" (not voice rest) to reduce continual vocal process trauma and antireflux therapy (preferably with a PPI). This regimen will result in healing in the majority of cases within 6 months. Although surgical removal is seldom necessary, it should be considered (1) when there is concern about the possibility of carcinoma, (2) when the lesion has matured and taken on the appearance of a fibroepithelial polyp, and (3) when the airway is obstructed.

39

NEUROGENIC AND FUNCTIONAL DISORDERS OF THE LARYNX

Christy L. Ludlow, PhD
Eric A. Mann, MD, PhD

Evaluation of Laryngeal Movement during Speech Using Videoendoscopy

Flexible fiberoptic examination is more useful than peroral endoscopic examination for evaluating neurogenic and functional voice disorders because movement of the vocal folds during speech and nonspeech gestures must be evaluated. During videoendoscopy, the vowel "ee" allows a better view of the larynx because the tongue is forward and high, opening the pharynx and bringing the epiglottis forward. Sniffing, whistling, and throat clearing are useful for identifying whether movement abnormalities affect nonspeech gestures. Strobo-scopic examination is useful for assessing the vibratory characteristics of the vocal folds but often is not useful when the patient cannot maintain a consistent vibratory cycle such as during tremor, breathiness, aphonia, and moderate hoarseness.

NEUROGENIC DISORDERS

Dysphonia can appear as the first sign of neurogenic disease. Caution should be used in treatment of neurogenic voice symptoms until it can be ensured that the laryngeal disorder is focal and not part of a progressive neurodegenerative disease. Referral for a neurologic examination is important before planning intervention in these disorders.

Upper Motor Neuron Disorders

Hypophonia In Parkinson's Disease

Reduced loudness and breathy vocal quality, referred to as hypophonia, is a hallmark of the voice disorder in early Parkinson's disease. Voice quality typically fades into breathiness in contextual speech. There may be reduced range and speed of vocal fold movement, particularly on the more affected side. In later stages of the disease, dysarthria becomes severe and the patient cannot voluntarily produce phonation. Also, severe "on-off" drug-related changes may occur. Glottal gap, asymmetries in closure, and bowing and thinning of the vocal folds are often noted on videoendoscopy.

Voice therapy, aimed at increasing vocal intensity, is of benefit in the earlier stages of the disease when combined with dopaminergic enhancement therapy. Recently, percutaneous collagen has been used to improve the breathy hypophonia of Parkinson's disease with vocal fold bowing and glottic insufficiency but does not improve overall speech in patients with preexisting dysarthria.

Parkinson Plus Syndromes: Progressive Supranuclear Palsy

Progressive supranuclear palsy (PSP) is a rare degenerative disorder with supranuclear ophthalmoplegia, complaints of falling backward, axial dystonia, pseudobulbar palsy, dysphagia, dysarthria, bradykinesia, masked facies, emotional lability, sleep disturbance, and cognitive decrements. Progressive supranuclear palsy may be differentiated from Parkinson's disease in that supranuclear ophthalmoplegia is characteristic of PSP, and the tremor present in parkinsonism is typically absent in PSP. Hypophonia is present, with unilateral vocal fold paresis.

Multiple Systems Atrophy

Multiple systems atrophy is another Parkinson plus syndrome. This is a rare degenerative movement disorder with lesions in the cerebellum, brainstem, and basal ganglia. In the Shy-Drager syndrome variant of this disorder, the most prominent feature is airway compromise secondary to bilateral abductor paresis. Patients often require tracheostomy in the late stages of the disease.

Pseudobulbar Palsy

Pseudobulbar palsy results from neuronal loss above the nucleus ambiguus involving the corticobulbar tracts bilaterally owing to vascular or degenerative lesions, tumors, or infections. Dysphonia is characterized by a strained-strangled, harsh voice, likely the result of hyperadduction of true and false vocal folds. Some persons have a breathy voice with vocal fold asymmetry.

Multiple Sclerosis

Multiple sclerosis (MS) is a progressive demyelinating disorder, having sensory and motor impairments, cognitive problems, spasticity, and tremor. Dysarthria and tremor occur with gait and limb ataxia in MS. Staccato speech, harsh voice quality, intermittent hyperadduction of the vocal folds, breathy voice, and vocal fold asymmetry are common findings.

Lower Motoneuron Disorders

Amyotrophic Lateral Sclerosis

Amyotrophic lateral sclerosis (ALS) is a degenerative disease of the corticobulbar tracts and lower motoneuron nuclei, which can produce a mixed dysarthria (flaccid-spastic paralysis). In flaccidity, there is hypoadduction of one or both vocal folds, pooling of saliva in the piriform sinuses, breathiness and hypernasality, reduced loudness, and "wet" phonation.

Dysphagia is common. In spasticity, voicing is strained and harsh because of hyperadduction. A mixed form of dysphonia can include both flaccid and spastic components. Speech symptoms may be the earliest signs in the bulbar type of ALS.

Myasthenia Gravis

Myasthenia gravis is a disorder of acetylcholine transfer at the myoneural junction, characterized by weakness and fatigability of striated muscle. This disorder causes a flaccid dysphonia, characterized by breathy, weak phonation. Sometimes stridor can develop with bilateral abductor muscle weakness. The extraocular muscles are usually the first affected, and laryngeal involvement is less frequent. Dysphagia can be severe.

Wallenberg's Syndrome

Occlusion of the posterior inferior cerebellar artery may produce infarction of the lateral medulla, resulting in Wallenberg's syndrome (lateral medullary syndrome). This syndrome is marked by dysarthria and dysphagia, ipsilateral impairment of pain and temperature sensation on the face, and contralateral loss of pain and temperature in the trunk and extremities. Vertigo, nausea, vomiting, intractable hiccupping, ipsilateral facial pain, and diplopia can occur. Unilateral vocal fold paralysis and flaccid dysphonia occur when the nucleus ambiguus or corticobulbar tracts leading to it are affected.

Postpolio Syndrome

Approximately 25% of survivors of the poliomyelitis epidemics experience progressive muscle weakness known as postpolio syndrome (PPS). Postpolio patients who complain of swallowing difficulties are at risk for unilateral or bilateral laryngeal paralysis. Progressive muscle weakness, fatigue, pain, and flaccid dysphonia occur.

DISORDERS OF THE PERIPHERAL NERVOUS SYSTEM

Phonosurgery for Vocal Fold Paralysis

Lesions of the tenth cranial nerve from the nucleus ambiguus to the musculature can cause paresis or paralysis of the laryngeal muscles. The glottic larynx must remain closed for airway protection during swallowing and be patent for respiration. Neither of these functions can be compromised by surgery aimed at improving phonation.

Perioperative Management

Perioperative control of underlying medical problems (chronic obstructive pulmonary disease, inhalant allergies, smoking, gastroesophageal reflux) is imperative before phonosurgery. Postoperatively, a short period of complete voice rest (less than 1 week) or modified voice rest is recommended. Whispering can be damaging after phonosurgery.

Unilateral Paralysis

Before phonosurgery, the primary cause of the dysfunction should be determined if possible. Vocal fold immobility may be attributable to damage to the recurrent laryngeal nerve (RLN) during thyroid or cancer surgery, tumor invasion of the nerve, neuromuscular disorders, neurodegenerative disease, or cricoarytenoid joint abnormalities. Procedures that are appropriate while waiting for recovery from RLN paralysis or compensation for it include thyroplasty to medialize the paralyzed vocal fold or collagen, Gelfoam, or fat injection to augment the paralyzed vocal fold. Voice and swallowing therapy should be initiated during this period. For patients with known terminal or unresectable disease, phonosurgery, if desired, should proceed at once.

Surgery for Glottic Incompetence

Augmentation. Vocal fold injection places material within or lateral to the vocal fold to move it medially. Direct laryngoscopy with the patient awake may be used for intraoperative assessment of results. Because of granulomas secondary to injection of Teflon paste, newer techniques and injection materials are preferred.

Gelfoam paste can be injected when only temporary results lasting 6 weeks to 3 months are desired. Autologous fat injection can have problems of resorption of the fat over time, leading most surgeons to overinject the vocal fold by 30 to 50%. Collagen injection is preferred for correction of gaps caused by vocal fold atrophy and other small defects. It should be injected into the deep layer of the lamina propria to prevent rapid resorption and to maintain correction beyond 3 months. Autologous collagen is a safer alternative to the bovine preparation, which may produce a hypersensitization reaction.

Medialization Thyroplasty. Laryngeal framework surgery provides methods to medialize, separate, shorten, or lengthen the vocal folds. These procedures are referred to as thyroplasty types I through IV. If the mobile vocal process contacts the paralyzed vocal process during phonation, type I thyroplasty is usually beneficial. If a wide posterior glottal gap is noted during phonation, a concomitant arytenoid adduction procedure may be required for voice optimization.

Arytenoid Adduction. This adduction procedure is used for vocal fold paralysis with a large posterior glottal chink or a difference in the level of the vocal folds during phonation.

Arytenoidopexy. This procedure more closely reflects the simultaneous, three-dimensional effects of the lateral cricoarytenoid, posterior cricoarytenoid, interarytenoid, and thyroarytenoid muscles on arytenoid position and stabilization during phonation.

Reinnervation. Reinnervation techniques succeed to the degree that they can reproduce the normal tone and action of the intrinsic laryngeal muscles. A nerve-muscle pedicle from the omohyoid muscle may restore adductory function to the thyroarytenoid muscle. Ansa cervicalis nerve transfer to the RLN for unilateral RNL paralysis has also been used.

Bilateral Vocal Fold Paralysis

Patients with bilateral vocal fold paralysis usually require treatment because of loss of abductor function leading to airway obstruction. Not only is the glottic chink narrowed by the resting position of the vocal folds, but also, with inspiration, the Bernoulli effect causes the folds to move medially as the velocity of the airflow increases.

Tracheostomy

Tracheostomy provides immediate, effective treatment. Although long-term tracheostomy is less appealing, it often stabilizes the patient with acute bilateral vocal fold paralysis.

Increasing Airway Caliber

Lateralization of one of the vocal folds and/or the removal of tissue from the posterior glottis enlarges the posterior glottis while preserving vocal quality.

Restoration of Function

Because of the trade-off between airway and vocal quality in other procedures, the ideal treatment of bilateral vocal fold paralysis remains reinnervation. Direct repair of the injured RLN is often unsatisfactory; vocal fold motion becomes uncoordinated and synkinetic. Tracheostomy and endoscopic procedures, particularly those that make use of the carbon-dioxide laser, are currently the mainstays of treatment for bilateral vocal fold paralysis.

Laryngeal Paralysis and Aspiration

Unilateral vocal fold paralysis rarely results in aspiration. When other motor or sensory dysfunctions also occur, the combination may impair the protective function of the larynx, leading to aspiration. Nonsurgical management of aspiration consists of discontinuing oral intake and providing alternative methods of alimentation. Enteral alimentation may be provided with a nasogastric feeding tube. For long-term feeding, gastrostomy or jejunostomy may be performed.

Other surgical techniques involve separation of the upper digestive tract from the upper respiratory tract. Although patients frequently lose their voice and may also require permanent tracheostomy, such procedures can be performed with low morbidity.

FUNCTIONAL VOICE DISORDERS

The term "functional voice disorder" is used to designate a voice disorder owing to misuse of the larynx for voice production. There are no structural abnormalities and no peripheral nerve injuries to account for abnormalities in laryngeal function. The disorder occurs only when the person attempts a particular function such as vocalization or breathing. These disorders are attributable to central nervous system disorders and/or behavioral abnormalities.

Functional voice disorders may be (a) idiopathic, (b) caused by misuse of the larynx for voice production (the development of compensatory behaviors), or (c) psychogenic, owing to psychological difficulties.

Idiopathic Disorders

Spasmodic Dysphonias

The spasmodic dysphonias include either *adductor* spasmodic dysphonia (uncontrolled closing of the vocal folds on vowels and voiced sounds), *abductor* or breathy spasmodic dysphonia (prolonged vocal fold opening for voiceless sounds extending into vowels), or *vocal fold tremor* (modulations in phonatory pitch and loudness most evident during prolonged vowels). Patients complain of increased effort, loss of control, and increased difficulties with stress. Coughing, crying, shouting, and laughter are unaffected. In some patients, particularly those with abductor spasmodic dysphonia, some degree of vocal fold asymmetry may be apparent within the first 6 to 12 months, suggesting injury. Movement abnormalities are observed on endoscopy in speech: during vowels in adductor spasmodic dysphonia, voiceless consonants (such as s, h, f, t, k) in abductor spasmodic dysphonia, and sustained vowels in vocal tremor.

Treatment.

RECURRENT LARYNGEAL NERVE SECTION. Section of one RLN results in initial dramatic reduction or elimination of voice spasms. Because of the high rate of symptom recurrence from reinnervation, RLN section is less preferred to botulinum toxin injections at the present time.

RECURRENT LARYNGEAL NERVE AVULSION. This involves more extensive removal of the recurrent nerve to reduce the risk of reinnervation but should be reserved for patients who do not benefit from or tolerate botulinum toxin injections or have failed prior RLN section.

SELECTIVE LARYNGEAL ADDUCTOR DENERVATION-REINNERVATION. This procedure involves bilateral section of the adductor RLN branches to the thyroarytenoid and lateral cricoarytenoid muscles with intentional reinnervation of the proximal thyroarytenoid branches using branches of the ansa cervicalis nerve. Because the procedure is technically difficult and produces permanent structural and functional changes in the larynx, it should be reserved for patients with relatively severe disease.

BOTULINUM TOXIN.   Either unilateral or bilateral thyroarytenoid injections is the treatment of choice for adductor spasmodic dysphonia. Restoration of normal voice occurs in 90% of patients for up to 3 months, followed by gradual symptom return within 4 to 5 months. The most commonly used method of injection is the percutaneous electromyography-guided approach through the cricothyroid membrane. Within 3 to 5 days of thyroarytenoid botulinum toxin injection, the breaks in phonation on vowels are reduced. Transient side effects, breathiness and swallowing difficulties, do not occur in all patients.

Botulinum toxin injections in either the cricothyroid or the posterior cricoarytenoid muscles are effective in only some patients with abductor spasmodic dysphonia. The effects of botulinum toxin injections on vocal tremor are also less predictable, and not all persons are benefited.

Paradoxical Vocal Fold Movement

Paradoxical vocal fold movement is the adduction of the vocal folds during the inspiratory phase of respiration, producing either a complete stoppage of air or stridor. These patients often have normal vocal fold movement during speech and can inspire during pauses while speaking.

Some patients have a focal laryngeal dystonia and can be treated using botulinum toxin injections into the thyroarytenoid muscles. Swallowing problems can be experienced as a result. Many patients are responsive to voice therapy, psychotherapy, and pharmacotherapy. However, caution must be exercised in diagnosis and treatment of this group of disorders, which can be life threatening.

Disorders of Vocal Misuse

Disorders of vocal misuse are best conceptualized as disorders of muscle use.

Muscular Tension Dysphonia

Increased muscular tension in the larynx and neck is associated with increased phonatory tension, elevation of the larynx in the neck, and an open posterior glottic chink between the arytenoid cartilages on phonation.

Rarely is voice production improved by psychological counseling alone. Usually, voice re-education and life management counseling can change voice use. These patients differ from adductor spasmodic dysphonia because of a consistent posture being used for voice production, which can be seen on fiberoptic videoendoscopy. In the spasmodic dysphonias, the abnormalities are intermittent and rapid, affecting only vowels in adductor spastic dysphonia and prolonged voiceless consonants in abductor spastic dysphonia. In muscular tension dysphonia, the laryngeal posture for voice is consistently abnormal and may be associated with inflammation or nodules. A trial of voice therapy by a speech pathologist experienced in treatment of these disorders is recommended before considering botulinum toxin. Botulinum toxin combined with voice therapy can train patients to eliminate these abnormal postures.

Voice Fatigue Syndrome

Voice fatigue syndrome is diagnosed only after excluding myasthenia gravis, Parkinson's disease, amyotrophic lateral sclerosis, and muscle atrophy associated with aging, Epstein-Barr virus, and sulcus vocalis. When a misuse disorder is present, patients use excessive muscular tension in one muscle group, which interferes with voice production for extended periods. Fiberoptic videotaping can be beneficial in retraining normal voice production, and a regimen of increased physical exercise may be beneficial in increasing vocal function.

Abnormal Pitch

A high pitch in males continuing past pubescent voice change is referred to as puberphonia or mutational falsetto. When this condition continues into adulthood, the misuse has become part of the voicing gesture. The combination of botulinum toxin in the cricothyroid muscles with voice retraining can benefit the most resistant cases.

False Vocal Fold Phonation (Dysphonia Plicae Ventricularis)

False vocal fold phonation is a muscle disorder involving excessive approximation of the ventricular folds. Phonation only with the ventricular folds is extremely rare. This usually follows injury to the true vocal folds from intubation, radiation, atrophy owing to vocal fold paralysis, or surgery for carcinoma. Fiberoptic videoendoscopy is used to demonstrate gestures such as throat clearing, humming, and sighing and to train glottal phonation independent of ventricular adduction.

Psychogenic Voice Disorders

Psychological processes in these patients result in inappropriate use of a normal vocal mechanism for speech communication. A psychogenic origin should be considered only when all other possible structural, neurogenic, or functional voice disorders have been excluded. Sometimes patients can have a psychological history similar to that usually found in patients with a psychogenic voice disorder but may have a neurogenic disorder. Many functional disorders, such as the spasmodic dysphonias, were considered psychogenic voice disorders until recently. Only the behavioral characteristics are available for differentiating among these disorders. Psychogenic voice disorders rarely produce secondary peripheral tissue abnormalities. Sometimes periods of abnormal voice production can be intermittent with normal periods of voice production. At least five types of voice disorders can be identified. Conversion reaction dysphonia is most commonly found in patients who are experiencing a strong emotional reaction to a traumatic experience or chronic depression. In malingering dysphonia, the patient is attempting to feign a voice disorder for secondary gain. Patients with psychogenic dysphonias exhibit inconsistent voice symptoms interspersed with periods of normal voice production. Elective mutism occurs most frequently in young children in response to traumatic events. Psychological overlay occurs when a patient with another voice disorder has symptom exaggeration usually to draw attention to the disorder or for some secondary gain.

In psychogenic voice disorders, management is most successful when vocal retraining, psychological or psychiatric counseling, and life situation change are simultaneously employed; otherwise, the voice symptoms may return intermittently. Because of the complexity and diagnostic uncertainty of most of the functional voice disorders, caution must be exercised. Usually, the disorder is not acute or life threatening, except in the case of acute airway obstruction in paradoxical vocal fold adduction. Therefore, a trial of voice therapy is often warranted before embarking on phonosurgery, botulinum toxin injection, pharmacologic management techniques, or psychological counseling.

40

NEOPLASMS OF THE LARYNX AND LARYNGOPHARYNX

Robert A. Weisman, MD
Kris S. Moe, MD
Lisa A. Orloff, MD

There are many types of benign tumors of the larynx and laryngopharynx, but, as a group, they are uncommon. In general, these neoplasms may be managed by observation or excision, depending on their location and individual behavior. Excision may be performed endoscopically in tumors of moderate size and accessible location. A decision to remove the tumor must take into account the morbidity of the procedure, which for tumors of neural origin will likely mean some loss of function. Paragangliomas are derived from neuroendocrine cells, are associated with the internal branch of the superior laryngeal nerve and posterior branch of the recurrent laryngeal nerve, and must be differentiated from laryngoceles using computed tomography (CT) or magnetic resonance imaging (MRI). Therapy, if required, is excision or, less frequently, radiation.

Schwannomas arise from the superior laryngeal nerve and may present in the aryepiglottic fold. The malignant form is rare. Neurofibromas are rare in the larynx and consist of a mixture of axonal or dendritic fibers and Schwann cell elements. Affected patients are typically young and often have syndromic neurofibromatosis, with multiple neurofibromas. The supraglottis is the typical site of origin.

Granular cell tumors also arise from the Schwann cell and are often multifocal in the head and neck, with the larynx being the second most common site.

Hemangiomas may occur in the larynx or pharynx and often present with significant bleeding. Diagnosis is typically made by appearance, and biopsy may be hazardous. Surgical excision often requires an external approach, and proximal and distal control of vessels may be necessary. Preoperative embolization should be considered.

The subglottic hemangioma presents in infancy, may be associated with multiple cutaneous or mucosal hemangiomas, and is often found in association with other congenital anomalies.

Lymphangiomas or cystic hygromas present in the supraglottis and hypopharynx. They may infiltrate extensively and often cause airway obstruction. Myogenic tumors presenting in this region include leiomyoma, myoma, and myoblastoma. Local excision is usually adequate therapy.

MALIGNANT NEOPLASMS

Laryngeal and laryngopharyngeal cancers are the most common malignancy of the head and neck. Laryngeal cancer has historically been a disease with a significant male predominance, although the gender distribution has been changing as more women have begun to smoke. There are approximately 10,000 new cases of laryngeal cancer and 2,500 new cases of hypopharyngeal cancer per year in the United States. The overall mortality rate for laryngeal cancer is 32%, with 25% of patients presenting with regional and 10% with distant metastasis. The majority of patients present between ages 55 and 65.

The most significant risk factors are the consumption of tobacco and alcohol. Cigarettes carry the greatest risk of laryngeal cancer, but cigar and pipe smoking are also risk factors. The primary carcinogens in tobacco are tars and polycyclic hydrocarbons. Only 1% of laryngeal carcinoma occurs in non-smokers. Inhabitants of urban areas are at greater risk than rural dwellers, and other possible etiologic factors include gastroesophageal reflux, exposure to wood dust, asbestos, volatile chemicals, nitrogen mustard, ionizing radiation, and immune system compromise. Ionizing radiation and radioactive iodine have been implicated. Human papillomavirus (HPV) may be a cofactor, and HPV 16 deoxyribonucleic acid (DNA) is commonly demonstrated in laryngeal cancers. Oral herpes infections may also predispose to laryngeal cancer, as may deficiencies in dietary intake of the B vitamins, vitamin A, betacarotene, and retinoids. Anatomic conditions such as sulcus vocalis and laryngoceles are associated with laryngeal carcinoma, and there is also an association with Plummer-Vinson syndrome (glossitis, achlorhydria, and atrophic gastritis). The development of laryngeal and laryngopharyngeal carcinomas is most likely multifactorial in origin.

Laryngeal cancer has one of the highest rates of second primary cancers. These second tumors occur synchronously in 1% of cases and metachronously in 5 to 10%. Second primaries are more common with supraglottic than glottic tumors, and the most common type is bronchogenic carcinoma. The risk of a second primary tumor in the lung is proportional to the smoking history and whether the patient continues to smoke.

The role of follow-up screening for primary or metastatic lung tumors is controversial. Although the tumors might be detected before they become symptomatic, overall survival is not likely to change much. Chest CT is highly sensitive but not specific, but the specificity of positron emission tomography may aid in earlier diagnosis of second tumors.

Pathology

The epithelium of the larynx is chiefly pseudostratified ciliated columnar with the exception of the true vocal folds where it is stratified squamous. The epithelium appears to undergo predictable changes as it progresses to invasive carcinoma. Hyperplasia refers to thickening owing to an increase in the number of cells. This is typically seen with chronic irritation or trauma. Hyperkeratosis denotes an increase in the depth of the overlying keratin layer. Both of these are benign changes. Dysplasia, however, is a premalignant disorder involving loss of the normal progressive maturation of cells from the basal layer to the superficial epithelium. This may range from mild to severe, the latter being synonymous with carcinoma in situ (Cis). Once Cis has progressed to penetrate the basement membrane, it becomes invasive carcinoma. Three percent of hyperkeratoses without dysplasia, 7% of mild dysplasias, 18% of moderate dysplasias, and 24% of severe dysplasias of the vocal cords will develop invasive carcinoma. Aneuploidy on flow cytometry predicts a high risk of progression from dysplasia to invasive carcinoma.

Cellular differentiation is also important in the prognosis of laryngeal carcinoma, with lymphatic metastases being more common in poorly differentiated tumors. Supraglottic tumors tend to be less differentiated than glottic tumors and behave aggressively early in their course. Additional pathologic characteristics that influence prognosis include infiltrating versus pushing borders, presence or absence of a local host inflammatory reaction, and vascular or perineural invasion.

Over 95% of laryngeal malignancies are squamous cell carcinoma. There are variants or subtypes of squamous carcinoma. These include verrucous, basaloid squamous, and spindle cell carcinoma. Verrucous carcinomas are extremely well differentiated and do not metastasize to lymph nodes. Basaloid squamous carcinoma is an aggressive tumor occurring more frequently in the hypopharynx. Spindle cell carcinoma tends to be pleomorphic with areas of standard squamous carcinoma or Cis. Spindle cell cancers are more resistant to radiation therapy and may undergo osteocartilaginous differentiation after radiation.

Nonsquamous malignancies of the larynx and laryngopharynx include adenoid cystic carcinoma, typical and atypical carcinoid, small cell carcinoma, and chondrosarcoma. Adenoid cystic carcinoma is rare, and most are subglottic or supraglottic owing to their origin in minor salivary or seromucinous glands. Perineural invasion is common, as are pulmonary and osseous metastases. Lymphatic invasion is rare, however, and elective neck dissection is not indicated. Typical carcinoid of the larynx is extremely rare and occurs almost exclusively in males. Surgery is typically curative. Atypical carcinoid is more common, exhibits more atypia and cellular necrosis, and is more aggressive. Regional and distant metastases are common, and chemotherapy and radiation therapy should be considered as an addition to surgery. Chondrosarcoma is a rare, slow-growing tumor and usually arises from the cricoid cartilage. Surgery is the primary therapy, and lymphatic metastasis is rare.

Anatomic Subsites and Patterns of Spread of Laryngeal Tumors

The spread of tumors within the larynx is not haphazard; rather, it occurs in a relatively predictable fashion under the influences of local subsites. These influences include anatomic defenses such as perichondrium and cartilage, as well as anatomic weaknesses such as blood vessels and lymphatic channels. Furthermore, the supraglottis arises from different embryologic anlage than the glottis and subglottis, thus producing unique routes of lymphatic spread. Understanding this allows the surgeon to anticipate tumor behavior and increase the chance of successful local therapy.

The majority of supraglottic tumors begin on the epiglottis and tend to advance by local invasion. Initial barriers to spread include the perichondrium and cartilage of the epiglottis, with deeper resistance to invasion including the thyroepiglottic ligament and finally the thyroid cartilage. The quadrangular membrane of the aryepiglottic fold may help to contain superior and lateral invasion. Supraglottic tumors tend to spread by lymphatic invasion, with over 30% of clinically N0 cases demonstrating involved lymph nodes on final pathology. The supraglottic lymphatic drainage is through the thyrohyoid membrane following the superior laryngeal veins to levels II and III in the neck.

Glottic tumors arise on the vocal fold or up to 10 mm inferior to it. The vocal folds are known to have very limited lymphatic drainage, and glottic tumors remain contained until lateral invasion allows entry into the paraglottic space, a vertical portal of spread to the rest of the larynx. Vocal fold tumors allow diagnosis at an early stage owing to ensuing hoarseness, and lateral invasion is manifested by vocal cord paresis or paralysis from interference with function of the thyroarytenoid muscle or cricoarytenoid joint. The anterior commissure of the vocal folds is an important area of relative vulnerability to tumor invasion. Here the anterior vocal ligament and vessels perforate the thyroid cartilage, violating the protective barrier of the perichondrium. Tumors that are relatively small in size can quickly gain T4 staging by penetration of the cartilage.

Subglottic tumors arise 10 mm or more below the glottis and are rare, comprising less than 1% of laryngeal tumors. Direct invasion may occur anteriorly through the cricothyroid membrane or inferiorly within or external to the trachea.

Transglottic tumors may involve all three subsites of the larynx. The spread of these tumors is dictated by the areas they invade.

Hypopharyngeal tumors may be divided into superior and inferior. Superior tumors arise on the lingual surface of the epiglottis, vallecula, or tongue base. Inferior tumors arise mainly in the piriform sinus. As tumors extend inferiorly in the pharynx, they have a greater tendency to spread via lymphatics and have a high rate of distant metastasis.

As a group, distant metastasis from laryngeal tumors is a late event, occurring after local and regional recurrences. Only 8 to 10% of patients present with distant metastases, whereas 25% already have regional nodal involvement. The primary sites of distant metastases are the lungs, liver, and bone.

Clinical Evaluation

The primary presenting symptom in carcinoma of the glottis is hoarseness. This occurs early in the disease process but has often been present for 3 or more months by the time of diagnosis. Patients with supraglottic carcinoma tend to remain asymptomatic until the tumor is locally advanced and often present owing to nodal metastasis. The rare patient with carcinoma of the subglottis typically presents with stridor or hemoptysis. Other symptoms of concern for laryngeal cancer are dyspnea, dysphagia, and pain (particularly when referred to the ear). Pain occurs with advanced tumors, owing to invasion through cartilage and extralaryngeal structures. Pain radiating to the ear may be caused by involvement of the glossopharyngeal or vagus nerves. Other symptoms are cough, hemoptysis, halitosis, and weight loss. Coughing is often attributable to the aspiration seen with glottic tumors, and weight loss is an ominous sign that often suggests distant metastases. Tenderness on palpation of the larynx may indicate extension through cartilage.

As the treatment of laryngopharyngeal tumors can be physically demanding, the overall health and ability of the patient to undergo treatment are very important. The patient's alcohol intake can have a direct bearing on the postoperative course, and the smoking history may have an impact on wound healing. Prior therapies such as local radiation are critical to ascertain.

A complete physical examination is required, with special attention to the entire upper aerodigestive tract and cervical region. Complete laryngoscopy is required, either with a mirror or a fiberoptic endoscope, and any abnormality in vocal fold motion should be noted. Videostroboscopy can be important in the evaluation of early glottic cancers as progression from Cis to invasive carcinoma will be demonstrated by tethering of the mucosa to the underlying stroma with dyskinesia of the mucosal wave. Documentation of the size, location, and fixation of any cervical lymph nodes is important.

Imaging Studies

The current modalities most commonly used for imaging of the upper aerodigestive tract in the United States are CT and MRI. These have been refined to the point that they can provide important information on invasion of cartilage, local spaces, and regional structures, as well as demonstrate lymph nodal metastases. Both technologies have sensitivities ranging from 60 to 80%, with specificities between 70 and 90%. Additional information on lymph node size, shape, and appearance may suggest involvement by metastatic disease. Positron emission tomography is based on differential uptake of radioactive [18^F] fluorodeoxyglucose. Tissues invaded by tumor typically take up greater concentrations of the tracer owing to their increased metabolic demands. Positron emission tomography has been demonstrated to be more sensitive, specific, and accurate than CT or MRI in detecting occult nodal disease. It alone does not provide detailed anatomic information, but it is currently being coupled with CT, which is expected to enhance the accuracy of tumor imaging in the future.

Panendoscopy

Panendoscopy is a systematic survey of the upper aerodigestive tract through laryngoscopy, esophagoscopy, and bronchoscopy. Detailed information on the exact extent of the primary tumor is obtained while concurrently searching for additional primary malignancies. During laryngoscopy, which is performed at the end of the procedure so that bleeding does not interfere with assessment of the other structures, the tumor is biopsied. For more precise evaluation, telescopes can be introduced through the laryngoscope, and suspension microlaryngoscopy may be performed for "hands-free" viewing under magnification.

Tumor Staging

When all clinical investigations have been performed, staging of the tumor is possible. The system used in the United States is the tumor, node, metastasis (TNM) classification created by the American Joint Committee on Cancer, which separates patients into stages I to IV, with higher stages carrying a poorer prognosis.

TREATMENT FOR CANCERS OF THE LARYNX AND LARYNGOPHARYNX

Early Glottic Cancer

"Early" glottic cancer refers to tumors ranging from Cis to T2 lesions that are grouped together in a prognostically favorable category because the greatest diminution in survival occurs with progression from T2 to T3 tumors. As a group, early glottic carcinomas are understaged 40% of the time. Carcinoma in situ without an invasive component is relatively rare. T1 lesions of the anterior commissure invade cartilage early, making them true T4 lesions in many instances.

In most institutions, radiation therapy (XRT) is favored over surgical treatment of early glottic carcinoma because it has been thought to result in superior vocal function while providing cure rates similar to surgery. Primary radiation therapy is delivered in single fractions over 6 to 7 weeks for a typical dose of 6,600 cGy and produces a cure rate for T1 cancers of 80 to 90%. Male gender and bilateral vocal fold involvement have been associated with poorer outcomes. T2 cancers have an overall cure rate of approximately 65% with

XRT, although there is great variability in the literature. Some of this variability may be attributable to mixing T2a lesions (normal vocal cord mobility) with T2b lesions (impaired mobility). Rates of 85% have been reported for the former, with a 20% drop for the latter.

The surgical treatment of early glottic carcinoma most commonly involves vertical hemilaryngectomy. More recently, endoscopic excision has gained favor and is used extensively in Europe. Studies of laser excision are demonstrating survival outcomes equal to or better than XRT, with a postoperative vocal quality that is comparable. In addition, 40% of these patients can be salvaged with laryngeal conservation surgery should the tumor recur, leaving XRT as an additional therapeutic option.

Early Supraglottic Cancer

True early supraglottic carcinoma is rare; even those tumors presenting as T1 or T2 have a high incidence of regional metastases, making them stage III or IV, with the management of regional disease having disproportionate importance in this group of tumors.

Surgery and XRT appear equally efficacious for the rare T1 tumors, with local control rates of 90%. T2 lesions also have similar control rates with both therapies.

Traditional surgical therapy for supraglottic tumors involves supraglottic laryngectomy, with resection of the epiglottis, aryepiglottic folds, and false vocal folds. Contraindications to the procedure include fixation of the vocal fold, extension of tumor to the anterior commissure, and thyroid cartilage invasion. Patients must have excellent pulmonary function to be candidates for this procedure.

As with early glottic carcinoma, laser excision of early supraglottic carcinoma is also becoming more widely used in the United States. New bivalved laryngoscopes have increased the visibility and accessibility of these tumors to transoral excision. The local control rates with laser excision appear to be equal to open procedures for T1 and T2 lesions.

For N0 patients, single-modality therapy for the primary and regional sites is adequate. Patients with regional metastases typically require combination therapy, and in these instances, XRT to the primary and combined therapy of the neck are a rational approach.

Management of Advanced Laryngeal Cancer

Advanced Supraglottic Cancer

T3 carcinoma of the supraglottic larynx implies invasion of the preepiglottic space, cartilage, medial wall of the piriform sinus, or fixation of the vocal fold. These tumors all have a high probability of lymphatic invasion. Treatment options include single-modality therapy, surgery and XRT, or chemotherapy and XRT. The choice of therapy must be individualized to the patient, taking into account the tumor size and location as well as the age, health, and wishes of the patient. Laryngeal function should be preserved whenever possible.

Supraglottic laryngectomy can be undertaken for T3 tumors without the following: fixation of the vocal cords, extensive involvement of the piriform sinus, thyroid or cricoid cartilage invasion, or invasion of the tongue base beyond the circumvallate papillae. With proper surgical selection, a 3-year disease-free survival rate of 75% is possible. Laser excision of supraglottic tumors is also possible, and reports have demonstrated less dysphagia and aspiration with this procedure than with open techniques. In addition, the voice results appear to be improved over extended supraglottic laryngectomies.

Surgical treatment of the neck is also necessary, and when two or more nodes are positive, or if extracapsular extension is present, adjuvant radiation therapy is indicated. Because the supraglottic lymphatic drainage is bilateral, levels II, III, and IV of both sides of the neck must be addressed. For N+ necks, level V should be treated as well.

Standard daily radiation therapy for T3 tumors results in higher local failure rates, lower survival, and lower rates of laryngeal preservation. Surgical salvage is possible in only 50% of these patients and usually requires laryngectomy. Hyperfractionated (more than one treatment per day) XRT appears to produce higher local control and cure rates than single-fraction schedules.

Advanced Glottic Cancer

Current therapies for advanced glottic carcinoma include single-modality (laryngectomy or XRT) and multimodality (XRT with chemotherapy or surgery with XRT) strategies. Radiation therapy can be administered in daily fractions or twice-daily fractions (hyperfractionated). Most trials have indicated an improvement in local tumor control with hyper-fractionation, but the impact on overall survival is less certain.

Extensive efforts are being directed at organ preservation protocols. The well-known Veterans Affairs Laryngeal Cancer Study Group compared laryngectomy with postoperative XRT to induction chemotherapy followed by XRT in patients exhibiting at least a partial response to chemotherapy. Survival rates were similar in the two groups, with 64% laryngeal preservation in the nonsurgical group. Studies are now demonstrating superior results with chemotherapy given concomitantly with XRT compared with sequential chemotherapy-XRT. Induction chemotherapy has also been used before surgery to downsize tumors requiring laryngectomy to a size amenable to partial laryngectomy or radiation. More investigation is required before the optimal therapy for advanced glottic cancer is known, and outcome studies that include quality of life data are required to assess each intervention.

Recurrent and Metastatic Laryngeal Carcinoma

Local recurrence of lesions managed initially by XRT or partial laryngectomy can at times be managed by salvage surgery, depending on the extent of the recurrence. Similarly, when XRT was not used as an initial modality, it remains a therapeutic option. Parastomal tumor recurrence portends a grave prognosis, and when paratracheal lymph nodes are involved, the disease is most likely incurable. Recurrences above the equator of the stoma are at times amenable to resection.

Lesions with the highest risk of distant metastasis are those in the supraglottis that extend to the hypopharynx and piriform sinus. This is especially true of patients with N2 and N3 neck disease. Glottic primaries are the least likely to metastasize. The most common site of distant metastasis is the lung (50 to 80% of metastases), followed by the liver and bone. Metastasis to bone is associated with a survival time of less than 4 months, whereas patients with pulmonary metastases have a mean survival of 12 months. Patients with incurable recurrences suffering from pain, dysphagia, or airway obstruction can sometimes be palliated by XRT or low-toxicity chemotherapy. These patients should be offered the assistance of hospice programs.

Complications of Treatment of Laryngeal Cancer

The complications of XRT for laryngeal cancer include skin desquamation, mucosal ulceration and dryness, hoarseness, dysphagia, dysgeusia, and esophageal stricture. Laryngeal chondroradionecrosis may also occur, is heralded by pain, and can be difficult to distinguish from recurrent carcinoma. Surgical complications include hemorrhage, infection, pharyngocutaneous fistula, aspiration pneumonia, and stenosis of the stoma, pharynx, or esophagus. With conservation surgery, glottic or supraglottic stenosis can also occur. The risk of surgical complications is somewhat higher after XRT.

Vocal Quality after Surgery for Laryngeal Carcinoma

For early cancers that do not invade the anterior commissure or vocal process, carbon-dioxide laser excision produces a near-normal or normal voice in the majority of patients. When the entire vocal fold must be removed, however, the resultant vocal quality is considerably less than that which can be achieved with XRT. After hemilaryngectomy, the vocal outcome is variable and probably depends in part on the method of reconstruction used. Studies comparing the quality of voice in these patients compared with those who underwent XRT have not been undertaken, owing in part to the fact that most patients undergoing hemilaryngectomy are XRT failures.

There are several voice rehabilitation options for patients who have had a total laryngectomy. An electrolarynx can be used soon after surgery, although the mechanical voice is of only fair to poor quality. Another option is esophageal speech, in which the patient swallows air and expels it through the pharynx while speaking. This is difficult for most patients to master and results in short phonatory times. Tracheoesophageal puncture is a third option, in which a prosthesis is placed in a surgically created tract between the upper tracheostoma and the pharynx. The patient then covers the stoma with a finger and exhales forcefully through the prosthesis into the pharynx. Phonation is generated in the pharyngoesophageal segment, as in esophageal speech, but the phonatory duration is much longer, and the intensity of speech can be partially modulated

41

NEOPLASMS OF THE NASOPHARYNX

Frank G. Ondrey, MD, PhD
Simon K. Wright, MD

NASOPHARYNGEAL CARCINOMA

Epidemiology

Nasopharyngeal carcinoma (NPC) is unique among squamous cell carcinomas of the head and neck (SCCHN) in its geographic epidemiologic profile. Although it is a rare tumor in most parts of the world, in regions of southeastern Asia, its incidence soars to 27.3 in 100,000. The highest incidence occurs in Taiwan, where 98% of the population is Chinese, 90% of whom originate from the Guangdong province. There is a decrease in incidence in northern China, falling to 3 in 100,000 in northern provinces. The Japanese, who trace their origins to the Mongoloid region, have an incidence of just 1 in 100,000 for both men and women. In Europe and North America, the incidence is 1 in 100,000. In China, the disease rate rises after age 20 and falls after age 60; the mean age is 40 to 50 years. The male-to-female ratio is 3 to 1.

Dietary Associations

Because of the strikingly high incidence of NPC among the "boat people" of southern China (54.7/100,000), speculation about their unique environmental exposures led to the examination of salted fish as a risk factor. Salted fish has been shown to contain strong carcinogens and mutagens. Animal studies support the association, demonstrating a dose-dependent relationship between salted fish intake and tumor development in rats.

Epstein-Barr Virus Associations

Epstein-Barr virus (EBV) is a double-stranded deoxyribonucleic acid (DNA) virus that, in addition to being the cause of infectious mononucleosis, is implicated in a variety of lymphoid neoplasms: endemic Burkitt's lymphoma, post-transplantation lymphoproliferative disorders, subsets of Hodgkin's disease, and nasal T-cell lymphoma. The connection between EBV and NPC was first made in the late 1960s, when serologic studies demonstrated elevated titers of immunoglobin (Ig)A and IgG titers against viral antigens. Two major lines of evidence for the role of EBV have been elucidated: serologic studies and nucleic acid studies.

Serologic Studies

Elevated levels of IgA and IgG antibodies directed against viral capsid antigen and early antigen in patients with NPC have been documented by many studies. Immunoglobulin A can be detected in 80 to 85% of patients with NPC. Response to treatment yields a corresponding decrease in levels; increasing titers are associated with progression of disease. Anti-EBV nuclear antigen 1 IgA has also proven to be a sensitive indicator of the presence of NPC.

Nucleic Acid Studies

Direct evidence for the role of EBV in the pathogenesis comes from studies of EBV ribonucleic acid (RNA) in NPC cells, the presence of which indicates infection with the virus.

Biomarkers

Vascular endothelial growth factor, a potent angiogenic growth factor, has been shown to be elevated in patients with metastatic NPC but not in patients with nonmetastatic NPC.

Histology

The World Health Organization (WHO) has classified NPC into three histopathologic groups. WHO type I is a keratinizing squamous cell carcinoma similar to others of the head and neck. It exhibits abundant keratin formation with intercellular bridges and various degrees of differentiation. It can be subdivided into well-differentiated (G1), moderately differentiated (G2), or poorly differentiated (G3) grades. WHO type II is a nonkeratinizing form with greater pleomorphism, scant keratin formation, and a variety of patterns. It exhibits a pavemented or stratified pattern with clear cell margins. WHO type III is an undifferentiated tumor, characterized by greater heterogeneity of cell size, indistinct cell borders, and prominent nucleoli. Types II and III both typically demonstrate lymphocytic infiltration; these are endemic forms of NPC and are classically associated with EBV. The clinical implications of the differential types are considerable. In a National Cancer Data Base study of 5,069 patients diagnosed with NPC in the United States between 1985 and 1989, there were substantial differences between 5-year survival of keratinizing (37%) versus nonkeratinizing (65%) and undifferentiated (64%) NPC.

Staging Systems

The epidemiologic idiosyncrasies of NPC are reflected in the controversies surrounding the staging of this disease. All staging of NPC begins with a thorough physical examination including endoscopy. Imaging studies, including computed tomography (CT) and magnetic resonance imaging (MRI), are performed to define soft tissue and bony extension. Ho developed a staging system based on his extensive experience treating NPC in endemic areas of southeastern Asia. His system divides all disease into three T categories that do not account for nasopharyngeal subsite involvement. Ho's staging system divides the neck into three zones, with increasing

N status from superior to inferior. The fourth edition of the American Joint Committee on Cancer (AJCC) staging was developed and applied in the United States, where NPC is nonendemic. It divides all disease into four T categories, including T2 accounting for multiple nasopharyngeal subsite involvement. The neck is treated similarly to other head and neck cancers. The fifth edition of the AJCC staging system sought to combine the value of each staging system by including components of the Ho and AJCC, producing a system simplifying the nasopharyngeal subsites and preserving the vertical stratification of lymph node involvement.

Clincical Presentation

Poor access and confounding early symptoms account for the high proportion of advanced disease at the time of diagnosis. Generally, symptoms fall into one of four general areas of complaint: aural, nasal, neck, and miscellaneous accounted for by cranial nerve (CN) involvement, the most common being CN VI. The classic presentation is a neck mass, particularly in the superior part of the posterior cervical triangle, and conductive hearing loss, often with bloody drainage. Nasopharyngeal carcinoma often arises from the lateral wall of the nasopharynx, near the fossa of Rosenmüller, inducing a serous otitis media as it enlarges and obstructs the eustachian tube.

Nodal involvement is extremely common in NPC, occurring in 75 to 90% of WHO type II and III histologies at the time of diagnosis. In type III, nodal involvement is bilateral in 60% of cases. Distant dissemination is reported by most major series to be between 5 and 11% at the time of presentation.

Diagnosis

The diagnosis of NPC begins with an accurate history and complete physical examination, including endoscopic visualization of the nasopharynx. This is followed by endoscopic examination of the nasopharynx under general anesthesia for the purposes of tumor staging. Patients who present with neck metastases with unknown primaries should have NPC ruled out by direct biopsy. Imaging studies are done for staging. Magnetic resonance imaging is useful for evaluation of muscle, nerve, or intracranial invasion, whereas CT demonstrates bony involvement more reliably. Chest roentgenogram, bone scan, complete blood count, serum chemistries, and liver function tests are recommended.

Treatment

Radiotherapy

Historically, external beam radiotherapy (XRT) has been the standard of treatment for locoregionally confined NPC. In such patients, it is administered with the intent to cure. The location of primary disease with respect to vital structures and the propensity toward bilateral lymphatic metastasis pattern along with the inherent radiosensitivity of NPC have made XRT the primary treatment modality. The entire nasopharynx and bilateral retropharyngeal, jugulodigastric, low neck, posterior chain, and supraclavicular lymph nodes are included in the initial XRT target. At least 45 to 50 Gy at 1.8 to 2.0 Gy per fraction (day) are delivered. The dose to the primary tumor is usually boosted to 66 to 70 Gy based on tumor stage. Because NPC is generally more radiosensitive than other SCCHN, moderate-dose XRT followed by neck dissection is not recommended. However, proven residual disease after full-course XRT should be addressed with neck dissection 6 to 8 weeks following completion of XRT. The M. D. Anderson Cancer Center has reported survival on a consecutive series of 378 patients. Respective actuarial survival rates at 5-, 10-, and 20-year follow-up were 48%, 34%, and 18%. Local control rates with radiation alone for T1, T2, T3, and T4 tumors are 85 to 95%, 80 to 90%, 60 to 75%, and 40 to 60% respectively.

Treatment of the N0 neck is guided by two principles. First, the high probability of neck involvement is unrelated to stage of the primary disease, and bilateral involvement is frequent. Thus, it is not possible to predict reliably a side of disease or which patients may have subclinical local metastases. Second, although salvage surgery of the untreated neck is effective in 80 to 90% of patients, the appearance of disease in the untreated neck is strongly associated with distant metastasis. Because patients without subclinical metastases cannot be distinguished from those with subclinical metastases, coupled with the fact that close surveillance and salvage surgery are associated with adverse outcomes, the elective treatment of the necks of all patients is warranted, even though, inevitably, some patients will be receiving treatment unnecessarily. Regional control rates with radiation alone are good: reported 5-year regional control rates for N0, N1 and 2, and N3 categories are 90 to 100%, 80 to 90%, and 60 to 80%, respectively. It is unclear whether local recurrence increases the risk of distant metastasis.

The ability to achieve focal exposure and relative ease of access to the nasopharynx have generated interest in endocavitary radiotherapy (brachytherapy) as a means of boosting the dose to the primary tumor site following external beam radiotherapy. No phase III studies have been performed to evaluate this modality, and definite indications for endocavitary radiotherapy await further clinical trials.

Predictors of Radiotherapy Failure. The ability to predict which patients are at greatest risk of failure would make it possible to focus more aggressive or adjuvant therapy on those who have the worst prognosis, while sparing those with a favorable outlook the morbidity of aggressive treatment. As expected, T category and N category are well-established predictors of survival. Interestingly, T category is unrelated to risk of distant metastasis; its impact on survival can be attributed to increasing risk of local failure. Conversely, N category exerts its influence on survival through increasing risk of distant metastasis, recognizing that, overall, the risk of neck failure is low. Other strong predictors of failure include more differentiated tumors (WHO type I) and CN involvement.

Complications of Radiotherapy. In modern clinical trials, mucositis is the most frequent radiotherapy acute toxicity, occurring in 18 to 84%. Grade 3 mucositis (< 50%) occurs in 20 to 28% of patients. Long-term complications of radiotherapy include skin and subcutaneous fibrosis, osteoradionecrosis, myelitis, brain necrosis, temporomandibular joint ankylosis, hypopituitarism, sensorineural hearing loss, and bone atrophy

Chemotherapy and Radiotherapy. Because NPC is considered both radiosensitive and chemosensitive, it stands to reason that treatment with chemotherapy and radiotherapy protocols would be tried. Problems with overlapping toxicities had precluded such treatments in the past. However, with advances in XRT delivery, chemotherapeutic agents, and supportive care, chemoradiotherapy protocols have been made possible. Although radiotherapy has been effective for treating early-stage disease, patients with bulky lymphadenopathy or supraclavicular metastases are at greater risk of distant metastases and experience a 5-year survival rate of 10 to 40% with radiotherapy alone. The high incidence of distant metastases combined with the chemosensitivity of NPC make this malignancy an ideal candidate for the addition of chemotherapy to the treatment regimen.

The goal of chemoradiotherapy is to enhance local control of tumor and to address distant metastases that are not included in the field of radiation. To obtain optimal local control results, the two modalities should be delivered as close in time as possible to achieve a synergistic effect. Toxicity becomes the limiting factor in this setting, and drugs with minimal overlapping toxicities with XRT and each other are favored. As for control of distant metastases, there is no synergistic effect, and the timing of administration is unrelated to XRT. The earlier the treatment, however, the smaller will be the micrometastatic tumor deposits.

Neoadjuvant Chemoradiotherapy. Radiation for stage I and II NPC generally does well. For patients with locoregionally advanced NPC with bulky lymph node metastases, in whom local failure and distant metastasis rates are high, the 5-year survival rate ranges from 10 to 40%. Knowing that NPC is chemosensitive, it is logical to add chemotherapy to the treatment regimen in this patient population. Early studies of neoadjuvant chemotherapy using three cycles of cisplatin-containing regimens yielded encouraging results with acceptable toxicities.

Clinical trials using either neoadjuvant or combined neoadjuvant and adjuvant chemoradiotherapy have shown at best an improvement in occurrence of distant metastasis. In one study, the incidence of treatment-related deaths was excessive. Thus, although neoadjuvant and adjuvant chemoradiotherapy may alter the natural history of locoregionally advanced NPC by prolonging disease-free survival, no randomized trials offer evidence of improving overall or disease-specific survival.

Concurrent Chemoradiotherapy. Cisplatin is a good candidate for concomitant treatment because its toxicities do not overlap with those of XRT: myelosuppression is uncommon. Cisplatin was used in a pilot concurrent chemoradiotherapy study with encouraging results. Based on this, a Head and Neck Intergroup study for patients with stage III/IV NPC was initiated; it randomized patients to a standard radiotherapy control arm (2 Gy/fraction to 70 Gy over 7 weeks) or to a concurrent cisplatin and adjuvant cisplatin and 5-fluorouracil group (5-FU) in which cisplatin was given every 3 weeks, totaling three doses during radiotherapy. This was followed by cisplatin and 5-FU for three cycles. After the first planned interim analysis with 138 evaluable patients, the trial was closed. About 25% of patients had type I histologies. At a mean follow-up of 2.7 years, 3-year overall survival rates were 78% and 47% for the chemoradiotherapy and radiotherapy arms. The median progression-free survival was 13 months in the radiotherapy arm compared with 52 months in the chemoradiotherapy arm. No fatal toxicity events related to planned treatment occurred; however, grade 3 to 4 toxicity occurred more frequently in the chemoradiotherapy arm (76 versus 50%). Both progression-free survival and 2-year overall survival were statistically significant in favor of concurrent chemoradiotherapy followed by adjuvant chemotherapy. Because of the rarity of this disease, all stage III and IV patients were included, thus representing a heterogeneous group with respect to T and N classification. Forty-four percent of patients in the radiotherapy arm and 45% of patients in the chemoradiotherapy arm exhibited type III histologies. The applicability of this heterogeneous study population to treatment of patients in endemic areas where up to 90% of histologies can be expected to be type III is unknown. Type I and types II and III differ in their association with EBV as well as in their reported response to radiotherapy, which confounds the applicability of this study to populations from endemic areas. A further limitation of this study is the combination of concomitant cisplatin and adjuvant cisplatin and 5-FU. The contribution of concurrent and adjuvant chemotherapy treatment cannot be separated in this study.

JUVENILE NASOPHARYNGEAL ANGIOFIBROMA

A clinical presentation of epistaxis and nasal obstruction in an adolescent male patient classically represents a juvenile nasopharyngeal angiofibroma (JNA) until proven otherwise. This is a relatively rare sporadic neoplasm that represents approximately 0.05% of all head and neck neoplasms.

Clinically, this tumor may be locally invasive, even eroding adjacent skull base bone. This tumor is nonencapsulated and is highly vascular but has not been shown to be metastatic. Incomplete excision of JNA may result in its recurrence, but often microscopic disease is left after excision, and in the majority of individuals, the neoplasms do not recur. Spontaneous regression of the neoplasm has been identified after incomplete gross excision, but untreated angiofibromas have not been shown to regress spontaneously. Several hypotheses regarding the source of this mass have been advanced, but the origin of this tumor as an aberrance of embryology or as part of a genetic syndrome has never been substantiated. The anatomic site of origin in nearly all cases appears to be in the nasopharynx at the superior aspect of the sphenopalatine foramen. The tumor develops and remains submucosal in a complicated anatomic compartment that defies simple surgical extirpation with generous margins.

Differential Diagnosis

The differential diagnosis of lesions within the nasopharynx in the age group affected by JNA includes both benign and malignant processes. Other benign conditions associated with nasal obstruction include adenoid and turbinate hypertrophy, nasal polyposis, antral choanal polyps, and nasopharyngeal cysts. Other benign neoplasms of the nasopharynx include chordomas, angiomatous polyps, teratomas (eg, dermoids), fibromas, hemangiomas, gliomas, fibrous dysplasia, chondromas, and rhabdomyomas. Soft tissue malignancies in the differential diagnosis include rhabdomyosarcomas, NPCs, and lymphomas.

Clinical Presentation

The average and median ages for the presentation of JNA are 12.5 and 14 years, respectively. Early lesions will present with epistaxis and nasal obstruction. Symptoms and signs have predictive value for the anatomic extent of the disease.

For example, lateral extension may cause serous otitis media, conductive hearing loss, facial deformity including a cheek mass, and proptosis. Cranial nerve findings are rare but may exist and be attributable to involvement of CN I to VI.

Diagnostic Workup

Once the clinical presentation suggests a possible differential diagnosis, a radiologic workup is performed. The MRI is particularly helpful in identifying soft tissue characteristics of the lesion that would increasingly suggest that it is a JNA as opposed to another neoplasm. The lesion will demonstrate contrast enhancement on CT scans and MRI, and any vascular flow voids within the lesion will be identified on MRI. The usual, nearly uniform enhancement of this lesion radiographically distinguishes it from other vascular entities such as arteriovenous malformations. Additionally, other accompanying features of soft tissue, including reactive inflammation of the sinus or nasal mucosa or postobstructive sinusitis, will be well delineated on MRI.

Because of the characteristic clinical presentation and radiographic appearance, few clinicians would feel compelled to obtain tumor biopsies as part of the workup. Clearly, a biopsy of this lesion could lead to massive hemorrhage and is discouraged. Lesions currently undergo preoperative embolization with carotid angiography at many major centers. This technique allows for a decrease in blood loss during surgery by 60 to 80%. Typically, embolization agents are directed via the external carotid circulation through the internal maxillary artery, but significant blood supply can be derived directly from the internal carotid artery and ethmoidal arteries.

Treatment

Surgery

Because JNAs can involve multiple anatomic sites at the skull base, surgical treatment options can be applied on a stage-specific basis. Additionally, the experience and surgical preference of the otolaryngologist or skull base team may affect which approach is chosen for a particular tumor. Endoscopic approaches have been suggested for small tumors, at least for the smallest stage I tumors, and this has become a preferred approach for selected tumors at some institutions. Transpalatal approaches have been used to remove JNA from the nasopharynx when there is limited lateral extent of the tumors. Other surgeons approach lesions of limited extent transfacially through a lateral rhinotomy and medial maxillectomy approach. Midfacial degloving techniques may also be used. Lesions with extension into areas outside the nasopharynx will often require a combination of skull base approaches to gain adequate exposure. Clearly, lateral approaches to the infratemporal fossa are required in resecting lesions with lateral extensions to that region.

Other Modalities

Juvenile nasopharyngeal angiofibromas are known to have recurrence rates up to 25%, and extension of disease into extranasopharyngeal sites correlates with increased rates of recurrence. For these reasons, several investigators have considered additional modalities of treatment for extensive JNA. Some institutions will employ radiation therapy as standard care for intracranial disease extension. Typically, 30 to 40 Gy are used in standard fractions to gain lesion control. Significant further growth of tumor is not noted, but lesions do not completely regress after treatment. Because these tumors are associated with puberty in young males, considerable effort has been expended in hormonal therapies as primary or adjunctive treatment for these tumors. Hormonal therapies for this lesion have included the use of diethylstilbestrol and flutamide.

42

NEOPLASMS OF THE ORAL CAVITY AND OROPHARYNX

Dennis H. Kraus, MD
John K. Joe, MD

This chapter focuses on squamous cell carcinoma, also called epidermoid carcinoma, of the oral cavity and oropharynx. Tumors affecting these regions have significant implications for respiration, deglutition, and speech. The propensity for locoregional recurrence of advanced cancers of the oral cavity or oropharynx necessitates combined therapy, usually surgery and adjuvant radiotherapy.

ANATOMY

The oral cavity is defined as the region from the skin–vermilion junction of the lips to the junction of the hard and soft palate above and to the line of the circumvallate papillae below. The oral cavity includes the lips, buccal mucosa, upper and lower alveolar ridges, retromolar trigone, hard palate, floor of the mouth, and anterior two-thirds of the tongue (oral tongue).

Regional lymph node groups in the neck are grouped into various levels for ease of description. The lateral neck is divided into levels I through V. Metastasis to regional lymph nodes occurs in a predictable fashion through sequential spread. Regional lymph nodes at highest risk for metastases from primary squamous cell carcinomas of the oral cavity include those at levels I, II, and III, collectively known as the supraomohyoid triangle.

The oropharynx is the midportion of the pharynx connecting the nasopharynx above with the hypopharynx below. The oropharynx extends from the plane of the inferior surface of the hard palate to the plane of the superior surface of the hyoid bone and opens anteriorly into the oral cavity. The oropharynx includes the base of the tongue, soft palate, tonsillar regions, and posterior pharyngeal wall.

The primary routes of lymphatic spread from primary tumors of the oropharynx, hypopharynx, and larynx involve deep jugular chain lymph nodes at levels II, III, and IV. Midline structures such as the base of the tongue, soft palate, and posterior pharyngeal wall commonly drain to lymphatic channels in both sides of the neck.

EPIDEMIOLOGY AND ETIOLOGY

In the United States, the incidence of oral cavity and pharyngeal cancer was estimated to number approximately 30,200 new cases in the year 2000, representing 2.5% of all new cases of cancer.

Both tobacco and alcohol abuse independently contribute to the development of cancer of the oral cavity and oropharynx. When present together, however, the combined effects of tobacco and alcohol abuse in the development of oral and oropharyngeal cancer are multiplicative, rather than simply additive.

Geographic differences in tobacco consumption may explain the higher proportion of cancers arising from the oral cavity and oropharynx worldwide, compared to that in the United States. Such cultural practices include reverse smoking, consumption of betel and paan, and bidi smoking.

Other risk factors implicated in carcinoma of the oral cavity and oropharynx include viral infection with human papillomavirus or human immunodeficiency virus (HIV), poor socioeconomic status, neglected oral hygiene, recurrent trauma from ill-fitting dentures, vocal abuse, gastroesophageal reflux, prolonged exposure to sunlight, ionizing radiation, and dietary deficiencies of vitamin A or riboflavin.

PATHOLOGY

The risk of second primary tumors for squamous cell carcinoma of the head and neck is approximately 4% annually, up to 25% at 10 years.

The development of malignant tumors appears to be the result of multiple accumulated genetic alterations. Genetic alterations in the progression to carcinogenesis include activation of proto-oncogenes and the inactivation of tumor suppressor genes. *P53* is a tumor suppressor gene that plays an important role in arresting cell growth in the presence of genetic damage to permit deoxyribonucleic acid (DNA) repair or lead to apoptosis. Mutations in and subsequent inactivation of the *P53* tumor suppressor gene may result in accumulation of DNA damage and uncontrolled cellular growth. It has been shown that the incidence of *P53* mutations increases throughout the progression from premalignant lesions to invasive carcinomas.

Akin to the progression of genetic events leading to phenotypic evidence of malignancy, various precancerous lesions affect the oral cavity and oropharynx, with the potential for malignant degeneration. Leukoplakia is a clinical descriptive term for a white patch in the oral cavity or pharynx that does not rub off. The prevalence of premalignant or malignant transformation is variable but has been estimated at approximately 3.1%.

Erythroplasia appears as a red, slightly raised, granular lesion in the oral cavity and oropharynx. In contrast to the variable incidence of cancer in patients with leukoplakia, erythroplasia has a much higher correlation with concurrent or subsequent malignancy.

Histologically, squamous cell carcinoma may be classified into the following categories: keratinizing, nonkeratinizing, spindle cell, adenoid squamous, and verrucous carcinoma.

Verrucous carcinoma presents as a slowly growing exophytic or warty neoplasm in the oral cavity. Verrucous carcinoma typically affects the buccal mucosa of elderly patients with a history of tobacco exposure or poor oral hygiene. True verrucous carcinoma does not have metastatic potential. The recommended treatment for verrucous carcinoma is wide surgical excision, although irradiation may be considered in selected patients. Anaplastic transformation of verrucous carcinoma has been reported to occur following radiation therapy, but this theory is controversial.

MECHANISMS OF CANCER SPREAD

In general, lesions in the posterior part of the oral cavity have a higher predilection for regional lymph node metastases than those lesions situated more anteriorly in the oral cavity. There is an increased risk for bilateral or contralateral metastases from primary tumors arising from midline structures, such as the midline lip, floor of the mouth, oral tongue, base of the tongue, soft palate, and posterior pharyngeal wall. The 5-year survival rate of patients with cervical lymph node metastases is approximately 50% that of patients without regional lymph node metastases.

Extracapsular spread of carcinoma in cervical lymph nodes portends a poor prognosis. Extracapsular extension has been associated with increased rates of regional nodal recurrence as well as significantly decreased survival rates. Other negative prognostic factors with regard to regional metastases include an increased number of involved lymph nodes, as well as spread of tumor to lymph node levels more inferiorly in the neck.

Distant metastases from cancers of the oral cavity and oropharynx generally do not occur until advanced stages of disease. Distant metastases typically involve first the lungs or bones.

EVALUATION

The first step when evaluating a patient with cancer of the oral cavity or oropharynx is a thorough history and comprehensive examination of the head and neck. The patient should be asked about symptoms of dysphagia, odynophagia, dysarthria, globus sensation, difficulty breathing, hemoptysis, otalgia (possibly referred), weight loss, or other constitutional symptoms and about consumption of tobacco and alcohol, occupational exposures (including exposure to sunlight), and previous radiation exposure.

There is no substitute for a systematic, comprehensive examination of the neck, but imaging techniques such as computed tomography (CT) or magnetic resonance imaging (MRI) may provide valuable supplemental information regarding the status of regional lymph nodes.

Pathologic confirmation by fine-needle aspiration biopsy is critical for any suspicious neck mass.

Evaluation of the mandible for bony invasion by tumor may be best accomplished by clinical examination, although useful supplemental information may be provided by panoramic films and DentaScan imaging.

Endoscopic examination of the upper aerodigestive tract under anesthesia provides both thorough inspection of the primary tumor and evaluation for second primary tumors, with the ability to biopsy suspicious sites. The oropharynx, hypopharynx, larynx, and esophagus should be examined in a systematic fashion.

TREATMENT

The primary objective in treating patients with squamous cell carcinoma of the oral cavity or oropharynx should focus on rendering the patient free of disease. In general, early-stage lesions may be treated by surgery or radiation with comparable results, and more advanced cancers are best approached with combined therapy. Further investigation into the benefit of chemotherapy for carcinoma of the oral cavity and oropharynx is warranted as it currently plays a supplemental role to the established treatment modalities, surgery and radiation.

An issue of ongoing controversy concerns the management of the neck in patients without clinical evidence of regional nodal metastases (the N0 neck). Elective neck dissection has been shown to improve locoregional control and may therefore positively impact the quality of the patient's survival. In light of the morbidity associated with the radical neck dissection, there has been a trend toward selective, rather than comprehensive, neck dissection, based on the predictable pattern of cervical lymph node metastases. Selective neck dissection has been demonstrated to be an oncologically sound procedure, providing effective treatment for the N0 neck. Supraomohyoid neck dissection (SOHND), selective lymphadenectomy clearing cervical nodal levels I, II, and III, has been recommended for N0 patients with primary squamous cell carcinomas of the oral cavity.

Based on the predictable spread of cervical nodal metastases, SOHND may not be sufficient for the N0 neck with a primary arising in the oropharynx. The risk for level IV spread is higher from primary tumors of the oropharynx compared with those arising from the oral cavity. Thus, an antero-lateral neck dissection encompassing levels II, III, and IV of the deep jugular chain has been advocated for N0 necks with an oropharyngeal primary.

For the clinically positive neck, the traditional surgical procedure of choice has been comprehensive neck dissection with preservation of cranial nerve XI when technically feasible. The continuing evolution of a more selective approach to the neck, however, has included the clinically positive neck as well. Comprehensive neck dissection, with preservation of cranial nerve XI, the sternocleidomastoid muscle, and the internal jugular vein, may be performed for N1, N2a, or N2b disease when technically feasible. Supraomohyoid neck dissection may be acceptable for N1 disease without extracapsular extension arising from primaries of the oral cavity, particularly when the involved node is at level I.

SPECIFIC SITES IN THE ORAL CAVITY

Squamous cell carcinoma of the *lip* by virtue of its location tends to present at an early stage. The lower lip is affected more commonly, presumably secondary to sunlight exposure. Comparable cure rates have been reported for small tumors using either surgery or radiation therapy, but surgical excision is the treatment of choice in most instances owing to its lower morbidity and better cosmetic result. Regional metastases from carcinoma of the lip are uncommon except in advanced lesions, recurrent lesions, or lesions arising at the oral commissure. When lymphatic spread arises from midline lip lesions, bilateral nodal metastases are more prevalent.

Treatment planning for carcinoma of the *buccal mucosa* is similar to that for cancers of the lip. Surgical resection is recommended for stage I and II tumors, with combination therapy using surgery and postoperative radiotherapy for stage III and IV tumors.

Tumors of the *alveolar ridge* typically present with soreness or gum pain, ulceration, intraoral bleeding, loosening of teeth, or ill-fitting dentures. Surgery is recommended as the primary treatment modality for early cancers, with the addition of postoperative radiotherapy for advanced lesions.

Branches from the glossopharyngeal (IX) nerve provide sensory innervation to the retromolar trigone, so patients with carcinoma of the *retromolar trigone* may present complaining of pain referred to the ipsilateral ear. Numbness in the distribution of the inferior alveolar nerve may be observed if tumor invades the mandible. Trismus may result from invasion of the pterygoid musculature. Extension into the pterygopalatine fossa may lead to disease at the skull base. The proximity of the structures of the oropharynx, including the base of the tongue, soft palate, and tonsil, places them at risk for tumor involvement by direct extension.

Presenting symptoms of cancer of the *hard palate* include pain, bleeding, improper denture fit, or altered speech. Patients often delay for 3 to 6 months before presenting for treatment. For early-stage lesions, no differences have been shown between single-modality treatment using either surgery or irradiation, so selection of therapy should be based on the anatomic location and extent of disease, the presence of second primaries, and associated patient comorbidities. Surgery followed by adjuvant radiotherapy is recommended for advanced-stage disease. Regional lymphatic drainage from the hard palate is sparse, so metastases to cervical lymph nodes are uncommon.

By virtue of their location, cancers of the *floor of the mouth* may remain undetected until progressing to advanced disease. Large bulky tumors may affect normal speech and deglutition. Patients may complain of pain referred to the ipsilateral ear from tumor involvement of the lingual nerve extending to the main trunk of the mandibular nerve (V3). Advanced tumors may invade the tongue or mandible by direct extension. Elective treatment of the neck is warranted in carcinoma of the floor of the mouth owing to the significant incidence of occult nodal metastases. The risk of contralateral nodal metastases is significant with floor of the mouth cancer, and multiple levels are often involved. Surgery is recommended for early-stage lesions, whereas combined surgery and postoperative radiotherapy are the treatment of choice for advanced floor of the mouth cancers.

Common presenting symptoms and signs for carcinoma of the *oral tongue* include localized pain and the presence of an ulcer, frequently at the middle third of the tongue. Patients may report dysarthria or pain with eating. As with the floor of the mouth, cancers of the oral tongue may present with referred pain in the ipsilateral ear owing to involvement of the mandibular nerve (V3). Surgical resection is typically employed for stage I and II lesions, whereas combined therapy using surgery and postoperative radiotherapy is indicated for stage III and IV disease. Occult metastases in regional lymphatics are common with carcinoma of the tongue, particularly when the depth of the primary tumor is greater than 2 mm thick. The risk of regional metastases approaches 40% in this group of patients, necessitating elective treatment of the N0 neck with carcinoma of the oral tongue.

The pectoralis major myocutaneous flap provides well-vascularized soft tissue for reconstructing oral cavity defects in a single stage. The radial forearm free flap and rectus abdominis free flap are two types of free tissue transfer useful for intraoral soft tissue reconstuction. Mandibular defects may be successfully reconstructed with composite bone flaps, including the fibular osteocutaneous free flap or iliac crest osteocutaneous free flap.

SPECIFIC SITES IN THE OROPHARYNX

Typical of cancers of the oropharynx, *base of the tongue* cancers often present at an advanced stage of disease. Overall, 62% of patients present with nodal metastases, and contralateral or bilateral nodal involvement is frequently seen.

A variety of treatment options for base of the tongue cancer have been proposed, including surgery with or without postoperative radiotherapy, primary external beam radiotherapy, external beam radiation therapy with brachytherapy implantation with or without neck dissection, and induction chemotherapy with external beam radiation therapy with or without brachytherapy.

For cancers of the *soft palate*, either surgery or radiotherapy provides good local control and survival rates in early-stage (stages I and II) tumors. Combination therapy, using surgical resection followed by adjuvant radiation therapy, is recommended for stage III and IV tumors.

Of all of the tumors in the oral cavity and oropharynx, cancers of the *tonsil* are the most radiosensitive, particularly exophytic lesions. Stage I and II tumors may be best approached with primary radiotherapy, recognizing the potential for occult nodal metastases. Treatment planning for stage III and IV tumors is slightly more complicated as the method of choice may differ depending on the particular situation. A small tonsil primary with extensive nodal metastases may be treated with primary radiotherapy with consideration for neck dissection. In contrast, a large primary tumor at the tonsillar region without regional lymph node metastases could be approached with combination surgery and postoperative radiotherapy or with combination chemotherapy and irradiation.

Cancers of the *posterior pharyngeal wall* commonly present with dysphagia and odynophagia. Alternatively, the patient may complain of a globus sensation or change in voice. Both surgery and radiation have been singly employed, often with disappointing results. Although the data are sparse, it appears that combination therapy of surgery and postoperative radiotherapy may be indicated, particularly for advanced disease.

Advanced lesions of the oropharynx necessitating a mandibulotomy approach with mandibular preservation may require flap reconstruction to resurface the inner portion of the mandible. The thin, pliable nature of the radial forearm free flap makes it a preferable choice over the pectoralis major myocutaneous flap for reconstruction in this region.

43

DISEASES OF THE SALIVARY GLANDS

William R. Carroll, MD
C. Elliott Morgan, DMD, MD

The spectrum of diseases involving the salivary glands includes infections, localized and systemic inflammatory processes, and benign and malignant tumors.

The *parotid gland* is located in the space between the ramus of the mandible and the external auditory canal and mastoid tip. The anterior portion of the gland overlies the masseter muscle, and the posterior portion overlies the sternocleidomastoid muscle. The deep, medial portion of the gland is adjacent to the parapharyngeal space. The parotid gland is covered by the parotid fascia. This layer is an extension of the superficial layer of the deep cervical fascia that splits to envelop the gland. The parotid duct (Stensen's duct) exits anteriorly, reaches the anterior aspect of the masseter muscle to pierce the buccinator muscle, and enters the oral cavity opposite the second upper molar tooth.

The position of the facial nerve is the dominant consideration in surgery of the parotid gland. As the nerve exits the stylomastoid foramen, it enters the posterior and medial portion of the gland, usually as a single trunk. Its primary bifurcation occurs at the pes anserinus with subsequent secondary division into five facial and cervical branches. The nerve lies within the substance of the gland. In our opinion, the most reliable way to find the main trunk of the facial nerve is by identification of the tympanomastoid suture. Looking at a skull, the tympanomastoid suture extends medially along the skull base until it ends at the stylomastoid foramen. The stylomastoid foramen is almost always within the suture line.

The *submandibular gland* is located within the submandibular triangle of the neck. Like the parotid gland, it is covered with a fascial capsule, which originates from the superficial layer of the deep cervical fascia. The marginal mandibular branch of the facial nerve often overlies the lateral aspect of the submandibular gland. It is positioned in a plane deep to the platysma muscle but superficial to the submandibular gland fascia.

The anterior border of the submandibular gland is folded over the posterior border of the mylohyoid muscle, creating portions of the gland both superficial and deep to the mylohyoid muscle. The lingual nerve is located just medial and superior to the gland within the sublingual space. The hypoglossal nerve courses between the medial portion of the submandibular gland and the hypoglossus muscle deep to the digastric muscle. The submandibular gland duct (Wharton's duct) arises from the medial aspect of the gland and proceeds submucosally in the floor of the mouth medial to the sublingual gland to reach its papilla at the side of the frenulum of the tongue.

The *sublingual glands* are located submucosally in the floor of the mouth. They are paired structures and nearly meet in the anterior part of the floor of the mouth. Typically, there is no single duct draining the submandibular glands. Rather, there are 10 to 12 smaller ducts that pass directly into the mucosa of the floor of the mouth.

There are hundreds of small, unnamed *minor salivary glands* distributed throughout the upper aerodigestive tract. These glands are both mucus and serous producing, and each has its own small duct draining directly to the mucous membrane. The minor salivary glands are most prominent in the oral cavity and are located in the hard and soft palate, lips, buccal mucosa, floor of the mouth, and tongue.

INFLAMMATORY DISEASES OF THE SALIVARY GLANDS

Viral Infections (Mumps)

Mumps (epidemic parotitis) is a disease of viral origin that most commonly occurs in the pediatric age group. Viral parotitis is usually caused by a paramyxovirus (specifically the *Rubulavirus*), but many viral pathogens may cause acute infections within salivary glands. Typical symptoms include fever, malaise, and headaches, followed by tenderness and enlargement of the parotid glands. The most common complication from paramyxovirus parotitis is orchitis, occurring in 20 to 30% of males. Oophoritis occurs in 5% of females. Involvement of the germinal tissues does not usually cause sterility. Aseptic meningitis is a complication in about 10% of patients with viral parotitis. Pancreatitis occurs in 5%. Treatment of viral salivary gland infection is supportive. Live attenuated mumps vaccine as part of mumps, measles, rubella (MMR) immunization is given to children after 12 months of age.

Sjögren's Syndrome

Sjögren's syndrome is a chronic autoimmune disorder of the exocrine glands, which affects predominantly, but not exclusively, the salivary glands. It is the second most common autoimmune disease, trailing only rheumatoid arthritis. Women in the fourth to fifth decade of life constitute 90% of cases.

The most common symptom of Sjögren's syndrome is xerostomia (dry mouth). The decreased salivation causes difficulty with swallowing, altered taste, and speech difficulties. Long-term xerostomia causes an increase in dental caries. Ocular involvement in Sjögren's syndrome is characterized as keratoconjunctivitis sicca. Sjögren's syndrome may progress to multisystem involvement. The systemic symptoms are linked to connective tissue disease. Rheumatoid arthritis occurs in 50% of patients with Sjögren's syndrome.

Asymmetric enlargement of the parotid that persists or is rapid in onset should raise suspicion of lymphoma. Patients have 44 times greater risk of developing lymphoma after developing Sjögren's syndrome. Parotid enlargement in the presence of splenomegaly, lymphadenopathy, immunosuppression, or previous radiation should raise suspicion for lymphoma.

Salivary tissue biopsy is the most commonly employed method for diagnosing Sjögren's syndrome. Histologic diagnosis is based on the presence of more than one cluster of greater than 50 lymphocytes per 4 mm^2. Lip biopsy has the highest specificity (95%), sensitivity (58 to 100%), positive predictive value, and negative predictive value of all tests for Sjögren's syndrome.

Human Immunodeficiency Virus

Patients infected with the human immunodeficiency virus (HIV) may develop a spectrum of salivary gland disorders, including diffuse infiltrative lymphocytosis, benign lymphoepithelial lesions, lymphoepithelial cysts, and malignant salivary gland tumors, including lymphoma, Kaposi's sarcoma, and adenoid cystic carcinoma.

Lymphoepithelial cysts may occur unilaterally or bilaterally in the parotid glands. Multiple lymphoepithelial cysts are so characteristic of HIV infection as to be considered almost pathognomonic. The pathogenesis of the cysts is unknown, and they can occur at any stage of the disease.

Sarcoidosis

The salivary glands are involved in 6 to 10% of patients with sarcoidosis. The parotid gland is involved most commonly.

Heerfordt's syndrome (uveoparotid fever) results from sarcoidosis and includes uveitis, lacrimal and salivary gland inflammation, and facial paralysis. The diagnosis is one of exclusion because the noncaseating granulomas are not pathognomonic for the disease. Anemia, thrombocytopenia, leukopenia, eosinophilia, decreased albumin, and hyperglobulinemia support the diagnosis. Elevated angiotensin converting enzyme levels, sedimentation rates, and calcium levels may also be present. Hilar adenopathy may be present on a chest radiograph. Corticosteroids are used to treat patients with more advanced forms of sarcoidosis.

Wegener's Granulomatosis

Wegener's granulomatosis is a systemic disorder often involving the respiratory tract from the nose to the lungs, as well as the kidneys. Wegener's granulomatosis affects both sexes equally, occurs in all ages, and is usually seen in Caucasians. Histologically, Wegener's granulomatosis is characterized by vasculitis of medium and small vessels.

More than 70% of the features associated with Wegener's granulomatosis are related to the ears, nose, and throat. Symptoms develop insidiously, with sinusitis being the most frequent presentation. Salivary gland enlargement may accompany the nasal and sinus symptoms, with the parotid or submandibular glands, or both, being affected. Subglottic stenosis commonly occurs. In the lower airway, pulmonary infiltrates or cavitary nodules are also noted. Renal involvement indicates systemic Wegener's granulomatosis and is the most frequent cause of death.

Intranasal biopsies should be taken with a generous section of viable nasal mucosa. These can be taken from the turbinate, septum, or lateral nasal wall. The specimen should be examined for fungal microorganisms as well. Wegener's granulomatosis must be differentiated from other granulomatous diseases including polymorphic reticulosis, Churg-

Strauss syndrome, lymphoma, sarcoidosis, scleroma, tuberculosis, relapsing polychondritis, and fungal disease.

The "gold standard" for treatment of Wegener's granulomatosis is cyclophosphamide and glucocortoids. Methotrexate has been used with corticosteroids in milder forms of Wegener's granulomatosis. Upper airway involvement responds well to trimethoprim and sulfamethoxazole used in combination with cyclophosphamide and glucocorticoids.

Acute and Chronic Bacterial Infections of the Salivary Glands

Acute bacterial sialadenitis may involve any salivary gland, although the parotid gland is affected most frequently. Suppurative infection of the salivary glands may be an isolated, acute event or a chronic event with recurrent acute exacerbations.

Acute bacterial infection of the salivary glands may occur either by retrograde transmission of bacteria from the oral cavity or by stasis of salivary flow. Saliva contains lysozyme and immunoglobulin A, which protect the salivary glands from infection. Stone formation (sialolithiasis) may cause mechanical obstruction of the salivary duct, causing stasis of flow with resultant bacterial infection. Elderly patients are at high risk for salivary gland infection owing to medications that decrease salivary flow. These medications include diuretics, antidepressants, beta blockers, anticholinergics, and antihistamines. Patients with chronic, debilitating conditions, patients with compromised immune function, HIV-positive patients, anorexic and bulimic patients, and depressed patients are at an increased risk for acute bacterial salivary gland infection. Xerostomia of any cause increases the risk for bacterial parotitis.

Staphylococcus aureus is the most common microorganism causing acute bacterial parotitis. Other microorganisms include beta-hemolytic streptococcus, *Haemophilus influen-*

zae, *Streptococcus pneumoniae*, and, less frequently, gram-negative microorganisms.

Symptoms of acute bacterial sialadenitis include rapid onset of pain, swelling, induration, and fever. The symptoms may worsen during eating. Examination reveals induration, erythema, edema and tenderness over the gland, and purulence at the ductal orifice. Bacterial sialadenitis may progress to abscess formation. Treatment of acute sialadenitis is directed at improving salivary flow. Antibiotic therapy should be directed toward the gram-positive and anaerobic microorganisms commonly involved.

Chronic Sialadenitis

Patients with chronic sialadenitis experience recurrent, low-grade inflammation and edema of the gland, minor pain, and sialorrhea that may be slightly purulent. *Streptococcus viridans* is the usual infecting microorganism. Measures to increase salivary flow should be instituted and appropriate antibiotics given. Attempts to identify stones or duct strictures should be made.

SALIVARY GLAND NEOPLASMS

Benign Salivary Gland Neoplasms

Pleomorphic Adenoma

Pleomorphic adenoma or benign mixed tumor is the most common salivary tumor, accounting for up to two-thirds of all salivary gland neoplasms. Approximately 85% of all pleomorphic adenomas are located in the parotid glands, 10% in the minor salivary glands, and 5% in the submandibular glands. Pleomorphic adenomas contain both mesenchymal and epithelial cells. Abnormalities are found in chromosome 8q12. This region is the site of the pleomorphic adenoma gene *PLAG1*. Grossly, the tumors appear encapsulated but, on close inspection, have pseudopod extensions into the surrounding tissues. This growth pattern is thought to be responsible for the high rate of local recurrence (approximately 30%) when these tumors are enucleated. Adequate surgical therapy involves nerve identification and protection with removal of the tumor and an adequate cuff of surrounding parotid gland parenchyma.

Warthin's Tumor

Warthin's tumor or papillary cystadenoma lymphomatosum is the second most common benign neoplasm of the salivary glands. Interestingly, Warthin's tumor occurs almost exclusively in the parotid glands. It typically involves the lower pole of the parotid gland and may be bilateral in up to 10% of cases. The most popular etiologic theory suggests that Warthin's tumor arises in salivary ducts that are trapped within intraparotid lymph nodes. The recommended treatment for Warthin's tumor is complete surgical excision similar to that described for pleomorphic adenoma.

Monomorphic Adenomas

Monomorphic adenomas include basal cell adenoma, clear cell adenoma, and glycogen-rich adenoma among other less common tumors. The most common monomorphic adenoma is the basal cell adenoma, which comprises 1 to 3% of salivary gland neoplasms. Treatment of monomorphic adenomas includes wide surgical excision with an adequate cuff of normal surrounding tissue.

Oncocytomas

Oncocytomas comprise less than 1% of all salivary gland neoplasms. Oncocytomas are grossly encapsulated, single lesions. Histologically, the tumors are composed of large cells with round nuclei. Treatment of oncocytoma involves wide local excision with a cuff of surrounding gland parenchyma. Rarely, malignant oncocytomas are detected. Cytologic differentiation from benign oncocytoma can be difficult, and malignancy is usually defined by invasive clinical and histologic features.

Hemangiomas

Hemangiomas are the most common tumor arising in the salivary gland from the connective tissue elements. They are the most common salivary gland tumor of any type in children and are often detected within the first year of life. Hemangiomas often occur over the angle of the mandible, and the overlying skin may contain a bluish discoloration. Engorgement of the lesion with crying or straining is often also seen. Most hemangiomas in the salivary glands undergo spontaneous resolution.

Malignant Tumors of the Salivary Glands

Salivary gland malignancies make up a relatively small percentage of all cancer occurring in the head and neck region. Spiro and colleagues analyzed over 7,000 reported salivary gland neoplasms. Seventy-eight percent of the parotid neoplasms, 54% of the submandibular neoplasms, and 35% of the minor salivary gland neoplasms were benign. Radiation exposure is one known risk factor, and there seems to be a dose-response relationship for the development of malignant tumors. Pain is present in 10 to 29% of patients with cancer in the parotid gland, and facial paralysis is detected in 10 to 15% of parotid gland malignancies. Of malignant neoplasms, 35% were mucoepidermoid carcinomas, 23% were adenoid cystic carcinoma, 18% were adenocarcinoma, 13% were malignant mixed tumor, and 7% were acinic cell carcinoma.

Mucoepidermoid Carcinoma

Mucoepidermoid carcinoma is the most common malignant salivary gland tumor. Approximately one-half of all mucoepidermoid carcinomas occur in the parotid gland, with the majority of the remainder occurring in minor salivary glands.

As the name implies, mucoepidermoid carcinomas are composed of both mucus and epidermoid cells. Histologic grading of mucoepidermoid carcinoma has correlated with prognosis. High-grade tumors recur locally nearly 60% of the time, develop lymph node metastases 40 to 70% and distant metastases 30% of the time, and have 5-year survival rates of 30 to 50%. In contrast, low-grade mucoepidermoid carcinomas have 5-year survival rates in the 80 to 95% range. They are much less likely to develop nodal or distant metastasis.

For low-grade mucoepidermoid carcinoma, treatment usually involves wide surgical excision. Neck dissection or adjuvant irradiation is used only when clinically evident metastases are detected or when there is evidence of bone, nerve, or extraglandular invasion. In contrast, high-grade mucoepidermoid carcinomas are treated more like squamous cell carcinomas. Wide surgical excision combined with regional lymph node dissection and adjuvant radiation therapy is commonplace.

Adenoid Cystic Carcinoma

Adenoid cystic carcinoma is the second most common malignancy of the salivary glands. It is the most common malignancy in the submandibular glands and minor salivary glands. The most common clinical presentation for adenoid cystic carcinoma is a painless, slowly enlarging mass. However, paresthesias and paralysis are more common with adenoid cystic carcinoma than other salivary malignancies. Indeed, perineural invasion and spread are hallmarks of adenoid cystic carcinoma. The prognosis of adenoid cystic carcinoma may be related to histologic grade. Those patients with low-grade tumors have slow disease progression and infrequent distant metastasis. Patients with high-grade malignancies experience much more rapid growth, with higher frequency of distant metastasis and decreased survival. The early trend toward better survival with low-grade lesions disappears as the patient follow-up exceeds 10 years. In other words, disease progression was slower and less fulminant but relentless and equally deadly. Fifteen- to 20-year survival rates are in the 30% range regardless of histologic grade.

Treatment of adenoid cystic carcinoma includes wide local excision of primary disease and therapeutic lymph node dissection. Elective node dissections are not typically recommended. Radiation therapy is usually recommended postoperatively. Fast neutron radiotherapy has proven effective for recurrent or unresectable adenocystic carcinoma. In the University of Washington series, when patients were able to undergo surgical resection (even if microscopic margins were not clear) and there was no direct skull base involvement, 5-year regional control rates of 80% were achieved.

Polymorphous Low-Grade Adenocarcinoma
Polymorphous low-grade adenocarcinoma (PLGA) typically arises from the minor salivary glands and is frequently seen in the oral cavity. The palate is the most common location for PLGA. It may be confused with pleomorphic adenoma on the benign side and with adenoid cystic carcinoma on the more malignant side. Proper treatment of PLGA is surgical.

Acinic Cell Carcinoma
Acinic cell carcinoma is reasonably rare and comprises roughly 1 to 3% of all salivary gland tumors. Most acinic cell carcinomas are found in the parotid gland, where they compose 12 to 17% of parotid malignancies. Bilateral parotid gland involvement has been reported in up to 3% of cases. The biologic behavior may range from slow indolent local growth to a more aggressive form with rapid growth and the potential for distant metastasis. Treatment of acinic cell carcinoma is wide surgical excision.

Malignant Mixed Tumors

This somewhat confusing group of tumors contains at least three distinct tumor types: carcinoma ex pleomorphic adenoma, malignant mixed tumor (carcinosarcoma), and benign metastasizing pleomorphic adenoma. Carcinoma ex pleomorphic adenoma is the most common of these three. This tumor represents malignant transformation of the epithelial component of a pleomorphic adenoma. The risk of malignant transformation increases from 1.5 to approximately 9.5% over the 5 to 15 years' duration of the pleomorphic adenoma. The biologic behavior of carcinoma ex pleomorphic adenoma is generally more aggressive than other salivary gland malignancies. Treatment is wide local excision with consideration of lymph node dissection and postoperative radiation therapy. Five- and 10-year survival rates are 40 and 24%, respectively.

Malignant mixed tumor is less common and contains malignant epithelial and mesenchymal components. This is a true carcinosarcoma, and both components of the malignancy are evident in metastatic sites. The sarcomatous component is often differentiated as a chondrosarcoma, but other types of sarcoma are also described. Treatment is wide surgical excision and radiation. Distant metastases are common, and the prognosis is poor.

Metastasizing pleomorphic adenoma represents an unusual lesion in which benign-appearing pleomorphic adenoma appears in regional lymph nodes. A 22% mortality rate is associated with this development. There is a suggestion that the risk of developing metastasizing pleomorphic adenoma increases with the longevity of the original tumor and with local recurrence.

Squamous Cell Carcinoma

Primary squamous cell carcinoma of the salivary glands is rare. Squamous cell carcinoma is much more commonly metastatic to the parotid gland parenchyma or intraparotid lymph nodes. The diagnosis of squamous cell carcinoma within the salivary gland should always trigger an intensive search for a primary lesion.

44

DISEASES OF THE THYROID AND PARATHYROID GLANDS

Robert A. Hendrix, MD

The normal adult thyroid gland weighs 20 to 25 g and is slightly larger in women. It contains two types of functioning endocrine cells of different origins. The follicular cells secrete L-thyroxine (T_4) and 3,5,3'-triiodothyronine (T_3), which influence a wide range of metabolic processes. The parafollicular cells or C cells influence calcium metabolism by secretion of calcitonin (CT).

The lumina of follicles of the thyroid contain the glycoprotein thyroglobulin as a colloid. The follicles secrete only 20% of serum T_3; dehalogenation of circulating T_4 produces the remainder. The concentration of unbound T_3 is about 10 times greater than unbound T_4 because of different affinities for thyroid-binding globulin (TBG) and other plasma proteins. Nonetheless, plasma proteins reversibly bind almost all of the serum T_3 and T_4, leaving only 0.3% of T_3 and 0.03% of T_4 (or one-tenth the level of T_3) free to act on receptor sites. The metabolic effects and the regulation of thyroid hormone depend solely on the concentration of free or unbound T_4 and T_3 in plasma. Approximately one-third of the T_4 is deiodinated to T_3, and *T_3 is three times more potent than T_4*. Thus, T_4 exerts most of its metabolic effects through its conversion to T_3.

Thyrotropin (thyroid-stimulating hormone, TSH) is a glycoprotein secreted by basophilic (thyrotropin) cells of the anterior pituitary gland. Thyroid-stimulating hormone mediates suprathyroid regulation of thyroid hormone secretion. Stimulation of the thyrotropin receptor leads to increase of cyclic adenosine monophosphate (cAMP) by activating the adenylate cyclase system. Follicular cell growth and function are both stimulated by the "second messenger" cAMP. Hypothalamic secretion of thyrotropin-releasing hormone (TRH) controls TSH secretion. Free thyroid hormones in serum exert negative feedback at the level of the pituitary by inhibiting TSH secretion and antagonizing TRH. At the level of the thyroid gland, iodine depletion enhances the responsiveness to TSH, whereas iodine enrichment inhibits the TSH response.

Calcitonin is a 32-amino-acid polypeptide transcribed from a locus on chromosome 11p, which is tightly linked with the gene for parathyroid hormone (PTH), parathormone. The action of CT is independent of PTH and vitamin D. The main endocrine effect is to decrease the number and activity of osteoclasts, thereby reducing bone resorption. Calcitonin affects fetal bone metabolism and skeletal growth and remains at high levels in cord blood as well as in young children. Levels are very low in older children and adults, in whom it has little consequence to metabolism.

Serum Tests Related to Thyroid Hormone

The most widely used serum assays of thyroid hormone are the T_4 radioimmunoassay (RIA), T_3 uptake of resin, and free T_4 (FT_4). Thyroxine RIA, as a measure of total serum T_4, has a normal range of 5 to 13 mg/dL. Free T_4 measures the metabolically effective fraction of circulating T_4. It provides the best assay of thyroid hormones in regard to function because it is not affected by TBG. Free T_4 may be estimated from the more commonly available FT_4 index, equal to the product of the T_4 and the T_3 uptake of resin. However, this calculation is unnecessary if the FT_4 test is available.

Thyroxine-binding globulin RIA is a specific test for T_4-binding abnormalities and is unaffected by changes in other serum proteins.

The measurement of serum TSH concentration by radioimmunoassay is useful to evaluate hyperfunction of the thyroid gland. Most evaluations of thyroid function should start with a sensitive thyrotropin assay. In a patient with little clinical probability of thyroid dysfunction, a normal TSH screen requires no further testing. If TSH is elevated, an FT_4 and possibly a thyroid antibody should be performed to evaluate for hypothyroidism. If TSH is low, then an FT_4 and possibly a T_3 should be performed to evaluate hyperthyroidism. However, in elderly patients, a low TSH assay may not be associated with hyperthyroidism.

In general, an elevated TSH and a low FT_4 suggest primary hypothyroidism, an elevated TSH and an elevated FT_4 suggest secondary (pituitary) hyperthyroidism or inappropriate T_4 ingestion, a low TSH and a high FT_4 suggest primary hyperthyroidism, and a low TSH and a low FT_4 suggest pituitary insufficiency.

Direct Tests of Function

The most commonly used direct test of gland function is the thyroid radioactive iodine uptake (RAIU). Iodine 123 (^{123}I) has become the agent of choice because of lower radiation dosages. It is administered orally in capsule form 24 hours before measurement of thyroid accumulation of isotope. In the thyroid suppression test, the RAIU is repeated after 7 days of daily administration of T_3. A decrease in the RAIU is evidence of the presence of thyroid suppression. This is of value in the assessment of glandular hyperfunction. In the thyrotropin stimulation test (RAIU performed following TSH administration), primary thyroid insufficiency can be distinguished from thyroid hypofunction caused by pituitary hypofunction.

Imaging of the Thyroid Gland

Closely related to the RAIU is the thyroid scintiscan by gamma camera 24 hours after administration of ^{123}I. To evaluate metastatic thyroid cancer or a substernal thyroid, ^{131}I should be used to overcome photon attenuation by bone.

B-mode (two-dimensional) ultrasonography is a useful adjunctive tool for the evaluation of thyroid masses, particularly in children or pregnant women in whom radioactive isotopes are undesirable. The chief importance of ultrasonography is to distinguish between cystic and solid lesions, particularly in goiter.

A computed tomographic (CT) scan with iodinated contrast interferes with performance of the radioactive iodide uptake and scan for up to 6 weeks. Thyroid scans and RAIU should therefore be performed before CT with contrast. Positron emission tomography is a promising modality. When measuring uptake of [^{18F}]-fluorodeoxyglucose in thyroid nodules, increased uptake was seen in malignant lesions.

Fine-Needle Aspiration Biopsy

Fine-needle aspiration biopsy has become the diagnostic study of choice for all solitary thyroid nodules, for nodules within multinodular goiters that grow rapidly or steadily or have a worrisome texture, or for diffusely enlarged thyroids with localized nodules. This office procedure requires a 10 mL syringe with a fine needle (21 or 22 gauge) passed through alcohol-prepared skin to a palpable nodule or area of interest in the thyroid during continuous aspiration. The specimen may be smeared on a slide and sprayed immediately with fixative or submitted in appropriate media (eg, Carbowax) for later examination. Sensitivity ranges from 75 to 93.5% and specificity from 75 to 100%. However, malignancy can be present in up to 15% of indeterminate specimens and 11% of negative specimens.

The gross appearance of aspirated fluid often yields diagnostic information: clear fluid suggests a parathyroid cyst; yellow fluid suggests a transudate; chocolate, green, or turbid fluid suggests degeneration; and bloody fluid suggests a rapidly growing tumor or the aspiration of a vessel.

Disorders of the Thyroid Glands

Goiter

Goiter is an enlargement of the thyroid gland resulting in swelling in the front of the neck. An enlarged thyroid gland becomes palpable when the volume of the gland is doubled, and a visible goiter is usually at least three times the normal thyroid mass of 20 g.

Simple (Nontoxic) Goiter. During puberty and pregnancy, the thyroid gland normally undergoes a diffuse enlargement. This is related in part to increased estrogens and subsequent increase in TBG. This condition is usually self-limited and rarely requires treatment. The term endemic goiter is applicable when 10% or more of the population has generalized or localized thyroid enlargement. It generally reflects a dietary deficiency of iodide particular to a geographic region, causing insufficient thyroid hormone secretion. Twenty-five percent of goiters occur in more developed countries. These so-called "sporadic goiters" arise largely from iodine-sufficient conditions including autoimmune thyroiditis, hypo- or hyperthyroidism, and thyroid carcinoma.

Nodular Goiter. The cause of nodular goiter is poorly understood but may be related to varying levels of TSH over a lifetime. Prevalence increases with advancing age. Multinodular goiter occurs in 4% in the United States (with a female-to-male ratio of 6.4 to 1.5). Large multinodular goiters are usually asymptomatic. They can, however, cause compression of neck structures, resulting in dysphagia, cough, or respiratory distress or a feeling of constriction in the throat. This may necessitate subtotal or total bilateral thyroidectomy. Thyroid cancer has been found in 4 to 17% of operated patients with multinodular goiter; however, excluding the selection bias for operation, the incidence of carcinoma is probably closer to 0.2%.

Hypothyroidism and Hyperthyroidism. Hypothyroidism results from insufficient thyroid hormone secretion. In infants, hypothyroidism causes cretinism with lethargy, stunted growth, mental retardation, and hearing loss. Hypothyroidism during pregnancy can apparently harm the neuropsychological development of the fetus. For women of childbearing age who are hypothyroid or who undergo thyroidectomy, it is necessary that they maintain a euthyroid state should they become pregnant. This is an exceedingly important responsibility of the thyroid surgeon to provide proper patient education in this regard.

Careful monitoring of patients on thyroid replacement is prudent to prevent hyperthyroidism with its associated reduction in bone density in postmenopausal women and atrial fibrillation in the elderly. In the absence of metastatic thyroid cancer, TSH suppression only to low normal is recommended. Given the deleterious effects of iatrogenic hyperthyroidism, treatment of cold nodules and euthyroid multinodular goiter with TSH suppression is generally out of favor.

Thyrotoxicosis is the clinical and physiologic response of the tissues to an excess supply of active thyroid hormone. Causes of this syndrome fall into one of three main categories: the most important category includes diseases in which the gland sustains overproduction of thyroid hormone, the second category involves the development of thyrotoxic states secondary to thyroiditis, and the third category is unusual and arises when a source of excess hormone arises from other than the thyroid gland.

If sustained hyperfunction of the thyroid gland leads to thyrotoxicosis, the condition is properly termed hyperthyroidism. In true hyperthyroidism, an increased RAIU is found. Young patients more commonly develop thyrotoxicosis from Graves' disease, whereas older patients develop toxic nodular goiter.

Graves' disease is a relatively common disorder consisting of a triad of hyperthyroidism with diffuse goiter, ophthalmopathy, and dermopathy. Graves' disease is more frequent in women and has a definite familial predisposition. The basic disorder is a disruption of homeostatic mechanisms caused by the presence of an abnormal immunoglobulin (Ig)G thyroid stimulator in the plasma, long-acting thyroid stimulator. Treatment of hyperthyroidism in Graves' disease has two approaches, both of which are directed to limit thyroid hormone production by the gland: the first approach uses antithyroid agents to blockade hormone synthesis chemically, the second approach is ablation of thyroid tissue either by surgery or by means of radioactive iodine. In the past, a major cause of mortality in Graves' disease was thyroid storm. Treatment with sympatholytic drugs, oxygen, intravenous glucose, iodide, and adrenal steroids has brought this serious problem under control. Surgical ablation of the thyroid gland in Graves' disease is recommended in patients who have had a relapse or recurrence after drug therapy, in patients with a large goiter or drug toxicity, and in patients who fail to follow a medical regimen or fail to return for periodic examinations.

Thyrotoxicosis caused by thyroid hormone secreted by an autonomous follicular adenoma is termed toxic adenoma. Radioiodide is generally an effective treatment for toxic adenoma, often sparing the normal remaining gland.

Toxic multinodular goiter (Plummer's disease) is a disease of aging that arises in a simple (nontoxic) goiter of long standing. Treatment is primarily medical, consisting of antithyroid drugs (propylthiouracil or methimazole), sympatholytic therapy, and radioiodide. In the absence of symptoms caused by mass effects of goiter, surgery is reserved for toxicity not controlled medically.

Thyroiditis. Bacterial thyroiditis is rare. Subacute (de Quervain's granulomatous) thyroiditis is a febrile illness in which the thyroid becomes tender often after an upper respiratory infection. Thyroid function remains normal, but microsomal and thyrogobulin antibodies do appear in low titers.

Hashimoto's disease (struma lymphomatosa) is the most common type of thyroiditis. Although this condition is associated with mild thyrotoxicosis in the early stages because of release of stored hormone from damaged follicles, most patients have depressed thyroid function (RAIU low to normal).

Riedel's struma (invasive fibrous thyroiditis) is a rare form of thyroiditis characterized by irreversible, profound hypothyroidism and a stony hard, irregular, fibrous gland. Symptoms include cough, dyspnea, and difficulty swallowing. Thyroid hormone replacement is the principal treatment.

Management of Thyroid Neoplasia

Solitary Nodule of the Thyroid

The most common indication for thyroidectomy (50% of cases) in the United States is the presence of a solitary thyroid nodule. Solitary nodules may occur in up to 4% of the population and are most often found in patients 30 to 50 years of age, with a four-fold increase in frequency in women. The most common cause of solitary thyroid nodules in children and adolescents is follicular adenoma, although malignancy is reported in 25.5% of cold nodules. Neck mass is the most common presenting symptom of papillary or follicular thyroid carcinoma in patients under 20 years of age.

Increased risk of malignancy is found in the following situations: (1) thyroid nodules associated with vocal cord paralysis; (2) solitary nodules in men; (3) solitary nodules in patients under 20 years old or over 50 years old; (4) solitary nodules in patients with a history of head and neck irradiation; (5) palpable lower or midcervical lymph nodes and apparently normal thyroid glands in young patients; (6) functioning or cold nodules on scintiscan or radionuclide uptake outside the thyroid gland; (7) solid or partially cystic lesions by ultrasonography; (8) recurrent cystic lesions following needle aspiration; (9) abnormal cytologic findings on needle aspiration biopsy; and (10) solitary nodules that fail to disappear in response to thyroid hormone suppression therapy.

In patients with chronic thyroid disease, high-risk patients who are candidates for surgery may be identified by the following criteria: (1) multinodular goiter containing cold nodules that enlarge in response to suppression with thyroid hormone, (2) rapidly enlarging nodules in chronic goiters with or without suppression, (3) goiters with vocal cord paralysis, (4) a history of head and neck irradiation, and (5) a history of neoplasia of the thyroid gland.

Malignant Lesions

Malignant tumors of the thyroid include papillary adenocarcinoma, follicular adenocarcinoma, Hürthle cell carcinoma, medullary carcinoma, and undifferentiated carcinomas (small cell carcinoma and giant cell carcinoma). Various miscellaneous malignant lesions include lymphoma, sarcoma, and teratoma.

Papillary Adenocarcinoma. Thyroid carcinomas comprise approximately 1% of all malignant tumors in the United States. Of these, 60 to 70% are papillary carcinomas. These account for 80 to 90% of radiation-induced thyroid carcinomas. Although usually sporadic, papillary thyroid carcinoma can occur in familial form and is sometimes associated with nodular thyroid disease. Approximately 25% of papillary carcinomas are occult, discovered incidentally at surgery, and of questionable clinical significance. The peak incidence is in the third and fourth decades, with a three-fold increase in frequency in women. This lesion generally has a prolonged course, and the overall mortality is estimated at 10% or less. The patient's age at diagnosis is the most important prognostic factor. Total ipsilateral lobectomy, isthmusectomy, and subtotal contralateral lobectomy probably comprise the most common procedure for papillary carcinoma confined to the thyroid gland. For more extensive well-differentiated disease, improved survival requires aggressive management of the primary and cervical lymph node disease by surgery, followed at 6 weeks by thyroid scan and high-dose ^{131}I administration for ablation of the remnant.

Follicular Carcinoma. Follicular carcinoma accounts for approximately one of five thyroid cancers, peaking in the fifth decade of life with a 3 to 1 female preponderance. Like papillary carcinoma, it is well differentiated, despite a worse prognosis. For patients under 40 years of age with encapsulated follicular carcinoma, isthmusectomy and lobectomy are performed, with total thyroidectomy reserved for patients over 40 years old. Some surgeons prefer to perform total thyroidectomy for all patients because follicular carcinoma, unlike papillary carcinoma, can undergo late anaplastic transformation. For invasive follicular carcinoma, total thyroidectomy is recommended, followed by ablative radioiodine. In the presence of palpable lymph nodes in the neck, modified radical neck dissection is recommended. Moderate elevations in thyroglobulin may be attributable to inadequate thyroid suppression therapy and may require assessment by careful assay of TSH levels. However, patients with elevated thyroglobulin levels despite adequate suppression therapy following definitive treatment of a well-differentiated carcinoma are at increased risk of recurrence.

Hürthle Cell Carcinoma. Hürthle cells observed in thyroid gland atrophy of Hashimoto's disease are a benign entity. Treatment of Hürthle cell carcinoma involves at least an isthmusectomy and lobectomy. If Hürthle cell carcinoma appears as a solitary thyroid nodule exceeding 2.0 cm or if it is bilateral, total thyroidectomy is recommended. Radical neck dissection is recommended for cervical nodal metastases.

Medullary Carcinoma with Amyloid Stroma. Medullary carcinoma accounts for 5 to 10% of thyroid carcinomas.

Lesions are capable of local invasion, spread to regional lymphatic vessels, or distant metastases. Calcitonin is an important tumor marker in medullary carcinoma. Multiple endocrine neoplasia type I (MEN-I) is characterized by parathyroid chief cell hyperplasia with pancreatic islet cell and pituitary adenomas. Multiple endocrine neoplasia type IIa (Sipple's syndrome) is manifested by medullary thyroid carcinoma with associated pheochromocytoma and parathyroid hyperplasia. Multiple endocrine neoplasia type IIb is characterized by medullary carcinoma of the thyroid, pheochromocytoma and multiple mucosal neuromas, ganglioneuromatosis, and a Marfan habitus. Further, a familial non-MEN (FN-MEN) is recognized in which hereditary medullary carcinoma of the thyroid occurs without associated endocrinopathy. Each of these is inherited as an autosomal dominant trait. Medullary carcinoma does not take up radioiodide, so this treatment is not recommended. Because of the propensity of medullary carcinoma for local microvascular invasion, late recurrence (up to 20 years after treatment), and metastatic disease, total thyroidectomy is recommended. Bilaterality is high, especially in familial syndromes. Most clinicians favor a radical neck dissection on the side of the primary neoplasm with a modified neck dissection on the contralateral side in the event of bilateral thyroid gland involvement.

Anaplastic Carcinoma. Anaplastic carcinoma, largely a disease of the elderly, accounts for less than 10% of malignant thyroid tumors. Anaplastic carcinoma is an often rapidly fatal, aggressive, enlarging, bulky mass that is rarely operable. Palliative radiation therapy and chemotherapy may prolong life.

The Parathyroid Glands

The parathyroid glands consist of four small, ovoid, yellowish-brown structures located between the posterior border of the thyroid gland and its capsule. These endocrine glands produce PTH, which acts to increase serum calcium. They are named anatomically with respect to laterality and superior or inferior position. Generally, PTH production is proportional to the mass of the gland.

The parathyroid glands are endoderm derivatives of the third and fourth pharyngeal pouches. Like the thymus, the inferior parathyroid glands (IPGs) are derivatives of the third pharyngeal pouch. Therefore, IPGs are also referred to as "parathyroids III." Similarly, the superior parathyroid glands (SPGs), derived from the fourth pharyngeal pouch, are referred to as "parathyroids IV." The SPGs are more constant in position than the IPGs. The SPG is usually located around the middle of the posterior border of the lateral lobe of the thyroid gland. Parathyroid glands can also exist as diffusely scattered collections of parathyroid tissue in connective tissue or fat or be represented as only three distinct glands. Generally, SPGs are deep and IPGs are superficial to the recurrent laryngeal nerves on each side.

Calcitonin and PTH-related peptide are important for calcium regulation in the fetus. In adults and children, calcium-phosphorous homeostasis is regulated principally by vitamin D and PTH. With inadequate serum levels of PTH (hypoparathyroidism) and consequential hypocalcemia, convulsive spasms of muscles (tetany) ensue. If laryngeal and respiratory musculature become involved, tetany can cause death. Treatment involves administration of intravenous or enteric calcium, calcitriol or vitamin D, and possibly magnesium.

The most common cause of surgical hypercalcemia is primary hyperparathyroidism, excessive PTH production from a primary defect of the parathyroid glands. Parathyroid adenoma is the cause of primary hyperparathyroidism in 80 to 85% of cases. Symptoms arise from effects on several systems: renal, with polyuria and renal colic owing to lithiasis; rheumatic, with bone and joint pain; neuronal, with fatigue, memory loss, and depression; and gastrointestinal, with dyspepsia, anorexia, and nausea. Thus arises the medical student's memory aid, rhyming the symptoms: "aching bones, renal stones, mental moans, abdominal groans."

Management of Hyperparathyroidism

The majority of patients in the United States with primary hyperparathyroidism are asymptomatic. The usual treatment is surgical removal of the abnormal parathyroid gland(s). There is currently no effective medical treatment.

Indications for parathyroidectomy with hypercalcemia include serum calcium levels consistently greater than 1 to 1.4 mg/dL above normal in patients under 50 years of age (eg, serum calcium 12.0 mg/dL), calcium renal calculi, urinary calcium greater than 400 mg/24hours or reduced renal function, bone density greater than 2 standard deviations from normal, or coexisting disease that would make observation inappropriate. Bone density improves up to 20% after parathyroidectomy. Parathyroidectomy prior to development of serious bone demineralization is beneficial. Improvement in glucose control attendant to parathyroidectomy suggests that diabetic patients with hyperparathyroidism should have surgery.

Pre- or intraoperative scanning with technetium Tc 99m sestamibi scintigraphy has become the preferred localization study, and it is of low cost as well as specific and sensitive for parathyroid adenomas.

Parathyroid Masses

Parathyroid carcinoma is rarely encountered but can be associated with uncontrollable hypercalcemia with metastases. Parathyroid carcinoma should be surgically excised with appropriate margins of normal tissue and regional dissection as necessary.

Parathyroidectomy

Currently, two markedly different techniques of parathyroidectomy are practiced for biochemically proven hyperparathyroidism: bilateral, open neck exploration and minimally invasive radioguided parathyroidectomy (MIRP).

For management of solitary parathyroid adenoma, unilateral, focused parathyroidectomy is a rapidly advancing and appealing alternative. Currently, only about 50% of patients are candidates for focused parathyroidectomy. Several important technological tools have become available to the parathyroid surgeon that make unilateral surgery feasible: imaging of parathyroid tissue by technetium Tc 99m sestamibi scintigraphy; use of a handheld, intraoperative gamma probe; and intraoperative rapid PTH assay. Possible contraindications to MIRP include presence of coexisting nodular thyroid disease, previous neck surgery or irradiation, suspicion of parathyroid hyperplasia, history of familial primary hyperparathyroidism, or other anatomic or medical contraindications.

Although expensive, intraoperative rapid PTH assay is helpful in focused parathyroidectomy. Excision of sufficient abnormal parathyroid tissue is correlated with assays performed prior to incision and at 5 and 10 minutes after excision that demonstrate a measured decrease of 59%. Intraoperative rapid PTH assay is most reliable in treatment of a single adenoma but is not as reliable in parathyroidectomy for hyperplasia.

Sestamibi has good affinity for hyperfunctioning parathyroid lesions as hot nodules. Lesions with mass greater than 250 mg are detected with this scintigraphy (sensitivity 85 to 90% with a specificity of nearly 100%), although hyperplastic glands are not imaged as effectively as adenomas. Recently, intraoperative assessment of adequacy of parathyroidectomy has been made by intraoperative radioactivity ratios. Twenty mCi of technetium Tc 99m sestamibi are injected 3.5 to 1.5 hours preoperatively and followed by parathyroid scan. If the scan confirms a single adenoma, patients are taken to the operating room immediately, and a general anesthesia or local anesthesia with sedation is administered. After excision, tissue samples are counted, and a simple percentage of background radioactivity is calculated. Whereas other tissues contained at most 2% of background, hyperplastic parathyroids contained $7.5 \pm 0.8\%$, with a maximum of 16%. Adenomas contained $56\% \pm 9\%$, with a range from 19 to 125%. This method eliminates the necessity of histopathologic evaluation of frozen sections of specimens.

Up to 65% of MIRP patients may be discharged within 5 hours of surgery compared with a mean stay of 1.35 days in traditional, open parathyroidectomy. Comparison of charges for traditional open neck exploration revealed lower costs for MIRP owing to decreased duration of the operation, anesthesia, hospitalization, and elimination of the need for histologic evaluation of frozen sections by use of intraoperative rapid PTH assay.

Complications of Thyroid Surgery

Unilateral recurrent laryngeal nerve injury is reported in 2.3% of cases. One in 400 cases may not have a recurrent nerve. An anomalous inferior laryngeal nerve occurs almost always on the right and is always associated with an anomalous retroesophageal right subclavian artery. In these cases, the inferior laryngeal nerve passes directly from the vagus to the larynx. Digital subtraction angiography can confirm this anomaly.

Iatrogenic injury to the superior laryngeal nerve occurs in 2.4% of patients undergoing surgery in the thyroid periapical region. The inferior thyroid artery is best divided near the capsule of the gland to prevent injury to the sympathetic trunk (with a resultant Horner's syndrome) and to preserve blood supply to the parathyroid glands.

In one-fourth of thyroidectomies, the patient has a transient mild decrease in serum calcium, which is generally asymptomatic. Transient hypocalcemia can be severe in 8% of patients over the first 96 hours postoperatively. Thus, the critical period for calcium monitoring is 24 to 96 hours postoperatively. It is also important to monitor serum magnesium levels postoperatively. Permanent hypoparathyroidism occurs in up to 8% after total thyroidectomy. Myxedema can occur 4 to 6 weeks after a thyroidectomy. The greatest cause of death in the past was thyroid storm, which can now be effectively controlled. The mortality rate of thyroidectomy today is approximately 0.1%.

Complications of Parathyroid Surgery

Complications of open exploration-type parathyroidectomy are essentially the same as those described for thyroidectomy except for problems arising from ablation of thyroid tissue. For MIRP, regarded as a safe and effective method of parathyroidectomy, the complication rate is described as low. Problems associated with MIRP can include hemorrhage or hematoma, infection, scarring, subcutaneous emphysema (although this is less likely with a gasless endoscopic approach), recurrent laryngeal nerve injury, failure to locate the parathyroid gland of interest (eg, in a previously operated neck), and, conceivably, pneumothorax.

45

LARYNGOSCOPY

Ellen S. Deutsch, MD
Jane Y. Yang, MD
James S. Reilly, MD

The larynx comprises the supraglottis, consisting of the epiglottis, aryepiglottic folds, false vocal folds, and laryngeal ventricle; the glottis or true vocal folds; and the subglottis, including the cricoid cartilage. Laryngeal disease generally presents with pain, stridor, or hoarseness. Hoarseness indicates that the abnormality involves, but is not necessarily limited to, the free margin of the vocal folds.

BENIGN MASSES

Vocal fold nodules, polyps, and cysts generally occur at the junction of the anterior and middle third of the vocal fold and involve the epithelial and superficial layers of the lamina propria. Vocal fold nodules, generally bilateral, are small, white, firm, sessile masses containing collagenous fibers and edema.

Vocal fold cysts, usually unilateral, comprise epithelial cysts and mucous retention cysts. Polyps, caused by vocal trauma, are usually unilateral, pedunculated, or sessile and may have evidence of preceding hemorrhage.

Reinke's edema, also known as polypoid corditis or polypoid degeneration of the vocal folds, is most commonly associated with tobacco use, although vocal misuse and extraesophageal reflux disease may contribute to this condition.

Granulomas commonly occur on the vocal process or inner surface of the body of the arytenoid cartilage and can be large enough to obstruct the airway. Primary etiologic factors include traumatic or prolonged intubation, vocal abuse, or extraesophageal reflux disease.

Benign neoplasms, including laryngeal rhabdomyomas, are less frequent causes of hoarseness.

Cartilaginous laryngeal neoplasms, such as chondromas, have a 5 to 1 male predominance; most occur in patients between the ages of 40 and 60 years. Granular cell tumor, previously referred to as granular cell myoblastoma, is a benign, slow-growing neoplasm that can often be removed endoscopically. Neurofibromas and neurilemomas or schwannomas are histologically similar, benign neurogenic tumors of the larynx originating from the aryepiglottic fold or from the false vocal folds. Paragangliomas and atypical carcinoids may have similar clinical appearances. Paragangliomas are the only laryngeal neoplasm with a female predominance. Both are of neuroendocrine origin, contain neurosecretory granules, and are distinguished by careful immunocytochemical and/or ultrastructural investigation. In contrast to other head and neck paragangliomas, such as chemodectomas, laryngeal paragangliomas do not secrete catecholamines.

Hemangiomas occur in both adult and infantile types. Infantile subglottic hemangiomas generally increase in size and symptom severity until 6 months of age, after which spontaneous regression occurs. The adult form occurs on or above the vocal folds and is often pedunculated, well demarcated, and reddish blue in color. Lipomas are usually solitary lesions, found in men during the seventh decade of life; most can be removed endoscopically. Extralaryngeal lesions, such as retropharyngeal abscesses, adjacent tumors, or postcricoid foreign bodies, may compress the airway and cause stridor by exerting a mass effect.

Autoimmune, immune, and idiopathic diseases may have laryngeal manifestations. Sarcoidosis is an idiopathic, chronic, noncaseating granulomatous disease that most commonly involves the supraglottis, particularly the epiglottis, and presents with dysphonia, dysphagia, globus sensation, and dyspnea.

Scleroma (rhinoscleroma) is a chronic granulomatous infectious disease caused by *Klebsiella rhinoscleromatis*, which primarily occurs in the nose and nasopharynx but may involve the larynx.

Wegener's granulomatosis is a necrotizing vasculitis typically involving a triad of organs: the sinuses, lungs, and kidneys. Glomerulonephritis may present with microhematuria, proteinuria, and red cell casts. Laryngeal involvement generally causes subglottic stenosis with dyspnea and stridor. Elevated cytoplasmic antineutrophil cytoplasmic antibodies (c-ANCA) are highly specific for Wegener's granulomatosis.

Amyloidosis is a disease of unknown etiology characterized by deposition of extracellular, fibrillar protein. It is classified by the name of the fibrillar protein (AL, AA, ATTR, or AB2M), the precursor protein (kappa or lambda light chain, apoSSA, transthyretin, or β_2-microglobulin), and the clinical presentation (primary, secondary multiple myeloma associated, familial, or hemodialysis associated). The larynx is the most common site of involvement in the upper aerodigestive tract.

Rheumatoid arthritis is an autoimmune disorder affecting 2 to 3% of the adult population. Both adult and juvenile rheumatoid arthritis may involve the cricoarytenoid joint.

Relapsing polychondritis is a multisystemic autoimmune inflammatory disorder of obscure etiology characterized by progressive inflammation and degeneration of cartilaginous structures and connective tissues. Respiratory tract involvement may be the presenting symptom in as many as 26% of patients, and up to 50% of patients will eventually develop respiratory complications. Laryngotracheobronchial involvement may cause life-threatening airway obstruction from acute inflammation, scarring, or airway collapse from cartilage dissolution. Medical management in the acute phases includes corticosteroids; dapsone and immunosuppresant agents, such as cyclophosphamide, may be helpful.

Examination of supraglottic allergic edema reveals pale, watery swelling of the epiglottis and aryepiglottic folds. Treatment may include subcutaneous epinephrine, intramuscular or intravenous corticosteroids, antihistamines, and inhaled racemic epinephrine. Fatal airway obstruction can occur when the larynx is affected; insertion of an oro- or nasopharyngeal airway, endotracheal intubation, or tracheostomy may be necessary.

Hereditary angioedema results from an autosomal dominant deficiency of active C1 esterase inhibitor leading to recurrent attacks of localized edema or severe abdominal pain, precipitated by trauma or stress. Airway occlusion is the most common cause of mortality. The deficiency of C1 esterase inhibitor protein is usually quantitative but can be qualitative. Standard therapies for allergy-mediated angioedema, such as epinephrine, antihistamines, and corticosteroids, are less successful; C1 inhibitor (C1-INH) concentrate is used for acute management, and mechanical control of the airway may be needed. Long-term prophylactic treatment may include attenuated androgens such as danazol or stanozolol; antifibrinolytic medications such as ε-aminocaproic acid and tranexamic acid; and C1-INH concentrate. Antifibrinolytic medications are the drugs of choice for children. Acquired angioneurotic edema is less common and generally begins during adulthood. Drug-induced angioedema most commonly occurs in patients taking angiotensin converting enzyme inhibitors.

Acute spasmodic laryngitis or nocturnal croup typically presents as a mild viral upper respiratory tract infection with nocturnal episodic wakening accompanied by inspiratory stridor and croupy cough in a toddler; it invariably subsides during the day.

Epiglottitis, or acute supraglottitis, is an acute bacterial infection of the epiglottis, aryepiglottic folds, and soft tissues of the arytenoid cartilages. Features include the dangerously rapid onset of sore throat, high fever, muffled voice, and signs and symptoms of airway obstruction, including inspiratory stridor, inability to swallow, respiratory distress, and restlessness. The classic presentation is a pale, shocky, restless, drooling child in an upright position with head forward and tongue protruding. Examination, which is deferred until equipment and personnel are available to secure the airway, reveals fiery red edema of epiglottis and aryepiglottic folds. Pediatric acute supraglottitis, now uncommon, was previously caused predominantly by *Haemophilus influenzae*. The disease is now more common in adults and may be life-threatening but is usually less severe, with slower onset and progression.

"Croup," or laryngotracheobronchitis, refers to a constellation of viral infections that may affect any or all segments of the pediatric airway and is the most common cause of airway obstruction in children; the majority of patients are between the ages of 6 months and 4 years. Patients usually have a characteristic "barking" cough, 60% have inspiratory stridor, and the voice may be hoarse but not muffled. Most patients respond to medical and supportive therapy including humidification, nebulized racemic epinephrine, and systemic glucocorticoids. Anterior-posterior airway radiographs may demonstrate subglottic swelling, which changes the appearance of the square-shouldered space below the vocal folds to that of a steeple or pencil; lateral neck radiographs may show subglottic haziness. Endoscopy is avoided during the acute phase of the illness but is indicated if the patient fails two extubation attempts or does not improve as expected. Interval endoscopy is indicated if the patient has other risk factors for subglottic stenosis, more than three episodes of croup, onset of croup prior to 6 months of age, or an atypical course.

Recurrent respiratory papilloma is a benign but very rapidly proliferating tumor that usually presents within the first few years of life with hoarseness, inspiratory stridor, and respiratory distress progressing over a period of weeks or months. Human papillomavirus (HPV) subtypes 6 and 11 are most commonly found in juvenile recurrent respiratory papilloma. Treatment consists of repeated excision using carbon-dioxide laser or a microdébrider. Recent trials of cidofovir appear promising. Malignant degeneration of recurrent respiratory papilloma is uncommon, but the risk is greater for patients with subtypes 16/18 and 31/33 and those treated with radiation therapy.

Bacterial or fungal laryngitis and tracheitis can cause sudden airway obstruction.

Laryngopharyngeal reflux, or extraesophageal reflux, denotes the entry of gastric contents above the upper esophageal sphincter. Otolaryngologic manifestations and sequelae of extraesophageal reflux include chronic intermittent hoarseness, vocal fatigue, sore throat, dysphagia, chronic cough, stridor, croup, subglottic stenosis, excessive mucus production, postnasal drip, globus sensation, a choking sensation resulting from laryngospasm, and frequent throat clearing. Laryngeal examination may reveal edema, which may be diffuse or limited to the vocal folds, obliteration of the ventricles, interarytenoid thickening, pseudosulcus, or vocal process granuloma. Effects within the posterior part of the larynx or trachea include erythema, edema, "cobblestoning," blunting of the carina, and friable mucosa.

Two mechanisms of injury may coexist: reflex mechanisms may cause laryngospasm, bronchospasm, or apnea, and prolonged direct contact with the gastric fluid may cause mucosal damage. Twenty-four-hour multichannel ambulatory esophageal pH monitoring is the most sensitive study for extraesophageal reflux; esophagoscopy with biopsy, barium esophagram, nuclear medicine scintiscan, and bronchoscopy with washings for fat-laden macrophages may be supportive. Treatment options include antireflux behavioral and dietary modifications; acid-suppressive medications, including histamine H_2-receptor antagonists and proton pump inhibitors; or surgical therapy such as Nissen fundoplication.

Acute airway obstruction from laryngeal or tracheal edema is possible after ingestion of acid, alkali, or corrosive substances; following inhalation of hot air, smoke, steam, or chemical fumes; or following direct mechanical trauma. Traumatic epiglottitis may be treated with fluids, humidified supplemental oxygen, nebulized epinephrine, and parenteral administration of corticosteroids; intubation may be necessary. Intraluminal trauma may occur from intubation or other causes and can result in acquired glottic or subglottic stenoses, subglottic cysts, synechiae, and webs. Pressure from endotracheal or tracheostomy tube cuffs may cause tracheomegaly.

External causes of laryngeal injury include blunt or penetrating trauma from motor vehicle crashes, falls, sporting injuries including "clothesline" injuries, or assaults. Penetrating injuries are most commonly caused by knives or bullets. Minor injuries may consist of edema, hematoma, contusion, abrasion, and small lacerations; major injuries may result in loss of soft tissue, large lacerations without approximation, fracture or dislocation of cricoid or thyroid cartilages, displacement of the arytenoid cartilages or epiglottis, and impaired vocal fold mobility. Airway obstruction may occur instantly, gradually over hours, or with great rapidity hours after the injury has occurred. Computed tomography is the radiologic modality of choice. Laryngoscopy is indicated when evidence of airway injury or obstruction occurs following trauma to the neck, even with minimal symptoms. Tracheostomy or intubation may be needed to maintain the airway.

Congenital laryngeal abnormalities include teratomas or hamartomas, laryngomalacia, subglottic stenosis, complete or partial laryngeal atresia including congenital laryngeal webs, laryngotracheoesophageal clefts, hemangiomas, and lymphangiomas.

Vocal fold paralysis may be congenital or acquired. Central bilateral vocal fold paralysis may result from increased intracranial pressure or congenital nerve compression. Peripheral causes of paralysis are usually associated with injury to the recurrent laryngeal nerves, particularly during cardiovascular, thoracic, or neck surgery; the left recurrent laryngeal nerve is more frequently injured.

Speech and swallowing disorders, including dysarthria, dysphagia, or aspiration, may result from a combination of neurologic, structural, cardiorespiratory, metabolic, and/or behavioral abnormalities.

MALIGNANCIES

The larynx is the second most common site of cancer in the upper aerodigestive tract. Each year, 12,500 new cases are diagnosed in the United States, with an estimated 5-year survival rate of 68% overall. Squamous cell carcinoma accounts for over 95% of all laryngeal malignancies, with a peak incidence in the sixth and seventh decades. Tobacco is the single most significant risk factor; ethanol is believed to have a synergistic effect with tobacco. Palliation and cure of laryngeal squamous cell carcinomas may be accomplished using radiation therapy, chemotherapy, laser, or open surgical resection, singly or in combination. Verrucous carcinoma, an exophytic, highly differentiated variant of squamous cell carcinoma, rarely metastasizes; surgical resection is the treatment of choice.

Pleomorphic carcinoma may histologically resemble other laryngeal supporting tissue neoplasms.

Rhabdomyosarcomas, usually of the embryonal type, are the most common type of laryngeal tumor in children and adolescents. Treatment may include chemotherapy alone or with radiation therapy. Surgery is usually reserved for diagnostic biopsy or for debulking lesions; extensive debilitating surgery is usually not indicated.

Well-differentiated laryngeal fibrosarcomas have a low mortality rate, whereas poorly differentiated laryngeal fibrosarcomas are fatal in more than half of the reported instances.

Primary tumors including adenocarcinoma, malignant fibrous histiocytoma, non-Hodgkin's lymphoma, malignant schwannoma, mucoepidermoid carcinoma, and primitive neuroectodermal tumor, as well as other sarcomas, such as synovial sarcoma, Ewing's sarcoma, chondrosarcoma, and "mixed" sarcoma, are rare. Metastases to the larynx are also rare.

RADIOLOGIC EVALUATION OF THE LARYNX

Routine radiologic evaluation comprises anterior-posterior and lateral neck images. The lateral view of the neck provides useful information about the base of the tongue, vallecula, thyroid and cricoid cartilages, posterior pharyngeal wall, prevertebral cervical soft tissues, and intralaryngeal structures including the epiglottis, aryepiglottic folds, arytenoid cartilages, false and true vocal folds, laryngeal ventricles, and subglottic space.

Fluoroscopy may be useful in assessing dynamic lesions. Adding radiologic contrast agents such as barium, or iohexol for tracheobronchography, may enhance visualization and further define airflow dynamics and distal anatomy. Spiral computed tomography and fast magnetic resonance techniques allow rapid acquisition of enhanced images of laryngeal structures, minimizing motion artifact. Direct spiral computed tomography of the neck is performed in the axial plane; coronal, sagittal, and three-dimensional reconstruction can be computer generated. Magnetic resonance has the advantage of multiplanar high-resolution imaging, with an increased ability to separate various soft tissues, and may be more sensitive for identifying early cartilage invasion.

46

BRONCHOESOPHAGOLOGY

Jane Y. Yang, MD
Ellen S. Deutsch, MD
James S. Reilly, MD

BRONCHOLOGY

Bronchology combines the history and physical examination with the knowledge of the pathologic possibilities and the findings of the radiologic evaluation and the specular examination of the airway to provide the patient with an accurate diagnosis and the best therapeutic option.

Indications for Bronchoscopy

Diagnostic bronchoscopy is indicated for patients with chronic cough; yield is increased if there is a history of tobacco use, chest radiograph abnormality, hemoptysis, or localized wheezing. For patients with hemoptysis, bronchoscopy facilitates control and protection of the airway; massive hemoptysis should be managed by rigid, open-tube endoscopy. Balloon tamponade can be accomplished using endoscopic guidance. Neodymium:yttrium-aluminum-garnet (Nd:YAG) lasers may be used to control bleeding from airway neoplasms. Adjunctive methods include instillation of vasopressin, sodium bicarbonate, epinephrine, or cold saline lavages. Stridor is caused by turbulent airflow resulting from an abnormality of the larynx, trachea, or bronchi. Stridor can be high or low pitched; inspiratory, expiratory, or biphasic; wet or dry. The suspected lesion, patient characteristics, and circumstances of the endoscopy are considered when determining whether to proceed with fiberoptic and/or rigid tracheobronchoscopy. Airway control may necessitate rigid endoscopy, intubation, or tracheostomy; reasonable preparations should be made prior to instrumenting the airway.

Following blunt or penetrating *chest trauma*, bronchoscopy is the most reliable means of establishing the site, nature, and extent of tracheal or bronchial disruption when a tracheal tear or bronchopleural fistula is suspected because of dyspnea, hemoptysis, subcutaneous and mediastinal emphysema, inspiratory stridor, hoarseness, coughing, localized pain or tenderness, or cyanosis. Tracheobronchial trauma can occur at every level of the trachea and major bronchi, but more than 80% of the injuries are within 2.5 cm of the carina.

Patients with thermal or chemical *inhalation injury* may have facial, oropharyngeal, or nasal burns; carbonaceous sputum; wheezing; rales; rhonchi; and hoarseness. Arterial blood gas measurements may indicate hypoxemia, hypercapnia, and the presence of carboxyhemoglobin. Close observation and bronchoscopy are indicated, and bronchoscopy may reveal erythema, edema, ulceration, necrosis, or soot deposits.

Bronchoscopy should be considered in adult patients with *respiratory infections* that do not respond adequately to empiric antibiotics covering the most common respiratory pathogens, including *Streptococcus pneumoniae, Staphylococcus aureus, Haemophilus influenzae, Mycoplasma pneumoniae,* and *Legionella pneumophila,* as well as in critically ill or immunocompromised patients. Bronchoscopy performed for evaluation of patients with *abnormal chest radiographs* is more likely to be diagnostic when the radiograph demonstrates lobar collapse and hilar abnormalities and is less likely to be diagnostic in evaluation of nodular lesions and infiltrates; persistent postobstructive consolidation is often caused by an endobronchial mass.

Biopsy of endobronchial lesions can be accomplished using rigid or fiberoptic bronchoscopy; transbronchial fine-needle aspiration may be more effective for tumors with necrotic centers. Brushings and biopsies may be obtained for both visible and bronchoscopically invisible parenchymal lung lesions; fluoroscopic guidance may be useful. Endoscopy is also useful in evaluating potential complications of intubation, such as granulomas, webs, stenoses, or necrosis.

Bronchoalveolar lavage is used in asthma, sarcoidosis, extraesophageal reflux disease, idiopathic pulmonary fibrosis, hypersensitivity pneumonitis, pulmonary alveolar proteinosis, hemosiderosis, histiocytosis X, and other interstitial lung diseases, as well as for identification of infectious lung diseases and confirmation of aspiration based on quantitative evaluation of lipid-laden macrophages.

Bronchopleural fistulae are usually iatrogenic but may also result from tuberculosis, pneumonia, empyema, lung abscess, or trauma. Most *tracheoesophageal fistulae* are congenital, but acquired lesions, such as posterior erosion of the trachea, may result from intubation or tracheostomy, particularly if a foreign body, such as a nasogastric tube, resides simultaneously in the esophagus.

A variety of *therapeutic procedures* can be performed endoscopically, avoiding the need for open surgical management. In adults with obstructing malignancies, *endobronchial stents* can be placed endoscopically as a temporizing measure. Complications include migration of the stent, inspissation of mucus, ingrowth of granulation tissue into metallic stents, and erosion of the wall of the airway and aortobronchial fistula, especially when inserted for treatment of airway obstruction secondary to compression by vascular structures.

Lasers can be used to resect or debulk tumors that obstruct the airway or to prepare the airway for insertion of airway stents. Carbon dioxide lasers allow precise destruction or excision of tissue, hemostasis of microcirculation, preservation of adjoining tissue, and minimal postoperative edema but can be applied only by using rigid instruments. Neodymium:yttrium-

aluminum-garnet lasers can be passed through fiberoptic bronchoscopes and applied using noncontact tips but can cause
submucosal damage that does not become fully evident until
after application is completed. Risks related to anesthesia
include hypoxemia, hypercarbia, and inadequate airway control. Risks related to the laser include airway burns and igni-
tion of the endotracheal tube; treatment includes immediate
extubation, paralysis of the patient, reintubation with a small
endotracheal tube, endoscopy to evaluate the injury and to
remove charred debris and foreign material, saline lavage, systemic corticosteroids and antibiotics, and careful monitoring
of pulmonary function.

Foreign-body aspiration is more common in young children than adults and most commonly comprises foods, particularly nuts. Adults may aspirate when drugs or trauma alter
their judgment or mental status or when neurologic disease or
physical conditions impair sensation or control of the food
bolus. Patients who aspirate foreign bodies may present with
gagging, coughing, and choking; however, over time, the
symptoms may become quiescent. Endoscopy is indicated if
there is a suggestive history despite a lack of radiographic
findings, if there is a suggestive radiographic finding despite
a lack of supportive history, or if pulmonary disease follows
an atypical course. Occasionally, a foreign body may be visible in radiographic images; sometimes only the sequelae are
demonstrated. A check-valve mechanism of airflow past a
foreign body can result in obstructive emphysema, and a stop-
valve mechanism can result in atelectasis. Lack of deflation
of a lung or bronchus may be demonstrated on inspiratory
and expiratory chest radiographs, lateral decubitus radiographs, or airway fluoroscopy.

Although fiberoptic bronchoscopic retrieval of foreign bodies has been performed successfully, rigid bronchoscopy, with
the capability of airway control, is preferred in most cases, especially in children. Airway foreign bodies must be grasped in a

secure manner and controlled during their removal. "Stripping off" a foreign body during its passage through the trachea or in the larynx may convert partial airway obstruction to total obstruction with an inability to ventilate the patient. In children, this risk is increased in the subglottis because of its intrinsic relative narrowness. If control over a foreign body is lost within the trachea or subglottis, the foreign body can be pushed into a main bronchus, allowing ventilation of at least one lung.

Bronchoscopy can be used to visualize, irrigate, and suction problematic secretions in critically ill patients who may not have the respiratory support and muscular strength to mobilize mucus plugs or other tenacious secretions interfering with ventilation. Bronchoscopy can be used to deliver medication, radioactive agents, or other therapies.

Tracheobronchial Conditions

Acute bronchiolitis, usually caused by respiratory syncytial virus, occurs in children under 2 years of age. Inflammatory airway obstruction has a greater impact on young children with narrower airways. *Bacterial tracheitis* may cause life-threatening sudden airway obstruction, particularly in children less than 3 years of age. Thick, copious secretions complicate mucosal swelling at the level of cricoid cartilage; *Staphylococcus aureus* is the most commonly isolated pathogen.

Initial management of *pneumonia* includes appropriate empiric antibiotic therapy based on the type of pneumonia and the patient's immunologic status. Bronchoscopy allows directed aspiration of secretions for culture; bronchoalveolar lavage and bronchoscopy-protected specimen brushing can retrieve specimens adequate for quantitative analysis. Bronchoscopy is indicated for lung abscesses unresponsive to postural drainage and chest physiotherapy to rule out an underlying carcinoma or foreign body, to obtain secretions for culture, and to drain the abscess.

Bronchiectasis, irreversible dilatation of the bronchial tree, may be postinflammatory, obstructive, or congenital and most commonly presents with chronic purulent sputum production and hemoptysis. *Mycetomas* are formed by the conglomeration of fungal elements, most commonly *Aspergillus* species, within a pulmonary cavity. The incidence of *Mycobacterium tuberculosis*, a bacillus transmitted by airborne inhalation of infected droplets, has declined in recent years; an increasing proportion of new cases occurs among immigrants. Bronchoscopy, with broncheoalveolar lavage and/or biopsy, has a high yield and should be considered in high-risk patients who have negative sputum cultures or patients who are unable to expectorate adequately.

Cystic fibrosis is the most common life-threatening genetic trait in Caucasians. Exocrine gland dysfunction manifests as a paucity of water in mucus secretions; difficulty clearing mucus secretions contributes to respiratory tract obstruction and infection, particularly with *Staphylococcus aureus* and *Pseudomonas aeruginosa*. Tracheobronchial suctioning or lavage may be temporarily helpful in treating atelectasis or mucoid impaction. Biopsy samples for evaluation of cystic fibrosis or other ciliary dysmotility disorders can be obtained from the carina with a cup forceps or by brushing; specimens are placed in glutaraldehyde for electron microscopy.

Interstitial lung disease encompasses a wide variety of pulmonary diseases characterized by diffuse parenchymal opacities. More than 160 causes have been reported; pneumoconiosis, drug-induced disease, and hypersensitivity pneumonitis account for over 80% of cases. A large variety of injurious inorganic dusts, chemicals, pharmacologic agents, and radiation therapy may contribute. Bronchoscopy with bronchoalveolar lavage may provide useful information in patients for whom open or thoracoscopic lung biopsy is not feasible.

Sarcoidosis is a non-necrotizing granulomatous disease, more common in African Americans, which usually causes hilar adenopathy demonstrable on chest radiograph and occasionally causes endobronchial granulomas or stenoses. Elevated serum angiotensin converting enzyme levels appear to correlate with disease activity. Fiberoptic bronchoscopy with transbronchial biopsy is the invasive procedure of choice for diagnosis. *Idiopathic pulmonary fibrosis* is a chronic fibrosing interstitial pneumonia of unknown etiology, associated with the histologic appearance of "usual" interstitial pneumonia. *Relapsing polychondritis* manifests with acute, recurrent, progressive inflammation and degeneration of cartilage and connective tissue. Serious airway manifestations, such as inflammation, stenosis, or dynamic collapse of the tracheobronchial tree, occur in about one-half of the patients. *Wegener's granulomatosis* is a necrotizing granulomatous vasculitis affecting both the upper and lower respiratory tracts and the kidneys.

Benign Neoplasms and Tumor-like Masses

Histologically benign neoplasms cause airway obstruction. *Recurrent respiratory papilloma* has a predilection for the larynx, but the trachea and bronchi may be involved by disseminated disease. In patients with *tracheopathia osteochondroplastica*, multiple submucosal nodules, consisting of cartilage and lamellar bone, can be seen projecting into the lumen of the tracheobronchial tree; right middle lobe collapse is a common finding.

Malignant Neoplasms

Bronchogenic carcinoma is the most common malignancy in the United States; approximately 87% of all cases of lung cancer are attributable to long-term tobacco use. Bronchoscopy has emerged as an integral tool for the diagnosis and staging of lung cancer. Bronchogenic carcinomas are divided histologically into small cell cancers and non-small cell cancers that include squamous cell carcinoma, adenocarcinoma, and large cell carcinoma. Only approximately 4% of primary lung tumors are not bronchogenic carcinomas. Bronchial *carcinoid* is a neuroendocrine neoplasm arising from Kulchitsky's cells, which may secrete hormones such as adrenocorticotropic hormone, antidiuretic hormone, gastrin, somatostatin, calcitonin, and growth hormone.

Other Tracheobronchial Disorders

Congenital *tracheal stenoses* may result from complete tracheal rings or other cartilage deformities. Acquired stenoses may result from inhalation thermal or chemical burns or from intubation. Definitive treatment involves surgical resection, expansion, and/or reconstruction.

Radiologic Evaluation

Specialized radiographic examinations, such as barium swallow, computed tomography, and magnetic resonance imaging or magnetic resonance angiography, may be useful to define airflow dynamics, distal anatomy, or the relationship between the airway and adjacent structures or masses. Tracheobronchography, with superimposition of three-dimensional anatomy, provides a unified view of the airway rather than a planar slice image. Radiographic tracheobronchial three-dimensional reconstruction and "virtual" endoscopy are being developed. Radiographic procedures can provide information about dynamic processes that is difficult to obtain by other methods but cannot provide tactile information or tissue samples.

Anomalies of the great vessels can affect the trachea and the esophagus. The anomalous innominate artery may obliquely compress the anterior tracheal wall. In addition, three typical patterns are demonstrated in patients with congenital vascular anomalies. A large posterior esophageal indentation in the presence of anterior tracheal compression suggests a vascular ring consisting of a double aortic arch or the complex of a right aortic arch, left ductus arteriosus, and aberrant left subclavian artery. An oblique small retroesophageal indentation with a normal trachea is usually the result of an aberrant right subclavian artery with a left aortic arch, which is generally asymptomatic, or, rarely, an aberrant left subclavian artery with a right aortic arch. The only vascular anomaly that passes between the trachea and the esophagus, causing an anterior esophageal indentation with a posterior tracheal indentation, is a "pulmonary sling," comprising an anomalous left pulmonary artery arising from the right pulmonary artery.

ESOPHAGOLOGY

Within the last few decades, improvements in lenses and illumination have allowed esophagoscopes to evolve into primary diagnostic and therapeutic tools for managing many esophageal disorders. Open-tube esophagoscopes are used to examine and treat esophageal disease; flexible fiberoptic upper gastrointestinal endoscopes also allow examination of the stomach and duodenum.

Indications for Esophagoscopy

Indications for esophagoscopy include complaints of dysphagia, odynophagia, regurgitation, pyrosis, and hematemesis; blunt trauma to the neck with associated subcutaneous air; penetrating neck trauma; radiographic evidence of esophageal masses or strictures; gastroesophageal reflux; caustic or foreign-body ingestion; congenital anomalies; vocal fold palsies; suspicion of aerodigestive malignancies (primary, synchronous, or secondary); esophageal involvement by autoimmune and idiopathic diseases; and mechanical obstruction or neuromuscular disorders. Interval evaluations may be indicated to monitor disease progression and treatment effects.

Therapeutic Esophagoscopy

Esophageal *strictures* may occur in patients with a history of caustic ingestion, Plummer-Vinson syndrome, Behçet's syndrome, gastroesophageal reflux, and Crohn's disease or as a result of tracheoesophageal fistulae or malignancies or their management. Rigid or fiberoptic esophagoscopes can be used to visualize the esophageal lumen for direct dilatation or to pass a guidewire or a *stent*.

Foreign bodies that become lodged in the esophagus require surgical removal. Meat is the most common esophageal foreign body found in adults, and coins are the most common in children. Patients may be asymptomatic, or they may have dysphagia or emesis or develop stridor, fever, or a cough aggravated by eating. Lodgment occurs most commonly just below the cricopharyngeus muscle and in the thoracic esophagus at the compression of the esophagus by the aortic arch or left bronchus or at a stricture.

Button batteries, sharp objects, and objects causing bleeding, acute or severe airway compromise, or significant pain or dysphagia should be removed emergently. Endoscopic removal of foreign bodies allows evaluation of any esophageal injury and visualization of multiple or radiolucent foreign bodies. Although some foreign bodies can be safely removed using a fiberoptic esophagoscope, rigid esophagoscopes with Hopkins rod telescopes remain the gold standard for evaluation and removal of esophageal foreign bodies. Complications of esophageal foreign bodies include edema, esophageal laceration, erosion or perforation, hematoma, granulation tissue, aortoesophageal or tracheoesophageal fistula, mediastinitis, paraesophageal or retropharyngeal abscess, migration of the foreign body into the fascial spaces of the neck, arterial-esophageal fistulae with massive hemorrhage, respiratory problems, strictures, and proximal esophageal dilation; fatalities have been reported.

Caustic Ingestion

Patients who ingest caustic substances are at risk of serious esophageal injury, even in the absence of oropharyngeal burns. Most ingestions occur in young children and are accidental; ingestions in adolescents and adults are often suicide gestures or attempts. Acid ingestion produces coagulative necrosis. Alkaline products, which produce liquefactive necrosis, account for the majority of ingestions and for the greatest number of serious injuries. Most authors report that the presence or absence of symptoms is an unreliable predictor of esophageal injury and advocate esophagoscopy to evaluate the extent and severity of injury for virtually all patients with caustic ingestions, to the upper limit of any full-thickness burn. Esophagoscopy is contraindicated in the presence of a severe burn with evidence of laryngeal edema and in patients who have been on high doses of corticosteroids. Management remains controversial and may include hospitalization, antibiotics, corticosteroids, analgesics, sedation, and antireflux therapy. Observation and selective esophagoscopy are reasonable for patients who ingest bleach or hair relaxers.

Esophageal Diseases

Achalasia is a motor disorder characterized by loss of peristalsis of esophageal smooth muscle and dysfunction of the lower esophageal sphincter causing incomplete relaxation. The esophagus eventually becomes dilated and retains food; at this point, barium contrast may demonstrate esophageal dilatation, with a smooth tapered bird-beak appearance of the lower esophageal sphincter because of incomplete relaxation. Histologically, the ganglion cells in Auerbach's plexus are significantly reduced in quantity or absent; esophageal cancer eventually develops in 2 to 8% of patients. Management options include dilation, surgical myotomy, or injection of botulinum toxin.

Patients with *amyloidosis* often have neural or muscular involvement, resulting in abnormal or absent peristalsis and impaired relaxation of the lower esophageal sphincter. *Pharyngoesophageal dysphagia*, caused by cricopharyngeal spasm, a cricopharyngeal bar, cervical osteophytes, or cervical diverticula, may result in discomfort, weight loss, or aspiration.

Esophageal *diverticula* are diagnosed radiographically with a barium swallow. Pharyngoesophageal ("Zenker's") diverticula are pulsion diverticula, related to spasm or disordered motility of the cricopharyngeus muscle and to congenital or acquired weakness of the muscular walls in Killian's dehiscence or triangle. Lower esophageal diverticula are also pulsion diverticula. Traction diverticula usually occur in the middle third of the esophagus, contain muscle, and result from inflammatory processes adjacent to the esophagus, causing contracture and deformity of the entire wall; they are frequently asymptomatic. Treatment options for Pharyngoesophageal diverticula include open cervical approaches such as diverticulectomy or diverticulopexy with cricopharyngeal myotomy or endoscopic procedures such as division of the esophagodiverticular wall including division of the cricopharyngeus muscle, often with endoscopic stapling.

Inflammation, Esophagitis, and Gastroesophageal Reflux Disease

An incompetent lower esophageal sphincter, increased intra-abdominal pressure, gastric outlet obstruction, dietary habits, or tobacco use may contribute to gastroesophageal reflux; the resultant contact between gastric acid and esophageal mucosa can cause chronic inflammation, strictures, webs, and dysmotility. Management may include dietary changes, weight loss, medications such as histamine H_2-receptor antagonists and proton pump inhibitors, or surgical procedures such as fundoplication.

Barrett's metaplasia, a premalignant condition, comprises replacement of the normal esophageal epithelium with gastric-type columnar mucosa as a consequence of prolonged chronic gastroesophageal reflux.

Infectious esophagitis, most commonly caused by herpes simplex virus, *Candida*, or cytomegalovirus, usually occurs in immunocompromised patients and diabetics. In bone marrow transplant patients with chronic *graft-versus-host disease*, an epithelial reaction of the esophageal mucosa can cause dysphagia and odynophagia.

Motility dysfunctions are the primary esophageal manifestations of *connective tissue disorders* such as scleroderma with progressive systemic sclerosis, polymyositis, dermatomyositis, systemic lupus erythematosus, rheumatoid arthritis, and mixed connective tissue disease. The xerostomia of Sjögren's syndrome can cause dysphagia.

Dermatologic vesicobullous diseases can also cause dysphagia. Epidermolysis bullosa comprises a group of hereditary disorders characterized by blister formation at sites of minor trauma. Pemphigus vulgaris is a rare intraepidermal bullous disease marked histologically by suprabasal acantholysis. Nikolsky's sign, separation of the epidermal layer from underlying tissue after applying lateral pressure to the skin, may be observed. *Benign mucous membrane (cicatricial) pemphigoid* is a chronic, bullous disease of the elderly, causing webs and strictures most commonly involving the oral cavity and conjunctiva. *Stevens-Johnson syndrome* is a severe systemic hypersensitivity erythema multiforme reaction that presents with iris-like, target lesions and vesicobullous lesions of skin and mucous membranes; the most common causative agents in adults are medications such as sulfonamides, phenytoin, barbiturates, phenylbutazone, digitalis, and penicillin and in children infections with microorganisms such as *Streptococcus*, herpes simplex virus, and *Mycoplasma*.

Benign Tumors

Benign esophageal tumors are less common than malignant esophageal tumors. *Squamous papillomas* are the only benign epithelial tumor. More than half of benign nonepithelial tumors are leiomyomas; other tumors include lipomas, fibromas, neurofibromas, gliomas, granular cell tumors, osteochondromas, hemangiomas, and adenomatous polyps.

Malignant Tumors

Squamous cell carcinoma is the most common malignant esophageal tumor. Screening endoscopy should be performed in patients with known risk factors such as alcohol and tobacco abuse, achalasia, Plummer-Vinson syndrome, tylosis (palmar and plantar keratoderma), chronic stricture from ingestion of lye or corrosive substances, and celiac disease. Symptoms include dysphagia, aspiration pneumonia, hoarseness, unilateral neck mass, cough, fever, or a choking sensation. Endoscopically, polypoid, ulcerative, or infiltrating lesions are usually found in the middle and lower third of the esophagus.

Adenocarcinoma is the second most common esophageal epithelial malignancy, usually occuring in the distal esophagus in association with Barrett's metaplasia. Other malignant epithelial tumors are rare and include variants of squamous cell carcinoma such as spindle cell carcinoma, verrucous carcinoma or pseudosarcoma, adenoid cystic carcinoma, mucoepidermoid carcinoma, argyrophyl cell carcinoma, and melanoma. Nonepithelial malignant esophageal tumors include leiomyosarcoma, rhabdomyosarcoma, and fibrosarcoma. Direct esophageal infiltration or compression may be caused by thyroid, lung, or lymphatic malignancies.

Hematemesis

Esophageal varices, usually limited to the distal half of the esophagus, develop as a result of portal hypertension. The principal clinical manifistation of esophageal varices is bleeding. Other causes of bleeding from the esophagus include the Mallory-Weiss syndrome and the Boerhaave's syndrome. Mallory-Weiss tears develop in the gastric cardia and gastroesophageal junction after an episode of retching, vomiting, and coughing and are usually limited to the mucosa. *Boerhaave's syndrome* describes the spontaneous, full-thickness esophageal tear that results most commonly from a prolonged bout of violent emesis. The patient may present with excruciating lower chest pain, shock, dyspnea, and extreme thirst. Survival is dependent on rapid diagnosis and treatment.

INDEX